적중 100

영어 기출 문제집

중 **3**

시사 | 박준언

Best Collection

구성과 특징

교과서의 주요 학습 내용을 중심으로 학습 영역별 특성에 맞춰 단계별로 다양한 학습 기회를 제공하여
단원별 학습능력 평가는 물론 중간 및 기말고사 시험 등에 완벽하게 대비할 수 있도록 내용을 구성

Words & Expressions

Step1
Key Words 단원별 핵심 단어 설명 및 풀이
Key Expression 단원별 핵심 숙어 및 관용어 설명
Word Power 반대 또는 비슷한 뜻 단어 배우기
English Dictionary 영어로 배우는 영어 단어

Step2 실력평가 단원별 수시평가 대비 주관식, 객관식 문제풀이

Step3 서술형 대비 학업성취도 및 수행능력평가 대비 서술형 문제풀이

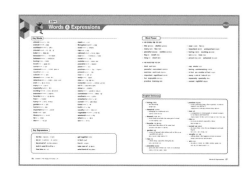

Conversation

Step1 핵심 의사소통 소통에 필요한 주요 표현 방법 요약
핵심 Check 기본적인 표현 방법 및 활용능력 확인

Step2 대화문 익히기 교과서 대화문 심층 분석 및 확인

Step3 교과서 확인학습 빈칸 채우기를 통한 문장 완성 능력 확인

Step4 기본평가 시험대비 기초 학습 능력 평가

Step5 실력평가 단원별 수시평가 대비 주관식, 객관식 문제풀이

Step6 서술형 대비 학업성취도 및 수행능력평가 대비 서술형 문제풀이

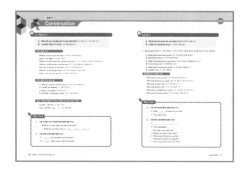

Grammar

Step1 주요 문법 단원별 주요 문법 사항과 예문을 알기 쉽게 설명
핵심 Check 기본 문법사항에 대한 이해 여부 확인

Step2 기본평가 시험대비 기초 학습 능력 평가

Step3 실력평가 단원별 수시평가 대비 주관식, 객관식 문제풀이

Step4 서술형 대비 학업성취도 및 수행능력평가 대비 서술형 문제풀이

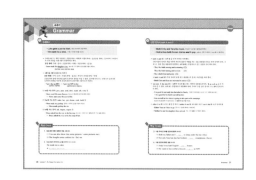

Reading

Step1 구문 분석 단원별로 제시된 문장에 대한 구문별 분석과 내용 설명
확인문제 문장에 대한 기본적인 이해와 인지능력 확인

Step2 확인학습A 빈칸 채우기를 통한 문장 완성 능력 확인

Step3 확인학습B 제시된 우리말을 영어로 완성하여 작문 능력 키우기

Step4 실력평가 단원별 수시평가 대비 주관식, 객관식 문제풀이

Step5 서술형 대비 학업성취도 및 수행능력평가 대비 서술형 문제풀이
교과서 구석구석 교과서에 나오는 기타 문장까지 완벽 학습

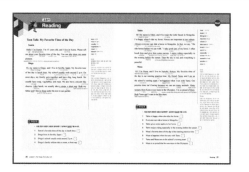

Composition

|영역별 핵심문제|

단어 및 어휘, 대화문, 문법, 독해 등 각 영역별 기출문제의 출제 유형을 분석하여 실전에 대비하고 연습할 수 있도록 문제를 배열

|단원별 예상문제|

기출문제를 분석한 후 새로운 시험 출제 경향을 더하여 새롭게 출제될 수 있는 문제를 포함하여 시험에 완벽하게 대비할 수 있도록 준비

|서술형 실전 및 창의사고력 문제|

학교 시험에서 점차 늘어나는 서술형 시험에 집중 대비하고 고득점을 취득하는데 만전을 기하기 위한 학습 코너

|단원별 모의고사|

영역별, 단계별 학습을 모두 마친 후 실전 연습을 위한 모의고사

교과서 파헤치기

- **단어Test1~3** 영어 단어 우리말 쓰기, 우리말을 영어 단어로 쓰기, 영영풀이에 해당하는 단어와 우리말 쓰기
- **대화문Test1~2** 대화문 빈칸 완성 및 전체 대화문 쓰기
- **본문Test1~5** 빈칸 완성, 우리말 쓰기, 문장 배열연습, 영어 작문하기 복습 등 단계별 반복 학습을 통해 교과서 지문에 대한 완벽한 습득
- **구석구석지문Test1~2** 지문 빈칸 완성 및 전문 영어로 쓰기

Contents

Lesson 1

All about Me

🎙 의사소통 기능

- 궁금증 표현하기
  Can you tell me about yourself?
- 가장 좋아하는 것 말하기
  What I like most is to take pictures.

🎙 언어 형식

- 동사의 강조
  I **do feel** good when I walk in the forest.
- 관계대명사 what
  Having fun is **what I want most.**

Words & Expressions

Key Words

- **advise**[ædváiz] 동 조언하다, 충고하다
- **among**[əmʌ́ŋ] 전 … 중에서
- **automatically**[ɔ̀:təmǽtikəli] 부 자동으로
- **barbecue**[bɑ́:rbikjù:] 명 바비큐
- **basement**[béismənt] 명 지하층[실]
- **cartoon**[kɑrtú:n] 명 만화
- **check**[tʃek] 동 확인하다
- **choice**[tʃɔis] 명 선택
- **comfortable**[kʌ́mfərtəbl] 형 편안한
- **contest**[kɑ́ntest] 명 대회
- **cool**[ku:l] 형 멋진
- **countryside**[kʌ́ntrisaid] 명 시골 (지역)
- **create**[kriéit] 동 만들다
- **designed**[dizáind] 형 그려진, 디자인된
- **designer**[dizáinər] 명 디자이너
- **different**[dífərənt] 형 다른, 다양한
- **do**[du] 조 (동사를 강조) 정말로
- **draw**(–**drew**–**drawn**)[drɔ:] 동 (그림을) 그리다
- **early adopter** 얼리 어답터 (남들보다 먼저 신제품을 사서 써 보는 사람)
- **enter**[éntər] 동 들어가다
- **exciting**[iksáitiŋ] 형 흥미로운
- **fantastic**[fænsǽstik] 형 환상적인, 매우 멋진
- **favorite**[féivərit] 형 가장 좋아하는
- **floor**[flɔ:r] 명 (건물의) 층
- **forest**[fɔ́:rist] 명 숲
- **forward**[fɔ́:rwərd] 부 앞으로
- **free**[fri:] 형 한가한, 다른 계획이 없는
- **furniture**[fɔ́:rnitʃər] 명 가구
- **garden**[gɑ́:rdn] 명 정원
- **goal**[goul] 명 목표
- **guest**[gest] 명 손님

- **hero**[híərou] 명 영웅, 히어로
- **homeroom teacher** 담임 선생님
- **humorous**[hjú:mərəs] 형 재미있는, 유머러스한
- **imagine**[imǽdʒin] 동 상상하다
- **interest**[íntərəst] 명 관심, 흥미
- **interesting**[íntərəstiŋ] 형 흥미로운, 재미있는
- **join**[dʒɔin] 동 가입하다
- **kind**[kaind] 명 종류
- **language**[lǽŋgwidʒ] 명 언어
- **motto**[mɑ́tou] 명 좌우명, 모토
- **nature**[néitʃər] 명 자연
- **nickname**[níknèim] 명 별명
- **not just** …: 단지 …가 아닌
- **others**[ʌ́ðərz] 대 다른 사람들
- **pet**[pet] 명 애완동물
- **photographer**[fətɑ́grəfər] 명 사진사
- **photo-taking** 사진촬영
- **poster**[póustər] 명 포스터
- **practice**[prǽktis] 동 연습하다
- **pretty**[príti] 부 매우, 꽤
- **product**[prɑ́dʌkt] 명 제품
- **real**[rí:əl] 형 진짜의
- **recognize**[rékəgnàiz] 동 인식하다
- **refreshed**[rifréʃt] 형 (기분이) 상쾌한
- **save**[seiv] 동 구하다, 절약하다
- **scene**[si:n] 명 장면
- **SF movie** 공상 과학 영화
- **skill**[skil] 명 기술
- **subject**[sʌ́bdʒikt] 명 과목, 주제
- **technology**[teknɑ́lədʒi] 명 기술
- **theater**[θí:ətər] 명 극장
- **wake up** (잠에서) 깨다, 일어나다

Key Expressions

- **be full of** …: …로 가득 차다
- **be filled with** …: …로 가득 차다
- **be good at**: …을 잘하다
- **be interested in**: …에 관심이 있다
- **go traveling**: 여행을 가다
- **get along with**: …와 잘 지내다

- **have free time**: 여가 시간을 가지다
- **here are**+복수명사: 여기에 …가 있다
- **look like**+명사: …처럼 보이다
- **stop –ing**: …하는 것을 그만두다
- **thank A for B**: B 때문에 A에게 감사하다
- **would like to**+동사원형: …하고 싶다

Word Power

※ 서로 반대되는 뜻을 가진 어휘
- □ **forward**(앞으로) ↔ **backward**(뒤쪽으로)
- □ **interesting**(재미있는) ↔ **uninteresting**(재미없는)
- □ **different**(다른) ↔ **same**(같은)
- □ **construct**(건설하다) ↔ **destroy**(파괴하다)

※ 서로 비슷한 뜻을 가진 어휘
- □ **enter** : **go into**(들어가다)
- □ **draw** : **sketch**(그리다)
- □ **humorous** : **funny**(재미있는)
- □ **recognize** : **identify**(인식하다, 확인하다)
- □ **fantastic** : **wonderful**(환상적인, 멋진)
- □ **advise** : **counsel**(조언하다, 충고하다)

English Dictionary

- □ **advise** 충고하다
  → to tell someone that they should do something
  누군가에게 무언가를 해야 한다고 말하다

- □ **among** ~ 중에서
  → in the middle of a group
  어떤 그룹의 한 가운데에

- □ **basement** 지하실[층]
  → part of a building that is under the level of the ground
  지면 아래에 있는 건물의 일부

- □ **choice** 선택
  → the possibility of choosing between two or more things
  두 가지 이상의 것 중에서 선택하는 가능성

- □ **countryside** 시골
  → land that is not in towns or cities and may have farms, fields, etc.
  도시에 있지 않고 농장, 밭 등이 있는 땅

- □ **create** 만들다, 창출하다
  → to make something happen or exist
  어떤 일이 일어나거나 존재하게 만들다

- □ **enter** 들어가다
  → to go into a place
  어떤 장소에 들어가다

- □ **fantastic** 환상적인
  → extremely good, attractive, or enjoyable
  매우 좋거나 매력적이거나 즐길 만한

- □ **forest** 숲
  → a large area of land that is covered with trees
  나무로 덮여 있는 넓은 지역의 땅

- □ **forward** 앞으로
  → towards a place or position that is in front of you
  당신 앞에 있는 장소나 위치를 향하여

- □ **furniture** 가구
  → things such as chairs, tables, and beds that you put into a room or building
  방이나 건물에 두는 의자, 탁자, 침대와 같은 물건

- □ **hero** 영웅
  → a very brave person, often a man, that a lot of people admire
  많은 사람들이 존경하는, 종종 남자로, 매우 용감한 사람

- □ **imagine** 상상하다
  → to form or have a mental picture or idea of something
  어떤 것에 대한 마음 속의 그림이나 생각을 형성하거나 가지다

- □ **motto** 좌우명, 모토
  → a short sentence or phrase that expresses a belief or purpose
  믿음이나 목적을 표현하는 짧은 문장이나 문구

- □ **pet** 애완동물
  → an animal that is kept in the home as a companion and treated kindly 집에서 동반자로 길러지고 친절하게 대접받는 동물

- □ **photographer** 사진사
  → a person who takes photographs, either as a job or hobby
  직업이나 취미로 사진을 찍는 사람

- □ **recognize** 인식하다, 알아차리다
  → to know someone or something because you have seen or heard him or her or experienced it before
  이전에 보거나 듣고 경험했기 때문에 사람이나 사물을 알다

01 다음 문장의 빈칸에 주어진 영어 설명에 해당하는 말을 쓰시오.

> • My dream house has a theater in the
> _____.

> part of a building that is under the level of the ground

02 다음 빈칸에 들어갈 말로 가장 적절한 것은?

> Nature is my good friend. I do feel good when I walk _____.

① in the building　② in the forest
③ on the street　④ across the road
⑤ with my pet dog

[03~04] 다음 설명에 해당하는 단어를 고르시오.

03

> to know someone or something because you have seen or heard him or her or experienced it before

① imagine　② enter
③ advise　④ recognize
⑤ create

04

> the possibility of choosing between two or more things

① choice　② check
③ motto　④ poster
⑤ goal

05 다음 우리말에 맞게 빈칸에 알맞은 단어를 쓰시오.

> 나의 꿈의 집에서, 나의 가족은 안전하고 편안하게 느껴.

➡ In my dream house, my family _____ safe and _____.

06 다음 빈칸에 공통으로 들어갈 말로 알맞은 것은?

> (A) I am an early _____ of new technology.
> (B) France is the biggest _____ of Korean orphans in Europe.

① plan　② choice
③ adopter　④ promise
⑤ condition

07 다음 짝지어진 단어의 관계가 같도록 빈칸에 알맞은 말을 쓰시오.

> enter : go into = advise : _____

08 다음 빈칸에 들어갈 말로 알맞게 짝지어진 것은?

> I like to use new technology. I do like to use new products and technology (A) _____ others. When I get near my house, the front door (B)_____ my face and opens automatically.

① with – captures　② after – recognizes
③ after – works　④ before – closes
⑤ before – recognizes

01 다음 빈칸에 들어갈 말을 〈보기〉에서 찾아 쓰시오. (필요하면 변형하여 쓰시오.)

┌─ 보기 ─┐
furniture   advise   excite   technology
└────────┘

(1) I like the scenes made with computer _____.

(2) The room is full of old _____.

(3) My dream house is filled with _____ things.

(4) Would you _____ me what I should do?

02 〈보기〉의 단어를 이용하여 문장의 빈칸을 완성하시오.

┌─ 보기 ─┐
along   interest   good   stop
└────────┘

(1) My goal this year is to _____ _____ fast food.

(2) I'm _____ _____ playing the drums.

(3) I'm _____ _____ the stars. I usually go out to see stars at night.

(4) I want to _____ _____ _____ everyone in the club.

03 다음 우리말과 같은 표현이 되도록 문장의 빈칸을 채우시오. (철자가 주어진 것은 주어진 철자로 시작하여 쓸 것.)

(1) 내가 가장 좋아하는 것은 새로운 언어를 배우는 것이다.
➡ What I like most is to learn a new _____.

(2) 너의 별명은 뭐니?
➡ What is your _____?

(3) 오늘 수업 시간에, 우리는 꿈의 집을 만들었다.
➡ Today, in class, we c_____ our dream house.

04 다음 영영풀이에 해당하는 단어를 〈보기〉에서 찾아 첫 번째 빈칸에 쓰고, 두 번째 빈칸에는 우리말 뜻을 쓰시오.

┌─ 보기 ─┐
imagine   fantastic   forward   forest
└────────┘

(1) _____ : extremely good, attractive, enjoyable: _____

(2) _____ : towards a place or position that is in front of you: _____

(3) _____ : to form or have a mental picture or idea of something: _____

05 다음 빈칸에 공통으로 알맞은 단어를 주어진 철자로 시작하여 쓰시오.

(1) • What k_____ of things do you want in your future?
   • The k_____ man helped us.

(2) • Our g_____ is to reduce our trash by ten percent.
   • Liverpool won by three g_____s to one.

Conversation

교과서

1 궁금증 표현하기

Can you tell me about yourself? 나에게 너에 대해 말해 줄 수 있니?

■ 'Can you tell me about + 명사[대명사]?' 또는 'Can you tell me 의문사+주어+동사 ~?'로 사실이나 원인, 어떤 상황에 대한 궁금증을 설명해 달라고 요청할 수 있다.

- Can you tell me about your family? 당신의 가족에 대해 얘기해 줄래요?
- Can you tell me about what happened? 무슨 일이 있었는지 말해 줄래요?
- Can you tell me why you were late yesterday? 어제 왜 늦었는지 말해 줄래요?
- Can you tell me why you don't love me? 왜 날 사랑하지 않는지 말해 줄래요?

■ 궁금증을 표현하는 다른 방법

'I'm really curious about ~.'은 '나는 ~에 대해서 정말 궁금해.'라는 의미로 새로운 정보에 대하여 궁금증을 표현하거나 보다 많은 정보를 알고 싶을 때 사용하는 표현이다. 'I'd like to know more about ~.', 'be interested in ~, want to know ~' 등으로도 표현할 수 있다.

- The cat was naturally curious about its new surroundings. 그 고양이는 원래 새로운 환경에 호기심이 있었다.
- We are curious about why you never called us. 우리는 왜 네가 우리에게 전화를 하지 않았는지 궁금하다.

핵심 Check

1. 다음 대화의 빈칸에 공통으로 들어갈 알맞은 것은?

- **A:** Can you tell me _____ the Wright Brothers?

  B: They invented the airplane.

- **A:** I am curious _____ this movie.

  B: So am I.

① in   ② of   ③ for

④ with   ⑤ about

② 가장 좋아하는 것 말하기

What I like most is to take pictures. 내가 가장 좋아하는 것은 사진을 찍는 것이다.

■ 'What I like most is ~.'는 '내가 가장 좋아하는 것은 ~이다.'라는 의미로 자신이 가장 좋아하는 것을 말할 때 사용하는 표현이며, 여기서 what은 관계대명사로 '~하는 것'의 의미를 가진다. 관계대명사 what은 the thing(s) that[which]로 바꾸어 쓸 수 있다. 즉, 'What I like most'는 'The thing that I like most'로 바꿀 수 있다.

■ 가장 좋아하는 것을 말하는 다른 표현은 'My favorite ~ is …' / 'I like … most.' / 'I prefer …' 등이 있다.

   • My favorite movie is *Titanic*. 내가 가장 좋아하는 영화는 *Titanic*이야.
   • I like pizza most. 나는 피자를 가장 좋아해.

■ 가장 좋아하는 것을 묻는 표현

'What's your favorite ~?'은 상대방이 가장 좋아하는 것을 묻는 표현으로 'Which[What] ~ do you like most?'나 'What do you like most?'라고 말할 수도 있다.

   • What's your favorite movie? 네가 가장 좋아하는 영화는 무엇이니?
   • Which food do you like most? 너는 어떤 음식을 가장 좋아하니?

■ 가장 좋아하는 것 묻고 표현하기

   A: What's your favorite subject? 네가 가장 좋아하는 과목이 뭐니?

   B: My favorite subject is English. / What I like most is English. 내가 가장 좋아하는 과목은 영어야.

핵심 Check

2. 다음 우리말에 맞도록 빈칸에 들어갈 알맞은 말을 쓰시오.

내가 가장 좋아하는 것은 보드 게임을 하는 거야.

_____ I like most is to play board games.

① Which   ② How   ③ What

④ When   ⑤ Whether

Listen & Speak 1 A-1

G: Jiho, how was your first day of third grade?

B: It was ❶pretty good. The teachers and my new classmates are all good.

G: That sounds good. Who is your homeroom teacher?

B: My homeroom teacher is Mr. Kim. He teaches math.

G: ❷Can you tell me more about him?

B: Yes. He is humorous and ❸told us some fun stories about math. It was interesting.

G: Cool! I hope you enjoy studying math.

G: 지호야, 너의 3학년 첫 날은 어땠어?

B: 꽤 좋았어. 선생님들과 새로운 반 친구들 모두 좋아.

G: 그거 좋네. 담임 선생님은 누구셔?

B: 내 담임 선생님은 김 선생님이셔. 그는 수학을 가르치셔.

G: 나에게 그에 대해 좀 더 말해 줄 수 있니?

B: 응. 그는 재미있고 우리에게 수학에 대한 재미있는 몇 가지 이야기를 해 주셨어. 그것은 흥미로웠어.

G: 멋지네! 네가 수학 공부를 즐기기 바라.

❶ 여기서 'pretty'는 부사로 '매우, 꽤'의 의미이다.
❷ 'Can you tell me about + 명사[대명사]?'는 궁금증을 표현할 때 사용하는 말이다.
❸ 'tell+간접목적어(…에게)+직접목적어(~을)' 형태이다.

Check(√) True or False

(1) Jiho's homeroom teacher is a math teacher.　　T ☐ F ☐

(2) Jiho's homeroom teacher isn't funny.　　T ☐ F ☐

Listen & Speak 2 A

1. G: I often go traveling with my family. ❶What I like most about traveling is trying new foods.

2. B: My favorite subject is music. I can play the drums and guitar. Among them, ❷playing the guitar is what I like most.

3. G: This is a picture of Dora. She is my best friend, not just a pet. ❸ Playing with her in my free time is what I like most.

1. G: 나는 가끔 나의 가족들과 여행을 가. 여행에 관해 내가 가장 좋아하는 것은 새로운 음식들을 먹어보는 거야.

2. B: 내가 가장 좋아하는 과목은 음악이야. 나는 드럼과 기타를 연주할 수 있어. 그것들 중에서, 기타를 연주하는 것이 내가 가장 좋아하는 거야.

3. G: 이것은 Dora 사진이야. 그녀는 단순히 애완동물이 아니라, 나의 가장 친한 친구야. 여가시간에 그녀와 함께 노는 것이 내가 가장 좋아하는 거야.

❶ 'What I like most is ~.'는 '내가 가장 좋아하는 것은 ~이다'라는 의미로 자신이 가장 좋아하는 것을 말할 때 사용하는 표현이다.
❷ playing the guitar는 동명사 주어로 '기타를 연주하는 것은'으로 해석한다. what I like most는 보어 자리에 사용된 관계대명사절로 '내가 가장 좋아하는 것'이라는 뜻이다.
❸ Playing with her는 동명사 주어이고, her는 애완동물인 'Dora'를 가리키는 말이다.

Check(√) True or False

(3) G likes going traveling with her family.　　T ☐ F ☐

(4) B prefers playing the drums to playing the guitar.　　T ☐ F ☐

(5) What G likes most is playing with Dora.　　T ☐ F ☐

🎤 **Listen & Speak 1 B**

A: ❶Can you tell me about your plan for this weekend?

B: Yes. ❷I am going to have a birthday party.

A: ❸Can you tell me about your goal for the year?

B: Yes. I want to ❹stop eating fast food.

A: 나에게 너의 이번 주말 계획에 대해 말해 줄 수 있니?

B: 응. 나는 생일 파티를 할 거야.

A: 나에게 너의 올해 목표에 대해 말해 줄 수 있니?

B: 응. 나는 패스트푸드를 그만 먹고 싶어.

❶ 이번 주의 미래의 계획을 묻는 표현이다.

❷ 'be going to+동사원형'은 '~할 예정이다'라는 의미로 미래의 계획을 말할 때 사용한다.

❸ 궁금증을 표현하는 표현이다.

❹ 'stop+동명사(v-ing)'는 '~하는 것을 그만두다'라는 의미이다. 'stop+to v'는 '~하기 위해 멈추다'라는 의미가 된다.

Check(√) True or False

(6) B is planning to have a birthday party this month.　　　　T ☐ F ☐

(7) B wants to stop eating fast food this year.　　　　T ☐ F ☐

🎤 **Real Life Talk**

Seho: Nice to meet you. ❶I'd like to join your photo club.

Bora: ❷Thank you for your interest in the club. Can you tell me about yourself?

Seho: Yes. My name is Kim Seho. I am in the third grade, class 8.

Andy: Tell me more. ❸What do you like to do most in your free time?

Seho: Well, ❹what I like most is to take pictures.

Bora: That's great. What is your dream for the future?

Seho: I want to be a photographer.

Andy: Then you made the right choice. You can learn a lot of photo-taking skills here. Welcome to our club.

Seho: Thank you. I'm so glad!

세호: 만나서 반가워. 나는 너희의 사진 동아리에 가입하고 싶어.

보라: 동아리에 관심을 가져 줘서 고마워. 너에 대해 말해 줄래?

세호: 응. 내 이름은 김세호야. 나는 3학년 8반이야.

Andy: 좀 더 말해 줘. 너는 여가 시간에 무엇을 하는 걸 가장 좋아하니?

세호: 음, 내가 가장 좋아하는 건 사진 찍는 거야.

보라: 멋지다. 너의 장래 희망은 뭐니?

세호: 나는 사진 작가가 되고 싶어.

Andy: 그러면 너는 정말 좋은 선택을 했구나. 너는 여기서 사진 찍는 기술을 많이 배울 수 있어. 우리 동아리에 온 걸 환영해.

세호: 고마워. 나도 기뻐!

❶ 'would like to v'는 '~하고 싶다'라는 의미이다.

❷ 'thank A for B' 구문으로 'B 때문에 A에게 고마워하다'라는 의미이다.

❸ 상대방이 가장 좋아하는 것이 무엇인지 묻는 표현이다.

❹ what은 관계대명사로 'the thing(s) that[which]'로 바꾸어 쓸 수 있다. 'to take pictures'는 보어 자리에 사용된 명사적 용법이다.

Check(√) True or False

(8) What Seho likes most in his free time is to take pictures.　　　　T ☐ F ☐

(9) Seho learned many photo-taking skills in the photo club.　　　　T ☐ F ☐

Warm Up

B1: Hello, my name is Kim Chanho. ❶I want to tell you about myself. I'm interested in music. ❷I'm good at playing the drums.

G1: Hi! I am Teri. I like running in the evening. ❸I feel refreshed when I exercise.

B2: Hello, my name is Jack. I'm interested in the stars. I ❹usually go out to see stars at night.

G2: I am Lee Bora. I want to be a designer in the future, so I ❺practice drawing when I have free time.

B3: I am Mark. I like dancing. I want to win first prize in the dance contest.

❶ want는 to부정사를 목적어로 취하는 동사이고, myself는 주어와 목적어가 같을 때 사용하는 재귀대명사이다.

❷ be good at은 '~을 잘하다'는 뜻이고, 전치사 at 뒤에는 동명사 playing을 사용한다.

❸ 'feel+형용사'로 '~하게 느끼다'라는 의미이다.

❹ 빈도부사 usually는 일반동사 앞에 사용한다.

❺ practice는 동명사(drawing)를 목적어로 취하는 동사이다.

Listen & Speak 1 A-2

G: Ted, look at this movie poster. I want to see this movie.

B: ❶It looks interesting. Can you tell me about it, Amy?

G: Yes. It is about a hero ❷who saves the Earth.

B: It ❸looks like an SF movie.

G: Yes, it is. Actually, SF is my favorite kind of movie. I like the scenes ❹made with computer technology. They are fantastic and look real.

B: That's cool. I am free this weekend. ❺Let's go to see it together.

G: Sounds good.

❶ 'look+형용사'는 '~하게 보이다'는 의미이다.

❷ 관계대명사절로 선행사 a hero를 수식하는 역할을 한다. 선행사가 단수명사인 a hero이므로 주격 관계대명사 뒤에 단수동사 saves를 사용해야 한다.

❸ 'look like+명사'로 '~처럼 보이다'는 의미이다.

❹ made는 '만들어진'의 의미로 명사 the scenes를 수식하는 수동의 의미를 가진 과거분사이다.

❺ 'Let's+동사원형' 형태로 '~하자'라는 권유의 표현이다.

Communication Task Step 2

A: What is your nickname?

B: My nickname is Speedy ❶because I can run fast.

C: What do you like most?

B: What I like most is to play baseball.

D: Can you tell me about your dream job?

B: I want to be a baseball player.

A: What is your motto?

B: My motto is "You can go ❷forward slowly, but never go back."

❶ because는 이유의 부사절 접속사로 뒤에 '주어+동사'가 온다. 'because of'는 전치사구로 뒤에 명사가 온다.

❷ forward는 부사로 '앞으로'의 의미로 동사 go를 수식한다.

Wrap Up

W: Today, we have a new student Hojun. Hojun, can you please introduce yourself to the class?

B: Yes. Hi, my name is Kim Hojun. I am from Busan. Nice to meet you.

W: ❶Can you tell us more about yourself?

B: Yes. I like sports, especially soccer. I want to join a sports club.

W: Is there anything else ❷you want to tell your new friends?

B: I want to get along with everyone. Please help me because I'm new here.

W: Thanks, Hojun. Welcome to our class.

❶ 궁금증을 표현하거나 보다 많은 정보를 알고 싶을 때 사용하는 표현이다. 'I'd like to know more about ~.'으로 표현할 수도 있다.

❷ anything else와 you 사이에 목적격 관계대명사 that이 생략되어 있다.

● 다음 우리말과 일치하도록 빈칸에 알맞은 말을 쓰시오.

Warm Up

B1: Hello, my name is Kim Chanho. I _____ _____ _____ you about _____. I'm _____ _____ music. I_____ _____ _____ _____ the drums.

G1: Hi! I am Teri. I like running in the evening. I feel _____ _____ I exercise.

B2: Hello, my name is Jack. I'_____ _____ in the stars. I _____ go out _____ _____ stars at night.

G2: I am Lee Bora. I want to be a _____ in the future, so I _____ _____ when I have free time.

B3: I am Mark. I like dancing. I want to _____ first prize in the dance _____.

Listen & Speak 1 A

1. **G:** Jiho, _____ was your first day of third _____?

   B: It was _____ good. The teachers and my new classmates are all good.

   G: That sounds _____. Who is your _____ _____?

   B: My homeroom teacher is Mr. Kim. He _____ math.

   G: _____ _____ _____ _____ more _____ him?

   B: Yes. He is _____ and _____ us some _____ about math. It was _____.

   G: Cool! I hope you _____ _____ math.

2. **G:** Ted, look at this movie poster. I want _____ _____ this movie.

   B: It _____ interesting. Can you tell me about it, Amy?

   G: Yes. It is _____ a hero _____ the Earth.

   B: It _____ _____ an SF movie.

   G: Yes, it is. Actually, SF is my _____ kind of movie. I like the _____ _____ with computer technology. They are _____ and look _____.

   B: That's _____. I am free this weekend. Let's go to see it together.

   G: _____ good.

 해석

B1: 안녕, 내 이름은 김찬호야. 너에게 나에 대해 말해주고 싶어. 나는 음악에 관심이 있어. 나는 드럼을 잘 쳐.

G1: 안녕. 나는 Teri야. 나는 저녁에 달리는 것을 좋아해. 나는 달릴 때 상쾌함을 느껴.

B2: 안녕, 내 이름은 Jack이야. 나는 별들에 관심이 있어. 나는 보통 밤에 별을 보러 나가.

G2: 나는 이보라야. 나는 미래에 디자이너가 되고 싶어서, 시간이 날 때 그림 그리는 연습을 해.

B3: 나는 Mark야. 나는 춤추는 걸 좋아해. 나는 춤 대회에서 1등을 하고 싶어.

1. G: 지호야, 너의 3학년 첫 날은 어땠어?

   B: 꽤 좋았어. 선생님들과 새로운 반 친구들 모두 좋아.

   G: 그거 좋네. 담임 선생님은 누구셔?

   B: 내 담임 선생님은 김 선생님이셔. 그는 수학을 가르치셔.

   G: 나에게 그에 대해 더 말해 줄 수 있니?

   B: 응. 그는 유머가 있으시고 우리에게 수학에 대한 재미있는 몇 가지 이야기를 해 주셨어. 그것은 흥미로웠어.

   G: 멋지네! 네가 수학 공부를 즐기기 바라.

2. G: Ted, 이 영화 포스터 좀 봐. 이 영화 보고 싶어.

   B: 그거 재미있어 보이네. 나에게 그것에 관해 말해 줄 수 있니, Amy?

   G: 응. 그것은 지구를 구하는 영웅에 대한 거야.

   B: 공상 과학 영화 같네.

   G: 응, 맞아. 사실 공상 과학은 내가 가장 좋아하는 영화 장르야. 나는 컴퓨터 기술로 제작된 장면들을 좋아해. 그 장면들은 환상적이고 진짜 같아 보여.

   B: 그거 멋지네. 나 이번 주말에 시간 있어. 같이 그거 보러 가자.

   G: 좋아.

Listen & Speak 1 B

A: Can you tell me _____ your plan for this weekend?

B: Yes. I am going to _____ a birthday party.

A: Can you tell me about your _____ for the year?

B: Yes. I want to _____ _____ fast food.

A: 나에게 너의 이번 주말 계획에 대해 말해 줄 수 있니?

B: 응. 나는 생일 파티를 할 거야.

A: 나에게 너의 올해 목표에 대해 말해 줄 수 있니?

B: 응. 나는 패스트푸드를 그만 먹고 싶어.

Listen & Speak 2 A

1. G: I often _____ _____ with my family. _____ I like _____ about traveling is trying new foods.

2. B: My _____ subject is music. I can play the drums and guitar. _____ them, _____ the guitar is _____ I like most.

3. G: This is a picture of Dora. She is my best friend, _____ _____ a pet. _____ with her in my free time is _____ I like most.

1. G: 나는 가끔 나의 가족들과 여행을 가. 여행에 관해 내가 가장 좋아하는 것은 새로운 음식들을 먹어보는 거야.

2. B: 내가 가장 좋아하는 과목은 음악이야. 나는 드럼과 기타를 연주할 수 있어. 그것들 중에서, 기타를 연주하는 것이 내가 가장 좋아하는 거야.

3. G: 이것은 Dora 사진이야. 그녀는 단순히 애완동물이 아니라, 나의 가장 친한 친구야. 여가시간에 그녀와 함께 노는 것이 내가 가장 좋아하는 거야.

Real Life Talk

Seho: Nice to meet you. I'_____ _____ _____ join your photo club.

Bora: Thank you _____ your interest in the club. Can you tell me _____ _____?

Seho: Yes. My name is Kim Seho. I am _____ the _____ grade, class 8.

Andy: Tell me _____. _____ do you like to do _____ in your free time?

Seho: Well, _____ I like most is _____ _____ pictures.

Bora: That's great. What is your dream for the future?

Seho: I want to be a _____.

Andy: Then you made the right _____. You can learn a lot of _____ skills here. Welcome to our club.

Seho: Thank you. I'm so _____!

세호: 만나서 반가워. 나는 너희의 사진 동아리에 가입하고 싶어.

보라: 동아리에 관심을 가져 줘서 고마워. 너에 대해 말해 줄래?

세호: 응. 내 이름은 김세호야. 나는 3학년 8반이야.

Andy: 좀 더 말해 줘. 너는 여가 시간에 무엇을 하는 걸 가장 좋아하니?

세호: 음, 내가 가장 좋아하는 건 사진 찍는 거야.

보라: 멋지다. 너의 장래 희망은 뭐니?

세호: 나는 사진 작가가 되고 싶어.

Andy: 그러면 너는 정말 좋은 선택을 했구나. 너는 여기서 사진 찍는 기술을 많이 배울 수 있어. 우리 동아리에 온 걸 환영해.

세호: 고마워. 나도 기뻐!

Communication Task Step 2

A: What is your _____?

B: My nickname is Speedy _____ I can run fast.

C: What do you like _____?

B: _____ _____ _____ _____ is to play baseball.

D: _____ _____ _____ _____ _____ your dream job?

B: I want to be a baseball player.

A: What is your _____?

B: My _____ is "You can go _____ slowly, but never go _____."

해석

A: 너의 별명이 뭐니?
B: 내 별명은 스피디인데 나는 빨리 달릴 수 있기 때문이야.
C: 너는 무엇을 가장 좋아하니?
B: 내가 가장 좋아하는 것은 야구를 하는 거야.
D: 나에게 네가 꿈꾸는 직업에 대해 말해 줄 수 있니?
B: 나는 야구 선수가 되고 싶어.
A: 너의 좌우명이 뭐니?
B: 나의 좌우명은 "앞으로 천천히 나아갈 수 있지만, 절대 물러설 수는 없다"야.

Wrap Up

W: Today, we have a _____ _____ Hojun. Hojun, can you please _____ _____ to the class?

B: Yes. Hi, my name is Kim Hojun. I am _____ Busan. Nice to meet you.

W: _____ _____ _____ _____ _____ about yourself?

B: Yes. I like sports, _____ soccer. I want to join a sports club.

W: Is there _____ else you want to tell your new friends?

B: I want to _____ _____ _____ everyone. Please help me _____ I'm new here.

W: Thanks, Hojun. _____ to our class.

W: 오늘, 새로 온 학생 호준이가 있어요. 호준아, 반 친구들에게 너를 소개해 주겠니?
B: 네. 안녕, 내 이름은 김호준이야. 나는 부산에서 왔어. 만나서 반가워.
W: 너에 대해 더 말해 줄 수 있니?
B: 네. 나는 스포츠, 특히 축구를 좋아해. 나는 스포츠 동아리에 가입하고 싶어.
W: 너의 새로운 친구들에게 더 말하고 싶은 게 있니?
B: 모두와 함께 잘 지내고 싶어. 나는 이곳에 새로 왔으니 도와주길 바라.
W: 고마워, 호준아. 우리 반에 온 것을 환영한단다.

01 우리말에 맞도록 주어진 단어를 이용하여 5단어로 쓰시오.

> • 그녀에 관해 말해 줄 수 있니? (tell, about)

➡ _____ _____ _____ _____ _____ her?

02 다음 대화의 빈칸에 공통으로 들어갈 말로 알맞은 것은?

> A: _____ your plan for this weekend?
> B: Yes. I am going to have a birthday party.
> A: _____ your goal for the year?
> B: Yes. I want to stop eating fast food.

① Are you curious about
② What's your favorite
③ What would you like for
④ Can you tell me about
⑤ Are you interested in

03 다음 글의 빈칸에 들어갈 말로 가장 알맞은 것은?

> My favorite subject is music. I can play the drums and guitar.
> Among them, _____ .

① I'd like to know how to play the drums
② I am having trouble with playing the guitar
③ my favorite subject is music
④ I wonder if I can play the guitar well
⑤ playing the guitar is what I like most

04 다음 대화의 밑줄 친 우리말에 맞게 문장의 빈칸을 채우시오.

> Hi! I am Teri. I like running in the evening. <u>운동을 할 때 상쾌함을 느껴</u>.

➡ I feel _____ _____ I exercise.

[01~02] 다음 글을 읽고 물음에 답하시오.

> Teri: I often go traveling with my family. (A) _____ I like most about (a)(travel) is trying new foods.
>
> Sumi: This is a picture of Dora. She is my best friend, not just a pet. (b)(Play) with her in my free time is (A)_____ I like most.

01 위 글의 빈칸 (A)에 공통으로 들어갈 말로 알맞은 것을 <u>모두</u> 고르시오.

① That[that]　　　② How[how]

③ What[what]　　　④ Whether[whether]

⑤ The[the] thing that

02 위 글의 괄호 (a)와 (b)의 단어를 알맞은 형태로 고치시오.

➡ (a) _____ (b) _____

03 다음 대화의 밑줄 친 우리말에 맞게 주어진 어구를 이용하여 영어로 쓰시오. (어형 변화 필수)

> G: Ted, look at this movie poster. I want to see this movie.
> B: It looks interesting. Can you tell me about it, Amy?
> G: Yes. <u>그것은 지구를 구하는 영웅에 관한 것이야.</u>
> B: It looks like an SF movie.
> G: Yes, it is.

> it / about / a hero / who / save / the Earth / is

➡ _____

[04~05] 다음 대화를 읽고 물음에 답하시오.

> A: We would like to know more about you, Minho. (A)_____
> B: I like pizza most.
> C: Can you tell me about your favorite subject?
> B: Art is (B)<u>내가 가장 좋아하는 것</u>. I want to become an art teacher like Mr. Kim.
> D: What do you like to do after school?
> B: I like to practice taegwondo and sing songs.

04 위 대화의 빈칸 (A)에 들어갈 말로 알맞은 것은?

① Do you like pizza?

② What's your favorite music?

③ What do you think of Italian food?

④ What is your favorite food?

⑤ What do you want to eat?

05 위 대화의 빈칸 (B)의 우리말에 맞게 4단어로 쓰시오.

➡ _____

06 다음 대화의 밑줄 친 부분의 의도로 알맞은 것은?

> G: Who is your homeroom teacher?
> B: My homeroom teacher is Mr. Kim. He teaches math.
> G: <u>Can you tell me more about him?</u>
> B: Yes. He is humorous and kind.

① 알고 있는지 묻기　　② 의무 표현하기

③ 확신 표현하기　　　④ 궁금증 표현하기

⑤ 의견 묻기

[07~08] 다음 대화를 읽고 물음에 답하시오.

Seho: Nice to meet you. I'ⓐd like to join your photo club.

Bora: Thank you ⓑfor your interest in the club. Can you tell me about yourself?

Seho: Yes. My name is Kim Seho. I am in the third grade, class 8.

Andy: Tell me more. What do you like to do most in your free time?

Seho: Well, ⓒthat I like most is to take pictures.

Bora: That's great. What is your dream for the future?

Seho: I want ⓓto be a photographer.

Andy: Then you made the right choice. You can learn ⓔa lot of photo-taking skills here. Welcome to our club.

Seho: Thank you. I'm so glad!

07 위 대화의 밑줄 친 ⓐ~ⓔ 중 어법상 어색한 것은?

① ⓐ ② ⓑ ③ ⓒ ④ ⓓ ⑤ ⓔ

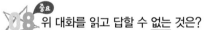**08** 위 대화를 읽고 답할 수 없는 것은?

① What does Seho want to do?

② What does Seho like to do most in his free time?

③ What skills does Andy have?

④ What is Seho's dream for the future?

⑤ What can Seho learn in the photo club?

서답형
09 다음 글의 빈칸에 들어갈 말에 대한 영어 풀이를 보고 주어진 철자로 시작하여 쓰시오.

> My favorite subject is music. I can play the drums and guitar. _____ them, playing the guitar is what I like most.

> in the middle of a group

➡ A_____

10 주어진 문장에 이어질 대화의 순서를 바르게 배열하시오.

> Can you tell me about your plan for this weekend?

> (A) Can you tell me about your goal for the year?
> (B) Yes. I am going to have a birthday party.
> (C) Yes. I want to stop eating fast food.

➡ _____

11 다음 두 사람의 대화가 어색한 것은?

① A: Can you tell me about your dream job?
   B: I want to be a soccer player.

② A: Can you tell us about yourself?
   B: My friends are all kind to me.

③ A: What is your favorite food?
   B: I like pizza most.

④ A: What do you like to do most in your free time?
   B: Well, what I like most is to take pictures.

⑤ A: I'd like to join your photo club.
   B: Thank you for your interest in the club.

서답형
12 다음 글의 밑줄 친 우리말에 맞게 주어진 단어를 알맞은 순서로 배열하시오.

> I often go traveling with my family. 여행에 관해 내가 가장 좋아하는 것은(traveling / what / like / most / I / about) is trying new foods.

➡ _____

[01~02] 다음 대화를 읽고 물음에 답하시오.

W: Today, we have a new student Hojun. Hojun, can you please introduce yourself to the class?

B: Yes. Hi, my name is Kim Hojun. I am from Busan. Nice to meet you.

W: (A)너에 관해 더 말해 줄 수 있니?

B: Yes. I like sports, especially soccer. I want to join a sports club.

W: Is there anything else you want to tell your new friends?

B: (B)나는 모두와 잘 지내고 싶어. Please help me because I'm new here.

W: Thanks, Hojun. Welcome to our class..

01 위 대화의 밑줄 친 (A)의 우리말에 맞게 주어진 단어를 활용하여 영작하시오.

> can / tell / us / more / yourself

➡ _____

02 위 대화의 밑줄 친 (B)의 우리말에 맞게 'get'과 'everyone'을 활용하여 영작하시오.

➡ _____

03 다음 대화의 빈칸에 들어갈 말로 자연스러운 것을 〈보기〉에서 찾아 쓰시오.

A: What is your nickname?

B: My nickname is Speedy (A)_____

C: What do you like most?

B: (B)_____

D: Can you tell me about your dream job?

B: I want to be a baseball player.

A: (C)_____

B: My motto is "You can go forward slowly, but never go back."

> 보기
> • What I like most is to play baseball.
> • because I can run fast.
> • What is your motto?

➡ (A) _____
  (B) _____
  (C) _____

[04~05] 다음 대화를 읽고 물음에 답하시오.

G: Ted, look at this movie poster. I want to see this movie.

B: It looks interesting. Can you tell me about it, Amy?

G: Yes. _____

B: It looks like an SF movie.

G: Yes, it is. Actually, SF is my favorite kind of movie. I like the scenes made with computer technology. They are fantastic and look real.

B: That's cool. I am free this weekend. Let's go to see it together.

G: Sounds good.

04 위 대화의 밑줄 친 질문에 대한 답을 주어진 단어를 활용하여 조건에 맞게 영작하시오.

> 조건
> • 전치사 about을 사용할 것
> • 관계대명사를 사용할 것.
> • 현재시제를 사용할 것
> (a hero, save, the Earth)

➡ It's _____.

05 위 대화의 내용을 정리할 때 빈칸에 알맞은 말을 쓰시오.

> • What Amy wants to see: a (a)_____
> • When Amy is going to see it with Ted:
> (b)_____

Grammar

① **동사 강조**

> - I **do love** swimming in the lake. 나는 호수에서 수영하는 것을 정말 좋아한다.
> - Sumin doesn't like horror movies, but she **does like** animated films.
>   수민이는 공포 영화를 좋아하지 않지만, 애니메이션 영화는 정말 좋아한다.

■ 문장에서 동사의 앞에 do를 배치해서 동사의 의미를 강조할 수 있다. 주어의 인칭과 수 및 시제에 맞춰 do/does/did 등을 활용하며, really의 의미로 해석한다.

- Ted **did see** the accident. Ted가 그 사고를 정말 봤다.
- Jane **does prefer** the mineral water. Jane은 미네랄 워터를 정말 선호한다.

■ 명령문을 강조할 때도 앞에 Do를 사용할 수 있다.

- Be kind to others! = **Do** be kind to others! 다른 사람들에게 정말 친절하게 대하라!

■ do는 동사를 강조하는 반면에 재귀대명사는 주어를 강조한다.

- Mary will do it **herself**. = Mary **herself** will do it. Mary가 직접 그것을 할 것이다.

■ It ~ that 강조구문에서는 주어와 목적어 및 부사(구/절)를 강조한다. 강조하려는 대상에 따라 that을 관계대명사 who/which 등으로 대체할 수 있다.

- Kevin stole the book from Susan's house yesterday. Kevin이 어제 Susan의 집에서 그 책을 훔쳤다.
  - → **It was** Kevin **that[who]** stole the book from Susan's house yesterday.
    어제 Susan의 집에서 그 책을 훔친 것은 바로 **Kevin**이었다.
  - → **It was** the book **that[which]** Kevin stole from Susan's house yesterday.
    Kevin이 어제 Susan의 집에서 훔친 것은 바로 **그 책**이었다.
  - → **It was** yesterday **that** Kevin stole the book from Susan's house.
    Kevin이 Susan의 집에서 그 책을 훔친 것은 바로 **어제**였다.
  - → **It was** from Susan's house **that** Kevin stole the book yesterday.
    어제 Kevin이 그 책을 훔친 것은 바로 **Susan의 집에서**였다.

핵심 Check

1. 괄호 안에서 알맞은 단어를 고르시오.
   (1) I (am / do) feel bad when I pass by smokers.
   (2) He (do / does) want to meet you today.

② 관계대명사 what

> • Tom gave her **what** he had bought. Tom은 그가 산 것을 그녀에게 줬다.
> • This is **what** she has wanted. 이것은 그녀가 원해 왔던 것이다.

■ what은 선행사를 포함하는 관계대명사이다.
- I will do **what** I can. = I will do **(all) the thing(s) that** I can. 나는 내가 할 수 있는 (모든) 것을 할 것이다.
- **What** she told me yesterday is true. = **The thing that** she told me yesterday is true. 그녀가 어제 나에게 말했던 것은 사실이다.

■ 관계대명사 what은 명사절을 이끈다.
- **What he said** to me was shocking. 그가 내게 말해 준 것은 충격적이었다. (주어)
- I can't believe **what she did** in such a short time. 그렇게 단시간에 그녀가 해낸 것을 나는 믿을 수 없다. (목적어)
- They are familiar with **what is baked** now. 그들은 지금 구워지는 것에 익숙하다. (전치사의 목적어)
- This is **what I told you** last Friday. 이것이 지난 금요일에 너에게 말한 것이다. (보어)

■ 의문대명사 what과 문장의 구조는 동일하며, 구분은 해석으로 한다. 관계대명사 what은 '~하는 것'으로, 의문대명사 what은 '무엇(을/이)'로 해석한다.
- She asked me **what** I hid in my hand. 그녀는 내가 손에 무엇을 감췄는지 물어보았다. (의문대명사)
- **What** I brought here is a puppy. 내가 여기 가져온 것은 강아지이다. (관계대명사)

■ 관계대명사 what의 관용적인 표현들
- A man should not be judged by **what he has**. 사람은 그의 재산으로 판단하면 안 된다.
- Abe is **what is called** a lazy worm. Abe는 말하자면 게으른 벌레이다.
- **What's better[worse]** is that she doesn't know the news. 더욱 좋은[나쁜] 것은 그녀가 그 소식을 모른다는 것이다.

핵심 Check

2. 다음 우리말에 맞게 괄호 안의 어구를 바르게 배열하시오.
(1) Janet은 그녀가 만든 것을 나에게 주었다. (what, had, me, made, Janet, she, gave)
➡ _____
(2) 그 공장에서 생산되는 것은 자동차이다. (the factory, what, cars, are, produced, in, are)
➡ _____

01 다음 문장에서 어법상 어색한 부분을 바르게 고쳐 쓰시오.

(1) She judged him by which he had.

_____ ➡ _____

(2) They does love the work of Gustav Climt.

_____ ➡ _____

(3) Shakira did felt very proud of her son.

_____ ➡ _____

(4) All what he said was a lie.

_____ ➡ _____

02 다음 중 어법상 바르지 않은 것은?

① What was taken by her camera was a UFO.

② The workers did built the museum about 100 years ago.

③ John does love what she paints.

④ What the letter says is that I should go back home.

⑤ They all do like her novel.

03 다음 대화의 밑줄 친 부분 중에서 어법상 잘못된 곳을 고르시오.

> A: ①Are you ②tired ③from the trip to Vietnam?
> B: No. I ④do ⑤feeling good.

04 다음 우리말에 맞게 주어진 단어를 바르게 배열하시오. (필요하면 어형을 바꿀 것)

(1) 그가 종이에 쓴 것은 흥미로웠다. (was, the paper, he, on, what, interesting, write)

➡ _____

(2) 그녀는 그녀의 엄마가 만드는 것을 정말 자랑스럽게 느낀다. (she, of, mother, feel, do, proud, her, make, what)

➡ _____

01 다음 빈칸에 알맞은 것은?

> Is this _____ you want to buy?

① which   ② those
③ where   ④ what
⑤ for what

02 중요 다음 문장에서 어법상 틀린 부분을 찾아 바르게 고쳐 쓰시오.

> He failed in his business, and that was worse, he fell ill.

_____ ➡ _____

03 다음 중 두 문장의 뜻이 같지 않은 것은?

① I do spend a lot of time watching TV these days.
→ I really spend much time watching TV these days.
② Jenny will show me what she took with her camera.
→ Jenny will show me the pictures that were taken with her camera.
③ Mom made me what I don't want.
→ Mom made me the thing that I don't want.
④ Sarah did break her leg at the basketball game.
→ Sarah really broke her leg at the basketball game.
⑤ King Arthur did find the legendary sword.
→ King Arthur was able to find the legendary sword.

04 중요 다음 빈칸에 알맞은 말이 순서대로 바르게 짝지어진 것은?

> • Jina _____ love skiing.
> • _____ I hope is to hear from you.

① was – That   ② did – How
③ does – What   ④ is – What
⑤ does – That

05 다음 빈칸에 알맞은 것은?

> It is the most boring magazine _____ I have ever read.

① who   ② where   ③ what
④ that   ⑤ whom

06 고난이도 다음 빈칸에 공통으로 들어갈 말로 알맞은 것은?

> • Kevin _____ feel at ease with her.
> • Mom always _____ the dishes right after dinner.

① does   ② has   ③ do
④ have   ⑤ doesn't

07 다음 중 밑줄 친 부분이 어법상 올바른 것은?

① The officer did warned them immediately.
② Do be quiet!
③ The girl did changed her mind.
④ She does believed it was not a dream.
⑤ Sam's uncles do looks happy.

08 다음 밑줄 친 what 중에서 나머지 넷과 용법이 다른 것은?

① What he said inspired the audience.

② Susan received what he had sent her.

③ I do like what was shown by the magician.

④ I don't know what Mother is cooking.

⑤ This is what they suggested at the meeting.

09 다음 중 어법상 옳은 문장은?

① Is this dog what you were looking for?

② He bought a new car his wife.

③ All the students think what the teacher is giving them special lessons.

④ The boy likes the toy what his aunt bought for him yesterday.

⑤ What she said him was really touching.

10 다음 중 어법상 어색한 문장을 모두 고르면?

① The fans believe what BTS said.

② That is not the thing which the president was trying to say.

③ She will see the movie that the director filmed.

④ This is not the book what she wanted to read.

⑤ Which he told his students at the graduation ceremony made them cry.

11 다음 밑줄 친 부분 중 어법상 어색한 것은?

① All of them do think he is guilty.

② James does teach art six years ago at the school.

③ He did cut his hair this morning.

④ She did find him behind the curtain soon.

⑤ Running a hotel does require a lot of time and energy.

12 다음 빈칸에 들어갈 말로 어색한 것은?

> A: Scott, you don't play Star Craft any longer, do you?
> B: No, but I _____ when I was young.

① used to play a lot

② played it a lot

③ did played it a lot

④ did play a lot

⑤ would play it a lot

13 다음 중 어법상 옳은 문장을 모두 고르면?

> ⓐ The kids are expected to do which their parents want them to do.
> ⓑ Taking a walk is an exercise what gives you more energy.
> ⓒ The thing cannot be cured must be endured.
> ⓓ That will make them think about what they should or shouldn't do.
> ⓔ I can't believe that I've just read in this book.
> ⓕ Making a plan for holidays, you should consider what you can do.
> ⓖ What you teach can be different from that you know.

➡ _____

14 다음 문장의 밑줄 친 부분을 강조하는 문장으로 알맞은 것은?

> Sandra <u>made</u> the plan yesterday.

① Sandra made the only plan yesterday.
② Sandra did made the plan yesterday.
③ Sandra made the very plan yesterday.
④ Sandra did make the plan yesterday.
⑤ Sandra makes did the plan yesterday.

15 다음 중 밑줄 친 부분의 쓰임이 주어진 문장의 밑줄 친 <u>do</u>와 같은 것은?

> The students <u>do</u> feel that something worse than before will happen today.

① Mom has lots of things to <u>do</u>.
② They <u>did</u> their role as extras.
③ I don't eat it, but she <u>does</u> enjoy it.
④ Everyone agrees you <u>did</u> your best at the contest.
⑤ I <u>do</u> not have much information.

16 다음 우리말을 영작할 때, 빈칸에 들어갈 알맞은 말을 쓰시오.

> 이제 그는 과거의 그가 아니다.

➡ Now, he is not _____ he _____ .

17 다음 밑줄 친 what의 용법이 나머지 넷과 다른 것은?

① The girl started to eat <u>what</u> they had given her.
② That volunteer work is <u>what</u> she wants to do.
③ She accepted <u>what</u> he offered.
④ I wonder <u>what</u> he gave her.
⑤ That's <u>what</u> I meant to say.

18 다음 중 어법상 옳은 문장은?

① What she do like to have right now is a piece of pizza.
② Frank did made what his father designed.
③ Sean does love what he is doing.
④ Tony did play the game what he was good at.
⑤ He does show her what he invented it.

19 Which of the following has the same usage as the underlined part below?

> He knows I <u>do</u> feel nervous on the stage.

① He doesn't teach how to swim, <u>does</u> he?
② The college students are <u>doing</u> some research on the bacteria.
③ What Kitty <u>did</u> was to jump off the roof into the pool.
④ Jane folds her ears and so <u>do</u> I.
⑤ I'm sure that I <u>did</u> lock the safe.

20 다음 우리말을, 주어진 단어들을 배열하여 영작할 때, 네 번째로 오는 단어는?

> 그녀가 하고 있는 말에 집중하라.
> (to, is, pay, she, saying, attention, what)

① pay   ② is   ③ she
④ what   ⑤ attention

21 다음 중 어법상 어색한 문장은?

① He forgot the thing what she did.
② They know the reason why it's cold.
③ She knew the way he solved the problem.
④ This is how he killed the big bear.
⑤ That is what Mike wants to buy.

01 다음 대화의 빈칸을 채우되, 동사를 강조하는 'do'를 활용하시오.

(1) A: Did the old man really build the huge sand castle by himself? It's amazing.

   B: Yeah. He _____ _____ it.

(2) A: She doesn't look good. Don't you think that she overworked yesterday?

   B: I _____ _____ so. I'm so worried about her.

(3) A: Can you believe Cindy wrote this letter to her boyfriend?

   B: She _____ _____ this letter to him, though he can't read it yet.

02 다음 문장에서 어법상 어색한 부분을 찾아 바르게 고쳐 다시 쓰시오.

(1) I don't believe that they said to me the other day.

   ➡ _____

(2) Show her that you put in your mouth.

   ➡ _____

(3) She did felt friendly to Mike.

   ➡ _____

(4) I do loved Susan, but she left me forever.

   ➡ _____

(5) What she asked him to help her was not true.

   ➡ _____

03 주어진 두 문장을 관계대명사 what을 이용하여, 하나의 문장으로 만드시오.

(1) • Sarah bought the things.
   • They were comic books.
   ➡ _____

(2) • Robert couldn't believe the thing.
   • The researchers explained it.
   ➡ _____

(3) • The thing was discussed.
   • It was shocking.
   ➡ _____

04 우리말과 일치하도록 괄호 안에 주어진 어휘를 활용하여, 글자 수에 맞게 영작하시오.

(1) 그녀가 동굴 안에서 발견한 것이 세상을 놀라게 했다. (find, cave, surprise, 10 단어)

   ➡ _____

(2) 이 방에서는 정말 조용해라! (quiet, do, 6 단어)

   ➡ _____

(3) 그녀가 시장에서 사온 것들은 모두 비싼 것이었다. (buy, expensive, from, all, 9 단어)

   ➡ _____

05 다음 각 문장을 밑줄 친 부분을 강조하는 문장으로 바꿔 쓰시오.

(1) Charlie found his missing child.

➡ _____

(2) He knows many K-pop singers.

➡ _____

(3) Jeremy wrote those essays last year.

➡ _____

06 다음 문장을 각각의 주어진 조건에 맞게 강조하는 문장으로 바꿔 쓰시오.

• Carl bought the hamster yesterday.

(1) Carl 강조. 재귀대명사 사용.

➡ _____

(2) the hamster 강조. It ~ that 구문 사용.

➡ _____

(3) bought 강조.

➡ _____

(4) yesterday 강조.

➡ _____

07 다음 문장에서 어법상 어색한 부분을 찾아 바르게 고쳐 다시 쓰시오.

(1) She finally accepted that he offered.

➡ _____

(2) He did felt satisfied with the result.

➡ _____

(3) It is quite different from which they have been waiting for.

➡ _____

(4) What I saw him yesterday is not true.

➡ _____

(5) What people believed in the past does surprises me.

➡ _____

08 다음 우리말을 영작할 때, 빈칸에 들어갈 알맞은 단어를 쓰시오.

(1) 그녀는 재즈 음악을 정말 좋아한다.
→ She _____ like jazz music.

(2) 그 회의에서 논의되는 것은 현재의 경제 상황에 매우 중요하다.
→ The thing _____ is being discussed at the meeting is critical for the current economic situation.

(3) 그 곰이 개를 정말 죽였다.
→ The bear did _____ the dog.

(4) 너에게 중요한 것들이 나에게는 중요하지 않다.
→ _____ are important to you _____ not important to me.

09 다음 그림을 보고, 우리말에 맞게 빈칸을 채우되, 괄호 안의 어휘를 이용하시오.

_____(John은 정말 치통을 느꼈기 때문에), he went to the dentist for treatment. (feel, do, as, a toothache)

➡ _____

Reading

My Dream House

Have you ever thought about your dream house? Today, in class, we

현재완료 – 경험
created our dream house. Here are some of the dream houses that we

Here are + 복수 주어   목적격 관계대명사(생략 가능)
made.

A House in Nature - Minho

Nature is my good friend. I do feel good when I walk in the forest.

feel 강조
I'd like to have a dream house in the countryside. It should have a big

~하고 싶다   = The dream house
garden with many flowers and trees. I am always excited by the sound

~이 있는   감정을 느낄 때 과거분사
of birds. It will be wonderful to wake up in the morning and listen to

가주어   진주어   wake up과 병렬구조
the songs of the birds. Also, I'd like to have many pets. It will be fun to

가주어   진주어
play with them!

A Fun Place - Julie

Welcome to my dream house! Having fun is what I want most, so my

동명사 주어   관계대명사 what(~하는 것)
dream house is full of exciting things. It has a theater in the basement.

신나는 감정을 유발할 때 현재분사
There, I can eat cookies and enjoy my favorite movies. My dream

= In the theater
house has a game room on the second floor. I can play many different
kinds of games there.

= in the game room

create: 만들다, 창작하다
forest: 숲
would like to V: ~하고 싶다
countryside: 시골 지역, 전원 지대
excited: 신이 난
wonderful: 아주 멋진, 신나는, 훌륭한
basement: 지하실, 지하층
floor: 층
favorite: 가장 좋아하는

확인문제

● 다음 문장이 본문의 내용과 일치하면 T, 일치하지 <u>않으면</u> F를 쓰시오.

1   The students made their dream house in class. ☐

2   Minho thinks that nature is his good friend. ☐

3   Walking in the forest makes Minho feel lonely. ☐

4   Minho's dream house has a theater. ☐

5   Julie's dream house enables her to play various kinds of games. ☐

My house also has a swimming pool. I want to do fun things with my
_{to부정사를 목적어로 취하는 동사}
friends in my house. You can be my guest!

A Place for Family - Misun

My family is the most important thing to me. In my dream house,
my family feels safe and comfortable. At the gate, you can find
_{2형식 동사(+형용사 보어)}
a beautifully designed sign with my family's picture on it. When
_{과거분사}   = the beautifully designed sign
you enter the house, you will see a large living room. My family
_{타동사(~로 들어가다)}
sometimes plays board games and sings there. It will have a garden
     = in the living room
with a large picnic table for family picnics. There, we will enjoy
_{~이 있는}   = In the garden
barbecues. Do you like my dream house?

A House with New Technology - Bryan

I am an early adopter of new technology. I do like to use new
_{like 강조}
products and technology before others. When I get near my house, the
_{= other people}
front door recognizes my face and opens automatically. The furniture
_{자동사(열리다)}
checks the weather conditions and advises me on what to wear. The
_{의문사+to V = 의문사+주어+should+V(무엇을 ~할지)}
bathroom mirror tells me my weight and the condition of my health.
_{4형식 동사+간접목적어(사람)+직접목적어(사물)}
A robot cleans the house and cooks for me. This is what I can imagine
_{관계대명사 what(~하는 것)}
about my dream house.

swimming pool: 수영장
guest: 손님
comfortable: 편안한
gate: 정문, 대문
picture: 사진
enter: ~로 들어가다
living room: 거실
early adopter: 남들보다 먼저 신기술을 사용하는 사람
product: 물건, 제품
technology: 기술
get near: 가까이 가다, 접근하다
recognize: 알아보다, 인식하다
automatically: 자동으로
furniture: 가구
advise: 조언하다
weight: 무게, 체중
imagine: 상상하다

📎 확인문제

● 다음 문장이 본문의 내용과 일치하면 T, 일치하지 <u>않으면</u> F를 쓰시오.

1 Julie doesn't want anyone to come to her dream house. ☐

2 Misun didn't make a living room in her dream house. ☐

3 Misun wants to enjoy barbecues with her family in her dream house. ☐

4 Bryan wants a house where the latest technologies are used. ☐

5 In Bryan's dream house, he has to clean the house and cooks for himself. ☐

● 우리말을 참고하여 빈칸에 알맞은 말을 쓰시오.

My Dream House

1 _____ you _____ _____ about your dream house?

2 Today, in class, we _____ our dream house.

3 Here _____ some of the dream houses _____ we made.

A House in Nature - Minho

4 _____ is my good friend.

5 I _____ _____ _____ when I walk in the forest.

6 I'd _____ _____ _____ a dream house _____ the countryside.

7 It _____ _____ a big garden _____ many flowers and trees.

8 I _____ always _____ the sound of birds.

9 It will be _____ _____ _____ _____ in the morning and _____ _____ the songs of the birds.

10 Also, I'd _____ _____ _____ many pets. It will be fun _____ _____ with them!

A Fun Place - Julie

11 Welcome _____ my dream house!

12 _____ _____ is _____ I want most, so my dream house _____ _____ _____ exciting things.

13 It has a theater _____ _____ _____.

14 There, I can eat cookies and _____ my favorite _____.

15 My dream house _____ a game room _____ the second _____.

내가 꿈꾸는 집

1 여러분은 꿈의 집에 대해 생각해 본 적이 있나요?

2 오늘, 우리는 수업 시간에 우리가 꿈꾸는 집을 만들었습니다.

3 여기 우리가 만든 몇몇 꿈의 집이 있습니다.

자연 속의 집 – 민호

4 자연은 나의 좋은 친구입니다.

5 나는 숲속에서 걸을 때 기분이 정말 좋습니다.

6 나는 시골에 꿈의 집을 갖고 싶습니다.

7 집에는 많은 꽃과 나무가 있는 큰 정원이 있을 것입니다.

8 나는 항상 새소리에 신이 납니다.

9 아침에 깨어나서 새들의 노래 소리를 듣는 것은 멋질 것입니다.

10 또한 나는 많은 애완동물을 갖고 싶습니다. 그들과 노는 것은 매우 재미있을 것입니다!

재미있는 장소 – Julie

11 나의 꿈의 집에 온 것을 환영합니다!

12 즐겁게 지내는 것은 내가 가장 원하는 것입니다. 그래서 내 꿈의 집은 흥미로운 것들로 가득합니다.

13 집에는 지하에 영화관이 있습니다.

14 그곳에서 나는 쿠키를 먹을 수 있고 내가 좋아하는 영화들을 즐길 수 있습니다.

15 내 꿈의 집에는 2층에 게임방이 있습니다.

16 I can play many different _____ _____ _____ there.

17 My house also has _____ _____ _____.

18 I want to _____ _____ _____ with my friends in my house. You can be _____ _____!

A Place for Family - Misun

19 My family is _____ _____ _____ _____ to me.

20 In my dream house, my family _____ _____ and _____.

21 _____ the gate, you can find a _____ _____ _____ with my family's picture _____ it.

22 When you _____ the house, you will _____ _____ _____ _____ _____.

23 My family sometimes plays _____ _____ and sings there.

24 It will have a garden with _____ _____ _____ _____ for family picnics.

25 There, we will _____ barbecues. _____ _____ _____ my dream house?

A House with New Technology - Bryan

26 I am _____ _____ _____ of new technology.

27 I _____ _____ to use new products and technology _____ others.

28 When I _____ _____ my house, the front door _____ my face and _____ automatically.

29 The furniture _____ the weather _____ and _____ me _____ what to wear.

30 The bathroom mirror _____ _____ my weight and the _____ of my health.

31 A robot _____ the house and _____ _____ me.

32 This is _____ _____ _____ _____ _____ about my dream house.

16 나는 그곳에서 많은 다양한 종류의 게임을 할 수 있습니다.

17 나의 집에는 또한 수영장이 있습니다.

18 나는 나의 집에서 친구들과 함께 즐거운 일들을 하고 싶습니다. 여러분도 나의 손님이 될 수 있습니다!

가족을 위한 장소 – 미선

19 나의 가족은 나에게 가장 중요한 것입니다.

20 내 꿈의 집에서 가족은 안전하고 편안함을 느낍니다.

21 현관에서 여러분은 가족 사진이 있는 아름답게 디자인된 문패를 발견할 수 있습니다.

22 여러분이 집에 들어서면 여러분은 큰 거실을 보게 될 것입니다.

23 나의 가족은 때때로 그곳에서 보드 게임도 하고 노래를 부르기도 합니다.

24 가족 소풍을 위한 커다란 피크닉 테이블이 있는 큰 정원을 갖게 될 것입니다.

25 그곳에서 우리는 바비큐를 즐길 것입니다. 내 꿈의 집이 마음에 드나요?

신기술이 있는 집 – Bryan

26 나는 남들보다 먼저 신기술을 써 보는 것을 좋아하는 사람입니다.

27 나는 새로운 제품이나 기술을 다른 사람보다 먼저 사용하는 것을 정말 좋아합니다.

28 내가 집 근처에 도착할 때, 현관문은 내 얼굴을 인식하고 자동으로 문을 엽니다.

29 가구는 날씨 상태를 확인하여 내게 무엇을 입을지 조언해 줍니다.

30 욕실 거울은 나에게 체중과 건강 상태를 알려 줍니다.

31 로봇은 집을 청소하고 나를 위해 요리합니다.

32 이것이 내가 나의 꿈의 집에 대해 상상할 수 있는 것입니다.

● 우리말을 참고하여 본문을 영작하시오.

My Dream House

1 여러분은 꿈의 집에 대해 생각해 본 적이 있나요?

➡ _____

2 오늘, 우리는 수업 시간에 우리가 꿈꾸는 집을 만들었습니다.

➡ _____

3 여기 우리가 만든 몇몇 꿈의 집이 있습니다.

➡ _____

A House in Nature - Minho

4 자연은 나의 좋은 친구입니다.

➡ _____

5 나는 숲속에서 걸을 때 기분이 정말 좋습니다.

➡ _____

6 나는 시골에 꿈의 집을 갖고 싶습니다.

➡ _____

7 집에는 많은 꽃과 나무가 있는 큰 정원이 있을 것입니다.

➡ _____

8 나는 항상 새소리에 신이 납니다.

➡ _____

9 아침에 깨어나서 새들의 노래 소리를 듣는 것은 멋질 것입니다.

➡ _____

10 또한 나는 많은 애완동물을 갖고 싶습니다. 그들과 노는 것은 매우 재미있을 것입니다!

➡ _____

A Fun Place - Julie

11 나의 꿈의 집에 온 것을 환영합니다!

➡ _____

12 즐겁게 지내는 것은 내가 가장 원하는 것입니다. 그래서 내 꿈의 집은 흥미로운 것들로 가득합니다.

➡ _____

13 집에는 지하에 영화관이 있습니다.

➡ _____

14 그곳에서 나는 쿠키를 먹을 수 있고 내가 좋아하는 영화들을 즐길 수 있습니다.

➡ _____

15 내 꿈의 집에는 2층에 게임방이 있습니다.

➡ _____

16 나는 그곳에서 많은 다양한 종류의 게임을 할 수 있습니다.
➡ _____

17 나의 집에는 또한 수영장이 있습니다.
➡ _____

18 나는 나의 집에서 친구들과 함께 즐거운 일들을 하고 싶습니다. 여러분도 나의 손님이 될 수 있습니다!
➡ _____

A Place for Family - Misun

19 나의 가족은 나에게 가장 중요한 것입니다.
➡ _____

20 내 꿈의 집에서 가족은 안전하고 편안함을 느낍니다.
➡ _____

21 현관에서 여러분은 가족 사진이 있는 아름답게 디자인된 문패를 발견할 수 있습니다.
➡ _____

22 여러분이 집에 들어서면 여러분은 큰 거실을 보게 될 것입니다.
➡ _____

23 나의 가족은 때때로 그곳에서 보드 게임도 하고 노래를 부르기도 합니다.
➡ _____

24 가족 소풍을 위한 커다란 피크닉 테이블이 있는 큰 정원을 갖게 될 것입니다.
➡ _____

25 그곳에서 우리는 바비큐를 즐길 것입니다. 내 꿈의 집이 마음에 드나요?
➡ _____

A House with New Technology - Bryan

26 나는 남들보다 먼저 신기술을 써 보는 것을 좋아하는 사람입니다.
➡ _____

27 나는 새로운 제품이나 기술을 다른 사람보다 먼저 사용하는 것을 정말 좋아합니다.
➡ _____

28 내가 집 근처에 도착할 때, 현관문은 내 얼굴을 인식하고 자동으로 문을 엽니다.
➡ _____

29 가구는 날씨 상태를 확인하여 내게 무엇을 입을지 조언해 줍니다.
➡ _____

30 욕실 거울은 나에게 체중과 건강 상태를 알려 줍니다.
➡ _____

31 로봇은 집을 청소하고 나를 위해 요리합니다.
➡ _____

32 이것이 내가 나의 꿈의 집에 대해 상상할 수 있는 것입니다.
➡ _____

[01~03] 다음 글을 읽고 물음에 답하시오.

My Dream House

Have you ever thought about your dream house? Today, in class, we created our dream house. Here are some of the dream houses that we made.

A House in Nature - Minho

Nature is my good friend. I do feel (A)_____ when I walk in the forest. I'd like to have a dream house in the countryside. It should have a big garden with many flowers and trees. I am always excited by the sound of birds. It will be wonderful to wake up in the morning and listen to the songs of the birds. Also, I'd like to have many pets. It will be fun to play with them!

01 다음 중 빈칸 (A)에 들어갈 말로 가장 적절한 것은?

① embarrassed   ② scared
③ terrible   ④ bored
⑤ good

02  What is Minho mainly talking about?

① the forest he visited last weekend
② the house that he lives in now
③ his dream for the future
④ a dream house he wants to have
⑤ pets that he raises

서답형

03 According to the passage, where does Minho want to have his dream house? Answer in English with a full sentence.

➡ _____

[04~06] 다음 글을 읽고 물음에 답하시오.

A Fun Place - Julie

Welcome to my dream house! ① Having fun is what I want most, so my dream house is full of exciting things. ② It has a theater in the basement. ③ There, I can eat cookies and enjoy my favorite movies. ④ My dream house has a game room on the second floor. ⑤ My house also has a swimming pool. I want to do fun things with my friends in my house. You can be my guest!

04 ①~⑤ 중 다음 주어진 문장이 들어가기에 가장 적절한 곳은?

I can play many different kinds of games there.

①   ②   ③   ④   ⑤

05 다음 중 Julie의 꿈의 집을 잘못 이해한 사람은?

① Amy: The house is perfect for Julie because she likes having fun.
② Brian: The house is filled with many exciting things.
③ Chris: It is a very good idea to have a theater on the ground floor.
④ David: It must be really exciting to have a game room in her house.
⑤ Emily: I want to swim in her swimming pool.

서답형

06 다음과 같이 풀이되는 말을 위 글에서 찾아 쓰시오.

someone who is visiting you because you have invited them

➡ _____

[07~09] 다음 글을 읽고 물음에 답하시오.

(A)_____ - Misun

My family is the most important thing to me. In my dream house, my family feels safe and comfortable. At the gate, you can find a beautifully designed sign with my family's picture on it. When you enter the house, you will see a large living room. My family sometimes plays board games and sings there. It will have a garden with a large picnic table for family picnics. There, we will enjoy barbecues. Do you like my dream house?

07 빈칸 (A)에 들어갈 말로 가장 적절한 것은?

① The Place Where I Live Now
② A Place for Family
③ Let Me Introduce My Family
④ Building a Safe House
⑤ A Comfortable Place for Herself

08 다음 중 위 글을 읽고 답할 수 있는 것은?

① How do Misun's friends feel about her dream house?
② How many family members does Misun have?
③ How large is the living room?
④ What does Misun's family do in the living room?
⑤ When did Misun make the dream house?

서답형
09 According to the passage, what is the most important thing to Misun? Answer in English with a full sentence.

➡ _____

[10~12] 다음 글을 읽고 물음에 답하시오.

A House with New Technology - Bryan

I am an early (A)[adapter / adopter] of new technology. I do like to use new products and technology before others. When I get (B)[near / away] my house, the front door recognizes my face and opens automatically. The furniture checks the weather conditions and advises me on (C)[when / what] to wear. The bathroom mirror tells me my weight and the condition of my health. A robot cleans the house and cooks for me. This is ⓐ_____ I can imagine about my dream house.

10 다음 중 빈칸 ⓐ에 들어갈 말과 같은 말이 들어가는 것은?

① This is the tip _____ I want to give you.
② The book _____ she read is here.
③ A bag is _____ Mary wants to have.
④ The man _____ is walking over there is famous in our town.
⑤ _____ she lied to us doesn't change.

11 (A)~(C) 중 글의 흐름상 적절한 것이 바르게 짝지어진 것은?

① adaptor – near – when
② adaptor – away – when
③ adopter – near – when
④ adopter – away – what
⑤ adopter – near – what

서답형
12 What does a robot do for Bryan in his dream house? Answer in English with a full sentence.

➡ _____
_____

[13~16] 다음 글을 읽고 물음에 답하시오.

My Dream House

Have you ever thought about your dream house? Today, in class, we created our dream house. Here are some of the dream houses that we made.

A House in Nature - Minho

Nature is my good friend. I do feel good when I walk in the forest. I'd like to have a dream house in the countryside. It should have a big garden with many flowers and trees. I am always excited by the sound of birds. It will be wonderful to wake up in the morning and listen to the songs of the birds. (A)Also, I'd like to have many pets. It will be fun to play with them!

13 다음 중 밑줄 친 (A)를 대신하여 쓸 수 있는 것은?

① However   ② Nevertheless
③ Therefore   ④ For example
⑤ In addition

14 다음 중 위 글에 이어질 내용으로 가장 적절한 것은?

① the reason why walking in the forest is good for our health
② how to get to Minho's dream house
③ the dream house that another student created
④ some reasons why Minho doesn't like to live in the city
⑤ benefits of waking up early in the morning

서답형
15 When did the students create their dream house? Answer in English.

➡ _____

16 다음 중 위 글을 바탕으로 알 수 있는 민호의 성향으로 가장 적절한 것은?

① selfish and greedy
② nature friendly
③ wise and considerate
④ talkative and generous
⑤ lonely and boring

[17~19] 다음 글을 읽고 물음에 답하시오.

A Fun Place - Julie

Welcome to my dream house! Having fun is what I want most, so my dream house is full (A)_____ exciting things. It has a theater in the basement. There, I can eat cookies and enjoy my favorite movies. My dream house has a game room on the second floor. I can play many different kinds of games there. My house also has a (B)swimming pool. I want to do fun things with my friends in my house. You can be my guest!

17 다음 중 빈칸 (A)에 들어갈 말과 같은 말이 들어가는 것은?

① He is interested _____ playing with toys.
② They didn't pay attention _____ his presentation.
③ The girl depended _____ her brother.
④ Who does this watch belong _____?
⑤ I want to get rid _____ this headache.

서답형
18 Write the things that Julie's dream house has. Answer in English.

➡ _____

19 다음 중 밑줄 친 (B)와 쓰임이 같은 것은?

① Did you see the crying baby?
② Where is my sleeping pill?
③ Is he riding a bike?
④ The dancing boy is my cousin.
⑤ The surprising news made us sad.

[20~21] 다음 글을 읽고 물음에 답하시오.

A Place for Family - Misun

My family is the most important thing to me. In my dream house, my family feels safe and comfortable. At the gate, you can find a beautifully designed sign with my family's picture on it. When you enter the house, you will see a large living room. My family sometimes plays board games and sings there. It will have a garden with a large picnic table for family picnics. There, we will enjoy barbecues. Do you like my dream house?

20 다음 중 위 글에서 반의어를 찾을 수 없는 것은?

① dangerous   ② small
③ big   ④ uncomfortable
⑤ unimportant

21 다음 중 위 글의 내용과 일치하는 것은?

① Misun thinks she will live in her dream house by herself.
② Misun thinks her family feels unpleasant in the dream house.
③ There is no living room in Misun's house.
④ Misun will enjoy barbecues in the garden with her family.
⑤ The picnic table is for birthday parties for friends.

[22~25] 다음 글을 읽고 물음에 답하시오.

A House with (A)_____ - Bryan
I am an early adopter of new technology. I do like to use ①new products and technology ②after others. When I get near my house, the front door ③recognizes my face and opens ④automatically. The furniture checks the weather conditions and ⑤advises me on what to wear. The bathroom mirror tells me my weight and the condition of my health. A robot cleans the house and cooks for me. This is (B)_____ I can imagine about my dream house.

서답형

22 빈칸 (A)에 알맞은 말을 위 글에서 찾아 쓰시오.

➡ _____

23 다음 중 빈칸 (B)에 들어갈 말로 가장 적절한 것은?

① that   ② how   ③ when
④ why   ⑤ what

24 ①~⑤ 중 글의 흐름상 어색한 것은?

①   ②   ③   ④   ⑤

25 다음 중 위 글을 읽고 답할 수 있는 것은?

① How many stories does the house have?
② What made Bryan become an early adopter?
③ What happens when Bryan gets near his dream house?
④ How many times a day does a robot clean the house?
⑤ How many rooms does the house have?

[01~04] 다음 글을 읽고 물음에 답하시오.

My Dream House

Have you ever thought about your dream house? Today, in class, we created our dream house. Here are some of the dream houses that we made.

A House in Nature - Minho

Nature is my good friend. I do feel good when I walk in the forest. I'd like to have a dream house in the countryside. It should have a big garden with many flowers and trees. I am always excited by the sound of birds. It will be wonderful to wake up in the morning and listen to the songs of the birds. Also, I'd like to have many pets. It will be fun to play with (A)them!

01 According to the passage, how does Minho feel when he walks in the forest? Answer in English with a full sentence.

➡ _____

02 What did they make in class today?

➡ _____

03 What can we find in the garden of Minho's house?

➡ _____

_____

04 중요 밑줄 친 (A)가 가리키는 것을 위 글에서 찾아 쓰시오.

➡ _____

[05~08] 다음 글을 읽고 물음에 답하시오.

A Fun Place - Julie

Welcome to my dream house! Having fun is what I want most, so my dream house is full of exciting things. It has a theater in the basement. There, I can eat cookies and enjoy my favorite movies. My dream house has a game room on the second floor. I can play many different kinds of games there. My house also has a swimming pool. I want to do fun things with my friends in my house. You can be my guest!

05 중요 According to the passage, what does Julie want most? Answer in English with a full sentence.

➡ _____

06 Where can we find a theater in Julie's dream house?

➡ _____

07 고난이도 다음 중 위 글의 내용과 일치하지 않는 것을 찾아 바르게 고쳐 쓰시오.

Julie's dream house is filled with strange things. It has a theater and a swimming pool. She wants to do fun things in her dream house.

➡ _____

08 Where can we find the game room? Answer in English with a full sentence.

➡ _____

[09~11] 다음 글을 읽고 물음에 답하시오.

A Place for Family - Misun

My family is the most important thing to me. In my dream house, (A)my family feels safe and comfortable. At the gate, you can find a beautifully designed sign with my family's picture on it. When you enter the house, you will see a large living room. My family sometimes plays board games and sings there. (B)It will have a garden with a large picnic table for family picnics. There, we will enjoy barbecues. Do you like my dream house?

09 밑줄 친 문장 (A)의 동사를 강조하여 다시 쓰시오.

➡ _____

10 What can we see at the gate of Misun's dream house? Answer in English with a full sentence.

➡ _____

_____

11 밑줄 친 (B)가 가리키는 것을 영어로 쓰시오.

➡ _____

[12~13] 다음 글을 읽고 물음에 답하시오.

A House with New Technology - Bryan

I am an early adopter of new technology. I do like to use new products and technology before others. When I get near my house, the front door recognizes my face and opens automatically. The furniture checks the weather conditions and advises me on what to wear. The bathroom mirror tells me my weight and the condition of my health. A robot cleans the house and cooks for me. This is what I can imagine about my dream house.

12 다음 빈칸에 들어갈 알맞은 말을 위 글에서 찾아 쓰시오.

Early adopters are people who _____
_____.

13 What does the furniture do in Bryan's dream house?

➡ _____

_____

[14~15] 다음 글을 읽고 물음에 답하시오.

To Jina, at some future time

(A)_____ I want to put into my memory box are my soccer ball, my school newspaper, and a letter from my best friend, Semin. I want to put in the soccer ball because I spend a lot of time playing soccer. I want to put in the school newspaper because I do want to remember what happened in my middle school days. Finally, I want to put in the letter from Semin because it shows what good friends we are. What I hope from you is to keep these three things forever.

From Jina

14 빈칸 (A)에 들어갈 알맞은 말을 쓰시오.

➡ _____

15 Write the reason why Jina wants to put the school newspaper in the memory box. Use the words 'It's because' and 'does'.

➡ _____

_____

After You Read -Read and Match

I like to use new products and technology.
목적어(to부정사의 명사적 용법)

There are many items that use new technology in my dream house. Every day
관계대명사(주격)   선행사가 items이므로 복수동사 use를 사용

my furniture checks the weather and tells me (□what to do / ☑what to wear).
확인하다. 점검하다   의문사+to부정사(무엇을 입을지): 명사구

A robot (☑ cooks / □cleans my classroom) for me.

해석

나는 새로운 제품과 기술을 사용하는 것이 좋다.

내가 꿈꾸는 집에는 새로운 기술을 이용하는 물건들이 많이 있다. 매일 내 가구들은 날씨를 확인해서 내가 무엇을 입을지 말해 준다. 로봇은 나에게 요리를 해 준다.

Project Step 1

A: We would like to know more about you, Minho.
   would like to+V: ~하고 싶다

   What is your favorite food?
   상대방이 가장 좋아하는 것 묻기

B: I like pizza most.
   '가장 (많이)'라는 최상급 표현

C: Can you tell me about your favorite subject?

B: Art is what I like most.
   관계대명사로 the thing that[which]으로 바꾸어 쓸 수 있다. '~하는 것'으로 해석한다.

   I want to become an art teacher like Mr. Kim.
   전치사로 '~처럼, ~와 같은'

D: What do you like to do after school?

B: I like to practice taegwondo and sing songs.
   practice와 sing은 병렬 관계다.

구문해설 • **favorite**: 가장 좋아하는 • **subject**: 과목. • **after school**: 방과 후에 • **practice**: 연습하다

A: 우리는 너에 대해서 더 많이 알고 싶어, 민호야. 네가 가장 좋아하는 음식은 뭐니?
B: 나는 피자를 가장 좋아해.
C: 나에게 네가 가장 좋아하는 과목에 대해 말해 줄 수 있니?
B: 미술이 내가 가장 좋아하는 거야. 나는 김 선생님과 같은 미술 선생님이 되고 싶어.
D: 너는 방과 후에 무엇을 하는 것을 좋아하니?
B: 나는 태권도를 연습하고, 노래 부르는 것을 좋아해.

Project Step 3

We made an M and an H with what Minho likes. Minho likes art and pizza, so
                                관계대명사(~하는 것)   결과를 이끄는 접속사(그래서)

we made an M with a paint brush, colored pencils, and a piece of pizza. We

made an H with a musical note and taegwondo.
수단을 나타내는 전치사(~로, ~을 써서)

구문해설 • **art**: 예술, 미술 • **paint brush**: 붓 • **colored pencil**: 색연필

우리는 민호가 좋아하는 것으로 M과 H를 만들었습니다. 민호는 미술과 피자를 좋아합니다. 그래서 우리는 붓, 색연필, 그리고 피자 조각으로 M을 만들었습니다. 우리는 음표와 태권도로 H를 만들었습니다.

영역별 핵심문제

01 다음 주어진 두 단어의 관계가 같도록 빈칸에 알맞은 단어를 쓰시오.

> wide : narrow = backward : _____

02 다음 글의 빈칸 (a)와 (b)에 들어갈 단어가 바르게 짝지어진 것은?

> • Today, in class, we (a)_____ our dream house. Here are some of the dream houses that we made.
> • My dream house is full of exciting things. I want to do fun things with my friends in my house. You can be my (b)_____!

① destroyed – host   ② destroyed – guest
③ created – host   ④ created – guest
⑤ made – pet

[03~04] 다음 영영 풀이에 해당하는 것을 고르시오.

03

> an animal that is kept in the home as a companion and treated kindly

① puppy   ② furniture
③ pet   ④ swallow
⑤ subject

04

> a short sentence or phrase that expresses a belief or purpose

① motto   ② sign
③ photographer   ④ hero
⑤ forest

05 (A)와 (B)의 빈칸에 공통으로 들어갈 말을 쓰시오.

> (A) There are many items that use new _____ in my dream house. Every day my furniture checks the weather and tells me what to wear.
> (B) Romans had very advanced _____ in producing concrete.

06 다음 밑줄 친 부분의 뜻이 <u>잘못된</u> 것은?

① You made the right <u>choice</u>. (선택)
② I like the <u>scenes</u> made with computer technology. (장면)
③ This is what I can <u>imagine</u> about my dream house. (상상하다)
④ I'd like to have many <u>pets</u>. (애완동물)
⑤ My dream house has a <u>theater</u> in the basement. (오락실)

07 다음 글의 빈칸에 들어갈 말로 적절한 것은?

> G1: Hi! I am Teri. I like running in the evening. I feel (a)_____ when I exercise.
> B2: Hello, my name is Jack. I'm (b)_____ in stars. I usually go out to see stars at night.

	(a)	(b)
①	bored	uninterested
②	tired	interested
③	tired	uninterested
④	refreshed	interested
⑤	refreshed	pleased

08 주어진 문장에 이어질 대화를 순서에 맞게 바르게 배열한 것은?

> G: Jiho, how was your first day of third grade?

(A)

> B: Yes. He is humorous and told us some fun stories about math. It was interesting.
> G: Cool! I hope you enjoy studying math.

(B)

> B: My homeroom teacher is Mr. Kim. He teaches math.
> G: Can you tell me more about him?

(C)

> B: It was pretty good. The teachers and my new classmates are all good.
> G: That sounds good. Who is your homeroom teacher?

① (A) – (B) – (C)　　② (B) – (A) – (C)
③ (B) – (C) – (A)　　④ (C) – (A) – (B)
⑤ (C) – (B) – (A)

[09~11] 다음 대화를 읽고 물음에 답하시오.

> Seho: Nice to meet you. I'd like to join your photo club. (①)
> Bora: Thank you for your interest in the club. Can you tell me about yourself? (②)
> Seho: Yes. My name is Kim Seho. I am in the third grade, class 8.
> Andy: Tell me more. (③)
> Seho: Well, what I like most is to take pictures. (④)
> Bora: That's great. (A)＿＿＿＿＿＿＿
> Seho: I want to be a photographer. (⑤)
> Andy: Then you made the right choice. You can learn a lot of photo-taking skills here. Welcome to our club.
> Seho: Thank you. I'm so glad!

09 주어진 문장이 들어갈 위치로 알맞은 것은?

> What do you like to do most in your free time?

①　　②　　③　　④　　⑤

10 위 대화의 빈칸 (A)에 들어갈 말로 알맞은 것을 <u>모두</u> 고르시오.

① Can you tell me about your dream job?
② What do you like most?
③ Can you tell me about your goal for next year?
④ What is your dream for the future?
⑤ What do you think of a photographer?

11 위 대화의 내용과 일치하지 <u>않는</u> 것은?

① Seho wants to join the photo club.
② Bora wants to know about Seho.
③ Seho already knows a lot of photo-taking skills.
④ Bora and Andy belong to the photo club.
⑤ The photo club teaches lots of photo-taking skills.

12 다음의 제시된 〈조건〉에 맞게 Carol의 질문에 대한 답을 완성하시오.

> ┤ 조건 ├
> (1) 관계대명사 what을 사용할 것
> (2) to부정사를 사용할 것
> (3) 'play baseball'을 이용할 것

> Andy: What is your nickname?
> Becky: My nickname is Speedy because I can run fast.
> Carol: What do you like most?
> Becky: ＿＿＿＿＿＿＿＿＿＿＿
> Dan: Can you tell me about your dream job?
> Becky: I want to be a baseball player.

➡ ＿＿＿＿＿＿＿＿＿＿＿＿＿＿＿

Grammar

13 다음 중 어법상 옳은 문장은?

① Jenny do look lovely.

② They are look handsome on the stage.

③ He does believes she's crazy.

④ I do met my cousins in Suwon.

⑤ She did make a fortune.

14 다음 우리말의 내용을 주어진 조건에 맞게 강조하는 문장으로 영작했을 때, 빈칸에 적절한 말을 쓰시오.

> • Peter가 지난 수업에서 그 문제들을 풀었다.
>
> (1) Peter 강조
>
>   = It was _____
>
>   in the last class.
>
> (2) '풀었다'라는 동사 강조
>
>   = Peter _____.
>
> (3) '지난 수업에서' 강조
>
>   = It was _____
>
>   _____.

15 다음 빈칸에 알맞은 말이 바르게 짝지어진 것은?

> • The photographer showed me _____
>   were taken in front of the White House.
> • Janet _____ start her own business.

① what – did

② that – does

③ whose – does

④ what – do

⑤ that – did

16 Which of the followings are grammatically incorrect? Choose all.

① The room does feel too cold.

② Do be careful when you drive.

③ Sam did believe what Will said.

④ My uncle do likes playing with me.

⑤ It did took three hours and a half.

17 다음 두 문장의 의미가 같도록 빈칸에 들어갈 알맞은 말을 쓰시오.

> • I didn't see the thing that he had done.
> = I didn't see _____ he had done.

[18~19] 다음 그림을 보고 빈칸에 맞는 단어를 채우시오.

18

➡ *The Old Man and the Sea* by Ernest Hemingway _____ make me impressed.

19

➡ The pyramids showed _____ the ancient Egyptians believed.

20 다음 밑줄 친 부분의 쓰임이 나머지와 다른 것은?

① The guards do protect well the actor.

② Can I do some laundry over there?

③ Barbara does work for the bank.

④ Paul did eat kimchi last night.

⑤ Laura does play the villain role.

21 다음 중 각각의 (A)와 (B)에서 밑줄 친 부분의 쓰임이 서로 일치하는 것을 고르면?

① (A) What should we do now?

   (B) He knows that I do believe her.

② (A) She did keep the promise.

   (B) They did something to correct it.

③ (A) Emily does as she wants.

   (B) He does buy the sneakers of the brand.

④ (A) Do be nice to others.

   (B) Do you know when he will come?

⑤ (A) Everyone wonders how he did it.

   (B) All the villagers don't trust him even if he does good things.

22 다음 중 어법상 어색한 문장을 모두 고르면?

① What Robert really wanted at that moment was to be left alone on the stage.

② Susan's cold face was what made her husband nervous.

③ That you said was dangerous, and we were all worried about it.

④ There are about 6 different songs what the musician composed.

⑤ Asking questions and finding out the answers are what scientists do.

Reading

[23~27] 다음 글을 읽고 물음에 답하시오.

My Dream House

Have you ever thought about your dream house? Today, in class, we created our dream house. Here are some of the dream houses (A)_____ we made.

A House in Nature - Minho

Nature is my good friend. I do feel good when I walk in the forest. I'd like to have a dream house in the countryside. (B)It should have a big garden with many flowers and trees. I am always excited by the sound of birds. It will be wonderful to wake up in the morning and listen to the songs of the birds. Also, I'd like to have many pets. (C)It will be fun to play with them!

23 다음 중 빈칸 (A)에 들어갈 말로 적절한 것을 모두 고르시오.

① which   ② why   ③ what

④ that   ⑤ who

24 밑줄 친 (B)가 가리키는 것을 위 글에서 찾아 쓰시오.

➡ _____

25 According to the passage, what always makes Minho excited? Answer in English with a full sentence.

➡ _____

26 다음 중 밑줄 친 (C)와 쓰임이 같은 것은?

① It is not that far from here to the mart.

② It was cold and windy outside.

③ It looks like a cucumber.

④ It is interesting to read the novel.

⑤ It is flying high in the sky.

27 다음 중 위 글의 내용과 일치하지 <u>않는</u> 것은?

① Minho's dream house was made in class today.

② Minho likes to walk in the forest.

③ Minho wants his dream house to be in the middle of a city.

④ Lots of flowers and trees can be found in the garden.

⑤ Minho wants to have many pets in his dream house.

[28~31] 다음 글을 읽고 물음에 답하시오.

> To Jina, at some future time
> Hi, Jina. What I want to ①put into my memory box are my soccer ball, my school newspaper, and a letter ②from my best friend, Semin. I want to put in the soccer ball because I spend a lot of time ③to play soccer. I want to put in the school newspaper because I ④do want to remember what happened in my middle school days. (A)Finally, I want to put in the letter from Semin because it shows ⑤what good friends we are. What I hope from you is to keep these three things forever.
> From Jina

28 ①~⑤ 중 어법상 바르지 <u>않은</u> 것은?

    ①   ②   ③   ④   ⑤

29 다음 중 밑줄 친 (A)를 대신하여 쓸 수 있는 것은?

① Fortunately   ② At first

③ Lastly   ④ Interestingly

⑤ Hardly

30 Write the reason why Jina wants to put in the letter from Semin. Use the phrase 'It's because.'

  ➡ _____

31 다음 중 위 글을 읽고 답할 수 <u>없는</u> 것은?

① How many things does Jina want to put into the box?

② How many letters does Jina want to put into the box?

③ Who is Jina's best friend?

④ Why does Jina want to put her soccer ball into the box?

⑤ When did Jina start to play soccer?

32 주어진 단어를 바르게 배열하여 다음 글의 주제를 쓰시오.

> To Jina, at some future time
> Hi, Jina. What I want to put into my memory box are my soccer ball, my school newspaper, and a letter from my best friend, Semin. I want to put in the soccer ball because I spend a lot of time playing soccer. I want to put in the school newspaper because I do want to remember what happened in my middle school days. Finally, I want to put in the letter from Semin because it shows that what good friends we are. What I hope from you is to keep these three things forever.
> From Jina

(Jina / put / wants / into / memory / her / things / to / box)

  ➡ _____

01 출제율 90%

다음 짝지어진 단어의 관계가 같도록 빈칸에 알맞은 말을 쓰시오.

> answer : reply = counsel : _____

02 출제율 90%

다음 영영 풀이에 해당하는 단어는?

> land that is not in towns or cities and may have farms, fields, etc.

① ground   ② countryside

③ space   ④ forest

⑤ castle

03 출제율 95%

다음 대화의 밑줄 친 (A)와 같은 의미의 문장을 주어진 단어를 활용하여 쓰시오.

> A: What is your nickname?
> B: My nickname is Speedy because I can run fast.
> C: What do you like most?
> B: What I like most is to play baseball.
> D: (A)Can you tell me about your dream job?
> B: I want to be a baseball player.

➡ I'm _____.

   (really / curious)

[04~05] 다음 대화를 읽고 물음에 답하시오.

> W: Today, we have a new student Hojun. Hojun, can you please introduce yourself to the class?
> B: Yes. Hi, my name is Kim Hojun. I am from Busan. Nice to meet you.
> W: Can you tell us more about yourself?
> B: Yes. I like sports, especially soccer. I want to join a sports club.

> W: (A)새 친구들에게 더 할 말 없니?
> B: I want to get along with everyone. Please help me because I'm new here.
> W: Thanks, Hojun. Welcome to our class.

04 출제율 100%

위 대화를 읽고 다음 빈칸에 Hojun에 관한 정보를 완전한 문장의 영어로 쓰시오.

(1) Hojun의 출신지: _____

(2) Hojun이 좋아하는 운동: _____

(3) Hojun이 새 친구들에게 하고 싶은 말:

_____

05 출제율 90%

위 대화의 밑줄 친 우리말에 맞게 주어진 어구를 알맞게 배열하시오.

> (there / anything / is / you / want / else / to tell / your new friends / ?)

➡ _____

06 출제율 90%

What does each student like most? (What으로 문장을 시작하여 쓰시오.)

> (1) Jiho: I often go traveling with my family. What I like most about traveling is trying new foods.
> (2) Bora: My favorite subject is music. I can play the drums and guitar. Among them, playing the guitar is what I like most.
> (3) Jenny: This is a picture of Dora. She is my best friend, not just a pet. Playing with her in my free time is what I like most.

➡ (1) _____

   (2) _____

   (3) _____

_____

G: Ted, look at this movie poster. I want to see this movie.

B: It looks (a)interesting. Can you tell me about it, Amy?

G: Yes. It is about a hero (b)who saves the Earth.

B: It (c)looks like an SF movie.

G: Yes, it is. Actually, SF is my favorite kind of movie. I like the scenes (d)making with computer technology. They are fantastic and (e)look real.

B: That's cool. I am free this weekend. Let's go to see it together.

G: Sounds good.

07 위 대화의 밑줄 친 부분 (a)~(e) 중 어법상 어색한 것은?

① (a) ② (b) ③ (c) ④ (d) ⑤ (e)

08 위 대화의 내용과 일치하지 않는 것은?

① They are talking about a movie.

② Amy wants to see the movie.

③ The movie is about a hero who helps people in need.

④ Amy likes SF movies a lot.

⑤ They are going to see the movie this weekend.

[09~11] 다음 대화를 읽고 물음에 답하시오.

Seho: Nice to meet you. I'd like to join your photo club. (①)

Bora: Thank you for your interest in the club. (A)_____

Seho: Yes. My name is Kim Seho. (②) I am in the third grade, class 8.

Andy: Tell me more. What do you like to do most in your free time? (③)

Seho: Well, (B)내가 가장 좋아하는 것은 사진을 찍는 거야.

Bora: That's great. What is your dream for the future? (④)

Seho: I want to be a photographer.

Andy: (⑤) You can learn a lot of photo-taking skills here. Welcome to our club.

Seho: Thank you. I'm so glad!

09 위 대화의 빈칸 (A)에 들어갈 말로 알맞은 것은?

① What's your favorite club?

② Can you tell me about yourself?

③ Let me introduce myself to you.

④ Do you know who I am?

⑤ Do you mind telling me about yourself?

10 위 대화의 밑줄 친 (B)의 우리말에 맞게 주어진 조건을 활용하여 대화를 완성하시오.

┌─ 조건 ─
│ (1) 관계대명사 what을 사용할 것
│ (2) to부정사를 사용할 것

➡ _____

11 위 대화의 (①)~(⑤) 중 주어진 문장이 들어갈 위치로 알맞은 것은?

Then you made the right choice.

① ② ③ ④ ⑤

12 다음 두 문장의 의미가 같도록 빈칸을 채우시오. (단, book 과 that은 사용 불가)

• What she bought at Sam's bookstore were the books about making hip-hop music.

= The _____ _____ she bought at Sam's bookstore were the books about making hip-hop music.

출제율 95%

13 다음 중 <u>어색한</u> 문장을 <u>모두</u> 고르시오.

① You are the only one what makes me happy.

② Edvard Munch did painted *The Scream* in 1893.

③ Jeremy did take good care of his youngest sister.

④ It were the books that he bought for Sumi yesterday.

⑤ All the citizens understood what the mayor announced.

출제율 100%

14 다음 주어진 문장의 밑줄 친 what과 같은 용법으로 쓰인 것을 <u>모두</u> 고르시오.

> • That is <u>what</u> she has taught for decades.

① <u>What</u> did you come here for?

② I don't know <u>what</u> these words mean.

③ <u>What</u> upset me was his attitude.

④ I wonder <u>what</u> you are interested in.

⑤ <u>What</u> was considered polite in the past is not always seen as such today.

출제율 90%

15 다음 두 문장을 관계대명사 what을 이용하여, 하나의 문장으로 만드시오.

(1) • That is not the thing.

 • Harry has always wanted it.

 ➡ _____

(2) • My parents already know the things.

 • They happened three weeks ago.

 ➡ _____

(3) • Tell her the things.

 • They have been bothering you.

 ➡ _____

[16~18] 다음 글을 읽고 물음에 답하시오.

To Jina, at some future time

 What I want to put into my memory box are my soccer ball, my school newspaper, and a letter from my best friend, Semin. I want to put in ⓐ_____ because I spend a lot of time playing soccer. I want to put in ⓑ_____ because I do want to remember what happened in my middle school days. Finally, I want to put in ⓒ_____ from Semin because it shows what good friends we are. (A)내가 너에게 바라는 것 is to keep these three things forever.

From Jina

출제율 90%

16 빈칸 ⓐ~ⓒ에 들어갈 알맞은 말을 위 글에서 찾아 쓰시오.

 ➡ ⓐ _____

 ⓑ _____

 ⓒ _____

출제율 95%

17 주어진 단어를 활용하여 밑줄 친 우리말 (A)를 영어로 쓰시오.

> (hope / from)

 ➡ _____

출제율 95%

18 다음 중 위 글의 내용과 일치하는 것은?

① Jina is making a memory box to send to Semin.

② Jina used to wite letters to Semin.

③ Jina puts in more than three things.

④ Jina would like to keep the memory box forever.

⑤ Jina wants Semin to accept the memory box.

[19~20] 다음 글을 읽고 물음에 답하시오.

A Place for Family - Misun

My family is the most important thing to me. In my dream house, my family feels ①safe and comfortable. ②At the gate, you can find a beautifully ③designed sign with my family's picture on it. When you ④enter into the house, you will see a large living room. My family sometimes plays board games and sings there. It will have a garden with a large picnic table ⑤for family picnics. There, we will enjoy barbecues. Do you like my dream house?

출제율 95%

19 밑줄 친 ①~⑤ 중 어법상 바르지 않은 것은?

① ② ③ ④ ⑤

출제율 100%

20 다음 중 위 글에서 찾아볼 수 없는 것은?

① the gate with a beautifully designed sign

② a large living room where Misun's family can sing

③ a kitchen with a large picnic table

④ a garden where Misun's family will enjoy barbecues

⑤ a large picnic table for her family picnics

[21~23] 다음 글을 읽고 물음에 답하시오.

A House with New Technology - Bryan

I am an early adopter of new technology. I do like to use new products and technology before others. When I get near my house, the front door recognizes my face and opens automatically. The furniture checks the weather conditions and advises me on what to wear. The bathroom mirror tells me my weight and the condition of my health. A robot cleans the house and cooks for me. This is what I can imagine about my dream house.

출제율 100%

21 다음 중 위 글의 내용과 일치하는 것은?

① Bryan is not interested in using new technology.

② Bryan opens the front door by using a remote control.

③ The front door can identify Bryan's face.

④ Bryan gets some advice on what to wear from the bathroom mirror.

⑤ A robot answers the phone for Bryan.

출제율 90%

22 다음과 같이 풀이할 수 있는 말을 위 글에서 찾아 쓰시오.

to know who someone is or what something is

➡ _____

출제율 90%

23 What does the bathroom mirror tell Bryan? Answer in English with a full sentence.

➡ _____

_____

01 다음 대화를 아래 〈조건〉에 따라 완성하시오.

> G: Jiho, (A) _____
>
> B: It was pretty good. The teachers and my new classmates are all good.
>
> G: That sounds good. Who is your homeroom teacher?
>
> B: My homeroom teacher is Mr. Kim. He teaches math.
>
> G: (B) _____
>
> B: Yes. He is humorous and told us some fun stories about math. It was interesting.
>
> G: Cool! I hope you enjoy studying math.

> ┤ 보기 ├
>
> (A) how를 이용하여 3학년 첫 날이 어떠했는지 묻는 말을 쓸 것.
>
> (B) Mr. Kim에 대해 더 많이 알고 싶어 하는 궁금증을 표현하는 말을 쓸 것.

02 다음 대화의 밑줄 친 우리말을 주어진 어휘를 배열하여 완성하시오.

> B: This movie looks like an SF movie.
>
> G: Yes, it is. Actually, SF is my favorite kind of movie. <u>나는 컴퓨터 기술로 만들어진 장면을 좋아해.</u> They are fantastic and look real.

> I / made / the scenes / with / computer technology / like

➡ _____

03 다음 대화를 읽고 물음에 영어로 답하시오.

> Seho: Nice to meet you. I'd like to join your photo club.
>
> Bora: Thank you for your interest in the club. Can you tell me about yourself?
>
> Seho: Yes. My name is Kim Seho. I am in the third grade, class 8.
>
> Andy: Tell me more. What do you like to do most in your free time?
>
> Seho: Well, what I like most is to take pictures.
>
> Bora: That's great. What is your dream for the future?
>
> Seho: I want to be a photographer.
>
> Andy: Then you made the right choice. You can learn a lot of photo-taking skills here. Welcome to our club.
>
> Seho: Thank you. I'm so glad!

(1) What does Seho like to do most in his free time?

➡ _____

(2) What can Seho learn in the photo club?

➡ _____

04 다음 우리말과 같은 뜻이 되도록 주어진 단어들을 이용하여, 제시된 글자 수에 맞게 영작하시오.

(1) 나는 내가 가진 것을 최대한 이용해야 한다. (most, make, must, of, have, 9 단어)

➡ _____

(2) 당신이 하는 것이 당신이 말하는 것보다 훨씬 중요하다. (say, than, much, important, 11 단어)

➡ _____

05 다음 주어진 문장을 밑줄 친 부분을 강조하는 문장으로 바꾸어 쓰시오.

(1) People in Hong Kong love freedom.

➡ _____

(2) Did he break the door yesterday?

➡ _____

(3) The wall was painted by Mr. Lee.

➡ _____

[06~08] 다음 글을 읽고 물음에 답하시오.

A House with New Technology - Bryan

I am an early adopter of new technology. I do like to use new products and technology before others. When I get near my house, the front door recognizes my face and opens automatically. The furniture checks the weather conditions and advises me on what to wear. The bathroom mirror tells me my weight and the condition of my health. A robot cleans the house and cooks for me. This is what I can imagine about my dream house.

06 다음 역할에 맞게 빈칸에 알맞은 말을 쓰시오.

(1) _____ : checking weather conditions

(2) _____ : cooking for Bryan

(3) _____ : telling the condition of Bryan's health

07 다음 물음에 조건에 맞게 답하시오.

Q: Does the front door really open automatically?

A: Yes. _____ by recognizing my face.
(동사를 강조하여 쓸 것)

08 다음 중 위 글의 내용과 일치하지 않는 것을 두 군데 찾아 바르게 고쳐 쓰시오.

There are many items that use new technology in my dream house. Every day my furniture checks the weather and tells me what to do. A robot cleans my classroom for me.

➡ _____

➡ _____

[09~10] 다음 글을 읽고 물음에 답하시오.

A Place for Family - Misun

My family is the most important thing to me. In my dream house, my family feels safe and comfortable. At the gate, you can find a beautifully designed sign with my family's picture on (A)it. When you enter the house, you will see a large living room. My family sometimes plays board games and sings there. It will have a garden with a large picnic table for family picnics. There, we will enjoy barbecues. Do you like my dream house?

09 밑줄 친 (A)가 가리키는 것을 위 글에서 찾아 쓰시오.

➡ _____

10 According to the passage, where will the family enjoy barbecues? Answer in English with a full sentence.

➡ _____

01 아래 표를 보고 (A)는 주말 계획을, (B)는 올해 목표에 관해 묻는 말과 답을 하나 골라 쓰시오.

(A) Plan for This Weekend	(B) Goal for the Year
• have a birthday party	• stop eating fast food
• go to a concert	• get good grades
• take a day trip	• make many friends

A: _____ your plan for this weekend?

B: Yes. I am going _____.

A: _____ your goal for the year?

B: Yes. I want to _____.

02 〈보기〉에 주어진 어휘를 활용하여, 관계대명사 what이 들어간 문장을 3개 이상 만드시오. 단, 각 그룹에서 하나 이상의 단어가 각 문장에 포함되어야 함.

> 보기
>
> A 그룹: see / look for / find / know / buy
> B 그룹: Jane / Brian / Ms. Smith / Kathy
> C 그룹: book / the bag / at the market / at the library / in the kitchen

(1) _____

(2) _____

(3) _____

03 지민의 추억 상자에 넣을 물건과 그 이유를 살펴보고 다음 편지를 완성하시오.

> dancing shoes – They are related to my future dream.
> the first prize from a dancing performance – I can remember my happiest moment.
> some pictures with friends – I don't want to forget my friends from middle school.

> To Jimin, at some future time
> Hi, Jimin. What I want to put into this memory box are _____, _____
> _____, and _____. I want to put in _____
> because _____. I want to put in _____
> because _____. Lastly, I want to _____
> because _____.

단원별 모의고사

01 다음 단어에 대한 영어 설명이 <u>어색한</u> 것은?

① hero: a very brave person, often a man, that a lot of people admire
② furniture: things such as chairs, tables, and beds that you put into a room or building
③ photographer: a person who takes photographs, either as a job or hobby
④ save: to make something happen or exist
⑤ advise: to tell someone that they should do something

02 다음 짝지어진 단어의 관계가 같도록 빈칸에 알맞은 말을 쓰시오.

enter : go into = sketch : _____

03 다음 영영풀이에 해당하는 단어를 고르시오.

a large area of land that is covered with trees

① forest   ② countryside
③ farm   ④ wood
⑤ furniture

04 다음 중 짝지어진 대화가 어색한 것은?

① A: Can you tell me about your plan for this weekend?
  B: Yes. I am going to have a birthday party.
② A: What is your dream for the future?
  B: I want to be a doctor.
③ A: Can you tell me about your goal for the year?
  B: Yes. I want to stop eating fast food.
④ A: Can you tell me about your favorite subject?
  B: I want to become an art teacher.
⑤ A: Can you please introduce yourself to the class?
  B: Yes. Hi, my name is Kim Hojun.

[05~06] 다음 대화의 빈칸에 들어갈 말로 알맞은 것을 고르시오. (06은 정답이 2개)

05
A: What is your nickname?
B: My nickname is Speedy because I can run fast.
C: _____
B: What I like most is to play baseball.

① What do you do in your free time?
② What are you doing?
③ What do you like most?
④ Do you like to play baseball?
⑤ Why do you like sports?

06
A: We would like to know more about you, Minho. What is your favorite food?
B: I like pizza most.
C: _____
B: Art is what I like most. I want to become an art teacher like Mr. Kim.

① What is your favorite color?
② Can you tell me about your favorite subject?
③ Who's your favorite teacher?
④ How about Korean art?
⑤ What subject do you like most?

[07~08] 다음 대화를 읽고 물음에 답하시오.

W: Today, we have a new student Hojun. Hojun, can you please introduce yourself to the class?

B: Yes. Hi, my name is Kim Hojun. I am from Busan. Nice to meet you.

W: Can you tell us more about yourself?

B: Yes. I like sports, especially soccer. I want to join a sports club.

W: Is there anything else you want to tell your new friends?

B: (A)_____ Please help me because I'm new here.

W: Thanks, Hojun. Welcome to our class.

07 빈칸 (A)에 들어갈 말로 알맞은 것은?

① I want to know more about you.
② I'm really curious about soccer.
③ I want to get along with everyone.
④ I want to know about Busan.
⑤ I don't feel like talking to you.

08 What does Hojun want to do? (7단어로 답할 것)

➡ _____

09 다음 대화의 빈칸에 'tell me'를 사용하여 상대방의 가장 친한 친구에 관한 궁금증을 나타내는 표현을 쓰시오.

A: _____

B: Yes. My best friend is Jiwoo. He is very good at surfing.

10 다음의 〈보기〉를 보고 Andy와 Teri가 가장 좋아하는 것을 묻고 답하는 문장을 완성하시오.

> ┤ 보기 ├
> Andy: listen to K-pop music
> Teri: travel by train

Andy: _____, Teri?

Teri: _____ is to travel by train. How about you?

Andy: _____ is to _____ K-pop music.

11 (A)와 (B)에 공통으로 들어갈 말로 알맞은 것은?

(A)
My favorite subject is music. I can play the drums and guitar. Among them, playing the guitar is _____.
(B)
This is a picture of Dora. She is my best friend, not just a pet. Playing with her in my free time is _____.

① what I don't want to do
② that I want to know what a friend is for
③ why I like music
④ what I like most
⑤ how we know each other

12 다음 대화의 빈칸에 들어갈 말로 적절하지 <u>않은</u> 것은?

A: Can you tell me about your dream job?
B: I want to be a baseball player.
A: What is your motto?
B: My motto is "_____."

① Actions speak louder than words
② Working hard is the mother of good luck
③ If you do not walk today, you will have to run tomorrow
④ You can go forward slowly, but never go back
⑤ There is no place like home

13 다음 두 문장을 같은 의미의 한 문장이 되도록 관계대명사 what을 사용하여 쓰시오.

(1) • I will read the words.
   • Sarah wrote them in her mail.
   = I will read _____.

(2) • Australia is the place.
   • Gloria wants to visit it someday.
   = Australia is _____.

14 다음 중 어법상 어색한 것을 고르시오.

① It was at the park that Mr. and Ms. Anderson first had a date.
② It was four months ago that Mary borrowed some books from me.
③ It was very hungry that Paul became after hard work.
④ Chinese people do love the number 8.
⑤ Sam Smith did compose all the songs.

15 다음 주어진 문장의 밑줄 친 부분과 쓰임이 같은 것을 모두 고르면?

> • Robert's mom does worry about his vision due to the PC games he is crazy for.

① She doesn't have any plans.
② Do we have to know your schedule?
③ They do think it's not fair.
④ Do not move an inch.
⑤ Susan did wash the dishes by herself.

16 우리말과 일치하도록 괄호 안의 어구를 바르게 배열하시오.

(1) 이것이 그녀가 작년에 일본인 목수로부터 구매한 것이다. (from, last year, she, a, what, this, carpenter, is, purchased, Japanese)
➡ _____
_____

(2) 그 무거운 상자를 옮겨 준 것은 바로 영어 선생님이었다. (the English teacher, moved, heavy, it, the, who, box, was)
➡ _____

(3) John이 그 사무실에서 수리한 것은 복사기 한 대였다. (machine, office, in, John, photocopy, a, fixed, what, the, was)
➡ _____
_____

[17~19] 다음 글을 읽고 물음에 답하시오.

> A House in Nature - Minho
> [A] It will be wonderful to wake up in the morning and listen to the songs of the birds. Also, I'd like to have many pets. It will be fun to play with them!
> [B] It should have a big garden with many flowers and trees. I am always excited by the sound of birds.
> [C] Nature is my good friend. I do feel good when I walk in the forest. I'd like to have a dream house in the countryside.

17 다음과 같이 풀이되는 말을 위 글에서 찾아 쓰시오.

> an animal that you keep in your home to give you company and pleasure

➡ _____

18 자연스러운 글이 되도록 [A]~[C]를 바르게 배열한 것은?

① [A] – [C] – [B]　　② [B] – [A] – [C]

③ [B] – [C] – [A]　　④ [C] – [A] – [B]

⑤ [C] – [B] – [A]

19 According to the passage, when does Minho feel good? Answer in English with a full sentence.

➡ _____

[20~21] 다음 글을 읽고 물음에 답하시오.

A: My name is Tanabat Suasawathe, but people call me Chang. It means an elephant.

B: My name is Alina Ivanovna Dmitrieva. My middle name Ivanovna says that my father's name is Ivan.

C: My name is Carl Hansen. My parents didn't make my name, but chose it from a list.

D: My name is Han Sujin. My sister's name is Han Mijin. Our family name is Han, and both of our names end with jin.

20 위 글의 내용과 일치하지 않는 것을 모두 고르시오.

① People call Tanabat by his name.

② By her middle name, we can guess what the name of Alina's father is.

③ Carl's name is made by his parents.

④ Sujin's family name is Han.

⑤ Sujin has a sister whose name ends with jin like her.

21 What does Chang mean? Answer in English with a full sentence.

➡ _____

[22~24] 다음 글을 읽고 물음에 답하시오.

A Fun Place - Julie

Welcome to my dream house! Having fun is what I want most, so my dream house is full of exciting things. It has a theater in the basement. There, I can eat cookies and enjoy my favorite movies. My dream house has a game room on the second floor. I can play many different kinds of games there. My house also has a swimming pool. I want to do fun things with my friends in my house. You can be my guest!

22 다음 중 위 글의 내용과 일치하지 않는 것은?

① It is easy to find exciting things in her dream house.

② The theater is located in the basement.

③ In order to enjoy her favorite movies, she has to go to the basement.

④ She wants to play various kinds of games in the game room.

⑤ The swimming pool is on the same floor as the game room.

23 Write the reason why Julie's dream house is full of exciting things. Use the phrase 'It's because.'

➡ _____

24 What can Julie do in the theater in her dream house?

➡ _____

Experience Different Cultures!

 의사소통 기능

- 조언 구하기
  Can I get your advice on what to bring?
- 경고하기
  Make sure you don't wrap the present in white or black paper.

 언어 형식

- 현재완료진행시제
  I **have been living** in America for three years.
- 분사
  You can wave to and smile at an elderly man **walking** on the street.

Words & Expressions

Key Words

- □ **address** [ədrés] 명 주소
- □ **advice** [ədváis] 명 충고, 조언
- □ **baht** [ba:t] 명 바트(태국의 화폐 단위)
- □ **bowl** [boul] 명 그릇
- □ **bring** [briŋ] 동 가져오다
- □ **bump** [bʌmp] 동 부딪치다
- □ **China** [tʃáinə] 명 중국
- □ **Chinese** [tʃàiníːz] 형 중국(어)의 명 중국어, 중국인
- □ **correctly** [kəréktli] 부 정확하게, 올바르게
- □ **cultural** [kʌ́ltʃərəl] 형 문화의, 문화적인
- □ **death** [deθ] 명 죽음
- □ **differ** [dífər] 동 다르다
- □ **difference** [dífərəns] 명 차이
- □ **difficult** [dífikʌlt] 형 어려운
- □ **elderly** [éldərli] 형 나이 든
- □ **entrance fee** 입장료
- □ **exchange** [ikstʃéindʒ] 동 교환하다, 환전하다
- □ **expensive** [ikspénsiv] 형 비싼
- □ **experience** [ikspíəriəns] 동 경험하다
- □ **finally** [fáinəli] 부 마지막으로
- □ **goods** [gudz] 명 상품, 제품
- □ **greet** [griːt] 동 ~에게 인사하다
- □ **guest** [gest] 명 손님
- □ **hand** [hænd] 동 건네주다
- □ **invite** [inváit] 동 초대하다
- □ **Japan** [dʒəpǽn] 명 일본
- □ **mean** [miːn] 동 의미하다
- □ **negative question** 부정의문문
- □ **pack** [pæk] 동 (짐을) 싸다, 꾸리다
- □ **pay** [pei] 동 지불하다
- □ **place** [pleis] 동 놓다
- □ **positive question** 긍정의문문
- □ **postal code** 우편 번호
- □ **present** [préznt] 명 선물
- □ **prepare** [pripέər] 동 준비하다
- □ **price tag** 가격표
- □ **rate** [reit] 명 율, 비율
- □ **receive** [risíːv] 동 받다
- □ **rude** [ruːd] 형 무례한
- □ **Russia** [rʌ́ʃə] 명 러시아
- □ **sales tax** 판매세
- □ **serve** [səːrv] 동 제공하다, 대접하다
- □ **share** [ʃɛər] 동 나누다, 공유하다
- □ **shorts** [ʃɔːrts] 명 반바지
- □ **since** [sins] 접 …한 이후로
- □ **soup** [suːp] 명 국, 수프
- □ **surprising** [sərpráiziŋ] 형 놀라운
- □ **state** [steit] 명 주
- □ **stay** [stei] 동 머물다
- □ **tag** [tæg] 명 꼬리표, 태그
- □ **Taiwan** [tàiwáːn] 명 대만, 타이완
- □ **tax** [tæks] 명 세금
- □ **temple** [témpl] 명 사원
- □ **tongue** [tʌŋ] 명 혀
- □ **traditional** [trədíʃənl] 형 전통적인
- □ **uncomfortable** [ənkʌ́mfətəbəl] 형 불편한
- □ **wave** [weiv] 동 (손을) 흔들다
- □ **wrap** [wæp] 동 포장하다, 싸다

Key Expressions

- □ **a pair of** 한 벌의
- □ **at first** 처음에
- □ **be regarded as** …로 여겨지다
- □ **between A and B** A와 B 사이에
- □ **each other** 서로
- □ **get off** 내리다
- □ **get used to …** 에 익숙해지다
- □ **have a bad effect on** …에 나쁜 영향을 미치다
- □ **in response to** …의 대답으로
- □ **make sure (that)**+주어+동사 … 반드시 …하다
- □ **place** 목적어 **together** …을 모으다
- □ **range from A to B** (범위가) A에서 B에 이르다
- □ **remember to V** …할 것을 기억하다
- □ **take a picture** 사진을 찍다
- □ **take off** …을 벗다
- □ **the same as …** …와 똑같은
- □ **Why don't you**+동사원형…? …하는 게 어때?
- □ **would like to V** …하고 싶다

Word Power

※ 명사(국가 이름) – 명사(국민, 언어) / 형용사
- □ **China**(중국) – **Chinese**(중국인, 중국어) / 중국의
- □ **Japan**(일본) – **Japanese**(일본인, 일본어) / 일본의
- □ **Korea**(한국) – **Korean**(한국인, 한국어) / 한국의
- □ **Russia**(러시아) – **Russian**(러시아인, 러시아어) / 러시아의
- □ **Taiwan**(대만) – **Taiwanese**(대만인, 대만어) / 대만의
- □ **France**(프랑스) – **French**(프랑스인, 프랑스어) / 프랑스의

※ 서로 비슷한 뜻을 가진 어휘
- □ **elderly** : **aged** (늙은, 나이 먹은)
- □ **hand** : **give** (건네주다)
- □ **rude** : **impolite** (무례한)
- □ **death** : **dying** (죽음, 사망)

※ 서로 반대되는 뜻을 가진 어휘
- □ **negative** (부정적인) ↔ **positive** (긍정적인)
- □ **expensive** (비싼) ↔ **cheap** (값싼)
- □ **difference** (차이) ↔ **similarity** (닮음)
- □ **bring** (가져오다) ↔ **take** (가져가다)

English Dictionary

□ **address** 주소
→ the number of the house, name of the road, and name of the town where a person lives or works, and where letters can be sent
집의 번호, 도로의 이름, 사람이 살거나 일하는 마을의 이름, 그리고 편지가 발송될 수 있는 곳

□ **advice** 충고, 조언
→ an opinion that someone offers you about what you should do or how you should act in a particular situation
어떤 상황에서 무엇을 해야 하는지, 어떻게 행동해야 하는지에 대해 누군가가 제안하는 의견

□ **bump** 부딪히다
→ to hurt part of your body by hitting it against something hard
무언가 단단한 것에 부딪혀서 신체의 일부를 다치게 하다

□ **correctly** 올바르게, 맞게
→ in a way that is in agreement with the true facts or with what is generally accepted
사실 또는 일반적으로 받아들여지는 것과 일치하는 방식으로

□ **entrance fee** 입장료
→ an amount of money that you pay in order to be allowed into a cinema, theater, etc.
영화관, 극장 등에 들어갈 수 있도록 지불하는 돈

□ **exchange** 교환하다
→ to give something to someone and receive something from that person
누군가에게 무언가를 주고 그 사람에게서 무언가를 받다

□ **goods** 상품, 제품
→ things for sale, or the things that you own
판매용 물건이나 당신이 소유한 물건

□ **invite** 초대하다
→ to ask or request someone to come to an event
누군가에게 어떤 행사에 오도록 부탁하거나 요청하다

□ **postal code** 우편번호
→ a short series of letters and numbers that is part of an address, and shows exactly where a place is
주소의 일부이며 장소가 정확히 어디에 있는지 보여주는 짧은 일련의 문자 및 숫자

□ **rude** 무례한
→ not polite 공손하지 않은

□ **sales tax** 판매세
→ a tax paid by people when they buy goods or services 상품이나 서비스를 살 때 지불하는 세금

□ **tag** 꼬리표
→ a small piece of paper, cloth, or metal with information on it, tied or stuck onto something larger 더 큰 무언가에 묶여 있거나 붙어 있는, 그 위에 정보가 있는 종이나 천, 금속의 작은 조각

□ **tax** 세금
→ money paid to the government that is based on your income or the cost of goods or services you have bought 당신의 수입이나 구입한 상품이나 서비스의 비용에 근거해서 정부에 지불되는 돈

□ **traditional** 전통적인
→ following or belonging to the customs or ways of behaving that have continued in a group of people or society for a long time without changing
오랜 기간 동안 사람들 또는 사회에서 변하지 않고 계속되어 온 관습이니 행동 방식을 따르거나 속해 있는

□ **uncomfortable** 불편한
→ not feeling comfortable and pleasant, or not making you feel comfortable and pleasant 편안하고 쾌적하지 않거나, 편안하고 쾌적하지 못하도록 하는

□ **wave** 흔들다
→ to raise your hand and move it from side to side as a way of greeting someone
누군가에게 인사하기 위한 방법으로 손을 들고 좌우로 움직이다

□ **wrap** 포장하다
→ to cover or surround something with paper, cloth, or other material
종이, 천 또는 기타 재료로 뭔가를 덮거나 둘러싸다

01 다음 글의 빈칸에 주어진 철자로 시작하는 단어를 쓰시오.

> Since Minhee's family moved to America, they have experienced many cultural d_____ between Korea and America.

02 다음 대화의 빈칸에 들어갈 말로 가장 적절한 것은?

> A: Can I get your _____ on how to write an address in English?
> B: Sure. You should write the street address first.

① letter　② choice
③ advice　④ tax
⑤ report

[03~04] 다음 설명에 해당하는 단어를 고르시오.

03
> an amount of money that you pay in order to be allowed into a cinema, theater, etc.

① sale　② tag
③ rate　④ sales tax
⑤ entrance fee

04
> not feeling comfortable and pleasant, or not making you feel comfortable and pleasant

① uncomfortable　② rude
③ traditional　④ cultural
⑤ colorful

05 다음 우리말에 맞게 빈칸에 알맞은 어휘를 쓰시오.

> 미국에서, 나이든 사람에게 손을 흔드는 것은 무례하다고 여겨지지 않는다.

➡ In America, waving to an older person is not _____ _____ rude.

06 다음 글의 빈칸에 공통으로 들어갈 말로 알맞은 것은?

> (A) Americans often ask _____ questions, such as "Aren't you coming?"
> (B) Scientists have a fairly _____ attitude to the theory.

① positive　② easy
③ different　④ negative
⑤ difficult

07 다음 짝지어진 단어의 관계가 같도록 빈칸에 알맞은 말을 쓰시오.

> Korea - Korean : China - _____

08 다음 빈칸에 들어갈 말이 알맞게 짝지어진 것은?

> Here in America, in most states, people pay a (A)_____ when they buy goods. It is called a sales tax. Sales tax rates differ by state. They (B)_____ from less than one percent to more than ten percent.

① tip – pay　② money – range
③ tip – differ　④ tax – pay
⑤ tax – range

01 다음 빈칸에 들어갈 말을 〈보기〉에서 찾아 쓰시오. (필요하면 변형하여 쓰시오.)

┌─ 보기 ─┐
tag   stay   make   share   culture
└─────────┘

(1) I bought a present for Ms. Han. I _____ at her house here in Korea.

(2) _____ sure you don't ask a person's age in Western cultures.

(3) In America, you usually need to pay more than the price on the _____.

(4) I have been learning about _____ differences since I came to America.

02 다음 글의 밑줄 친 우리말에 해당하는 말을 주어진 단어 개수에 맞게 쓰시오.

┌─────────────────────────────┐
(A) ~의 대답으로(3단어) negative questions, such as "Don't you like apple pie?" you should answer "No," if you don't like it. And you should answer "Yes," if you like it. These answers are (B) ~와 같은(3단어) the answers to (C) 긍정의 questions, such as "Do you like apple pie?"
└─────────────────────────────┘

➡ (A) _____ (B) _____
   (C) _____

03 다음 우리말과 같은 표현이 되도록 문장의 빈칸을 채우시오.

(1) 연장자에게 한 손으로 무언가를 주는 것은 무례한 것으로 여겨진다.

➡ Giving something to older people with one hand is regarded as _____.

(2) 그를 위해 작은 선물을 준비하고 싶어.

➡ I want to _____ a small gift for him.

(3) 사원을 방문할 때 반바지를 입어서는 안 된다.

➡ You shouldn't wear _____ when you visit a _____.

04 다음 영영풀이에 해당하는 단어를 〈보기〉에서 찾아 첫 번째 빈칸에 쓰고, 두 번째 빈칸에는 우리말 뜻을 쓰시오.

┌─ 보기 ─┐
exchange   wave   correctly
└─────────┘

(1) _____ : to raise your hand and move it from side to side as a way of greeting someone: _____

(2) _____ : in a way that is in agreement with the true facts or with what is generally accepted: _____

(3) _____ : to give something to someone and receive something from that person: _____

05 빈칸에 공통으로 알맞은 단어를 주어진 철자로 시작하여 쓰시오.

(1) • They also take g_____ care of us and protect us.
   • The shop put all its g_____s in the shopwindow that day.

(2) • Make sure you use two h_____s when you h_____ it to her.

Conversation

① 조언 구하기

> **Can I get your advice on what to bring?** 무엇을 가져갈지에 대해 너의 조언을 구할 수 있을까?

- 충고를 구할 때는 어려운 상황을 말한 다음 'Can I get your advice on ~?'으로 말할 수 있다. Can I get your advice on my bad habit?(내 나쁜 버릇에 대해서 충고 좀 해줄래?)

- 조언을 구하는 다양한 표현들
  - How can I speak English well? 어떻게 하면 영어를 잘할 수 있을까?
  - What should I do to pass the exam? 시험에 합격하기 위해 무엇을 해야 하니?
  - What can I do to lose weight? 체중을 줄이기 위해 무엇을 할 수 있니?
  - What's your advice? 네 충고는 무엇이니?
  - What do you advise me to do? 넌 내가 무엇을 하라고 충고하니?
  - If you were me, what would you do? 네가 나라면 어떻게 할래?

- 조언을 할 때
  - (I think) You should apologize. (내 생각에는) 넌 사과해야 해.
  - Make sure you wash your hands. 손을 꼭 닦도록 해.
  - I suggest you read it again. 넌 그것을 다시 읽어야 해.
  - You need to read a lot. 넌 독서를 많이 할 필요가 있어.
  - You have to go to bed early. 넌 일찍 잠자리에 들어야 해.

  - Why don't you ~?나 How[What] about ~?의 제안하는 표현을 이용하여 조언을 할 수도 있다.
  - Why don't you help her? 그녀를 도와주지 그래?
  - How about inviting Ann? Ann을 초대하는 게 어때?

핵심 Check

1. 다음 대화의 빈칸에 들어갈 말로 <u>어색한</u> 것은?

   A: You look worried. What's wrong?

   B: I can't get a good grade. _____

   A: How about making a study plan?

   B: That's a good idea.

   ① What should I do?

   ② What can I do to get a good grade?

   ③ What do you advise me to do?

   ④ If you were me, what would you do?

   ⑤ Make sure you study harder.

❷ 경고하기

Make sure you don't wrap the present in white or black paper. 절대 선물을 흰색이나 검정색 종이로 포장하지 않도록 해.

■ 상대방에게 경고나 당부하는 표현으로 '반드시 ~하도록 하다, ~을 확실히 하다'라는 의미의 'make sure ~'를 사용한다. make sure 다음에 접속사 that을 생략할 수 있고 당부하고자 하는 내용을 주어와 동사를 갖춘 문장으로 쓴다. 다시 말해, sure 다음에는 '(that+)주어+동사'를 쓴다. 유사한 의미를 가진 표현으로 'had better+동사원형 ~', 'Don't forget to+동사원형 ~', 'remember to+동사원형 ~' 등이 있다.

■ 경고하기 표현
  - **A:** Make sure you don't cook it for over ten minutes. (그것을 10분 넘게 조리하지 마.)
    B: Okay, I will. (알겠어요, 그럴게요.)
  - **A:** I think I caught a cold. (나 감기에 걸린 것 같아.)
    B: That's too bad. Make sure you take some medicine and relax. (안됐구나. 꼭 약을 먹고 쉬렴.)
  - Remember to call me when you leave. (떠날 때 나에게 전화하는 것을 기억해라.)
  - Don't forget to call me when you arrive. (도착하면 나에게 전화하는 것을 잊지 마.)
  - You had better call me when you arrive. (너는 도착하면 나에게 전화하는 것이 좋겠다.)

■ 상대방의 경고나 당부를 받아들일 때 make sure 다음에 긍정문이 오면 'OK. I will.'로 답하고, 부정문이 오면 'OK. I won't.'로 답한다.
  - **A:** Make sure you give me a call when you get home. (집에 도착하면 내게 꼭 전화해.)
    B: Okay, I will. (응. 그렇게 할게.)
  - **A:** Make sure you won't be late for the class again. (다시는 지각하지 마.)
    B: Okay, I won't. (네, 안 할게요.)

핵심 Check

2. 다음 대화의 빈칸에 들어갈 알맞은 것은?

   A: Mom, can I play soccer with my friends after school?
   B: Sure, but _____.

   ① you don't have to play soccer
   ② you can't play soccer
   ③ you had better not play soccer
   ④ don't forget to stay home after school
   ⑤ make sure you come home before dinner

Listen & Speak 1 A-1

G: I want to send this to my aunt in the USA.

B: What is it?

G: It's her *hanbok*. ❶Can I get your advice on how to write an address in English?

B: Sure. You should write the street address first.

G: ❷Like this?

B: Yes. ❸Then, write the name of the city and the state and then the postal code. Finally, write the country.

G: Thanks for your help.

G: 나는 이것을 미국에 계신 이모에게 보내고 싶어.

B: 그게 뭔데?

G: 이모의 한복이야. 영어로 주소를 어떻게 쓰는지에 대해 너의 조언을 구할 수 있을까?

B: 물론이지. 먼저 거리 주소부터 적어야 해.

G: 이렇게?

B: 응. 그러고 나서, 도시 이름과 주 그리고 그 다음에 우편 번호를 적어. 마지막으로 국가를 적어.

G: 도와줘서 고마워.

❶ 충고를 구할 때 쓰는 표현으로, 'how to+동사원형'은 '어떻게 ～하는지, ～하는 방법'으로 해석한다.

❷ like는 전치사로 '～처럼'의 뜻이다.

❸ 순서대로 해야 할 일을 열거할 때 사용하는 표현이다.

Check(√) True or False

(1) G knows how to write an address in English.　　　　　T ☐　F ☐

(2) G has to write the name of the country finally when she writes an address in English.　　T ☐　F ☐

Listen & Speak 2-1

B: Sena, I bought a present for Ms. Han. I have stayed at her house here in Korea.

G: That's great. What did you buy her?

B: ❶I bought her a hat. Do you think she'll love it?

G: Yes. ❷Make sure you use two hands when ❸you hand it to her.

B: Why?

G: ❹Because giving something to older people with one hand is regarded as rude in Korea.

B: Okay. I'll remember that.

B: 세나야, 나 한 씨 아주머니께 드릴 선물을 샀어. 이곳 한국에서 그녀의 집에 머물고 있거든.

G: 그거 잘 됐네. 그녀를 위해 무엇을 샀니?

B: 모자를 샀어. 그녀가 그것을 좋아할 거라고 생각하니?

G: 응. 그녀에게 그것을 건넬 때 반드시 두 손으로 건네도록 해.

B: 왜?

G: 연장자에게 한 손으로 무언가를 주는 것은 한국에서 무례한 것으로 여겨지거든.

B: 알겠어. 그걸 기억할게.

❶ buy+간접목적어(～에게)+직접목적어(－을)'의 4형식으로 'I bought a hat for her.'로 바꾸어 쓸 수 있다.

❷ 상대방에게 경고하는 표현으로 '반드시 ～하도록 하다'라는 의미이다. Make sure 뒤에 '(that+)주어+동사'를 사용한다.

❸ hand는 동사로 '건네주다'라는 의미이다. 직접목적어가 대명사(it)일 때는 'you hand her it.'처럼 4형식으로 사용하지 않는다.

❹ 이유의 부사절 접속사로 'Because+주어+동사 ～'의 어순을 취한다. giving은 동명사 주어로 동사는 단수 is가 온다. be regarded as는 '～로 여겨지다'라는 의미이다.

Check(√) True or False

(3) Sena will give a hat to Ms. Han.　　　　　T ☐　F ☐

(4) Koreans should not give something to the elderly with one hand.　　T ☐　F ☐

Listen & Speak 1 B

G: Look at the people ❶wearing traditional Moroccan clothes. They are really beautiful. I want to take pictures of them.

M: Wait. ❷There is an important thing you need to know before taking pictures.

G: Oh, really? Can I get your advice on it?

M: Yes. You shouldn't take pictures of Moroccan people ❸without asking.

G: Why?

M: They believe it may ❹have a bad effect on them when someone takes their picture.

G: 모로코 전통 의상을 입고 있는 사람들을 보세요. 그들은 매우 아름다워요. 그들의 사진을 찍고 싶어요.

M: 잠깐. 네가 사진을 찍기 전에 알아야 할 중요한 것이 있어.

G: 오, 정말요? 그것에 대해 조언을 구할 수 있을까요?

M: 응. 너는 물어보지 않고 모로코 사람들의 사진을 찍으면 안 돼.

G: 왜요?

M: 그들은 누군가가 자신의 사진을 찍으면 그것이 그들에게 나쁜 영향을 끼칠 것이라고 믿어.

❶ wearing은 명사 the people을 수식하는 현재분사이다.
❷ thing과 you 사이에 목적격 관계대명사 that[which]이 생략되어 있다. There is an important thing (that) you need to know ~. before는 전치사로 뒤에 동명사 taking이 온다.
❸ 전치사 without+동명사(asking): 물어보지 않고서
❹ have an effect on ~: ~에 영향을 미치다

Check(√) True or False

(5) G wants to take pictures of the people wearing traditional Moroccan clothes.   T ☐ F ☐

(6) In Morocco, you can take pictures of Moroccan people freely.   T ☐ F ☐

Listen & Speak 2 A-2

B: ❶Did you pack everything you need for the trip to Thailand tomorrow?

G: Not yet. What should I take?

B: ❷Remember to bring a pair of long pants or a long skirt.

G: Why? It's very hot in Thailand, ❸isn't it?

B: Yes, but there are many temples in Thailand. You shouldn't wear shorts when you visit a temple.

G: Okay. Is there anything else?

B: ❹Make sure you exchange Korean won to Thai baht.

B: 너는 내일 태국 여행에 필요한 모든 것을 챙겼니?

G: 아니 아직. 무엇을 가져가야 할까?

B: 긴 바지나 긴 치마를 한 벌 가져가는 것을 기억해.

G: 왜? 태국은 매우 덥잖아, 그렇지 않니?

B: 응, 하지만 태국에는 절이 많아. 너는 절을 방문할 때 반바지를 입으면 안 돼.

G: 알겠어, 다른 것이 또 있니?

B: 반드시 한국 원화를 태국 바트로 환전하도록 해.

❶ everything과 you 사이에 목적격 관계대명사 that[which]이 생략되어 있다.
❷ remember+to부정사: ~할 것을 기억하다 / remember+V-ing(동명사): ~한 것을 기억하다
❸ 평서문이 be동사의 긍정문이므로, 부가의문문에는 부정문 isn't와 대명사 it을 사용한다.
❹ 상대방에게 경고하는 표현으로 '반드시 ~하도록 하다'라는 의미이다. Make sure 뒤에 '주어+동사'를 사용한다.

Check(√) True or False

(7) G packed everything she needs for the trip to Thailand.   T ☐ F ☐

(8) G shouldn't wear shorts when she visits temples in Thailand.   T ☐ F ☐

Warm Up

1. People show their tongues in Tibet.
2. ❶People place their hands together and say "Namaste" in India.
3. ❷Men bump their noses in the United Arab Emirates.

❶ place+목적어+together: ~을 모으다 ❷ bump: 부딪히다

Listen & Speak 1 B

A: ❶Can I get your advice on visiting the Netherlands?
B: Sure. ❷You shouldn't stand on a bike path.
A: Can I get your advice on visiting the USA?
B: Sure. You should sit in the back seat in the taxi.

❶ 상대방의 조언을 구할 때 사용하는 표현이다. 전치사 on 뒤에 동명사가 와야 한다.
❷ shouldn't는 조동사의 부정문으로 '~해서는 안 된다'라는 의미이다.

Communication Task-Step 2

A: ❶Which country would you like to visit?
B: ❷I'd like to visit Malaysia. Can I get your advice on traveling there?
C: Sure. Make sure you don't use ❸your left hand to hand something to someone.
B: Okay. Thanks.

❶ which는 의문사로 명사 country를 수식하는 역할을 한다.
❷ 'I'd(=would) like to'는 '~하고 싶다'라는 뜻이다.
❸ your left hand의 'hand'는 명사로 '손'이고, to hand의 'hand'는 동사로 '건네주다'라는 뜻이다.

Real Life Talk

Seho: My Chinese friend invited me to his house for dinner this Friday.
Bora: That's good. ❶I hope you enjoy having dinner at his house.
Seho: I want to prepare a small gift for him. You lived in China for several years. Can I get your advice on what to bring?

Bora: How about some tea?
Seho: Tea?
Bora: Yes. Most Chinese people like to receive tea ❷as a present. They enjoy drinking tea. Also, they usually serve tea to guests.
Seho: Oh, thanks. Is there anything else that I need to know?
Bora: ❸Make sure you don't wrap the present in white or black paper. White and black mean death in China.
Seho: Okay. I'll remember that. Thank you for the advice.

❶ 'I hope (that+)주어+동사 ~'로 접속사 that이 생략되어 있다. enjoy는 목적어로 동명사(having)를 취한다.
❷ as는 전치사로 '~로'의 의미이다.
❸ 상대방에게 경고하는 표현으로 '반드시 ~하도록 하다'라는 의미이다. Make sure 뒤에 '(that+)주어+동사'를 사용한다.

Wrap Up 1

B: I'm going to Japan this summer. Can I get some advice on visiting there?
G: Make sure you pay when you get off the bus.
B: Oh, I didn't know that. Are there any other things I should remember?
G: Pick up the bowl and hold it ❶while eating. Also, ❷when having soup, you should drink it without a spoon.
B: Okay. Thanks

❶ 'while eating'은 '~하는 동안'의 의미로 'while you are eating'에서 주어와 be동사가 생략된 형태이다.
❷ when having soup는 when you are having soup에서 주어와 be동사가 생략된 형태이다.

Wrap Up 2

M: ❶I want to give flowers to my friend from Russia. ❷Is there anything I should remember?
W: Make sure you don't give flowers in even numbers.

❶ give A to B: B에게 A를 주다, from: ~출신인
❷ anything과 I 사이에는 목적격 관계대명사 that[which]이 생략되어 있다.

● 다음 우리말과 일치하도록 빈칸에 알맞은 말을 쓰시오.

Warm Up

1. People _____ _____ _____ in Tibet.
2. People _____ their hands _____ and say "Namaste" in India.
3. Men _____ _____ _____ in the United Arab Emirates.

Listen & Speak 1 A

1. G: I want _____ _____ this to my _____ in the USA.
   B: _____ is it?
   G: It's her *hanbok*. Can I _____ your _____ on _____ _____ _____ an _____ in English?
   B: Sure. You should write the _____ _____ first.
   G: _____ this?
   B: Yes. Then, write the name of the city and the _____ and then the _____ _____. _____, write the country.
   G: Thanks for your help.

2. G: _____ _____ the people _____ _____ Moroccan clothes. They are really beautiful. I want _____ _____ _____ _____ them.
   M: Wait. _____ _____ an important thing you need to know _____ _____ pictures.
   G: Oh, really? Can I get your _____ _____ it?
   M: Yes. You shouldn't _____ _____ _____ _____ people _____ _____.
   G: Why?
   M: They believe it may have _____ _____ _____ them _____ someone takes their picture.

Listen & Speak 1 B

A: _____ _____ _____ your _____ on _____ the Netherlands?
B: Sure. You _____ stand on a bike _____.
A: Can I _____ _____ _____ _____ _____ _____ the USA?
B: Sure. You _____ _____ in the _____ _____ in the taxi.

Listen & Speak 2 A

1. **B:** Sena, I bought a _____ for Ms. Han. I _____ _____ at her house here in Korea.

   G: That's great. _____ did you _____ her?

   B: I _____ her a hat. Do you think she'll love it?

   G: Yes. _____ _____ you use two hands when you _____ it _____ her.

   B: Why?

   G: Because _____ something to older people with one hand _____ _____ _____ _____ in Korea.

   B: Okay. I'll remember that.

2. **B:** Did you _____ everything you need for the trip to Thailand tomorrow?

   G: Not _____. What should I _____?

   B: _____ _____ _____ a pair of long pants or a long skirt.

   G: Why? It's very hot in Thailand, _____ it?

   B: Yes, but _____ _____ many _____ in Thailand. You shouldn't wear _____ when you visit a _____.

   G: Okay. Is there anything _____?

   B: _____ _____ you _____ Korean won _____ Thai baht.

Listen & Speak 2 B

A: Is there anything I need to _____ when I eat in _____?

B: Yes. _____ _____ you _____ your hands _____ the table _____ _____ _____.

A: Is there _____ I need to remember _____ I eat in Uzbekistan?

B: Yes. _____ _____ you don't _____ _____ your hat or shoes _____ _____ a meal.

Real Life Talk

Seho: My _____ friend _____ me to his house for dinner this Friday.

Bora: That's good. I hope you enjoy _____ dinner at his house.

해석

1. B: 세나야, 나 한 씨 아주머니께 드릴 선물을 샀어. 이곳 한국에서 그녀의 집에 머물고 있거든.
   G: 그거 잘 됐네. 그녀를 위해 무엇을 샀니?
   B: 모자를 샀어. 그녀가 그것을 좋아할 거라고 생각하니?
   G: 응. 그녀에게 그것을 건넬 때 반드시 두 손으로 건네도록 해.
   B: 왜?
   G: 연장자에게 한 손으로 무언가를 주는 것은 한국에서 무례한 것으로 여겨지거든.
   B: 알겠어. 그걸 기억할게.

2. B: 너는 내일 태국 여행에 필요한 모든 것을 챙겼니?
   G: 아니 아직. 무엇을 가져가야 할까?
   B: 긴 바지나 긴 치마를 한 벌 가져가는 것을 기억해.
   G: 왜? 태국은 매우 덥잖아, 그렇지 않니?
   B: 응, 하지만 태국에는 절이 많아. 너는 절을 방문할 때 반바지를 입으면 안 돼.
   G: 알겠어. 다른 것이 또 있니?
   B: 반드시 한국 원화를 태국 바트로 환전하도록 해.

A: 내가 프랑스에서 식사할 때 기억해야 할 것이 있니?
B: 응. 반드시 항상 손을 식탁 위에 올려두도록 해.

A: 내가 우즈베키스탄에서 식사할 때 기억해야 할 것이 있니?
B: 응. 식사할 때 모자나 신발을 절대 벗지 않도록 해.

세호: 나의 중국인 친구가 이번 주 금요일 저녁 식사에 나를 집으로 초대했어.
보라: 좋네. 그 친구 집에서 네가 즐거운 저녁 식사하기를 바라.

Seho: I want to _____ a small gift for him. You lived in China for _____ years. Can I get your _____ on _____ _____ _____?

Bora: _____ _____ some tea?

Seho: Tea?

Bora: Yes. _____ Chinese people like to _____ tea _____ a _____. They enjoy _____ tea. Also, they usually _____ tea to _____.

Seho: Oh, thanks. Is there anything else _____ I need to know?

Bora: _____ _____ you don't _____ the present in white or black paper. White and black _____ _____ in China.

Seho: Okay. I'll remember that. Thank you for the _____.

Communication Task Step 2

A: _____ country would you like to visit?

B: I'd like to visit Malaysia. Can I _____ your _____ on _____ there?

C: Sure. _____ _____ you don't use your left _____ to hand something to someone.

B: Okay. Thanks.

Wrap Up

1. **B:** I'm _____ to Japan this summer. Can I _____ some advice on _____ there?

   G: Make sure you _____ when you _____ _____ the bus.

   B: Oh, I didn't know that. Are there any other things I should _____?

   G: _____ up the bowl and hold it _____ _____. Also, _____ _____ soup, you should drink it _____ a spoon.

   B: Okay. Thanks.

2. **M:** I want _____ _____ flowers to my friend _____ Russia. Is there anything I should _____?

   W: _____ _____ you don't give flowers in even numbers.

해석

세호: 그에게 줄 작은 선물을 준비하고 싶어. 너는 몇 년 동안 중국에 살았지. 무엇을 가져가야 할지 조언을 구해도 될까?

보라: 차를 가져가는 게 어때?

세호: 차?

보라: 응. 중국 사람들 대부분은 선물로 차를 받는 것을 좋아해. 그들은 차 마시는 것을 즐기거든. 또 그들은 대개 손님들에게 차를 대접해.

세호: 오, 고마워. 내가 알아야 할 또 다른 것이 있을까?

보라: 선물을 흰색이나 검은색 종이로 포장하지 않도록 해. 흰색과 검은색은 중국에서 죽음을 의미해.

세호: 알겠어. 기억할게. 조언해 줘서 고마워.

A: 너는 어떤 나라를 방문하고 싶니?

B: 나는 말레이시아를 방문하고 싶어. 그곳을 여행하는 것에 대해 너의 조언을 구할 수 있을까?

C: 물론이지. 누군가에게 무엇을 건넬 때 절대 왼손을 사용하지 않도록 해.

B: 알겠어. 고마워.

1. B: 나는 이번 여름에 일본에 갈 거야. 그곳을 방문하는 것에 대해 몇 가지 조언을 구할 수 있을까?

   G: 반드시 버스에서 내릴 때 돈을 내도록 해.

   B: 오, 그걸 몰랐어. 내가 기억해야 할 다른 것들이 또 있니?

   G: 먹는 동안에는 그릇을 들어올리고 그것을 잡고 있어. 또한 국을 먹을 때, 숟가락 없이 그것을 마셔야 해.

   B: 알겠어. 고마워.

2. M: 나는 러시아에서 온 내 친구에게 꽃을 주고 싶어. 내가 기억해야 하는 것이 있니?

   W: 짝수로 꽃을 주지 않도록 해라.

Conversation 시험대비 기본평가

01 우리말에 맞도록 주어진 단어를 이용하여 쓰시오.

> • 무엇을 입을지에 대해 제가 당신의 조언을 구할 수 있을까요?
> (can / get / advice / to / wear)

➡ _____

02 다음 대화의 빈칸에 들어갈 말로 <u>어색한</u> 것은?

> A: Is there anything I need to remember when I eat in France?
> B: Yes. _____ on the table at all times.

① Remember to keep your hands
② You'd better keep your hands
③ Make sure you keep your hands
④ Don't forget to keep your hands
⑤ Don't keep your hands

03 다음 대화의 빈칸에 들어갈 말로 알맞은 것은?

> A: _____
> B: Sure. You should never stand on a bike path.

① Do you know when to visit the U.S.A?
② Can I get your advice on what to bring?
③ Can I get your advice on visiting the Netherlands?
④ Which country would you like to travel to?
⑤ Did you enjoy riding a bike?

04 다음 우리말과 같도록 문장의 빈칸을 채우시오.

> 인도에서는 사람들이 손을 모으고 '나마스테'라고 말한다.

➡ People _____ their hands _____ and say "Namaste" in India.

[01~02] 다음 대화를 읽고 물음에 답하시오.

> **Girl:** I want to send this to my aunt in the USA.
> **Boy:** What is it?
> **Girl:** It's her *hanbok*. Can I get your advice on (A)_____?
> **Boy:** Sure. You should write the street address first.
> **Girl:** Like this?
> **Boy:** Yes. Then, write the name of the city and the state and then the postal code. Finally, write the country.

 01 위 대화의 빈칸 (A)에 들어갈 말로 알맞은 것은?

① what to wear
② how to wear *hanbok*
③ how to write an address in English
④ what gift to buy
⑤ which way to go

02 위 대화의 내용과 일치하지 <u>않는</u> 것은?

① The girl's aunt lives in the USA.
② The girl wants to decide whether to wear *hanbok*.
③ The girl wants to know how to write an address in English.
④ The boy knows how to write an address in English.
⑤ The girl has to write the street address first.

03 다음 주어진 문장에 이어질 대화 순서로 알맞은 것은?

> **A:** Which country would you like to visit?

> (A) Okay. Thanks.
> (B) I'd like to visit Malaysia. Can I get your advice on traveling there?
> (C) Sure. Make sure you don't use your left hand to hand something to someone.

① (A)–(B)–(C)
② (B)–(A)–(C)
③ (B)–(C)–(A)
④ (C)–(A)–(B)
⑤ (C)–(B)–(A)

 04 다음 대화의 빈칸에 들어갈 말로 알맞은 것을 고르시오.

> **A:** _____
> **B:** Sure. You should never chew gum on the street.

① Can I get your advice on getting a job in Singapore?
② Do you think I should visit Singapore?
③ Can you tell me when you will visit Singapore?
④ What would you like to do in Singapore?
⑤ Can I get some advice on visiting Singapore?

서답형
05 다음 대화의 빈칸에 들어갈 두 단어의 말을 쓰시오.

> **M:** I want to give flowers to my friend from Russia. Is there anything I should remember?
> **W:** _____ _____ you don't give flowers in even numbers.
>
> *even number 짝수

06 다음 대화 중 어색한 것은?

① A: Which country would you like to visit?

B: I'd like to visit Malaysia.

② A: Can I get your advice on visiting the USA?

B: Sure. You should sit in the back seat in the taxi.

③ A: Can I get your advice on making Mattang?

B: Sure. Don't add too much sugar.

④ A: Do you think she'll like it?

B: Make sure you use two hands when you hand it to her.

⑤ A: Can I get some advice on visiting Japan?

B: Make sure you pay when you get off the bus.

07 다음 대화의 밑줄 친 우리말에 맞게 주어진 단어를 이용하여 영어로 쓰시오. (어형 변화 필수)

> B: Did you pack everything you need for the trip to Thailand tomorrow?
>
> G: Not yet. What should I take?
>
> B: 긴 바지나 긴 치마를 한 벌 가져가는 것을 기억해.

> remember / bring / a long skirt / long pant / a pair of / or

➡ _____

08 다음 대화의 밑줄 친 부분의 의도로 알맞은 것은?

> A: Can I get your advice on traveling there?
>
> B: Sure. Make sure you don't use your left hand to hand something to someone.
>
> A: Okay. Thanks.

① 조언 구하기　　　② 경고하기

③ 확신 표현하기　　④ 궁금증 표현하기

⑤ 가능성 묻기

[09~10] 다음 대화를 읽고 물음에 답하시오.

> Seho: My Chinese friend invited me to his house for dinner this Friday.
>
> Bora: That's good. I hope you enjoy having dinner at his house. (①)
>
> Seho: I want to prepare a small gift for him. You lived in China for several years. Can I get your advice on what to bring? (②)
>
> Bora: How about some tea?
>
> Seho: Tea? (③)
>
> Bora: Yes. Most Chinese people like to receive tea as a present. They enjoy drinking tea. Also, they usually serve tea to guests.
>
> Seho: Oh, thanks. (④)
>
> Bora: Make sure you don't wrap the present in white or black paper. White and black mean death in China. (⑤)
>
> Seho: Okay. I'll remember that. Thank you for the advice.

09 위 대화의 ①~⑤ 중 주어진 문장이 들어갈 위치로 알맞은 것은?

> Is there anything else that I need to know?

①　　②　　③　　④　　⑤

10 위 대화를 읽고 답할 수 없는 것은?

① Who invited Seho to dinner?

② What did Bora suggest as a present for Seho's Chinese friend?

③ Why did Bora suggest some tea as a gift?

④ Why shouldn't Seho wrap the present in white or black paper?

⑤ In what color should Seho wrap the present?

Conversation 서술형 시험대비

[01~02] 다음 대화를 읽고 물음에 답하시오.

Seho: My Chinese friend invited me to his house for dinner this Friday.

Bora: That's good. I hope you enjoy having dinner at his house.

Seho: I want to prepare a small gift for him. You lived in China for several years. (A)
_____

Bora: How about some tea?

Seho: Tea?

Bora: Yes. Most Chinese people like to receive tea as a present. They enjoy drinking tea. Also, they usually serve tea to guests.

Seho: Oh, thanks. Is there anything else that I need to know?

Bora: (B)선물을 흰색이나 검은색 종이로 포장하지 않도록 해. White and black mean death in China.

Seho: Okay. I'll remember that. Thank you for the advice.

01 위 대화의 빈칸 (A)에 주어진 조건에 맞게 영어로 쓰시오.

┤ 조건 ├
• 조언을 구하는 표현을 쓸 것.
• 'can, get, on, what, bring'을 사용할 것.
• to부정사를 사용할 것.

➡ _____

02 위 대화의 밑줄 친 (B)의 우리말을 보고 주어진 조건에 맞게 영어로 쓰시오.

┤ 조건 ├
• Make sure를 사용하여 경고하는 표현을 쓸 것.
• 'the present', 'in', 'or'를 사용할 것.

➡ _____
_____

03 다음 대화의 빈칸에 들어갈 말로 자연스러운 것을 〈보기〉에서 찾아 문장을 쓰시오.

B: Did you pack everything you need for the trip to Thailand tomorrow?

G: Not yet. (A)_____

B: Remember to bring a pair of long pants or a long skirt.

G: Why? It's very hot in Thailand, isn't it?

B: Yes, but there are many temples in Thailand. (B)_____

G: Okay. Is there anything else?

B: (C)_____

┤ 보기 ├
• You shouldn't wear shorts when you visit a temple.
• What should I take?
• Make sure you exchange Korean won to Thai baht.

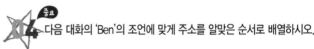

04 다음 대화의 'Ben'의 조언에 맞게 주소를 알맞은 순서로 배열하시오.

Jihee: I want to send this to my aunt in the USA.

Ben: What is it?

Jihee: It's her *hanbok*. Can I get your advice on how to write an address in English?

Ben: Sure. You should write the street address first.

Jihee: Like this?

Ben: Yes. Then, write the name of the city and the state and then the postal code. Finally, write the country.

USA, California 94101, San Francisco, 123 Van Ness Street

➡ _____

Grammar

① 현재완료진행시제

> • They **have been searching** for the missing child for 3 days. 그들은 미아를 3일간 수색 중이다.
> • Mom **has been knitting** since last winter. 엄마는 작년 겨울부터 뜨개질을 하고 있는 중이다.

■ 과거에 시작한 일이 현재까지 계속 진행되고 있는 경우를 나타낼 때 사용한다.
 • My sister Sumi **has been running** on the ground for 6 hours. 내 동생 Sumi는 6시간 동안 운동장을 달리고 있는 중이다.
 • Two giant typhoons **have been heading** toward Japan. 거대한 태풍 2개가 일본을 향해 가고 있는 중이다.

■ 현재완료 '계속' 용법과 비슷하지만, 현재완료진행은 '상태'가 아닌, '동작'을 나타낸다.
 • Tommy and Susan **have known** each other since they were young. (상태의 계속 – 현재완료진행 불가)
 • Jonathan **has been studying** quantum physics. Jonathan은 양자물리학을 공부해 오고 있는 중이다. (동작의 계속 – 현재완료진행 가능)

■ 현재완료진행형 문장과 자주 쓰이는 부사구는 'for(~ 동안)'와 'since(~ 이후로)'이다.
 • John's family **have been staying** at Highclass Hotel **since** last Friday. John의 가족은 지난 금요일 이후로 Highclass 호텔에 체류하는 중이다.
 • Mom **has been talking** on the phone with Aunt Mary **for** four hours. 엄마는 Mary 이모와 4시간 동안 전화로 얘기하는 중이다.

■ 현재완료진행형은 의미상 두 문장으로 나누어 쓸 수 있다. (과거+현재진행)
 • The members of the committee **have been discussing** the issue for 2 days.
  → The members of the committee **began** to discuss the issue **2 days ago**. (과거) + They're still **discussing** it. (현재진행형)

■ 현재완료시제는 과거에서 현재까지의 동작의 완료, 경험, 결과 또는 계속을 의미한다.
 • Susan **hasn't finished** her part of the project yet. Susan은 아직 프로젝트에서의 그녀 몫을 끝내지 못했다. 〈완료〉
 • **Have** you ever **been** to Science Fair? 과학 박람회에 가본 적 있나요? 〈경험〉
 • My wife **has** just **lost** her traffic card. 내 아내가 방금 교통카드를 잃어버렸다. 〈결과〉
 • It **has rained** since last weekend. 지난 주말부터 계속 비가 오고 있다. 〈계속〉

핵심 Check

1. 괄호 안에서 알맞은 것을 고르시오.
 (1) I have been feeling bad (for / since) I saw Abe.
 (2) He has been playing the trumpet (for / since) two and half hours.

2 분사

> Look at the dog **barking** at the strangers. 낯선 사람들을 향해 짖고 있는 개를 보아라.
>
> I know the girls **smiling** at me over there. 나는 저기에서 나를 향해 미소 짓고 있는 소녀들을 안다.

■ 현재분사는 '동사원형+-ing' 형태로 형용사처럼 명사를 앞 또는 뒤에서 꾸며준다. 일반적으로는 명사 앞에서, 다른 어구와 함께 구(phrase)를 이룰 때는 명사 뒤에서 꾸민다.
  - **The crying** baby kicked the blanket. 울고 있는 아기가 이불을 발로 찼다.
  - Do you know the baby **crying** in the blanket? 이불 속에서 울고 있는 아기를 아니?

■ 현재분사(-ing)는 능동/진행, 과거분사(p.p.)는 수동/완료의 의미를 갖는다.
  - The researchers are **searching** for the evidence of evolution. 연구진들은 진화의 증거를 찾고 있는 중이다.
  - Would you introduce me to the girl **dancing** on the stage? 무대에서 춤추고 있는 소녀를 소개해 주실래요?
  - Watch out the **broken** window! 깨진 창문을 조심하세요!
  - Some actors **invited** to the film festival didn't show up. 영화제에 초대된 일부 배우들이 나타나지 않았다.

■ 명사를 뒤에서 꾸며 주는 분사구는 '주격 관계대명사+be동사'가 생략된 것으로 볼 수 있다.
  - The girl (**who is**) **wearing** her school uniform is my niece. 교복을 입고 있는 그 소녀는 내 조카딸이다.
  - The professor wants to buy the book (**which was**) **written** by Leonardo da Vinci. 그 교수는 Leonardo da Vinci에 의해 쓰인 책을 사고 싶어한다.

■ 분사는 명사를 꾸며주는 역할 외에도, 주어나 목적어의 보충 설명을 하는 서술 용법이 있다. 이 경우, 주격 보어 또는 목적격 보어가 된다.
  - A lady stood **looking** at the picture. 한 숙녀가 그림을 보며 서 있었다.
  - The injured soldier lay **surrounded** by the enemies. 그 부상당한 군인이 적들에게 둘러싸인 채로 누워 있었다.
  - I am sorry to have kept you **waiting** so long. 그렇게 오래 기다리시게 해서 미안합니다.
  - Forest Gump heard his name **called**. Forest Gump는 그의 이름이 불리는 것을 들었다.
  - Finally, Sandra had her dream house **built** in her hometown. 마침내 Sandra는 그녀의 고향에 자신의 꿈의 집이 건축되도록 했다.

핵심 Check

2. 괄호 안에서 알맞은 것을 고르시오.
  (1) I must have the car (repaired / repairing) by noon.
  (2) Julie had her leg (breaking / broken) in the bike accident.

01 다음 문장에서 어법상 어색한 부분을 바르게 고쳐 쓰시오.

(1) She wants to make herself understanding in French.

_____ ➡ _____

(2) I have gone to Washington D.C. before.

_____ ➡ _____

(3) Shane has been studied mathematics since last year.

_____ ➡ _____

(4) The leader of the boy band received a letter writing in Spanish.

_____ ➡ _____

02 다음 중 어법상 바르지 않은 것은?

① My daughter has been using the smartphone for six hours.

② Roberto has been singing since this morning.

③ John's friends have been watching a horror movie.

④ The two families have been knowing each other since 1990s.

⑤ They all have been digging the hole to survive.

03 다음 대화의 밑줄 친 부분 중에서 어법상 잘못된 것을 고르시오.

A: ①Are you ②tiring ③from the trip to Switzerland?
B: No. I ④do ⑤feel good.

04 다음 우리말에 맞게 주어진 단어를 바르게 배열하시오. (필요하면 어형을 바꿀 것)

(1) Peter가 찍은 사진은 흥미로웠다. (was, by, the, Peter, picture, take, interesting)

➡ _____

(2) Billy의 엄마는 네 시간째 요리를 해오고 있는 중이다. (cook, hours, mom, been, have, for, five, Billy)

➡ _____

01 다음 빈칸에 알맞은 것은?

> Jimin began writing a poem half an hour ago, and she is still writing it now.
> = Jimin ＿＿＿＿＿＿ a poem for half an hour.

① has begun
② has wrote
③ has been writing
④ has been
⑤ has been written

02 다음 문장에서 어법상 틀린 부분을 찾아 바르게 고쳐 쓰시오.

> She bought a bag making in Philippines.

＿＿＿＿＿＿ ➡ ＿＿＿＿＿＿

03 다음 예시와 같이 두 문장을 한 문장으로 연결할 때, 빈칸에 알맞은 말을 넣으시오.

> • The little girl is reading a book in an armchair. She is my cousin.
>   → The little girl reading a book in an armchair is my cousin.

(1) There were many people.
   They were watching fireworks.
   → There were ＿＿＿＿＿ ＿＿＿＿＿ fireworks.
(2) The warehouse is very large.
   It was built by my father.
   → The warehouse ＿＿＿＿ ＿＿＿＿ ＿＿＿＿ ＿＿＿＿ very large.

04 다음 괄호 안의 단어의 알맞은 형태가 순서대로 바르게 짝 지어진 것은?

> • The girl (pick) up trash is my daughter.
> • The money (spend) for our vacation is too much.
> • The lecture was (bore) for the kids.

① picking – spending – boring
② picking – spent – bored
③ picking – spent – boring
④ picked – spending – bored
⑤ picked – spent – boring

05 다음 두 문장을 한 문장으로 표현할 때, 빈칸에 들어갈 알맞은 말을 쓰시오.

> • Sam started to play the cello 16 years ago.
> • He's still playing the cello now.

➡ Sam ＿＿＿＿ ＿＿＿＿ ＿＿＿＿ the cello ＿＿＿＿ 16 years.

06 다음 중 밑줄 친 부분의 쓰임이 다른 하나는?

① The girl standing next to me is Julie.
② They tried opening the box.
③ The sleeping lion seemed like a baby.
④ The boy watching TV got excited.
⑤ We saw a talking horse in Thai.

07 Translate the following Korean into English as directed below.

> • 노란 티셔츠를 입고 있는 아이가 단풍나무 아래에 앉아 있다.

> <Directions>
> • Use the words: T-shirt, the, wear, maple, be, under (Change the form if necessary.)
> • Complete it with 12 words in total.

➡ The kid ＿＿＿＿ ＿＿＿＿ ＿＿＿＿
＿＿＿＿ ＿＿＿＿ ＿＿＿＿ ＿＿＿＿
＿＿＿＿ ＿＿＿＿ tree.

08 다음 밑줄 친 ⓐ, ⓑ를 어법상 알맞게 고친 것이 차례대로 짝 지어진 것은?

> • She warned the baby not to touch the ⓐburn fire.
> • The students ⓑpass by bowed to the principal politely.

① burning – passed
② burnt – have been passing
③ burning – having been passed
④ burnt – being passed
⑤ burning – passing

09 다음 중 어법상 어색한 것을 모두 고르면?

① The little girl reads a storybook under the big tree is Sally.
② Kahn has been searching for a new item for his business since last year.
③ The member of the committee raising her hand was Jenny.
④ Sam Smith has been lied to all of us.
⑤ The people my family meeting there were so kind and gentle.

10 다음 중 어법상 옳은 것은?

① Steve has been losing his first job.
② The old man who sitting next to Mr. Brown was the mayor of the city.
③ The boy rides a horse over there is Frank.
④ There was no cake leaving for me.
⑤ This is the road leading to the castle.

11 다음 각 문장에서 어법상 어색한 부분을 하나씩 찾아서 알맞게 고치시오.

(1) William bought a book writing in ancient Greek from a second-hand bookstore.

➡ _____

(2) These are the cookies making with the oven James bought last week.

➡ _____

(3) Who will take care of the baby cried alone in the dark room?

➡ _____

12 다음 중 밑줄 친 부분의 쓰임이 〈보기〉와 다른 것은?

> ┤ 보기 ├
> She has been elected mayor twice.

① David hasn't heard of the word "ZZang-Nan-Dah" before.
② My family has been to Europe many times.
③ Have you witnessed the crime scene even once?
④ Michael has driven a jet-boat before.
⑤ Emily has gone to Hawaii with her family.

13 다음 중 밑줄 친 부분의 쓰임이 어색한 것을 모두 고르면?

① Yesterday was the most excited day of my life.
② The lecture by Professor Thomas may be the most boring one in this college.
③ The children were so curious that they tried to open the locked door.
④ Most of the audience there thought the film had lots of touched scenes.
⑤ My aunt Mariah loves collecting fallen leaves every autumn.

14 다음 문장의 빈칸에 들어갈 말로 가장 알맞은 것은?

> It _____ since last weekend.

① rained　　　　② is raining

③ was raining　　④ has been rained

⑤ has been raining

15 다음 문장의 빈칸에 들어갈 수 없는 것을 고르시오.

> The kids in the kindergarten have been playing block games _____.

① since 1 o'clock　　② all this afternoon

③ for an hour　　　　④ up to now

⑤ until 30 minutes ago

16 다음 〈보기〉에서 알맞은 동사를 한 번씩만 선택하여, 현재완료진행형으로 빈칸을 채워 문장을 완성하시오.

> ┤ 보기 ├
>
> paint listen take travel teach

(1) James _____ _____ _____ to the radio program since last summer.

(2) The volunteers _____ _____ _____ the walls of the underdeveloped village for 15 years.

(3) Sumin _____ _____ _____ math for free to help the poor children since last spring.

(4) The patient with a heart problem _____ _____ _____ the medicine as her family doctor advised.

(5) The newlyweds _____ _____ _____ in Europe since they got married last year.

17 다음 〈보기〉에 주어진 동사를 한 번씩만 사용하여 어법에 맞게 바꿔 빈칸을 완성하시오.

> ┤ 보기 ├
>
> know, relate, write, name

> I'd like to introduce you to the novel (A)_____ about a pianist. She is well (B)_____ as a role model among young people. She is one of the most promising pianists in Europe (C)_____ Ebony Janelle. A film (D)_____ to her will also be made.

18 다음 중 밑줄 친 부분의 쓰임이 〈보기〉와 다른 것은?

> ┤ 보기 ├
>
> The Jacksons have lived in this city since 1990s.

① We have known each other since we're born at the same hospital.

② Father has finished cleaning all the tables.

③ Thomas and Butler have been friends for 20 years.

④ It has been quite windy these days.

⑤ Sean has stayed in Austria since he went there to study music 4 years ago.

19 다음 우리말을 아래의 어휘들을 배열하여 현재완료진행시제를 이용하여 영작할 때, 4번째와 9번째 단어를 쓰시오.

> • 당신은 여기에 차분하게 앉아 있으면서, 그들을 돕기 위해 아무것도 안하고 있는 건가요?
>
> (nothing / sitting / here / doing / have / to / been / calmly / them / and / help / you)?

➡ _____, _____

01 괄호 안의 어구들을 바르게 배열하여 우리말을 영작하시오.

(1) David은 저녁식사를 하고 나서 1시간 동안 계속 껌을 씹고 있는 중이다.

(has / after / gum / been / David / chewing / an hour / dinner / for)

➡ _____

(2) Margaret은 인터넷을 처음 시작한 이후, 계속 블로그를 해 오고 있는 중이다.

(since / has / she / been / blogging / first / the Internet / Margaret / started)

➡ _____
_____

(3) 우리 팀원들은 6시간이 넘도록 체육관에서 계속 운동을 하고 있는 중이다.

(out / working / in / six hours / team / the gym / been / members / for / our / over / have)

➡ _____
_____

02 다음에 주어진 각 두 문장을 현재완료진행시제를 이용하여 한 문장으로 만드시오. 단, 반드시 전치사 for를 사용할 것.

(1) • Yujay started to practice playing the drums 6 weeks ago.
• He is still practicing it nowadays.

➡ Yujay _____
_____ .

(2) • Rachel began writing letters at 9:00 this morning.
• She keeps writing letters until now, at noon.

➡ Rachel _____ .

03 다음 우리말을 참고하여 빈칸에 알맞은 말을 쓰시오.

(1) I often take a picture of _____ birds.
(날고 있는 새들의 사진)

(2) Look at the man _____ the car. (세차하고 있는 남자)

(3) The woman _____ in front of me is Ms. Brown. (내 앞에 서 있는 여인)

(4) The dog _____ in the corner is cute.
(구석에 앉아 있는)

(5) She looked out of the _____window.
(닫힌 창문에서)

(6) Keep all the e-mails _____ to you. (너에게 보내진 모든 이메일)

(7) The story _____ by Tom was interesting. (Tom에 의해 쓰여진 이야기)

04 다음 괄호 안의 단어들을 바르게 배열하여 문장을 완성하시오. (단, 동사를 어법상 알맞은 형태로 변형할 것.)

(1) The _____ is waiting for her old friends. (the / stand / old lady / street / across)

(2) Who are the _____?
(on / perform / boys / stage / that)

(3) Louise is watering _____.
(the / an / in / boat / flowers / plant / old)

05 다음 〈보기〉의 각 문장에서 어법상 어색한 부분들을 하나씩 찾아 모두 고치고, 우리말로 해석하시오.

> ┤ 보기 ├
>
> ⓐ The super player calling Hoop King was really good at playing basketball.
> ⓑ We could see many tourists taken pictures in an old square in Austria.
> ⓒ The watches producing in Switzerland are enjoying the greatest fame in the world.
> ⓓ All the people attending the book concert found the title of the book writing by his little daughter.
> ⓔ Groups of migratory birds flown over the sky were making sounds of encouragement.

➡ ⓐ _____
해석: _____
_____

ⓑ _____
해석: _____
_____

ⓒ _____
해석: _____

ⓓ _____
해석: _____
_____

ⓔ _____
해석: _____
_____

06 다음 세 문장을 〈조건〉에 맞게 한 문장으로 다시 쓰시오.

> • Peter, Frank's son, brought home his mathematics homework three hours ago.
> • As soon as he arrived home, Peter showed Frank his homework, and Frank immediately started to do the homework instead of his son.
> • He is still doing it.

> ┤ 조건 ├
>
> • 완전한 영어 문장으로 쓸 것.
> • 접속사, 연결어, since 등은 사용하지 말 것.
> • for / son's / Frank를 반드시 포함하되, 총 10 단어를 초과하지 않을 것.

➡ _____
_____

07 다음 그림을 보고, 괄호 안의 어휘를 이용하여 우리말에 맞게 빈칸을 채우시오.

As he (A)_____ _____ _____ (suffer) from the toothache, he decides to have his tooth (B)_____(pull) out at the dentist's.
(그는 치통으로 고통을 겪고 있는 중이기 때문에, 치과에서 이를 뽑기로 결심한다.)

08 다음 각 두 문장을 '분사'를 활용하여 한 문장으로 만들 때, 괄호 안의 조건에 맞게 빈칸에 적절한 단어를 넣어 채우시오.

(1) Jaemin wanted to play with the baby. She was crying. (명사 앞에서 수식)
→ Jaemin wanted to play _____
_____ _____ _____.

(2) There was a truck. The truck was illegally parked. (명사 앞에서 수식)
→ There was _____ _____ _____
_____.

(3) We watched the birds. They were flying over the buildings. (명사 뒤에서 수식)
→ We watched _____ _____
_____ _____ _____ _____.

Let's Learn about Cultural Differences
let's+동사원형: ~하자(권유문)

    Hi! My name is Kim Minhee. I have been living in America for three
현재완료진행   기간을 이끄는 전치사

years. Since my family moved here, I have experienced many cultural
접속사(~한 이래로)

differences between Korea and America. I would like to share some of

them with you.

cultural differences between Korea and America

Minhee: Look at this shirt. I like it.

Linda: It looks nice. How much is it?

Minhee: It's 19 dollars and 99 cents.

Linda: That's not expensive.

Minhee: Yes, I agree. I want to buy it.

Clerk: That'll be 21 dollars and 20 cents.

Minhee: Really? But the price tag says it's only 19 dollars and 99 cents.
says (that): 명사절을 이끄는 접속사 that 생략

    Here in America, in most states, people pay a tax when they buy goods.
시간을 이끄는 접속사(~할 때)

It is called a sales tax. Sales tax rates differ by state. They range from
수동태(~라고 불리다)   range from A to B: A에서 B까지 이르다

less than one percent to more than ten percent. So when you buy goods

in America, you usually need to pay more than the price on the tag.
빈도부사(일반동사 앞. be동사나 조동사 뒤에 위치)

Jessica: Hi, Mrs. Johnson!

Minhee: Hello, Mrs. Johnson!

Mrs. Johnson: Hi, Jessica! Hi, Minhee! How are you?

Jessica: Fine, thank you. We are here for a burger. Enjoy your meal.

Mrs. Johnson: Thank you. You, too!

Minhee: Jessica, why did you wave to Mrs. Johnson?

cultural: 문화와 관련된, 문화의
difference: 차이
experience: 경험하다
would like to V: V하고 싶다
share: 공유하다
expensive: 비싼
tag: 꼬리표
goods: 상품
rate: 비율
range: (범위가 ~에서 …에) 이르다
more than: ~보다 많이, ~ 이상
differ by: ~에 따라 다르다

확인문제

● 다음 문장이 본문의 내용과 일치하면 T, 일치하지 않으면 F를 쓰시오.

1   Minhee went to America alone to study English. ☐

2   Minhee hasn't experienced cultural differences since she moved to America. ☐

3   Minhee greeted Mrs. Johnson by waving. ☐

In America, people often greet each other by waving. Waving to an
<u>by Ving</u>(~함으로써) <u>동명사 주어</u>
older person is not <u>regarded</u> as rude. When you come to America, you
<u>be regarded as</u>: ~라고 간주되다[여겨지다]
may <u>feel uncomfortable</u> about it at first, but <u>why don't you try it</u>? You
<u>2형식 동사+형용사 보어</u>   <u>Why don't you 동사원형? (권유하는 말)</u>
can wave to and smile at <u>an elderly man</u> walking on the street. He
<u>전치사 to와 at의 공통 목적어</u> <u>현재분사(an elderly man 수식)</u>
may wave back.

Andy: Minhee, try this apple pie.
Minhee: No, thanks. I don't want to.
Andy: Why not? <u>Don't you like</u> apple pie?
<u>부정의문문(~하지 않니?)</u>
Minhee: Yes.
Andy: Then, try some. It's delicious.
Minhee: No. I just <u>said</u> I don't like apple pie.
Andy: What? said (that): 명사절 접속사 that 생략

Americans often ask negative questions, <u>such as</u> "Aren't you
<u>~와 같은</u>
coming?" and "Didn't you go to the hospital?" <u>It</u> can be difficult <u>to</u>
<u>가주어 it</u>
<u>answer</u> negative questions correctly. Here is some <u>advice</u>.
<u>진주어</u>   <u>셀 수 없는 명사</u>
In response to negative questions, such as "Don't you like apple pie?"
<u>~의 대답으로</u>
you should answer "No," if you don't like it. And you should answer
"Yes," if you like it. These answers are <u>the same as</u> the answers to
<u>~와 똑같은</u>
positive questions, such as "Do you like apple pie?"

	Like	Don't like
Do you like apple pie?	Yes, I do.	No, I don't.
Don't you like apple pie?	Yes, I do.	No, I don't.

<u>Which</u> cultural difference is most <u>surprising</u> to you? <u>I have been</u>
<u>선택의문문에 사용하는 의문사(어느, 어떤)</u> <u>놀라움을 유발하므로 현재분사</u>
learning about cultural differences <u>since</u> I came to America. Some
<u>현재완료진행</u>   <u>접속사(~한 이래로)</u>
surprised me at first, but now I am <u>getting used to</u> them.
<u>get used to N: ~에 익숙해지다</u>

확인문제

● 다음 문장이 본문의 내용과 일치하면 T, 일치하지 <u>않으면</u> F를 쓰시오.

1 Waving to an older people is not regarded as impolite. ☐

2 Minhee didn't want to try the apple pie because she was full. ☐

3 Negative questions are hardly used in America. ☐

4 Minhee is not familiar with cultural differences yet. ☐

---

greet: 인사하다
wave: 손을 흔들다
regard: ~로 여기다
elderly: 연세가 드신
be regarded as: ~로 여겨지다
rude: 무례한
uncomfortable: 불편한
try: 먹어보다
negative: 부정적인
positive: 긍정적인
advice: 충고, 조언
response: 대답, 응답

● 우리말을 참고하여 빈칸에 알맞은 말을 쓰시오.

Let's Learn about Cultural Differences

1 Hi! My name is Kim Minhee. I _____ _____ _____ in America for three years.

2 _____ my family moved here, I _____ _____ many cultural differences _____ Korea _____ America.

3 I _____ _____ _____ _____ some of them with you.

4 Minhee: Look _____ this shirt. I like _____.

5 Linda: It _____ _____. How _____ is it?

6 Minhee: It's 19 _____ and 99 _____.

7 Linda: That's _____ _____.

8 Minhee: Yes, I agree. I want _____ _____ _____.

9 Clerk: That'll _____ 21 _____ and 20 _____.

10 Minhee: Really? But _____ _____ _____ it's only 19 dollars and 99 cents.

11 Here in America, in most states, people _____ _____ _____ when they buy _____.

12 It _____ _____ a sales tax. Sales tax _____ by state.

13 They _____ from _____ one percent to _____ _____ ten percent.

14 So when you _____ _____ in America, you _____ _____ _____ _____ more than the price on the tag.

15 Jessica: Hi, _____ Johnson! Minhee: Hello, _____ Johnson!

16 Mrs. Johnson: Hi, Jessica! Hi, Minhee! _____ are you?

17 Jessica: Fine, thank you. We are here _____ a burger. _____ _____ _____.

18 Mrs. Johnson: Thank you. You, _____!

19 Minhee: Jessica, why _____ you _____ to Mrs. Johnson?

문화적 차이에 대해서 배우자

1 안녕! 내 이름은 김민희야. 나는 미국에 3년 동안 살고 있어.

2 우리 가족이 이곳으로 이민을 온 이후로 나는 한국과 미국의 많은 문화적 차이를 경험하고 있어.

3 나는 그것들 중 몇 가지를 너희들과 공유하고 싶어.

4 민희: 이 셔츠를 봐. 마음에 들어.

5 Linda: 멋져 보인다. 얼마야?

6 민희: 19달러 99센트야.

7 Linda: 비싸지 않네.

8 민희: 응, 나도 그렇게 생각해. 그것을 사고 싶어.

9 점원: 21달러 20센트입니다.

10 민희: 정말이요? 하지만 가격표에는 단지 19달러 99센트라고 쓰여 있는데요.

11 이곳 미국에서는 대부분의 주에서 사람들이 물건을 구입할 때 세금을 내.

12 그것은 판매세라고 불려. 판매세의 비율은 주마다 달라.

13 판매세는 1퍼센트 미만부터 10퍼센트 이상까지 다양해.

14 그래서 미국에서 상품을 살 때, 대개 가격표에 있는 가격보다 더 많은 돈을 지불해야 해.

15 Jessica: 안녕하세요, Johnson 할머니! 민희: 안녕하세요, Johnson 할머니!

16 Mrs. Johnson: 안녕, Jessica! 안녕, 민희! 잘 지내지?

17 Jessica: 잘 지내요, 감사합니다. 저희는 여기 버거 먹으러 왔어요. 식사 맛있게 하세요.

18 Mrs. Johnson: 고맙구나. 너희들도!

19 민희: Jessica, 왜 너는 Johnson 할머니께 손을 흔들었니?

20 In America, people _____ _____ _____ _____ by waving.

21 _____ to an older person _____ not _____ _____ rude.

22 When you come to America, you may _____ _____ about it at first, but why don't you _____ _____?

23 You can _____ _____ and _____ _____ an elderly man walking on the street. He may _____ _____.

24 Andy: Minhee, _____ this apple pie.

25 Minhee: No, thanks. I don't _____ _____.

26 Andy: Why not? _____ you like apple pie?

27 Minhee: _____.

28 Andy: Then, _____ _____. It's _____.

29 Minhee: No. I just said I _____ _____ apple pie.

30 Andy: _____?

31 Americans often ask _____ _____, such as "_____ you coming?" and "_____ you _____ to the hospital?"

32 It can be difficult _____ _____ negative questions correctly. Here _____ some advice.

33 In response to _____ _____, such as "Don't you like apple pie?" you should _____ "_____," if you don't like it.

34 And you should _____ "_____," if you like it.

35 These answers are _____ _____ _____ the answers _____ _____ _____, such as "Do you like apple pie?"

36 _____ _____ _____ is most surprising to you?

37 I _____ _____ _____ about cultural differences _____ I came to America.

38 Some _____ me at first, but now I _____ _____ _____ them.

---

20 미국에서 사람들은 종종 손을 흔들며 서로에게 인사해.

21 나이가 많은 사람에게 손을 흔드는 것은 무례하다고 여겨지지 않아.

22 네가 미국에 오면 처음에는 그것에 대해 불편하게 느낄 수 있어. 하지만 한번 시도해 보지 않을래?

23 너는 길을 걷고 있는 연세가 많으신 할아버지께 손을 흔들며 미소를 지어도 돼. 그도 너한테 답례로 손을 흔들지도 몰라.

24 Andy: 민희, 이 사과 파이 좀 먹어 봐.

25 민희: 아니야, 고마워. 먹고 싶지 않아.

26 Andy: 왜 안 먹어? 너는 사과 파이를 좋아하지 않니?

27 민희: 응.

28 Andy: 그러면, 좀 먹어 봐. 맛있어.

29 민희: 아니. 내가 사과 파이를 좋아하지 않는다고 방금 말했잖아.

30 Andy: 뭐라고?

31 미국 사람들은 종종 "너 안 오니?", "너 병원 안 갔니?"와 같은 부정의문문으로 질문해.

32 부정의문문에 바르게 대답하는 것은 어려울 수 있어. 여기 약간의 충고 사항이 있어.

33 "너는 사과 파이를 좋아하지 않니?"와 같은 부정의문문의 대답으로 만약 사과 파이를 좋아하지 않는다면 너는 "No."라고 대답해야 해.

34 그리고 만약 그것을 좋아한다면 "Yes."라고 대답해야 해.

35 이 대답들은 "너는 애플파이를 좋아하니?"와 같은 긍정의문문에 대한 대답들과 같아.

36 어떤 문화적인 차이가 너에게 가장 놀랍니?

37 나는 미국에 온 이후로 문화적인 차이에 대해 계속 배우고 있어.

38 어떤 것들은 처음에 나를 놀라게 했지만, 지금은 그것들에 익숙해지고 있어.

● 우리말을 참고하여 본문을 영작하시오.

1 안녕! 내 이름은 김민희야. 나는 미국에 3년 동안 살고 있어.
➡ _____

2 우리 가족이 이곳으로 이민을 온 이후로 나는 한국과 미국의 많은 문화적 차이를 경험하고 있어.
➡ _____

3 나는 그것들 중 몇 가지를 너희들과 공유하고 싶어.
➡ _____

4 민희: 이 셔츠를 봐. 마음에 들어.
➡ _____

5 Linda: 멋져 보인다. 얼마야?
➡ _____

6 민희: 19달러 99센트야.
➡ _____

7 Linda: 비싸지 않네.
➡ _____

8 민희: 응, 나도 그렇게 생각해. 그것을 사고 싶어.
➡ _____

9 점원: 21달러 20센트입니다.
➡ _____

10 민희: 정말이요? 하지만 가격표에는 단지 19달러 99센트라고 쓰여 있는데요.
➡ _____

11 이곳 미국에서는 대부분의 주에서 사람들이 물건을 구입할 때 세금을 내.
➡ _____

12 그것은 판매세라고 불려. 판매세의 비율은 주마다 달라.
➡ _____

13 판매세는 1퍼센트 미만부터 10퍼센트 이상까지 다양해.
➡ _____

14 그래서 미국에서 상품을 살 때, 대개 가격표에 있는 가격보다 더 많은 돈을 지불해야 해.
➡ _____

15 Jessica: 안녕하세요, Johnson 할머니! 민희: 안녕하세요, Johnson 할머니!
➡ _____

16 Mrs. Johnson: 안녕, Jessica! 안녕, 민희! 잘 지내지?
➡ _____

17 Jessica: 잘 지내요, 감사합니다. 저희는 여기 버거 먹으러 왔어요. 식사 맛있게 하세요.
➡ _____

18 Mrs. Johnson: 고맙구나. 너희들도!
➡ _____

19 민희: Jessica, 왜 너는 Johnson 할머니께 손을 흔들었니?
➡ _____

20 미국에서 사람들은 종종 손을 흔들며 서로에게 인사해.
➡ _____

21 나이가 많은 사람에게 손을 흔드는 것은 무례하다고 여겨지지 않아.
➡ _____

22 네가 미국에 오면 처음에는 그것에 대해 불편하게 느낄 수 있어. 하지만 한번 시도해 보지 않을래?
➡ _____

23 너는 길을 걷고 있는 연세가 많으신 할아버지께 손을 흔들며 미소를 지어도 돼. 그도 너한테 답례로 손을 흔들지도 몰라.
➡ _____

24 Andy: 민희, 이 사과 파이 좀 먹어 봐.
➡ _____

25 Minhee: 아니야, 고마워. 먹고 싶지 않아.
➡ _____

26 Andy: 왜 안 먹어? 너는 사과 파이를 좋아하지 않니?
➡ _____

27 Minhee: 응.
➡ _____

28 Andy: 그러면, 좀 먹어 봐. 맛있어.
➡ _____

29 Minhee: 아니. 내가 사과 파이를 좋아하지 않는다고 방금 말했잖아.
➡ _____

30 Andy: 뭐라고?
➡ _____

31 미국 사람들은 종종 "너 안 오니?", "너 병원 안 갔니?"와 같은 부정의문문으로 질문해.
➡ _____

32 부정의문문에 바르게 대답하는 것은 어려울 수 있어. 여기 약간의 충고 사항이 있어.
➡ _____

33 "너는 사과 파이를 좋아하지 않니?"와 같은 부정의문문의 대답으로 만약 사과 파이를 좋아하지 않는다면 너는 "No."라고 대답해야 해.
➡ _____

34 그리고 만약 그것을 좋아한다면 "Yes."라고 대답해야 해.
➡ _____

35 이 대답들은 "너는 애플파이를 좋아하니?"와 같은 긍정의문문에 대한 대답들과 같아.
➡ _____

36 어떤 문화적인 차이가 너에게 가장 놀랍니?
➡ _____

37 나는 미국에 온 이후로 문화적인 차이에 대해 계속 배우고 있어.
➡ _____

38 어떤 것들은 처음에 나를 놀라게 했지만, 지금은 그것들에 익숙해지고 있어.
➡ _____

[01~02] 다음 글을 읽고 물음에 답하시오.

Hi! My name is Kim Minhee. I have been living in America for three years. (A) _____ my family moved here, I have experienced many cultural differences between Korea and America. I would like to share some of them with you.

01 다음 중 빈칸 (A)에 들어갈 말로 가장 적절한 것은?

① Although   ② For
③ If   ④ Since
⑤ As soon as

02 다음 중 위 글에 이어질 내용으로 가장 적절한 것은?

① Minhee's life in Korea
② common mistakes made by Korean people
③ some cultural differences Minhee experienced
④ the reason why Minhee moved to America
⑤ the reasons why cultural differences exist

[03~05] 다음 글을 읽고 물음에 답하시오.

Minhee: Look at this shirt. I like it.
Linda: It looks nice. How much is it?
Minhee: It's 19 dollars and 99 cents.
Linda: That's not expensive.
Minhee: Yes, I agree. I want to buy it.
Clerk: (A)That'll be 21 dollars and 20 cents.
Minhee: Really? But the price tag says it's only 19 dollars and 99 cents.
Here in America, in most states, people pay a tax when they buy goods. It is called a sales tax. Sales tax rates differ by state. They range from less than one percent to more than ten percent. So when you buy goods in America, you usually need to pay more than the price on the tag.

03 위 글에 따르면, 밑줄 친 (A)와 같이 말한 이유로 가장 적절한 것은?

① Because the clerk didn't like the shirt.
② Because a sales tax was added to the shirt.
③ Because the shirt was not on sale at that time.
④ Because the clerk didn't know the price of the shirt.
⑤ Because the clerk didn't want to sell the shirt to Minhee.

서답형
04 다음 빈칸에 들어갈 알맞은 말을 위 글에서 찾아 쓰시오.

Some large countries such as the USA are divided into smaller areas called _____.

05 다음 중 위 글의 내용을 바르게 이해한 사람은?

① 지유: 판매세는 셔츠에만 부과되는 거야.
② 경효: 원래 가격이 21달러 20센트였던 것을 19달러 99센트로 잘못 보았구나.
③ 유이: 미국에서 물건을 살 땐 가격표에 명시된 금액을 내면 되는 거야.
④ 예지: 물건을 살 때 지불하는 세금이 판매세구나.
⑤ 은별: 모든 주의 판매세가 똑같으니 계산하기 쉽겠어.

[06~08] 다음 글을 읽고 물음에 답하시오.

Jessica: Hi, Mrs. Johnson!

Minhee: Hello, Mrs. Johnson!

Mrs. Johnson: Hi, Jessica! Hi, Minhee! How are you?

Jessica: Fine, thank you. We are here for a burger. Enjoy your meal.

Mrs. Johnson: Thank you. You, too!

Minhee: Jessica, why did you wave to Mrs. Johnson?

In America, people often greet each other by waving. Waving to an older person is not regarded as (A)_____. When you come to America, you may feel uncomfortable about it at first, but why don't you try it? You can wave to and smile at an elderly man walking on the street. He may wave back.

06 다음 중 빈칸 (A)에 들어갈 말로 가장 적절한 것은?

① polite   ② friendly   ③ fun
④ rude   ⑤ considerate

07 다음 중 위 글의 내용과 일치하는 것은?

① Jessica doesn't know who Mrs. Johnson is.
② Jessica and Minhee are there to meet Mrs. Johnson.
③ Jessica is going to have a burger with Minhee.
④ Minhee waved to Mrs. Johnson.
⑤ Mrs. Johnson wants to meet Jessica.

서답형
08 According to the passage, how do people in America greet each other? Answer in English with a full sentence.

➡ _____

[09~11] 다음 글을 읽고 물음에 답하시오.

Andy: Minhee, (A)try this apple pie.

Minhee: No, thanks. I don't want to.

Andy: Why not? Don't you like apple pie?

Minhee: Yes.

Andy: Then, try some. It's delicious.

Minhee: No. I just said I don't like apple pie.

Andy: What?

① Americans often ask negative questions, such as "Aren't you coming?" and "Didn't you go to the hospital?" ② It can be difficult to answer negative questions correctly. ③ In response to negative questions, such as "Don't you like apple pie?" you should answer "No," if you don't like it. ④ And you should answer "Yes," if you like it. ⑤

 중요
09 ①~⑤ 중 주어진 문장이 들어가기에 가장 적절한 곳은?

Here is some advice.

①   ②   ③   ④   ⑤

10 다음 중 밑줄 친 (A)와 쓰임이 같은 것은?

① Please try me for the job.
② Don't try to explain.
③ Let me try a cup of tea.
④ Try whether you can do it or not.
⑤ I will try my best.

서답형
11 위 글을 참고하여 다음 상황에서 Minhee가 할 말을 빈칸에 알맞게 쓰시오.

Tom brought some chocolate cookies. He said to Minhee, "Don't you want to have some cookies?" But Minhee didn't like cookies. In this situation, what could Minhee say to Tom?

Minhee: _____, _____

[12~15] 다음 글을 읽고 물음에 답하시오.

Hi! My name is Kim Minhee. I have been living in America for three years. Since my family moved here, I have experienced many cultural (A)[similarities / differences] between Korea and America. I would like to share some of them with you.

Minhee: Look at this shirt. I like it.

Linda: It looks nice. How much is it?

Minhee: It's 19 dollars and 99 cents.

Linda: That's not expensive.

Minhee: Yes, I agree. I want to buy it.

Clerk: That'll be 21 dollars and 20 cents.

Minhee: Really? But the price tag says it's only 19 dollars and 99 cents.

Here in America, in most states, people pay a tax when they (B)[sell / buy] goods. It is called a sales tax. Sales tax rates differ by state. They range from less than one percent to more than ten percent. So when you buy goods in America, you usually need to pay (C)[more / less] than the price on the tag.

12 (A)~(C)에서 글의 흐름상 적절한 것끼리 바르게 짝지은 것은?

① similarities – sell -- more
② differences – sell – less
③ similarities – buy – more
④ differences – buy – more
⑤ similarities – buy – less

13 다음 중 위 글을 읽고 답할 수 있는 것은?

① How many states in America make people pay a sales tax?
② What is the color of the shirt?
③ Who made the sales tax?
④ What is the range of sales tax rates?
⑤ How did Minhee feel about a sales tax?

서답형

14 According to the passage, what do we need to pay when we buy things in America? Answer in English with a full sentence.

➡ _____

서답형

15 주어진 단어를 활용하여 다음 물음에 완전한 문장의 영어로 답하시오.

Q: When did Minhee move to America?
(ago)

➡ _____

[16~18] 다음 글을 읽고 물음에 답하시오.

Jessica: Hi, Mrs. Johnson!

Minhee: Hello, Mrs. Johnson!

Mrs. Johnson: Hi, Jessica! Hi, Minhee! How are you?

Jessica: Fine, thank you. We are here for a burger. Enjoy your meal.

Mrs. Johnson: Thank you. You, too!

Minhee: Jessica, why did you wave to Mrs. Johnson?

In America, people often greet each other by waving. Waving to an older person is not regarded as rude. When you come to America, you may feel uncomfortable about ⓐit at first, but why don't you try it? You can wave to and smile at an elderly man walking on the street. (A)_____

16 글의 흐름상 빈칸 (A)에 들어갈 말로 가장 적절한 것은?

① He may think that you are rude.
② He may wave flags and cheer.
③ He may wave back.
④ He may be upset and walk away.
⑤ He may wonder who you are.

서답형
17 밑줄 친 ⓐ가 의미하는 것을 위 글에서 찾아 쓰시오.

➡ _____

18 다음 중 위 글의 대화문에서 찾아볼 수 <u>없는</u> 것은?

① Minhee who is with Jessica
② Jessica waving to Mrs. Johnson
③ Mrs. Johnson having her meal
④ Minhee saying hi to Mrs. Johnson
⑤ Mrs. Johnson talking with her friends

[19~24] 다음 글을 읽고 물음에 답하시오.

Americans often ask negative questions, such as "Aren't you coming?" and "Didn't you go to the hospital?"

[A] And you should answer "Yes," if you like it. These answers are the same as the answers to positive questions, such as "Do you like apple pie?"

	Like	Don't like
Do you like apple pie?	Yes, I do.	No, I don't.
Don't you like apple pie?	Yes, I do.	No, I don't.

[B] In response to negative questions, such as "Don't you like apple pie?" you should answer "No," if you don't like it.

[C] It can be difficult to answer negative questions correctly. Here is some advice.

Which cultural difference is most surprising to you? I have been learning about cultural differences since I came to America. Some surprised me at first, but now I am getting used to them.

19 자연스러운 글이 되도록 [A]~[C]를 바르게 배열한 것은?

① [A]–[C]–[B]　　② [B]–[A]–[C]
③ [B]–[C]–[A]　　④ [C]–[B]–[A]
⑤ [C]–[A]–[B]

서답형
20 위 글을 읽고 다음 질문에 바르게 답하시오.

When you are hungry, your friend say to you "Aren't you hungry?" In this situation, what would you say to her?

➡ _____

21 다음 중 위 글의 내용과 일치하는 것은?

① "Do you like to play the violin?" is a negative question.
② Americans hardly use negative questions.
③ The writer learns about cultural differences by reading books.
④ When you are asked "Didn't you come to the party?", you should answer "Yes," if you didn't come to the party.
⑤ The answers to negative questions are the same as the answers to positive questions.

서답형
22 다음과 같이 풀이되는 말을 위 글에서 찾아 쓰시오.

relating to a particular society and its ideas, customs, and art

➡ _____

서답형
23 According to the passage, what has the writer been learning about? Answer in English with a full sentence.

➡ _____

24 문화적 차이에 대한 글쓴이의 현재 반응으로 가장 적절한 것은?

① surprised　② familiar　③ scared
④ shocked　⑤ amused

[01~02] 다음 글을 읽고 물음에 답하시오.

Hi! My name is Kim Minhee. I have been living in America for three years. Since my family moved here, I have experienced many cultural differences between Korea and America. I would like to share some of them with you.

01 How long has Minhee been living in America? Answer in English with a full sentence.

➡ _____

02 What does Minhee want to share with us? Answer with a full sentence and use the words below.

(want / between)

➡ _____
_____

[03~06] 다음 글을 읽고 물음에 답하시오.

Minhee: Look at this shirt. I like it.
Linda: It looks nice. How much is it?
Minhee: It's 19 dollars and 99 cents.
Linda: That's not expensive.
Minhee: Yes, I agree. I want to buy it.
Clerk: That'll be 21 dollars and 20 cents.
Minhee: Really? But the price tag says it's only 19 dollars and 99 cents.

Here in America, in most states, people pay a tax when they buy goods. It is called a sales tax. Sales tax rates differ by state. They range from less than one percent to more than ten percent. So when you buy goods in America, you usually need to pay more than the price on the tag.

03 According to the price tag, how much is the shirt?

➡ _____

04 When do people in America pay a sales tax? Answer in English with a full sentence.

➡ _____

05 다음 중 위 글의 내용과 일치하지 않는 것을 찾아 바르게 고치시오.

I went shopping with my friend. I picked a shirt and tried to pay the price on the tag. However, the clerk wanted me to pay more than the price on the tag, saying I needed to pay a sales tax. He said sales tax rates are equal in most states.

➡ _____

06 다음 질문에 알맞은 답을 주어진 단어를 활용하여 쓰시오.

Q: What doesn't the price on the tag include?
A: (include / it)

➡ _____

[07~09] 다음 글을 읽고 물음에 답하시오.

Jessica: Hi, Mrs. Johnson!
Minhee: Hello, Mrs. Johnson!
Mrs. Johnson: Hi, Jessica! Hi, Minhee! How are you?
Jessica: Fine, thank you. We are here for a burger. Enjoy your meal.
Mrs. Johnson: Thank you. You, too!
Minhee: Jessica, why did you wave to Mrs. Johnson?

In America, people often greet each other by waving. Waving to an older person is not regarded as rude. When you come to America, you may feel uncomfortable about it at first, but why don't you try it? You can (A)_____ to and smile at an elderly man walking on the street. He may wave back.

07 위 글의 흐름상 빈칸 (A)에 들어갈 알맞은 말을 위 글에서 찾아 쓰시오.

➡ _____

08 According to the passage, who waved to Mrs. Johnson? Answer in English with a full sentence.

➡ _____

09 위 글의 내용에 맞게 빈칸에 알맞은 말을 쓰시오.

_____ is not familiar with the way people _____ _____ _____ _____ _____ in America.

[10~13] 다음 글을 읽고 물음에 답하시오.

Andy: Minhee, try this apple pie.
Minhee: No, thanks. I don't want to.
Andy: Why not? Don't you like apple pie?
Minhee: (A)Yes.
Andy: Then, try some. It's delicious.
Minhee: No. I just said I don't like apple pie.
Andy: What?

Americans often ask negative questions, such as "Aren't you coming?" and "Didn't you go to the hospital?" It can be difficult to answer negative questions correctly. Here is some advice.

In response to negative questions, such as "Don't you like apple pie?" you should answer "No," if you don't like it. And you should answer "Yes," if you like it. These answers are the same as the answers to positive questions, such as "Do you like apple pie?"

	Like	Don't like
Do you like apple pie?	Yes, I do.	No, I don't.
Don't you like apple pie?	Yes, I do.	No, I don't.

10 주어진 단어를 바르게 배열하여 위 글의 제목을 완성하시오.

(correctly / to / negative / how / questions / answer)

➡ _____

11 위 글의 내용을 참고하여 밑줄 친 (A)의 답변을 민희의 의도에 맞게 바르게 표현하시오.

➡ _____

12 위 글의 내용에 맞게 빈칸에 알맞은 대답을 쓰시오.

I found a book boring. If someone asks me, "Didn't you find the book boring?", I would answer, "_____, _____ _____."

13 위 글의 내용에 맞게 빈칸에 알맞은 말을 쓰시오.

_____ _____ _____ is not that difficult. When you are in America, just remember this. Response to negative questions is _____ _____ as response to _____ _____.

Project Step 1

A: Can I get your advice on correct English expressions?
　　　　　　　　～에 대해 조언을 구할 수 있니?

B: Make sure you say window shopping instead of eye shopping.
　　'반드시 ～해라'라는 의미로 'Make sure (that)+주어+동사'　　　… 대신에

C: Make sure you don't say Y-shirt. You should say dress shirt instead.
　　　Make sure (that)+주어+동사　　　　　　　　　　　　부사: 그 대신에

구문해설 • correct: 옳은 • expression: 표현 • window shopping: 윈도 쇼핑(눈으로만 구경하는 쇼핑)
• instead of: … 대신에 • instead: 그 대신에

해석

A: 옳은 영어 표현에 대해 너의 조언을 구할 수 있을까?

B: 반드시 아이 쇼핑 대신 윈도 쇼핑(구경만 하는 쇼핑)이라고 말하도록 해.

C: 절대 와이셔츠라고 말하지 않도록 해. 대신 정장용 셔츠라고 말해야 해.

Project Step 3

Today, I realized I have been using many incorrect English expressions. For
　　　　realized 다음에 that 생략　　　　현재완료진행

example, we should say dress shirt instead of Y-shirt. Eye shopping is also an
예를 들어　　　　　　　　　　　　　　～ 대신에

incorrect expression. Make sure you don't use it.
　　　　　　　　　　　　Make sure (that)　　　eye shopping

구문해설 • incorrect: 잘못된, 틀린 • expression: 표현

오늘, 나는 내가 많은 잘못된 영어 표현을 사용해 왔다는 것을 알았습니다. 예를 들어, 우리는 Y-shirt 대신에 dress shirt라는 말을 써야 합니다. 아이 쇼핑도 또한 잘못된 표현입니다. 그것을 사용하지 않도록 명심하세요.

Enjoy Writing

Holi That I Can't Miss

There are many interesting festivals around the world. Among them, I'd like to
　　　　　　흥미로운 : 명사를 꾸며주는 분사　　　　　～중에서　　　　= I want to

attend Holi. People in India have been celebrating this festival for many years.
　　　　　　　　　현재완료진행형: 축제를 개최해오는 중이다　　　여러 해 동안

Holi is held in March. I think that if I go, I'll experience a lot of things.
be held 개최되다. 열리다　　　　　　　조건문: 내가 간다면

First, there are people throwing colored powder and water on each other. It
there are+복수명사: ～가 있다　　현재분사　　　　　　　　서로에게

will be fantastic! Second, I want to dance with other people on the street. I'll

also taste traditional Holi dishes. It's going to be very exciting. I can't wait for
　　　　　　　　　　　　　　　　　　　　　　　～가 기대된다

the day!

구문해설 • attend: 참여하다 • celebrate: 기념하다, 축하하다 • experience: 경험하다
• throw: 던지다 • taste: 맛보다

놓칠 수 없는 홀리
세계에는 많은 흥미로운 축제들이 있다. 그 중에서, 나는 홀리에 참여하고 싶다. 인도 사람들은 오랫동안 이 축제를 열어오고 있는 중이다. 홀리 축제는 3월에 열린다. 나는 내가 간다면, 많은 것들을 경험할 것이라고 생각한다. 첫째, 서로에게 색색의 가루와 물을 던지는 사람들이 있다. 그것은 환상적일 것이다. 둘째, 나는 거리에서 다른 사람들과 춤을 추고 싶다. 나는 또한 전통적인 홀리 요리를 맛볼 것이다. 그것은 정말 신날 것이다. 나는 그 날이 정말 기대된다!

01 다음 주어진 두 단어의 관계가 같도록 빈칸에 알맞은 단어를 쓰시오.

> difference – similarity = negative – _____

02 다음 글의 빈칸 (a)와 (b)에 들어갈 단어로 바르게 짝지어진 것은?

> I have been living in America for three years. (a)_____ my family moved here, I have experienced many cultural differences between Korea and America. I would like to (b)_____ some of them with you.

① Because – share   ② When – differ
③ Because – differ   ④ Since – wrap
⑤ Since – share

[03~04] 다음 영영 풀이에 해당하는 것을 고르시오.

03

> the number of the house, name of the road, and name of the town where a person lives or works, and where letters can be sent

① tax   ② postal code
③ address   ④ sales tax
⑤ entrance fee

04

> money paid to the government that is based on your income or the cost of goods or services you have bought

① tax   ② expense
③ goods   ④ advice
⑤ tag

05 빈칸에 공통으로 들어갈 말을 영어 설명을 읽고 알맞은 형태로 변형해서 쓰시오.

> In America, people often greet each other by _____. _____ to an older person is not regarded as rude.
> <영어 설명> to raise your hand and move it from side to side as a way of greeting someone

06 다음 밑줄 친 부분의 뜻이 잘못된 것은?

① Americans often ask negative questions, such as "Aren't you coming? (~와 같은)
② It can be difficult to answer negative questions correctly. (올바르게)
③ Which cultural difference is most surprising to you? (문화의)
④ Cultural differences surprised me at first, but now I am getting used to them. (~에 사용되다)
⑤ When we buy goods, we pay the price on the tag. (가격표)

07 다음 대화의 빈칸에 들어갈 말로 적절한 것은?

> A: Can I get your _____ on visiting the USA?
> B: Sure. You should sit in the back seat in the taxi.

① goods   ② advice
③ price   ④ hope
⑤ present

08 다음 문장을 읽고, 소녀가 민수에게 경고하는 표현을 사용하여 대화의 빈칸을 완성하시오.

> Minsu asks an American girl how old she is. The girl is unhappy because it's not polite to ask someone's age in Western cultures.

Minsu: How old are you?
Girl: _____ a person's _____ in Western cultures.

[09~11] 다음 대화를 읽고 물음에 답하시오.

Seho: My Chinese friend invited me to his house for dinner this Friday.
Bora: That's good. I hope you enjoy having dinner at his house. (①)
Seho: I want to prepare a small gift for him. You lived in China for several years. (②)
Bora: How about some tea?
Seho: Tea?
Bora: Yes. Most Chinese people like to receive tea as a present. They enjoy drinking tea. Also, they usually serve tea to guests. (③)
Seho: Oh, thanks. Is there anything else that I need to know? (④)
Bora: (A)_____ White and black mean death in China. (⑤)
Seho: Okay. I'll remember that. Thank you for the advice.

09 주어진 문장이 들어갈 위치로 알맞은 것은?

> Can I get your advice on what to bring?

① ② ③ ④ ⑤

10 위 대화의 빈칸 (A)에 들어갈 말로 알맞은 것을 고르시오.

① Make sure you use two hands when you hand it to her.
② Make sure you exchange Korean won to Thai baht.
③ Don't wrap the present in white or black paper.
④ Make sure you don't take pictures.
⑤ Don't touch the exhibits.

11 위 대화의 내용과 일치하지 않는 것은?

① Seho was invited by his Chinese friend.
② You can guess Bora knows well about the Chinese culture.
③ Bora suggested some tea as a present.
④ White and black mean death in China.
⑤ Seho will be served tea by Bora.

12 다음 대화의 밑줄 친 (A)와 같은 의미가 되도록 본문에 나오는 단어를 이용하여 8단어로 쓰시오.

> B: I'm going to Japan this summer. Can I get some advice on visiting there?
> G: Make sure you pay when you get off the bus.
> B: Oh, I didn't know that. Are there any other things I should remember?
> G: Pick up the bowl and hold it while eating. Also, when having soup, (A)you should drink it without a spoon.
> B: Okay. Thanks

➡ _____

13 다음 중 어법상 올바른 문장은?

① A kitten naming Toto is so cute.

② The teacher recommended the movies directing by Bong-Junho.

③ Those are the jeans produced in Vietnam through OEM.

④ Please show me the device which invented by Professor Sergio Teslar.

⑤ Some of the celebrities inviting to the festival didn't show up.

14 다음 Peter에 대한 정보를 읽고, 〈보기〉에서 알맞은 단어를 선택하여 빈칸에 알맞게 채우시오. (동사는 변형 가능)

> • Peter는 올해 Harvard 대학교에 입학한 이후로, 수학계에서 가장 어려운 문제들 중의 하나를 풀기 위해 지금까지 노력해 오고 있는 중이다.

─ 보기 ─
for / since / before / by / solve / play / try / be / pass / have / to

> Peter (A) _____ _____ _____ _____ _____ one of the most difficult questions in the world of mathematics (B) _____ he entered Harvard University this year.

15 다음 빈칸에 알맞은 말이 바르게 짝지어진 것은?

> • The photographer showed me what was _____ in London.
> • Janet has been picking up the _____ leaves after the storm passed by.

① taken – fallen
② taking – falling
③ taking – fell
④ took – fallen
⑤ took – falling

16 Which of the followings are grammatically <u>incorrect</u>? Choose all.

① The room has been feeling too cold.

② Dorothy has been driving since she got her driver's license.

③ Sam has been running for an hour.

④ My uncle has once played ice hockey.

⑤ I have been being falling in love with the girl group, G-idle.

17 다음 두 문장을 분사를 이용하여 한 문장으로 만드시오.

> • The lady is Ms. Baker.
> • She stays in Kenya to study wild animals.

➡ The lady _____

_____.

18 다음 그림을 보고 괄호 안의 단어를 활용해서 빈칸에 맞게 채우시오.

(1)

➡ I found a _____ (move) sentence in *The Old Man and the Sea* by Ernest Hemingway.

(2)

➡ The most famous Egyptian pyramids are those _____ (find) at Giza in Egypt.

19 다음 밑줄 친 부분의 쓰임이 나머지와 다른 것은?

① The guards <u>protecting</u> the actor were doing their best not to hurt crazy fans.

② John's father was busy <u>doing</u> the laundry that afternoon.

③ Barbara <u>working</u> for the bank fell in love with the police officer.

④ Paul <u>eating</u> pizza every day after midnight got another 5 pounds this week.

⑤ Laura was <u>playing</u> a good character.

20 다음 우리말을 영어로 옮긴 것 중 어법상 어색한 것을 고르시오.

① Paul의 엄마는 팔짱을 낀 채로 그의 아들들에게 얘기를 시작했다.

→ Paul's mom started to tell her sons with her arms folded.

② 우리는 눈을 감은 채로 노래를 불렀다.

→ We sang with our eyes closed.

③ Minsu는 다리를 꼰 상태로 교장 선생님을 보았다.

→ Minsu looked at the principal with his legs crossing.

④ 그녀는 창문을 열어 둔 채로 잠이 들었다.

→ She fell asleep with the window open.

⑤ Tom은 셔츠가 흠딱 젖은 채로 사무실에 왔다.

→ Tom came to the office with his shirts all wet.

21 다음 밑줄 친 부분 중 어법상 옳지 않은 것을 고르시오.

① We <u>have been living</u> here for quite a long time.

② I <u>have been studying</u> Spanish because I'm planning to go to Spain next year.

③ He <u>has been taking</u> care of Peter's little brothers since 3 hours ago.

④ My mom <u>has been owning</u> the bag since I was born.

⑤ Bella <u>has been cooking</u> for her friends until now.

Reading

[22~25] 다음 글을 읽고 물음에 답하시오.

Hi! My name is Kim Minhee. I have been living in America for three years. ⓐ<u>Since</u> my family moved here, I have experienced many cultural differences between Korea and America. I would like to share some of them with you.

Minhee: Look at this shirt. I like it.

Linda: It looks nice. How much is it?

Minhee: It's 19 dollars and 99 cents.

Linda: That's not expensive.

Minhee: Yes, I agree. I want to buy it.

Clerk: That'll be 21 dollars and 20 cents.

Minhee: Really? But the price tag says it's only 19 dollars and 99 cents.

Here in America, in most states, people pay a tax when they buy goods.

(A) They range from less than one percent to more than ten percent.

(B) It is called a sales tax. Sales tax rates differ by state.

(C) So when you buy goods in America, you usually need to pay more than the price on the tag.

22 자연스러운 글이 되도록 (A)~(C)를 바르게 배열하시오.

➡ _____

23 다음 중 밑줄 친 ⓐ와 쓰임이 <u>다른</u> 하나는?

① Peter hasn't phoned me <u>since</u> he went to Seoul.
② It has been 5 years <u>since</u> I met her.
③ <u>Since</u> you are alone at home, it is no wonder that you are very scared.
④ She has been ill in bed <u>since</u> the letter arrived.
⑤ I haven't seen her <u>since</u> I moved out of the apartment.

24 According to the passage, what is a sales tax? Answer in English with a full sentence.

➡ _____
_____

25 다음 중 위 글을 읽고 답할 수 있는 것은?

① Why did Minhee move to America?
② What is the most shocking difference between Korea and America?
③ Where was Minhee born?
④ How did Minhee think about the price on the tag?
⑤ How much money did Minhee have when she wanted to buy a shirt?

[26~29] 다음 글을 읽고 물음에 답하시오.

There are many interesting ①festivals around the world. Among ②them, I'd like to attend Holi. People in India have been celebrating this festival ③since many years. Holi is held in March. I think that if I go, I'll experience ④ a lot of things. First, there are people throwing colored powder and water on each other. It will be fantastic! Second, I want to dance with other people on the street. I'll also taste traditional Holi ⑤dishes. It's going to be very exciting. I can't wait for the day!

26 다음은 위 글의 제목이다. 빈칸에 알맞은 말을 위 글에서 찾아 어법에 맞게 쓰시오.

Holi, an _____ _____ in India

27 ①~⑤ 중 어법상 바르지 <u>않은</u> 것은?

① ② ③ ④ ⑤

28 In Holi, what do people throw on each other? Answer in English with a full sentence.

➡ _____

29 다음 중 위 글의 내용과 일치하는 것은?

① Holi is held in summer.
② You cannot attend Holi in India.
③ People will celebrate Holi for the first time this year.
④ The writer is looking forward to dancing with people on the street.
⑤ The writer isn't interested in tasting Holi dishes.

출제율 100%

01 다음 짝지어진 단어의 관계가 같도록 빈칸에 알맞은 말을 쓰시오.

> Russia - Russian = Japan - _____

출제율 90%

02 다음 영영 풀이에 해당하는 단어는?

> an opinion that someone offers you about what you should do or how you should act in a particular situation

① thought   ② advice
③ praise   ④ tag
⑤ tax

출제율 95%

03 다음 대화의 밑줄 친 (A)와 같은 의미의 문장을 주어진 단어를 활용하여 쓰시오.

> A: I'd like to visit Malaysia. Can I get your advice on traveling there?
> B: Sure. (A)You'd better not use your left hand to hand something to someone.
> A: Okay. Thanks.

➡ Make _____

[04~05] 다음 대화를 읽고 물음에 답하시오.

> G: I want to send this to my aunt in the USA.
> B: What is it?
> G: It's her *hanbok*. Can I get your advice on how to write an address in English?
> B: Sure. You should write the street address first.
> G: Like this?
> B: Yes. Then, write the name of the city and the state and then the postal code. Finally, write the country.

출제율 90%

04 To whom does the girl want to send the *hanbok*?

➡ _____

출제율 90%

05 What does the girl need to get advice on?

➡ She needs to get advice on _____
_____.

출제율 90%

06 다음 그림을 보고 아래 질문에 대해 주어진 단어를 이용하여 조언의 말을 쓰시오.

> Q: Can I get your advice on how to greet each other in Tibet?

➡ _____ in Tibet.
(sure / show / tongue)

[07~08] 다음 대화를 읽고 물음에 답하시오.

> G: (A)모로코 전통 의상을 입고 있는 사람들을 보세요. They are really beautiful. I want to take pictures of them.
> M: Wait. There is an important thing you need to know before taking pictures.
> G: Oh, really? Can I get your advice on it?
> M: Yes. You shouldn't take pictures of Moroccan people without asking.
> G: Why?
> M: They believe (B)_____ when someone takes their picture.

07 위 대화의 밑줄 친 (A)의 우리말에 맞게 주어진 어구를 알맞게 배열하시오. (필요하면 어형을 바꿀 것)

> (people / traditional / look at / the / wear / Moroccan clothes)

➡ _____

08 위 대화의 빈칸 (B)에 들어갈 말로 알맞은 것은?

① taking pictures is a popular hobby
② they should pay for it
③ it is similar to making a movie
④ it may have a bad effect on them
⑤ they will sell their pictures

09 대화의 빈칸 (A)에 들어갈 말로 알맞은 것은?

> B: Sena, I bought a present for Ms. Han. I have stayed at her house here in Korea.
> G: That's great. What did you buy her?
> B: I bought her a hat. Do you think she'll love it?
> G: Yes. (A)_____
> B: Why?
> G: Because giving something to older people with one hand is regarded as rude in Korea.
> B: Okay. I'll remember that.

① Make sure you keep your hands on the table at all times.
② Make sure you use two hands when you hand it to her.
③ Make sure you keep quiet.
④ Make sure you don't fight with your friends.
⑤ Don't wrap the present in white or black paper.

[10~11] 다음 대화를 읽고 물음에 답하시오.

> B: Did you (a)pack everything you need for the trip to Thailand tomorrow?
> G: Not yet. (A)What should I take?
> B: (b)Remember to bring a pair of long pants or a long skirt.
> G: Why? It's very (c)hot in Thailand, isn't it?
> B: Yes, but there are many temples in Thailand. You (d)should wear shorts when you visit a temple.
> G: Okay. Is there anything else?
> B: Make sure you (e)exchange Korean won to Thai baht.

10 위 대화의 밑줄 친 (a)~(e) 중 문맥상 어색한 것은?

① (a)　② (b)　③ (c)　④ (d)　⑤ (e)

11 위 대화의 밑줄 친 (A)와 같은 표현을 쓸 때 빈칸에 알맞은 말을 쓰시오.

> What should I take?
> = Can I _____ _____ _____ on what _____ _____ ?

12 다음 중 어법상 어색한 것을 고르시오.

① What have you been trying to find here?
② Kyle has been walking for 3 hours.
③ Donald's relatives have been playing poker during the last winter party.
④ Everyone has been watching the soccer game on TV since this morning.
⑤ Sarah's parents have been enjoying drawing pictures since last year.

13 다음 각 문장에서 어법상 <u>어색한</u> 부분을 하나씩 골라 고치시오.

출제율 100%

ⓐ They have been making some gifts since two months.

ⓑ The instructor taught us how to swim was almost drowned.

ⓒ The Spanish language speak in most of Latin American countries is not hard to learn.

ⓓ Prices have been risen steadily for 5 months.

➡ ⓐ _____ ⓑ _____

ⓒ _____ ⓓ _____

출제율 95%

14 다음 중 밑줄 친 부분의 성격이 나머지 넷과 <u>다른</u> 것은?

① All the students in my class came to see the works of Van Gogh <u>displayed</u> in this art museum.

② I know the pretty girl <u>smiling</u> at me in the middle of the field trip.

③ A kettle is used for <u>boiling</u> water.

④ Uncle Brian came home with a huge box <u>filled</u> with tropical fruits.

⑤ Street cleaners are collecting the leaves <u>fallen</u> on the road.

[15~18] 다음 글을 읽고 물음에 답하시오.

Hi! My name is Kim Minhee. I have been living in America for three years. Since my family moved here, I have experienced many cultural differences between Korea and America. I would like to share some of them with you.

Minhee: Look at this shirt. I like it.

Linda: It looks nice. How much is it?

Minhee: It's 19 dollars and 99 cents.

Linda: That's not expensive.

Minhee: Yes, I agree. I want to buy it.

Clerk: That'll be 21 dollars and 20 cents.

Minhee: Really? But the price tag says it's only 19 dollars and 99 cents.

Here in America, in most states, people pay a tax when they buy goods. It is called a sales tax. Sales tax rates differ by state. They range from less than one percent to more than ten percent. So when you buy goods in America, you usually need to pay (A)_____.

출제율 95%

15 빈칸 (A)에 들어갈 말로 가장 적절한 것은?

① more than the sales tax on the tag

② as much as a sales tax on the tag

③ much less than the price on the tag

④ as much as the price on the tag

⑤ more than the price on the tag

출제율 90%

16 다음과 같이 풀이되는 말을 위 글에서 찾아 쓰시오.

an amount of money that you have to pay to the government so that it can pay for public services

➡ _____

출제율 90%

17 위 글의 내용에 맞게 빈칸에 알맞은 말을 쓰시오.

Sales tax rates differ by state _____ _____ _____ one percent _____ _____ _____ ten percent.

18 다음 중 위 글의 내용과 일치하는 것은?

① Minhee moved to Korea three years ago.
② Minhee got so familiar with American cultures.
③ Minhee went to buy a shirt by herself.
④ People in Korea pay a sales tax like people in America.
⑤ Every state has its own sales tax rate.

[19~22] 다음 글을 읽고 물음에 답하시오.

Andy: Minhee, try this apple pie.
Minhee: No, thanks. I don't want to.
Andy: Why not? Don't you like apple pie?
Minhee: Yes.
Andy: (A)Then, try some. It's delicious.
Minhee: No. I just said I don't like apple pie.
Andy: What?

Americans often ask negative questions, such as "Aren't you coming?" and "Didn't you go to the hospital?" It can be difficult (B)to answer negative questions correctly. Here is some advice.

In response to negative questions, such as "Don't you like apple pie?" you should answer "No," if you don't like it. And you should answer "Yes," if you like it. These answers are the same as the answers to positive questions, such as "Do you like apple pie?"

	Like	Don't like
Do you like apple pie?	Yes, I do.	No, I don't.
Don't you like apple pie?	Yes, I do.	No, I don't.

Which cultural difference is most surprising to you? I have been learning about cultural differences since I came to America. Some surprised me at first, but now I am getting used to (C)them.

19 Andy가 민희에게 밑줄 친 (A)와 같이 말한 이유로 가장 적절한 것은?

① Because he understood Minhee doesn't like apple pie.
② Because he understood Minhee doesn't want to talk with him.
③ Because he understood Minhee likes him.
④ Because he understood Minhee likes apple pie.
⑤ Because he wanted Minhee to try harder.

20 다음 중 밑줄 친 (B)와 쓰임이 같은 것은?

① She ran fast to catch him.
② I am so happy to see you here.
③ It made me nervous to interview him.
④ The bird flew high to reach the top.
⑤ The boys needed something to play with.

21 밑줄 친 (C)가 가리키는 것을 위 글에서 찾아 쓰시오.

➡ _____

22 According to the passage, what has the writer been learning about since she came to America? Answer in English with a full sentence.

➡ _____

01 다음 그림을 보고 아래 〈조건〉에 따라 대화를 완성하시오.

┤ 조건 ├
(A) 'Can I'를 이용하여 대만을 방문하는
    것에 대해 조언을 구하는 표현을 쓸 것.
(B) 'eat food or drink water in the
    subway'를 대답에 활용할 것.

➡ A: _____ Taiwan?
   B: Sure. You should _____
   _____ .

02 다음 대화를 읽고 아래 질문에 대한 답을 본문에서 찾아 영어
로 쓰시오.

B: Did you pack everything you need for
   the trip to Thailand tomorrow?
G: Not yet. What should I take?
B: Remember to bring a pair of long
   pants or a long skirt.
G: Why? It's very hot in Thailand, isn't
   it?
B: Yes, but there are many temples in
   Thailand. You shouldn't wear shorts
   when you visit a temple.
G: Okay. Is there anything else?
B: Make sure you exchange Korean won
   to Thai baht.

Q: Why should she pack a pair of long
   pants or a long skirt?

➡ Because _____
   _____ .

03 다음 대화를 읽고 물음에 영어로 답하시오.

Seho: My Chinese friend invited me to
      his house for dinner this Friday.
Bora: That's good. I hope you enjoy
      having dinner at his house.
Seho: I want to prepare a small gift for
      him. You lived in China for several
      years. Can I get your advice on
      what to bring?
Bora: How about some tea?
Seho: Tea?
Bora: Yes. Most Chinese people like to
      receive tea as a present. They enjoy
      drinking tea. Also, they usually
      serve tea to guests.
Seho: Oh, thanks. (A)내가 알아야 할 또 다
      른 것이 있을까?
Bora: Make sure you don't wrap the
      present in white or black paper. White
      and black mean death in China.

(1) Q: Why did Bora suggest some tea as a
       gift?
   ➡ Because _____
   _____ .

(2) 밑줄 친 (A)의 우리말을 보고 주어진 〈조건〉
   과 단어를 이용하여 영어로 쓰시오.
   ┤ 조건 ├
   • 관계대명사를 사용할 것.
   • there / anything / else / need

   ➡ _____

04 다음 우리말과 같은 뜻이 되도록 주어진 어휘를 사용하여 글자
수에 맞게 영작하시오. (단어 변형 불가, 숫자는 영어로만 쓸 것.)

나는 한 인도 중학교에서 한국어를 13년 동안 가
르치고 있는 중이다. (teaching, for, Indian
middle, been, 13 단어)

   ➡ _____
   _____

05 다음 중 밑줄 친 부분을 어법에 맞게 고치고, 고친 단어의 종류가 <u>다른</u> 하나를 찾아, 그 이유를 설명하시오.

> ⓐ The boy <u>cry</u> at the corner of the street was Jane's youngest brother.
> ⓑ You should wait for the train <u>leave</u> at 5:00 here.
> ⓒ These days, people don't want to buy <u>sleep</u> bags for camping.
> ⓓ My wife saw a beautiful wall of a building <u>cover</u> with ivy.
> ⓔ Robert memorized a poem <u>write</u> by Ralph Waldo Emerson.

➡ ⓐ _____ ⓑ _____ ⓒ _____
ⓓ _____ ⓔ _____
이유: _____

[06~08] 다음 글을 읽고 물음에 답하시오.

Americans often ask negative questions, such as "Aren't you coming?" and "Didn't you go to the hospital?" It can be difficult to answer negative questions correctly. Here is some advice.

In response to negative questions, such as "Don't you like apple pie?" you should answer "No," if you don't like it. And you should answer "Yes," if you like it. These answers are the same as the answers to (A)_____, such as "Do you like apple pie?"

	Like	Don't like
Do you like apple pie?	Yes, I do.	No, I don't.
Don't you like apple pie?	ⓐ _____	ⓑ _____

Which cultural difference is most surprising to you? I have been learning about cultural differences since I came to America. Some surprised me at first, but now I am getting used to them.

06 빈칸 (A)에 알맞은 말을 쓰시오.

➡ _____

07 빈칸 ⓐ와 ⓑ에 적절한 말을 쓰시오.

➡ ⓐ _____ ⓑ _____

08 다음 상황을 읽고 빈칸에 알맞은 말을 위 글의 내용에 맞게 세 단어로 쓰시오.

> Julian came home late last night. If his mother says this morning, "Didn't you come late last night?", he will answer, "_____."

[09~10] 다음 글을 읽고 물음에 답하시오.

There are many (A)_____ festivals around the world. Among them, I'd like to attend Holi. People in India have been celebrating this festival for many years. Holi is held in March. I think that if I go, I'll experience a lot of things. First, there are people (B)_____ colored powder and water on each other. It will be fantastic! Second, I want to dance with other people on the street. I'll also taste traditional Holi dishes. It's going to be very exciting. I can't wait for the day!

09 주어진 단어를 어법에 맞게 빈칸 (A)와 (B)에 쓰시오.

> (interest / throw)

➡ (A) _____ (B) _____

10 According to the passage, what have people in India been celebrating for many years? Answer in English with a full sentence.

➡ _____

01 다음 (A)는 방문할 나라이고, (B)는 그 나라에서 유의해야 할 내용을 경고하는 문장이다. 아래의 대화를 완성하시오.

(A)	(B)
• Russia	• not / give flowers in even numbers
• the USA	• sit in the back seat in the taxi
• Malaysia	• not / use your left hand to hand something to someone
• Thailand	• not / touch someone's head

A: _____

B: Sure. _____ you _____.

02 다음 그림들을 보고, 괄호 안에 주어진 어휘를 모두 활용하여 현재완료진행형 문장을 쓰시오. (인칭과 시제 등에 유의하여 활용할 것.)

(John, eat, sing, since, lunch)   (Susan, clean, towel, table, brother, ten minutes)

(1) _____

(2) _____

03 주어진 단어를 활용하여 세계 축제 홍보 책자를 완성하시오.

Where: in Italy
What: Pizza Festival
When: in June
What you can do is …
① try different kinds of pizza from all around the world
② select the best chef

Pizza Festival that I Can't Miss
There are many interesting festivals around the world. Among them, I'd like to attend _____. People in _____ have been celebrating this festival for many years. Pizza Festival is held _____. I think that if I go, I will experience a lot of things. First, I will _____. Second, I will take part in _____. It's going to be very exciting. I can't wait for the day!

단원별 모의고사

01 다음 단어에 대한 영어 설명이 <u>어색한</u> 것은?

① bump: to hurt part of your body by hitting it against something hard
② rude: not polite
③ goods: things for sale, or the things that you own
④ sales tax: money paid to the government that is based on your income or the cost of goods or services you have bought
⑤ tag: a small piece of paper, cloth, or metal with information on it, tied or stuck onto something larger

02 다음 짝지어진 단어의 관계가 같도록 빈칸에 알맞은 말을 쓰시오.

> elderly : aged = rude : _____

03 다음 빈칸에 알맞은 것으로 짝지어진 것은?

> • Take _____ your shoes here.
> • _____ first I thought he was an Englishman.

① off – For
② off – At
③ on – To
④ on – With
⑤ over – From

04 다음 중 짝지어진 대화가 <u>어색한</u> 것은?

① A: Which country would you like to travel to?
　B: I'd like to visit Singapore.
② A: Is there anything I should know about the country?
　B: Yes. Make sure you don't chew gum on the street.

③ A: Aren't you hungry?
　B: Yes, I'm not.
④ A: Hi, Jessica! Hi, Minhee! How are you?
　B: Fine, thank you. We are here for a burger.
⑤ A: Look at this shirt. I like it.
　B: It looks nice. How much is it?

[05~06] 다음 대화의 빈칸에 들어갈 말로 알맞은 것을 고르시오.

05

> A: _____
> B: Make sure you say window shopping instead of eye shopping.

① Can I get some advice on visiting there?
② Are there any other things I should buy?
③ What is the best thing about shopping?
④ Can I get your advice on correct English expressions?
⑤ What is the name of the shopping mall?

06

> B: I'm going to Japan this summer. Can I get some advice on visiting there?
> G: Make sure you pay when you get off the bus.
> B: Oh, I didn't know that. _____
> G: Pick up the bowl and hold it while eating. Also, when having soup, you should drink it without a spoon.
> B: Okay. Thanks

① What should I take there?
② Can you tell me about your favorite food?
③ What are you going to eat?
④ How about Japanese food?
⑤ Are there any other things I should remember?

[07~08] 다음 대화를 읽고 물음에 답하시오.

Seho: My Chinese friend invited me to his house for dinner this Friday.

Bora: That's good. I hope you enjoy (a)having dinner at his house.

Seho: I want to prepare a small gift for him. You lived in China for several years. Can I get your advice on (b)what to bring?

Bora: How about some tea?

Seho: Tea?

Bora: Yes. Most Chinese people like to receive tea (c)as a present. They enjoy drinking tea. Also, they usually serve tea to guests.

Seho: Oh, thanks. Is there anything else (d)that I need to know?

Bora: (e)Make sure don't wrap the present in white or black paper. White and black mean death in China.

Seho: Okay. I'll remember that. Thank you for the advice.

07 위 대화의 밑줄 친 (a)~(e) 중 어법상 어색한 것은?

① (a) ② (b) ③ (c) ④ (d) ⑤ (e)

08 Why shouldn't Seho wrap the present in white or black paper? (7단어로 쓸 것)

➡ Because _____ .

09 다음 대화의 빈칸에 들어갈 알맞은 표현을 쓰시오.

> A: Is there anything I need to remember when I eat in France?
>
> B: Yes. _____ _____ you keep your hands on the table at all times.

[10~11] 다음 대화를 읽고 물음에 답하시오.

G: Look at the people wearing traditional Moroccan clothes. They are really beautiful. I want to take pictures of them.

M: Wait. (A)네가 사진을 찍기 전에 알아야 할 중요한 것이 있어.

G: Oh, really? (B) _____

M: Yes. You shouldn't take pictures of Moroccan people without asking.

G: Why?

M: They believe it may have a bad effect on them when someone takes their picture.

10 위 대화의 밑줄 친 (A)의 우리말 해석에 맞게 주어진 어구를 알맞은 순서로 배열하시오.

(an / before / important / is / thing / there / need / you / taking pictures / to / know)

➡ _____
_____

11 위 대화의 빈칸 (B)에 들어갈 말로 알맞은 것은?

① Who are you taking pictures of?
② Can I get your advice on it?
③ Is there anything else?
④ Can I get your advice on what to take?
⑤ Can I take pictures of Moroccan people?

12 다음 두 개 이상의 문장들을 주어진 〈조건〉에 맞게 한 문장으로 쓰시오.

조건
- 현재완료진행시제를 사용할 것.
- 분사가 명사의 뒤에서 수식할 것.
- for를 반드시 사용할 것.
- 10단어를 넘지 않을 것.

(1) • I started to read the novel last Sunday.
 • Sarah wrote the novel.
 • Today's Tuesday and I'm still reading it.
  = I _____

  _____ days.

(2) • Minsu got a job at a bank last month.
 • Bill founded the bank.
 • Minsu is still working there.
  = Minsu _____

  _____ a month.

13 다음 주어진 문장의 빈칸을 괄호 안의 단어를 사용하여 어법에 맞게 쓸 때, 〈보기〉의 빈칸에 들어갈 말과 쓰임이 같지 않은 것은?

보기
• Ethan purchased some drones _____ (make) in Indonesia for his next experiment.

① She has another box _____ (design) to keep fruit fresh.
② We have to put off the meeting _____ (schedule) on Saturday, Oct 26.
③ They decided to help the elderly _____ (live) alone.
④ Don't touch the statue _____ (place) in front of the square.
⑤ Sue gathered the dishes _____ (break) by her mistake.

14 우리말과 일치하도록 괄호 안의 단어를 바르게 배열하시오.

오늘 오전부터 나의 영어 선생님이 그 무거운 상자들을 옮기고 있는 중이다.
(morning, boxes, English, carrying, been, my, the, heavy, since, teacher, this, has).

➡ _____

_____

15 다음 중 밑줄 친 단어의 쓰임이 어법상 옳은 것은?

① We all remember the legendary singer Mr. Shin <u>calling</u> 'Mawang, the Devil King'.
② Can't you see that girl <u>worn</u> a rainbow evening dress.
③ There were a lot of bats <u>hanging</u> upside down from the ceiling.
④ These are old pictures <u>taking</u> 60 years ago.
⑤ I can recite the poem <u>writing</u> by Yoon-Dongju.

[16~18] 다음 글을 읽고 물음에 답하시오.

Hi! My name is Kim Minhee. I have been living in America for three years. Since my family moved here, I have experienced ① <u>many cultural differences</u> between Korea and America. I would like to ②<u>share</u> some of them with you.

Minhee: Look at this shirt. I like it.

Linda: It looks nice. How much is it?

Minhee: It's 19 dollars and 99 cents.

Linda: That's not expensive.

Minhee: Yes, I agree. I want to buy it.

Clerk: That'll be 21 dollars and 20 cents.

Minhee: Really? But the price tag says it's only 19 dollars and 99 cents.

Here in America, in most states, people ③pay a tax when they buy goods. It is called a sales tax. Sales tax rates ④differ by state. They range from less than one percent to more than ten percent. So when you buy goods ⑤in Korea, you usually need to pay more than the price on the tag.

16 민희가 위 글을 쓴 목적으로 가장 적절한 것은?

① to share some information about how to buy a shirt cheaply

② to introduce some cultural differences she has experienced

③ to complain about how hard it is to live in America

④ to introduce some people she made friends with in America

⑤ to write letters to friends in Korea

17 다음 중 위 글의 내용을 바르게 이해한 사람은?

① Amie: It must be really hard for Minhee to move to Korea.

② Brian: I think it is difficult for Minhee to live alone in America.

③ Clara: Like Minhee, I don't know anything about Korea.

④ David: I think people in Korea pay as much as the price tag says.

⑤ Edward: Korea has also a sales tax, so they always pay more than the price on the tag.

18 ①~⑤ 중 글의 흐름상 어색한 것은?

①   ②   ③   ④   ⑤

[19~21] 다음 글을 읽고 물음에 답하시오.

Jessica: Hi, Mrs. Johnson!

Minhee: Hello, Mrs. Johnson!

Mrs. Johnson: Hi, Jessica! Hi, Minhee! How are you?

Jessica: Fine, thank you. We are here for a burger. Enjoy your meal.

Mrs. Johnson: Thank you. You, too!

Minhee: Jessica, why did you wave to Mrs. Johnson?

In America, people often greet each other ① _____ waving. Waving to an older person is not regarded as (A)[polite / rude]. When you come to America, you may feel (B)[comfortable / uncomfortable] about it ② _____ first, but why don't you try it? You can wave ③ _____ and smile ④ _____ an elderly man walking ⑤ _____ the street. He may (C)[wave / turn] back.

19 다음 중 빈칸 ①~⑤에 들어갈 수 없는 것은?

① by   ② at   ③ to   ④ at   ⑤ for

20 (A)~(C)에서 글의 흐름상 자연스러운 것끼리 바르게 짝지어진 것은?

① polite – comfortable – wave

② rude – comfortable – turn

③ polite – uncomfortable – wave

④ rude – uncomfortable – wave

⑤ polite – uncomfortable – turn

21 According to the passage, how did Jessica greet Mrs. Johnson? Answer in English with six words.

➡ _____

Future Dreams, Future Jobs

 ## 의사소통 기능

- 확실성 정도 표현하기
  I'm quite sure you could become a great soccer player.
- 의견 표현하기
  It seems to me that you belong to the realistic type.

 ## 언어 형식

- It is[was] ~ that 강조 구문
  It is the growth ring in a fish **that** interests me.
- have+목적어+과거분사
  It's my responsibility to **have each song played** the same way every time.

Words & Expressions

교과서

Key Words

- **among**[əmʌ́ŋ] 전 ~ 중에서
- **analyst**[ǽnəlist] 명 분석가
- **analyze**[ǽnəlàiz] 동 분석하다
- **animator**[ǽnəmèitər] 명 만화 영화 제작자
- **attend**[əténd] 동 출석하다, 참석하다
- **audition**[ɔːdíʃən] 동 오디션을 보다
- **banker**[bǽŋkər] 명 은행가, 은행원
- **bank teller** 은행 창구 직원
- **brush**[brʌʃ] 명 붓, 솔
- **calm**[kɑːm] 동 진정시키다, 평온하게 하다
- **cast**[kæst] 명 출연자들
- **clear**[kliər] 형 명백한, 투명한
- **conduct**[kəndʌ́kt] 동 지휘하다, 처신하다
- **create**[kriéit] 동 창조하다
- **creature**[kríːtʃər] 명 생물, 생명체
- **data**[déitə] 명 자료
- **detail**[ditéil] 명 세부, 세목
- **developer**[divéləpər] 명 개발자
- **dish**[diʃ] 명 요리
- **engineer**[èndʒiníər] 명 기술자
- **enough**[inʌ́f] 부 충분히 형 충분한
- **figure**[fígjər] 명 인물, 형상, 사람 모양의 장난감
- **fix**[fiks] 동 고치다
- **florist**[flɔ́ːrist] 명 플로리스트, 화초 연구가
- **gardener**[gáːrdnər] 명 정원사
- **greenery**[gríːnəri] 명 화초, 푸른 잎
- **guide**[gaid] 동 안내하다
- **hairdresser**[héərdrèsər] 명 미용사
- **handle**[hǽndl] 동 다루다
- **highly**[háili] 부 매우, 대단히
- **historian**[histɔ́ːriən] 명 역사가, 역사학자
- **include**[inklúːd] 동 포함하다
- **information**[ìnfərméiʃən] 명 정보

- **lawyer**[lɔ́ːjər] 명 변호사
- **lead**[liːd] 동 이끌다, 인도하다
- **machine**[məʃíːn] 명 기계
- **mail carrier** 우편집배원
- **microphone**[máikrəfòun] 명 마이크
- **office worker** 회사원
- **orchestra**[ɔ́ːrkəstrə] 명 오케스트라, 관현악단
- **performance**[pərfɔ́ːrməns] 명 공연
- **personality**[pə̀ːrsənǽləti] 명 성격
- **poet**[póuit] 명 시인
- **police station** 경찰서
- **popular culture** 대중 문화
- **realistic**[rìːəlístik] 형 현실적인
- **recommend**[rèkəménd] 동 추천하다
- **record**[rékɔːrd] 명 기록 동 [rikɔ́ːrd] 녹화하다, 기록하다
- **reduce**[ridjúːs] 동 줄이다, 완화하다
- **report**[ripɔ́ːrt] 명 보고서
- **reporter**[ripɔ́ːrtər] 명 기자, 리포터
- **resource**[ríːsɔːrs] 명 자원
- **responsibility**[rispànsəbíləti] 명 책임
- **run**[rʌn] 동 실행하다
- **seem**[siːm] 동 ~인 것 같다
- **select**[silékt] 동 선택하다, 고르다
- **social worker** 사회복지사
- **someday**[sʌ́mdei] 부 언젠가
- **specialist**[spéʃəlist] 명 전문가
- **stethoscope**[stéθəskòup] 명 청진기
- **strength**[streŋkθ] 명 힘, 강점
- **tour guide** 관광 가이드
- **traditional**[trədíʃənl] 형 전통의, 전통적인
- **type**[taip] 명 유형
- **veterinarian**[vètərənέəriən] 명 수의사
- **weakness**[wíːknis] 명 약함, 약점

Key Expressions

- **be happy with** ~ ~에 만족하다
- **be interested in** ~ ~에 관심이 있다
- **belong to** (단체, 조직에) 소속하다, 속하다
- **by - ing** ~함으로써
- **care for** ~을 보살피다

- **come true** 실현되다
- **dream of** ~ ~을 꿈꾸다
- **I'm sure that** ~ ~을 확신하다
- **It seems that** ~ ~처럼 보이다, ~일 것 같다
- **make the best use of** ~을 최대한 활용하다

Word Power

※ 서로 비슷한 뜻을 가진 어휘

☐ **run : operate** (실행하다, 작동시키다)
☐ **fix : repair** (고치다)
☐ **handle : deal with** (다루다)
☐ **select : choose** (고르다, 선택하다)

☐ **highly : greatly** (매우, 대단히)
☐ **include : involve** (포함하다)
☐ **guide : lead** (안내하다, 이끌다)
☐ **recommend : propose** (추천하다)

※ 서로 반대되는 뜻을 가진 어휘

☐ **weakness** (약함, 약점) ↔ **strength** (강함, 강점)
☐ **include** (포함하다) ↔ **exclude** (제외하다)
☐ **clear** (분명한) ↔ **unclear** (불확실한)

☐ **increase** (증가하다) ↔ **decrease** (감소하다)
☐ **construct** (건설하다) ↔ **destroy** (파괴하다)
☐ **lead** (이끌다) ↔ **follow** (따르다)

English Dictionary

☐ **analyst** 분석가
→ someone whose job is to analyze and examine something
어떤 것을 분석하고 조사하는 일을 하는 사람

☐ **analyze** 분석하다
→ to study or examine something in detail, in order to discover more about it
어떤 것에 대해 더 많은 것을 발견하기 위해 자세히 연구하거나 조사하다

☐ **audition** 오디션을 보다
→ to give a short performance in order to show that you are suitable for a part in a film, play, show, etc.
영화, 연극, 쇼 등의 어떤 한 역할에 적합하다는 것을 보여주기 위해 짧은 공연을 하다

☐ **bank teller** 은행 창구 직원
→ a person whose job is to pay out and take in money in a bank
은행에서 돈을 지급하고 수납하는 것이 직업인 사람

☐ **belong to** 소속하다, 속하다
→ to be a member of an organization
조직의 일원이 되다

☐ **care for** 보살피다
→ to protect someone or something and provide the things they need, especially someone who is young, old or ill
누군가나 무언가를 보호하고 특히 어리거나, 늙거나, 병든 사람을 위해서 그들이 필요로 하는 것들을 제공해 주다

☐ **cast** 출연자
→ the actors in a film, play, or show
영화, 연극, 또는 쇼에 나오는 배우들

☐ **collect** 모으다
→ to take things and put them together
물건을 가져가서 한데 모으다

☐ **data** 자료
→ facts or information that can be analysed
분석될 수 있는 사실이나 정보

☐ **developer** 개발자
→ a person or company that creates new products, especially computer products such as software
특히 소프트웨어와 같은 컴퓨터 제품을 신제품으로 만드는 사람 또는 회사

☐ **greenery** 푸른 잎, 화초
→ green plants or branches, especially when cut and used as decoration
특히 잘려서 장식으로 사용되는 녹색 식물이나 가지

☐ **include** 포함하다
→ to contain something as a part of something else, or to make something part of something else
무언가를 다른 것의 일부로 포함하거나 다른 것의 일부로 만들다

☐ **lead** 이끌다
→ to bring a person or thing to a state or place
사람이나 사물을 어떤 상태나 장소로 데려오다[가져오다]

☐ **make the best use of** 최대한 활용하다
→ to use something as much as you can
당신이 할 수 있는 만큼 많이 무언가를 사용하다

☐ **personality** 성격
→ the type of person you are, shown by the way you behave, feel, and think
당신이 어떤 사람인지, 행동하고 느끼고 생각하는 방식으로 보여지는 것

☐ **responsibility** 책임
→ your job or duty to deal with something or someone
어떤 것 또는 어떤 사람을 처리해야 할 일이나 의무

☐ **resource** 자원
→ a useful or valuable possession or quality of a country, organization, or person
국가, 조직 또는 개인의 유용하거나 가치 있는 소유물 또는 자질

01 중요 다음 문장의 빈칸에 공통으로 들어갈 말로 가장 알맞은 것은?

- Ted and I _____ the same school.
- My parents are out of town to _____ the wedding.

① record
② develop
③ create
④ attend
⑤ select

02 서답형 다음 글의 빈칸에 들어갈 알맞은 말을 쓰시오.

A _____ is someone who creates beautiful things with flowers.

[03~04] 다음 설명에 해당하는 단어를 고르시오.

03
to be a member of an organization

① reduce
② belong to
③ make up
④ come true
⑤ make the best use of

04 중요
a useful or valuable possession or quality of a country, organization, or person

① source
② personality
③ resource
④ cast
⑤ developer

05 서답형 다음 우리말에 맞게 빈칸에 알맞은 단어를 쓰시오.

나는 내 팀의 강점과 약점을 보여 주기 위해서 그 자료들을 분석합니다.

➡ I _____ the data to show my team's _____s and _____es.

06 다음 빈칸에 공통으로 들어갈 말로 가장 알맞은 것은?

(A) Children's pictures _____ the walls of the classroom.
(B) It is a lot of fun to _____ your house with beautiful flowers.

① include
② increase
③ select
④ care for
⑤ decorate

07 서답형 다음 짝지어진 단어의 관계가 같도록 빈칸에 알맞은 말을 쓰시오.

fix : _____ = deal with : handle

08 중요 다음 빈칸에 들어갈 말로 알맞게 짝지어진 것은?

As a director of a musical theater, I do a lot of things. I _____ the actors and I look for good, strong voices. After selecting the _____, I teach them the songs for each scene. Then, I put the cast and orchestra together for practice.

① lead – gardener
② conduct – cast
③ record – actor
④ audition – cast
⑤ analyze – analyst

01 다음 빈칸에 들어갈 말을 〈보기〉에서 찾아 쓰시오.

┌─ 보기 ├─
among field reduce belong to calm
└─

(1) She helps them _____ stress and _____ themselves.
(2) What are you most interested in _____ the things on this list?
(3) Most people _____ one of six personality types. Realistic is one of the types.
(4) I am an ocean scientist. Ocean science is a big _____ .

02 다음 글의 밑줄 친 우리말에 해당하는 말을 쓰시오. (주어진 단어를 활용하여 쓰시오.)

I am happy when I create (A)다채로운 무언가를 with fresh flowers and greenery. If you like plants and the arts, I (B)강력히 추천합니다(high) you become a florist.

➡ (A) _____
　 (B) _____

03 다음 우리말과 같은 표현이 되도록 문장의 빈칸을 채우시오.
(1) 나는 스포츠 데이터 분석가입니다.
　 ➡ I am a sport data _____ .
(2) 나의 일은 녹화된 경기를 보고 자료를 수집하기 위해 컴퓨터 프로그램을 실행하는 것입니다.
　 ➡ My job is to watch _____ games and run a computer program to collect data.

(3) 공연 동안에, 나는 오케스트라 석에 있고 지휘를 합니다.
　 ➡ _____ the _____, I am in the orchestra area and conduct.

04 영영풀이에 해당하는 단어를 〈보기〉에서 찾아 첫 번째 빈칸에 쓰고, 두 번째 빈칸에는 우리말 뜻을 쓰시오.

┌─ 보기 ├─
greenery collect personality
└─

(1) _____ : to take things and put them together: _____
(2) _____ : the type of person you are, shown by the way you behave, feel, and think: _____
(3) _____ : green plants or branches, especially when cut and used as decoration: _____

05 빈칸에 공통으로 들어갈 단어를 쓰시오.

┌─
• To _____ an orchestra, you have to be able to hear the music in your head.
• The police officers _____ a school violence prevention campaign in Incheon four times a year.
└─

교과서

Conversation

1 확실성 정도 표현하기

> **I'm quite sure you could become a great soccer player.**
> 나는 네가 훌륭한 축구선수가 될 수 있을 거라고 꽤 확신한다.

- 'I'm sure (that) ~.'은 '나는 ~을 확신해.'라는 의미로 that절의 내용에 대해 자신의 확신을 나타내며, 'I'm (quite/fairly/absolutely) sure[certain] ~.'으로 표현할 수 있다.

- 확실성 정도 표현하기(긍정)
  - I was quite sure (that) you would be a successful fashion designer.
    나는 네가 성공적인 디자이너가 될 거라고 꽤 확신했다.
  - I have no doubt that you will become a great soccer player.
    나는 네가 훌륭한 축구선수가 될 것이라고 의심하지 않는다.

- 확실성 정도 표현하기(부정)
  - I'm not sure you will become a great soccer player.
    나는 네가 훌륭한 축구선수가 될 수 있을 거라고 확신하지 않는다.

- 상대방에게 확신 여부를 물을 때는 '확실해?'를 의미하는 'Are you sure?'를 쓴다.
  - **A:** Where is Kevin? Kevin은 어디에 있니?
    B: He's on the left. 그는 왼쪽에 있어.
    A: Are you sure? 확실해?
    B: Yes, I am. 응. 그래.

핵심 Check

1. 다음 대화의 빈칸에 들어갈 말로 알맞은 것을 <u>모두</u> 고르시오.

   A: I'm interested in art. Which job would be right for me?

   A: _____ a designer could be a good job for you.

   ① I'm fairly certain that
   ② I have no doubt that
   ③ I wonder whether
   ④ I'm quite sure that
   ⑤ Make sure that

2 의견 표현하기

It seems to me that you belong to the realistic type. 너는 현실적인 타입에 속하는 것 같다.

- 'It seems to me that ~.'은 '~인 것 같다'라는 의미로 자신의 의견이나 생각을 나타내는 표현이다. 'It seems to me ~'와 유사한 표현으로 'In my opinion, ~', 'I think ~', 'I believe ~', 'In my view, ~', 'For me, ~' 등이 있다.

- 의견을 표현하는 방법
내 생각에, 너는 현실적인 타입에 속하는 것 같다.
= I think that you belong to the realistic type.
= In my view, you belong to the realistic type.
= In my opinion, you belong to the realistic type.

  - **A:** What do you think about bringing cell phones to school? 너는 휴대전화를 학교에 가져오는 것에 대해 어떻게 생각하니?
  B: In my opinion, it is helpful in case of an emergency. 내 생각에, 그것은 응급상황인 경우에 도움이 돼.

  - **A:** What do you think about a water saving movement? 물 절약 운동에 대해서 어떻게 생각해?
  B: It seems to me that it is important to save water. 물을 절약하는 것은 중요한 것 같아.

핵심 Check

2. 다음 대화의 빈칸에 들어갈 말로 <u>어색한</u> 것은?

   A: I want to be a fashion designer. What would help me become one?

   B: _____ going to fashion shows would be helpful.

   ① In my opinion,
   ② It seems to me that
   ③ In my view,
   ④ For me,
   ⑤ You have to believe that

Listen & Speak 1 A-1

B: Anne, ❶I'm planning to visit the police station to see my uncle. He is a police officer.

G: Oh, I want to become a police officer someday.

B: ❷You do? Me, too. ❸I have dreamed of becoming a police officer since I was ten.

G: Can I come with you, Matt? I want to meet your uncle and ask him something.

B: Sure. What are you going to ask?

G: I want to ask him ❹what I need to do to become a police officer.

B: I see. ❺I'm sure he would like to meet you.

B: Anne, 나는 우리 삼촌을 보러 경찰서에 갈 예정이야. 그는 경찰관이거든.

G: 오, 나는 언젠가 경찰관이 되고 싶어.

B: 그래? 나도야. 나는 10살 때부터 경찰관이 되는 것을 꿈꿔 왔어.

G: 내가 너와 함께 갈 수 있을까, Matt? 나 너희 삼촌을 만나서 몇 가지 물어보고 싶어.

B: 물론이지. 무엇을 물어볼 거니?

G: 나는 경찰관이 되기 위해 내가 무엇을 해야 하는지 물어보고 싶어.

B: 알겠어. 나는 그가 널 만나고 싶어할 거라고 확신해.

❶ 'be planning to+동사원형'은 미래의 계획을 말할 때 사용하는 표현으로 '~할 예정이다'로 해석한다. to see는 부사적 용법의 목적으로 '~하기 위해'라는 뜻이다.

❷ do는 want to become a police officer를 대신하는 대동사다.

❸ 'since+주어+과거동사'는 '~한 이후로'의 의미로 현재완료와 주로 사용된다. 'dreamed of(전치사)+동명사(V-ing)' 형태를 사용한다.

❹ ask의 직접목적어 자리에 사용된 간접의문문으로 '의문사+주어+동사'의 어순을 취한다.

❺ 'I'm sure (that) ~.'은 '나는 ~을 확신해.'라는 의미로 확실성의 정도를 표현하는 말이다.

Check(√) True or False

(1) Anne wants to be a police officer.   T ☐ F ☐

(2) Matt has dreamed of becoming a police officer since he was ten.   T ☐ F ☐

Listen & Speak 2 A-1

G: I'm glad to meet you, Mr. Han. Could you please tell me what you do?

M: Okay. I guide travelers to different places in China and give them information about ❶where they should visit.

G: What else do you do?

M: I tell them about popular culture and traditional food in China.

G: ❷It seems to me knowing a lot about China is very important. Are you happy with your job?

M: Yes. I really love my job.

G: 만나 뵙게 되어 반갑습니다, Mr. Han. 당신이 어떤 일을 하시는지 말해 주실 수 있나요?

M: 그래. 나는 중국에 있는 다양한 장소로 여행객들을 안내하고 그들이 방문해야 할 곳에 대한 정보를 제공해.

G: 그 외에 또 어떤 일을 하시나요?

M: 나는 그들에게 중국의 대중문화와 전통 음식에 대해 말해 줘.

G: 중국에 대해 많이 아는 것이 매우 중요한 것 같네요. 당신의 직업에 만족하시나요?

M: 응. 나는 내 직업을 정말 사랑해.

❶ 전치사 about의 목적어 자리에 사용된 간접의문문이다.

❷ 'It seems to me that ~.'은 '~인 것 같다'라는 의미로 자신의 의견이나 생각을 나타내는 표현이다.

Check(√) True or False

(3) Mr. Han must be a tour guide.   T ☐ F ☐

(4) The girl isn't interested in Han's occupation.   T ☐ F ☐

Listen & Speak 1 A-2

M: What's wrong, Jisu?

G: I want to be an animator, but my drawing skill is not ❶good enough.

M: Hmm... ❷Being an animator is not just about being a good artist.

G: What should I do to become an animator?

M: Read a lot of books to make good stories and practice drawing every day.

G: Okay, I'll do so.

M: ❸I'm quite sure that you can be a good animator if you try hard.

G: Thank you very much.

M: 무슨 문제 있니, 지수야?
G: 저는 만화 영화 제작자가 되고 싶은데, 그리기 실력이 좋은 편이 아니에요.
M: 음... 만화 영화 제작자가 되는 것은 단순히 그림을 잘 그린다고 되는 것만은 아니란다.
G: 만화 영화 제작자가 되기 위해서 제가 무엇을 해야 하나요?
M: 좋은 이야기를 만들기 위해 책을 많이 읽고, 그림 그리는 것을 매일 연습하렴.
G: 알겠어요. 그렇게 할게요.
M: 나는 네가 열심히 노력하면 훌륭한 만화 영화 제작자가 될 수 있다고 아주 확신해.
G: 정말 감사해요.

❶ enough는 부사로 형용사 뒤에서 수식을 한다.
❷ Being은 동명사 주어로 단수 취급하고, 전치사 about 뒤에도 동명사 being을 사용한다.
❸ '나는 ~을 아주 확신해.'라는 의미로 that절의 내용에 대한 자신의 확신을 나타내는 표현이다.

Check(√) True or False

(5) Jisu is very good at drawing.   T ☐ F ☐

(6) The man advised Jisu to read lots of books and practice drawing every day.   T ☐ F ☐

Listen & Speak 2 A-2

B: Did you finish the report about your role model?

G: Yes, I did. I wrote about my role model, Ms. Shin. ❶I want to be like her.

B: ❷What does she do?

G: ❸She teaches people how to stretch. She also ❹helps them reduce stress and calm themselves.

B: Good. ❺It seems that she helps to keep both their mind and body healthy.

G: Yes, and I think it's great.

B: 네 롤 모델에 관한 기사 다 썼니?
G: 응, 다 썼어. 나는 나의 롤 모델인 신 씨에 관해 썼어. 나는 그녀처럼 되고 싶어.
B: 그녀는 무슨 일을 하니?
G: 그녀는 사람들에게 스트레칭하는 방법을 가르쳐. 그녀는 또한 그들이 스트레스를 완화하여 평온해지도록 도와 줘.
B: 좋구나. 그녀가 사람들의 몸과 마음을 둘 다 건강하게 유지하도록 돕는 것 같아.
G: 맞아, 그리고 나는 그것이 훌륭하다고 생각해.

❶ want는 to부정사를 목적어로 취하는 동사이고, 'be like'는 '~처럼 되다'는 의미로 이때의 like는 전치사이다.
❷ 직업을 묻는 표현이다.
❸ 'teach+간접목적어+직접목적어(how to stretch)' 구문이다.
❹ 'help+목적어+목적보어(동사원형/to부정사)' 구문으로 '…가 ~하도록 돕다'라는 뜻이다.
❺ 'It seems that+주어+동사 ~'는 '~처럼 보이다, ~인 것 같다'는 의미로 '주어+seem(s) to부정사'로 문장을 전환할 수 있다. help는 to부정사와 동사원형을 목적어로 가질 수 있다.

Check(√) True or False

(7) The girl wants to be like Ms. Shin.   T ☐ F ☐

(8) Ms. Shin helps people cure their disease.   T ☐ F ☐

Listen & Speak 1 B

- A: I'm interested in technology. ❶Which job would be right for me?

  B: ❷I'm quite sure that an app developer could be a good job for you.

- A: I'm interested in writing. Which job would be right for me?

  B: I'm quite sure that a writer could be a good job for you.

❶ which는 명사를 수식하는 의문형용사로 '어느, 어떤'의 의미다.
❷ an app developer: 앱 개발자

Listen & Speak 2 B

- A: I want to be a radio program writer. What would ❶help me become one?

  B: ❷It seems to me writing your own stories would be helpful.

- A: I want to be a social worker. What would help me become one?

  B: It seems to me reading books to kids at a hospital would be helpful.

❶ help+목적어+동사원형: 목적어가 ~하는 것을 돕다 one=a writer
❷ It seems to me (that) ... 구문이다. writing은 동명사로 would be의 주어이다.

Real Life Talk

Bora: ❶What are you most interested in among the things on this list?

Jessie: I'm most interested in ❷working outside and playing sports.

Bora: Well, ❸it seems to me that you belong to the realistic type.

Jessie: What do you mean?

Bora: Most people belong to ❹one of six personality types. Realistic is one of the types.

Jessie: Oh, that's interesting. ❺What kind of jobs do they recommend for realistic types?

Bora: A farmer, a police officer, a soccer player, and so on.

Jessie: Oh, I have always wanted to be a soccer player.

Bora: That's good. ❻I'm quite sure you could become a great soccer player.

❶ be interested in ~: ~에 관심이 있다. most는 최상급으로 '가장'의 의미다.
❷ 전치사 in 다음에 동명사 'working ~ and playing ~'이 온다.
❸ belong to는 '~에 속하다'는 의미로 수동태를 사용하지 않는다.
❹ 'one of+복수명사'는 '~ 중 하나'라는 의미이다.
❺ 'What kind of 명사 ~?'는 '어떤 종류의 ~?'라는 의미이다.
❻ 확실성의 정도를 표현하는 말이다.

Wrap Up 1

B: Hello, what are you doing, Sumi?

G: I'm looking for a good recipe on the Internet. I need it for my family dinner today.

B: That is nice. Do you cook often?

G: Yes, ❶I try to cook every weekend. I want to be a chef someday.

B: What are you doing ❷to make your dream come true?

G: I'm ❸taking a cooking class. I try to think of new and creative dishes.

B: ❹I'm quite sure you could be a good chef.

❶ try+to부정사: ~하려고 애쓰다[노력하다], try+V-ing: 시험 삼아 ~해 보다
❷ to make는 부사적 용법의 목적으로 '~하기 위해서'라는 뜻이다. 여기서 make는 사역동사로 '목적어(your dream)+동사원형(come)' 형태를 취한다.
❸ 'take a class'는 '수업을 듣다'는 뜻이다.
❹ 'I'm quite sure ~'는 확실성의 정도를 표현하는 말이다.

● 다음 우리말과 일치하도록 빈칸에 알맞은 말을 쓰시오.

Listen & Speak 1 A

1. B: Anne, I'm _____ to visit the _____ _____ to see my uncle. He is a police _____

   G: Oh, I want _____ _____ a police officer _____.

   B: You _____? Me, too. I have _____ of _____ a police officer _____ I was ten.

   G: Can I come _____ you, Matt? I want to meet your uncle and _____ him _____.

   B: Sure. What are you _____ to ask?

   G: I want to ask him _____ I need _____ _____ to become a police officer.

   B: I see. I'm _____ he _____ _____ _____ meet you.

2. M: What's _____, Jisu?

   G: I want to be an _____, but my _____ skill is not good _____.

   M: Hmm... _____ an animator is not just about _____ good _____.

   G: What should I do to become an _____?

   M: Read _____ _____ _____ books to make good stories and _____ _____ every day.

   G: Okay, I'll do so.

   M: I'm _____ _____ _____ you can be a good animator _____ you try hard.

   G: Thank you very much.

Listen & Speak 1 B

● A: I'm _____ in _____. _____ job would be _____ for me?

   B: I'm quite _____ that an app _____ could be a good job for you.

● A: I'm interested _____ _____. _____ _____ would _____ _____ me?

   B: I'm _____ _____ that a writer could _____ _____ _____ _____ _____ you.

해석

1. B: Anne, 나는 우리 삼촌을 보러 경찰서에 갈 예정이야. 그는 경찰관이거든.
   G: 오, 나는 언젠가 경찰관이 되고 싶어.
   B: 그래? 나도야. 나는 10살 때부터 경찰관이 되는 것을 꿈꿔왔어.
   G: 내가 너와 함께 갈 수 있을까, Matt? 나 너희 삼촌을 만나서 몇 가지 물어보고 싶어.
   B: 물론이지. 무엇을 물어 볼 거니?
   G: 나는 경찰관이 되기 위해 내가 무엇을 해야 하는지 물어보고 싶어.
   B: 알겠어. 나는 그가 널 만나고 싶어할 거라고 확신해.

2. M: 무슨 문제 있니, 지수야?
   G: 저는 만화 영화 제작자가 되고 싶은데, 그리기 실력이 좋은 편이 아니에요.
   M: 음... 만화 영화 제작자가 되는 것은 단순히 그림을 잘 그린다고 되는 것만은 아니란다.
   G: 만화 영화 제작자가 되기 위해서 제가 무엇을 해야 하나요?
   M: 좋은 이야기를 만들기 위해 책을 많이 읽고, 그림 그리는 것을 매일 연습하렴.
   G: 알겠어요. 그렇게 할게요.
   M: 나는 네가 열심히 노력하면 훌륭한 만화 영화 제작자가 될 수 있다고 아주 확신해.
   G: 정말 감사해요.

• A: 나는 기술에 관심이 있어. 어떤 직업이 나에게 맞을까?
   B: 나는 앱 개발자가 너에게 좋은 직업이 될 수 있을 거라고 아주 확신해.
• A: 나는 쓰기에 관심이 있어. 어떤 직업이 나에게 맞을까?
   B: 나는 작가가 너에게 좋은 직업이 될 수 있을 거라고 아주 확신해.

Listen & Speak 2 A

1. **G:** I'm _____ to meet you, Mr. Han. Could you please tell me _____ _____ _____?

   M: Okay. I _____ travelers to different places in China and give them _____ about where they should _____.

   G: What _____ do you do?

   M: I tell them about _____ _____ and _____ food in China.

   G: _____ _____ to me _____ a lot about China is very important. Are you _____ _____ your job?

   M: Yes. I really love my job.

2. **B:** Did you finish the report about your _____ _____?

   G: Yes, I did. I wrote about my role model, Ms. Shin. I want to _____ _____ her.

   B: What _____ she _____?

   G: She teaches people _____ _____ _____. She also helps them _____ stress and _____ _____.

   B: Good. _____ _____ _____ she helps _____ _____ _____ their mind _____ body healthy.

   G: Yes, and I think it's great.

Listen & Speak 2 B

- **A:** I want to be a radio _____ _____. What would help me _____ one?

  B: It seems to me _____ your own stories would be _____.

- **A:** I want to be a _____ _____. What would _____ _____ _____ one?

  B: It _____ to me _____ _____ _____ _____ at a hospital would _____ _____.

Real Life Talk

Bora: What are you _____ _____ in _____ the things on this list?

Jessie: I'm most interested in _____ outside and playing sports.

---

1. G: 만나 뵙게 되어 반갑습니다, Mr. Han. 당신이 어떤 일을 하시는지 말해 주실 수 있나요?
   M: 그래. 나는 중국에 있는 다양한 장소로 여행객들을 안내하고 그들이 방문해야 할 곳에 대한 정보를 제공해.
   G: 그 외에 또 어떤 일을 하시나요?
   M: 나는 그들에게 중국의 대중문화와 전통 음식에 대해 말해 줘.
   G: 중국에 대해 많이 아는 것이 매우 중요한 것 같네요. 당신의 직업에 만족하시나요?
   M: 응. 나는 내 직업을 정말 사랑해.

2. B: 네 롤 모델에 관한 기사 다 썼니?
   G: 응, 다 썼어. 나는 나의 롤 모델인 신 씨에 관해 썼어. 나는 그녀처럼 되고 싶어.
   B: 그녀는 무슨 일을 하니?
   G: 그녀는 사람들에게 스트레칭하는 방법을 가르쳐. 그녀는 또한 그들이 스트레스를 완화하여 평온해지도록 도와 줘.
   B: 좋네. 그녀가 그들의 몸과 마음을 둘 다 건강하게 유지하도록 돕는 것 같아.
   G: 맞아, 그리고 나는 그것이 훌륭하다고 생각해.

- A: 나는 라디오 방송 작가가 되고 싶어. 내가 그것이 되는 데 뭐가 도움이 될까?
  B: 너 자신만의 이야기를 쓰는 것이 도움이 될 것 같아.
- A: 나는 사회복지사가 되고 싶어. 내가 그것이 되는 데 뭐가 도움이 될까?
  B: 병원에서 아이들에게 책을 읽어 주는 것이 도움이 될 것 같아.

보라: 너는 이 목록에 있는 것들 중에서 무엇에 가장 관심이 있니?
Jessie: 나는 밖에서 일하는 것과 스포츠 하는 것에 가장 관심이 있어.

Bora: Well, _____ _____ _____ _____ _____ you _____ _____ the _____ type.

Jessie: What do you _____?

Bora: Most people _____ _____ one of six _____ _____. _____ is one of the _____.

Jessie: Oh, that's _____. _____ _____ _____ jobs do they _____ for realistic types?

Bora: A farmer, a police officer, a soccer player, _____ _____ _____.

Jessie: Oh, I have always wanted _____ _____ a soccer player.

Bora: That's good. _____ _____ _____ you could become a great soccer player.

Communication Task Step 2

A: I have _____ _____, _____ _____, 1 I, and _____ _____.

B: It _____ _____ me that you _____ _____ Type S.

C: Yes. _____ _____ are _____ for Type S are teacher, nurse, librarian or counselor.

A: Cool. I _____ _____ _____ to be a teacher.

D: That _____ great. I'm _____ _____ _____ _____ _____ be a good teacher.

Wrap Up 1

B: Hello, what are you _____, Sumi?

G: I'm looking for a good _____ on the Internet. I need it for my family dinner today.

B: That is nice. Do you _____ often?

G: Yes, I try _____ _____ every weekend. I want to be a _____ someday.

B: What are you doing to _____ your dream come true?

G: I'm _____ a cooking class. I try _____ _____ _____ new and _____ dishes.

B: _____ _____ _____ you could be a good chef.

보라: 음, 내 생각에 너는 현실적인 타입에 속하는 것 같아.
Jessie: 무슨 의미야?
보라: 대부분의 사람들은 여섯 가지 성격 유형 중 한 가지에 속해. 현실적인 타입도 그중 하나야.
Jessie: 오, 재미있다. 현실적인 타입의 사람들에게 그들이 추천하는 직업은 뭐야?
보라: 농부, 경찰관, 축구 선수 같은 거야.
Jessie: 오, 나는 항상 축구 선수가 되고 싶어 해 왔어.
보라: 멋지다. 나는 네가 훌륭한 축구 선수가 될 수 있을 거라고 아주 확신해.

A: 나는 S가 3개, A가 2개, I가 1개, E가 1개 있어.
B: 너는 S 타입에 속해 있는 것 같아.
C: 응. S 타입에게 추천되는 직업은 선생님, 간호사, 사서, 상담사야.
A: 멋지다. 나는 항상 선생님이 되고 싶었어.
D: 그거 멋지네. 나는 네가 좋은 선생님이 될 수 있다고 아주 확신해.

B: 안녕, 뭐 하고 있니, 수미야?
G: 나는 인터넷으로 좋은 요리법을 찾아보고 있어. 나는 오늘 우리 가족의 저녁 식사를 위해 그것이 필요해.
B: 그거 멋지네. 너는 요리를 자주 하니?
G: 응, 나는 매주 주말에 요리를 하려고 노력해. 나는 언젠가 요리사가 되고 싶어.
B: 네 꿈을 이루기 위해서 무엇을 하고 있니?
G: 나는 요리 수업을 듣고 있어. 새롭고 창의적인 요리를 생각해 내기 위해 노력해.
B: 나는 네가 좋은 요리사가 될 것이라고 아주 확신해.

01 우리말 해석에 맞도록 문장의 빈칸에 알맞은 말을 쓰시오.

• 너는 현실적인 타입에 속하는 것 같다.

➡ _____ _____ to me _____ you belong to the realistic type.

02 다음 대화의 빈칸에 들어갈 말로 알맞은 것은?

A: I'm interested in art. Which job would be right for me?
B: _____ a designer could be a good job for you.

① I question whether
② You may think that
③ I'm quite sure that
④ I'm very annoyed that
⑤ You should think

03 다음 대화의 빈칸에 들어갈 말로 가장 알맞은 것은?

A: I want to be a radio program writer. What would help me become one?
B: _____

① It seems to me going to fashion shows would be helpful.
② It seems that she helps to keep both their mind and body healthy.
③ I'm quite sure that you could be a radio program writer.
④ It seems to me you are a cook.
⑤ It seems to me writing your own stories would be helpful.

04 다음 대화의 밑줄 친 말의 의도로 알맞은 것은?

A: Jihun is good at painting.
B: Yes, he is. I'm sure he will be a great painter.

① 관심 표현하기   ② 확실성 정도 표현하기
③ 의견 표현하기   ④ 동의 표현하기
⑤ 반복 요청하기

[01~02] 다음 대화를 읽고 물음에 답하시오.

B: Anne, I'm (a)planning to visit the police station to see my uncle. He is a police officer.
G: Oh, I want (b)to become a police officer someday.
B: You do? Me, too. I have dreamed of (c)become a police officer since I was ten.
G: Can I come with you, Matt? I want to meet your uncle and ask him something.
B: Sure. What are you going to ask?
G: I want to ask him (d)what I need to do to become a police officer.
B: I see. (e)I'm sure he would like to meet you.

01 위 대화의 밑줄 친 (a)~(e) 중, 어법상 어색한 것은?

① (a) ② (b) ③ (c) ④ (d) ⑤ (e)

02 위 대화의 내용으로 알 수 없는 것은?

① Matt is going to meet his uncle this weekend.
② Anne wants to become a police officer.
③ Matt has wanted to be a police officer since he was ten.
④ Anne wants to ask Matt's uncle something.
⑤ Anne and Matt are going to go to the police station.

03 주어진 문장에 이어질 대화의 순서로 알맞은 것은?

A: I'm interested in animals. Which job is right for me?

(A) That's a person who works at a pet hair salon. He or she designs different hairstyles for pets.
(B) What is a pet hairdresser?
(C) I think a pet hairdresser can be a good job for you.
(D) That sounds nice.

① (B)–(A)–(C)–(D) ② (B)–(C)–(A)–(D)
③ (C)–(A)–(D)–(B) ④ (C)–(B)–(A)–(D)
⑤ (D)–(B)–(C)–(A)

04 다음 대화의 빈칸에 들어갈 말로 알맞은 것을 고르시오.

A: I want to be a fashion designer.
_____
B: It seems to me going to fashion shows would be helpful.

① Can I get your advice on fashion shows?
② Do you think I could be a fashion designer?
③ What would help me become one?
④ What would you like to do at fashion shows?
⑤ What do I like to be?

05 다음 대화의 밑줄 친 문장과 같은 의미가 되도록 주어진 단어를 이용하여 세 단어로 쓰시오.

A: It seems to me he is a cook.
B: That's right.

➡ _____, he is a cook. (opinion)

06 다음 두 사람의 대화가 <u>어색한</u> 것은?

① A: Can you imagine what jobs there will be in the future?

B: It seems to me that there will be space travel planners.

② A: Why are you applying to be a self-driving car mechanic?

B: I am interested in new technologies and cars.

③ A: Hello, what are you doing, Sumi?

B: I'm looking for a good recipe on the Internet.

④ A: What are you doing to make your dream come true?

B: I'm taking a cooking class.

⑤ A: I'm interested in technology. Which job would be right for me?

B: I'm quite sure that you could become a great soccer player.

서답형

07 다음 대화의 밑줄 친 우리말에 맞게 주어진 어구를 이용하여 영어로 쓰시오. (단어 2개를 추가하고, 어형 변화 필수)

> M: What's wrong, Jisu?
>
> G: I want to be an animator, but my drawing skill is not good enough.
>
> M: Hmm... 만화 영화 제작자가 되는 것은 단순히 그림을 잘 그린다고 되는 것만은 아니란다.

> be / an animator / not just / about / a good artist.

➡ _____

08 다음 대화의 밑줄 친 부분의 의도로 알맞은 것은?

> A: I want to be a radio program writer. What would help me become one?
>
> B: <u>It seems to me writing your own stories would be helpful.</u>

① 조언 구하기　　② 의견 표현하기

③ 확신 표현하기　　④ 궁금증 표현하기

⑤ 가능성 묻기

[09~10] 다음 대화를 읽고 물음에 답하시오.

> Bora: What are you most interested in among the things on this list?
>
> Jessie: I'm most interested in working (a)<u>outside</u> and playing sports.
>
> Bora: Well, it seems to me that you (b)<u>belong to</u> the realistic type.
>
> Jessie: What do you mean?
>
> Bora: Most people belong to one of six personality types. (c)<u>Realistic</u> is one of the types.
>
> Jessie: Oh, that's interesting. What kind of jobs do they (d)<u>recommend</u> for realistic types?
>
> Bora: A farmer, a police officer, a soccer player, and so on.
>
> Jessie: Oh, I have always wanted to be a soccer player.
>
> Bora: That's good. (e)<u>I'm not sure</u> you could become a great soccer player.

09 위 대화의 밑줄 (a)~(e) 중 어색한 것은?

① (a)　② (b)　③ (c)　④ (d)　⑤ (e)

10 위 대화를 읽고 답할 수 <u>없는</u> 것은?

① What is Jessie most interested in among the things on the list?

② What personality type does Jessie belong to?

③ What kind of job did Bora suggest to Jessie?

④ What has Jessie always wanted to be?

⑤ What jobs do they recommend for the realistic type?

[01~02] 다음 대화를 읽고 물음에 답하시오.

B: Anne, I'm planning to visit the police station to see my uncle. He is a police officer.

G: Oh, I want to become a police officer someday.

B: You do? Me, too. (A)나는 10살 때부터 경찰관이 되는 것을 꿈꿔왔어.

G: Can I come with you, Matt? I want to meet your uncle and ask him something.

B: Sure. What are you going to ask?

G: I want to ask him what I need to do to become a police officer.

B: I see. (B)_____

01 위 대화의 우리말 (A)에 맞게 주어진 어구를 알맞은 순서로 배열하시오. (부사절을 문장 뒤에 쓸 것.)

I / have / ten / becoming / a police officer / of / since / was / dreamed / I

➡ _____
_____

 위 대화의 빈칸 (B)에 들어갈 말을 주어진 〈조건〉에 맞게 쓰시오.

┌─ 조건 ┐
• 삼촌이 Anne을 만나길 바라실 거라는 확실성 정도를 표현하는 말을 쓸 것.
• 대명사와 would like to를 사용할 것.
└───────┘

➡ _____

03 다음 대화의 빈칸에 들어갈 말로 자연스러운 것을 〈보기〉에서 찾아 문장을 쓰시오.

G: I'm glad to meet you, Mr. Han.
(A)_____

M: Okay. I guide travelers to different places in China and give them information about where they should visit.

G: (B)_____

M: I tell them about popular culture and traditional food in China.

G: (C)_____
Are you happy with your job?

M: Yes. I really love my job.

┌─ 보기 ┐
• What else do you do?
• It seems to me knowing a lot about China is very important.
• Could you please tell me what you do?
└───────┘

04 다음 대화의 빈칸에 주어진 〈조건〉에 맞게 영어로 쓰시오.

┌─ 조건 ┐
(A) 동사 'do'를 사용하여 직업을 묻는 말을 쓸 것.
(B) 'seem'을 사용하여 의견을 표현하는 말을 쓸 것.
└───────┘

B: Did you finish the report about your role model?

G: Yes, I did. I wrote about my role model, Ms. Shin. I want to be like her.

B: (A)_____

G: She teaches people how to stretch. She also helps them reduce stress and calm themselves.

B: Good. (B)_____ she helps to keep both their mind and body healthy.

G: Yes, and I think it's great.

Grammar

교과서

1 It is[was] ~ that 강조구문

> • **It** is a puppy **that** I want to get for my birthday gift.
> 내가 생일 선물로 받고 싶은 것은 바로 강아지이다.
> • **It** was at the concert **that** Jane met Sean for the first time.
> Jane이 처음으로 Sean을 만난 것은 바로 콘서트에서였다.

■ It+be동사+[명사]+that+불완전한 문장: 주어나 목적어인 명사를 강조한다.

  • **Steve** invented **the machine**.
  → It was **Steve** that invented the machine. 그 기계를 발명한 것은 바로 Steve였다.
  → It was **the machine** that Steve invented. Steve가 발명한 것은 바로 그 기계였다.

■ It+be동사+[부사(구/절)]+that+완전한 문장: 부사(구/절)를 강조한다.

  • I met her at the party.
  → It was **at the party** that I met her.
  내가 그녀를 만난 것은 바로 파티에서였다.

■ 'It is[was] ~ that' 강조구문에서 강조하는 대상이 명사일 경우, that을 관계대명사 who 또는 which 등으로 대체할 수 있다.

  • Dr. King took care of my ants.
  → **It was** Dr. King **that[who]** took care of my ants. 나의 개미들을 돌봤던 이는 바로 King 박사였다.
  → **It was** my ants **that[which]** Dr. King took care of. King 박사가 돌봤던 것은 바로 나의 개미들이었다.

핵심 Check

1. 괄호 안에서 알맞은 것을 고르시오.

  (1) It was Susan's car (who / which) Rooney bought last week.
  (2) It was at the theater (that / which) Mom met Daddy for the first time.

② have+목적어+목적보어

> The orchestra practices hard to **have** each song **played** the same way every time.
> 그 오케스트라는 각각의 곡이 항상 같은 방식으로 연주되도록 하기 위해 열심히 연습한다.
>
> Brian **had** his electric scooter **repaired** at the shop. Brian은 가게에서 그의 전기 스쿠터를 수리시켰다.

■ have/has/had+목적어+목적보어: have는 '~하게 시키다, ~하게 하다'는 의미의 사역동사로 목적어의 능동/수동 여부에 따라 목적보어 자리에 원형동사 또는 과거분사가 온다.

- The researchers **had** students **fill** the questionnaire.
  연구진들은 학생들이 그 질문지에 답하도록 시켰다. (능동: 동사원형)
- The researchers **had** the questionnaire **filled** by students.
  연구진들은 그 질문지가 학생들에 의해 답변되도록 시켰다. (수동: 과거분사)
- Please **have** Mr. Trump **come** in. Trump씨가 들어오게 해주세요. (능동)
- Get out of my place, or I'll **have** you **arrested**.
  내 집에서 나가시오. 그렇지 않으면 당신이 체포되도록 하겠소. (수동)

■ have/has/had+목적어+목적보어(과거분사): 좋지 않은 일의 경우, '~ 당하다'의 뜻으로 해석한다.

- He **had** his bag **stolen** by a thief. 그는 도둑에게 가방을 도난당했다.
- Karl **had** his hat **blown** off by the wind. 바람에 Karl의 모자가 날아갔다.
- Sally **had** her ankle **broken** in a car accident. Sally는 자동차 사고로 발목이 부러졌다.

■ 그 밖의 5형식 표현 동사들

- Her teacher **made** her **read** that book. 그녀의 선생님은 그녀에게 그 책을 읽게 했다.
  → She **was made to read** that book by her teacher.
- I could not **make** people **understand** me in Spanish. 나는 스페인어로 사람들에게 내 말을 이해시킬 수 없었다.
  → I could not **make** myself **understood** in Spanish (by people).
- Jane **heard** the chairman **call** her name. Jane은 의장이 그녀의 이름을 부르는 것을 들었다.
  → Jane **heard** her name **called** by the chairman.
  → The chairman **was heard to call** Jane's name. 의장이 Jane의 이름을 부르는 것이 들렸다.
- She **got** her son **to fix** the door. 그녀는 그녀의 아들이 문을 고치도록 시켰다.
  → She **got** the door **fixed** by her son.

핵심 Check

2. 다음 우리말에 맞게 괄호 안의 단어를 바르게 배열하시오.

(1) Peter는 여러 번 다리가 부러졌다. (legs, had, times, Peter, several, broken, his)

➡ _____

(2) 나는 이번 토요일에 머리를 깎을 것이다. (hair, will, have, this, cut, I, Saturday, my)

➡ _____

01 다음 문장에서 어법상 어색한 부분을 바르게 고쳐 쓰시오.

(1) The researchers had the girl watched the other student.

_____ ➡ _____

(2) I got my knee injure in a soccer game.

_____ ➡ _____

(3) It was last Friday which they lost their puppy.

_____ ➡ _____

(4) It is my uncle that encourage me to study.

_____ ➡ _____

02 다음 중 어법상 바르지 않은 것은?

① It was two years ago that Christine wrote that novel.
② It was in May that the baby saw the fireworks for the first time.
③ It was James who broke window yesterday.
④ It was the taxi that Frank proposed to Nancy.
⑤ It is when people praise her talent that the actress feels happy.

03 다음 빈칸에 들어갈 말로 알맞은 것은?

| Mom _____ me take out the garbage. |

① told   ② set   ③ asked
④ had   ⑤ got

04 다음 문장의 밑줄 친 부분을 강조하여 문장을 다시 쓰시오.

| Barbara has always wanted to buy <u>those books</u>. |

➡ _____

중요

01 다음 문장의 밑줄 친 단어들 중 'It is[was] ~ that' 구문으로 강조할 수 <u>없는</u> 단어는?

> Jonathan wrote the touching story yesterday
> ①   ②   ③   ④
> afternoon at the cafe.
>   ⑤

02 다음 중 밑줄 친 부분의 쓰임이 나머지와 <u>다른</u> 것은?

① It was the lamp <u>that</u> Shelly broke this morning.

② It is my youngest sister <u>that</u> I always take care of.

③ It is his idea <u>that</u> you should join his soccer club.

④ It was at the mall <u>that</u> Lisa bought the stationery.

⑤ It was Minsu <u>that</u> met the mayor at the park last week.

중요

03 다음 중 어법상 어색한 문장은?

① The woman had her house paint.

② Will you let her go like this?

③ Tom had his hair cut by a barber last Saturday.

④ She'll make my dream come true.

⑤ Aunt Mary always helped me to do my homework when I lived with her.

04 다음 중 어법상 <u>어색한</u> 문장은?

① Tylor's daddy had him drive his truck yesterday.

② My mother allowed me to buy the smartphone yesterday.

③ Sarah Conner had her car fix by the mechanic.

④ The crowd let the little girl play the piano on the street.

⑤ Walking a little fast helps you to relieve some stress from your daily lives.

서답형

05 다음 대화의 문맥에 맞게, 괄호 안에 주어진 단어를 강조하는 'It is[was] ~ that' 구문의 문장을 영작하시오. (7 단어)

> Mom: Did you tear the letter in two?
> Jinwoo: No, _____.
>   (Poppy)

서답형

06 다음 〈보기〉의 문장 중 어법상 <u>어색한</u> 것들을 <u>모두</u> 골라 기호를 쓰고, 고치시오.

> ┤ 보기 ├
> ⓐ Those pictures behind you make me think of my golden days.
> ⓑ The director of the film ordered the actress gain 10 kilograms.
> ⓒ Let his son to take your laptop to his school for just a few days.
> ⓓ Mariah helped the new singer performing on the debut stage.
> ⓔ The teacher of Korean literature had Abdullah memorize the poems written by Yun Dongju.
> ⓕ No one could get the addict stops using drugs.

➡ _____

_____

[07~08] 다음 중 'It ~ that'의 쓰임이 나머지 넷과 다른 것은?

07
① It is my twin sister that you see in this picture.
② It was 30 years ago that Mr. Miles came to govern the region.
③ It is certain that she fell in love with the stranger at first sight.
④ It was in the street that Laura bought the fruit which made them sick.
⑤ It was the skirt that Christine's aunt made on her birthday.

08 중요
① It is the trumpet that Michelle usually enjoys playing in her free time.
② It was no wonder that Frank got accepted to Harvard University.
③ It was in the warehouse that the secret meeting was held.
④ It was Comet Halley that we happened to see last night.
⑤ It was only a minute ago that the train carrying her family left for LA.

09 중요 다음 중 어법상 어색한 문장은?

① He would not have his mind change by his son's accident.
② The storm made all the items on the shelves fall onto the floor.
③ My grandfather had my daddy take care of the old pine trees in his garden.
④ The fire fighters let everyone inside the building leave at once.
⑤ The Highclass Academy makes its students practice English so hard.

10 다음 문장의 빈칸 (A)~(D)에 들어갈 말로 가장 적절한 것은?

• The guards at the front gate had the guest (A)_____ the mansion. (enter)
• The general ordered our soldiers (B)_____ back a few meters. (step)
• The webtoons Sarah watches every day make her (C)_____. (smile)
• All of my classmates are expecting Haon (D)_____ Highschool Rapper. (win)

	(A)	(B)	(C)	(D)
①	to enter	to step	smile	win
②	to enter	step	to smile	win
③	enter	step	smile	to win
④	enter	to step	to smile	win
⑤	enter	to step	smile	to win

11 중요 다음 중 어법상 옳은 문장은?

① The manager of the hotel had the cleaning crew to wash the floor.
② Dayna's teacher always tells her eat vegetables.
③ The principal let the students to use the computers to prepare for the game.
④ Father always allows me to take pictures with his high-end camera.
⑤ I asked the P.E. teacher help me with the basketball practice.

서답형
12 다음 우리말을 괄호 안의 조건에 맞게 영작하시오.

• Laura는 Tom에게 그녀의 남편이 세탁기를 수리하는 것을 돕도록 시켰다.
(to, had, husband, the washing machine, repair 사용, 총 11단어로 할 것.)

➡ _____

_____

서답형

13 다음 대화가 자연스럽도록 주어진 단어를 모두 활용하여 문장을 완성하시오. (단어들 중 1 단어만 변형할 것.)

> Father: Has anyone done something to my plants? I think someone must have watered them too much.
>
> Daughter: _____
>
> _____ .
>
> (James / responsible / care / for / it / plants / take / is / is / of / who)

중요

14 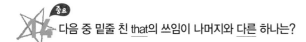 다음 중 밑줄 친 that의 쓰임이 나머지와 다른 하나는?

① It was in this cake that Michael hid the ring for his proposal.

② It was his bike that Julie's little brothers broke yesterday.

③ It was in 2015 that Leo won the Academy Award of Best Actor.

④ It was her pet kitty that woke Jessy up this morning.

⑤ It was her belief that ghosts were following her anywhere she went.

15 다음 중 밑줄 친 that을 다른 단어로 대체하여 바꿔 쓸 수 없는 문장은?

① It was the robot arm that carried out the difficult task.

② It is true that the team eventually reached the top of the mountain.

③ It was the suspect that met the police officer the other night.

④ It is he that solved the problem.

⑤ It was Mike that found this book in her room.

중요

16 다음 중 어법상 올바른 문장의 개수는?

ⓐ The famous actor living next door had the refrigerator fix by a repairman.

ⓑ Bill's sisters asked him clean their desks.

ⓒ A lot of crowd watched the boys dancing on the street to the sound of K-pop music.

ⓓ It was soft that Susan bought a scarf.

ⓔ The police officer helped an old lady to cross the street with no traffic signal.

ⓕ Lisa got her son pick up the delivery box.

ⓖ It was my dog that bit her leg.

ⓗ Sean must get this work do on time.

① 1개   ② 2개   ③ 3개   ④ 4개   ⑤ 5개

17 다음 우리말을 바르게 영작한 것을 모두 고르시오.

> • 그 가수는 콘서트에서 팬들에게 자신의 사진을 찍도록 했다.

① The singer ordered her fans to take pictures of themselves at the concert.

② The singer let her pictures be taken her fans at the concert.

③ The singer had her fans take pictures of her at the concert.

④ The singer had her fans to take pictures of her at the concert.

⑤ The singer had her pictures taken by her fans at the concert.

서답형

18 다음 문장에서 어법상 어색한 부분을 하나만 찾아서 고치시오.

> • The soccer player had his leg break and got a scar on his forehead during the match.

➡ _____

01 다음 문장을 밑줄 친 부분을 강조하여, 각각 It으로 시작하는 문장으로 바꾸어 쓰시오.

> • <u>John</u> is going to buy <u>the masks</u> <u>at a</u>
>   (A)   (B)
> <u>party</u> <u>this Friday</u>.
>   (C)   (D)

➡ (A) _____

   _____

   (B) _____

   _____

   (C) _____

   _____

   (D) _____

   _____

02 다음 그림을 보고, 우리말에 맞게 괄호 안의 단어를 배열하여 빈칸을 채우시오.

> • As my daddy _____
> pancakes, I was standing with a ladle.
> (help, make, to, him, have, me, 변형 가능)
> 아빠가 내게 아빠를 도와 팬케이크를 만들도록
> 시키셔서, 나는 국자를 들고 서 있었다.

03 다음 각 문장에서 어법상 어색한 부분을 모두 찾아 바르게 고치시오. 단, 강조 구문 자체가 어색할 경우, 전체를 다시 쓰시오.

(1) It is the Hongdae street that the band gives a street performance.

   ➡ _____

(2) It was carefully that he rescued the injured.

   ➡ _____

(3) It was chairman of the council who Bush was.

   ➡ _____

(4) It was the playground that the boy was injured severely.

   ➡ _____

(5) It is her mistake who she doesn't recognize.

   ➡ _____

04 〈보기〉의 단어들 중 가장 적절한 것을 골라 다음 문장의 빈칸에 써 넣으시오. (어형 변화 가능하며, 각 단어는 1회만 사용할 것)

> ┤ 보기 ├
>
> look / cry / come / clean / go

(1) Mom had Karl _____ his room.

(2) They felt some smoke _____ out of the conference hall.

(3) Shelly heard a baby _____ out loud.

(4) Her boss let Joen _____ scuba diving.

(5) That diet will allow you _____ slim.

05 다음 주어진 문장과 뜻이 같도록 빈칸을 알맞게 채우되, it을 반드시 사용하시오.

> • March 14, 1879 is the day Einstein was born on.

➡ It was _____ born.

06 다음 각 문장에서 어법상 어색한 단어를 한 개씩 찾아 올바르게 고치시오.

(1) The customs officers at the airport had the baggage check while a passenger was passing through.

➡ _____

(2) The host of the show got the singer sing that song again.

➡ _____

(3) Her father allowed Gabrielle meet the young boy to find out who he was.

➡ _____

(4) Will you let the boys playing here?

➡ _____

(5) Susan was broke her legs during the practice of the ballet movement.

➡ _____

(6) Those make-ups made you looks more healthy and alive.

➡ _____

07 다음 〈보기〉와 같이 두 문장이 같은 의미가 되도록 주어진 단어를 활용하여 제시된 글자 수에 맞게 쓰시오. (어형 변화 가능)

> ┤ 보기 ├
> Please tell the kids not to make noise here. (make, quiet / 5 단어)
> → Make them be quiet here.

(1) The teacher said to Susan, "Clear all the mess on your desk." (have, clean, Susan / 7 단어)

➡ _____

(2) His father looked a lot younger when he put the tie on. (make, much / 8 단어)

➡ _____

(3) Please don't stop the girl from watching the film. (allow, enjoy / 6 단어)

➡ _____

08 다음 문장을 읽고, 각 질문에 'It is[was] ~ that' 강조 구문을 사용하여 답하시오. 답할 수 없는 질문은 '답변 불가'라고 쓰시오.

> • Alicia had John's phone repaired at the repair shop two weeks ago.

(1) Who repaired John's phone?

➡ _____

(2) Who got John's phone repaired?

➡ _____

(3) When did Alicia have John's phone repaired?

➡ _____
_____

(4) How many weeks did it take to repair John's phone?

➡ _____

(5) Where was John's phone repaired two weeks ago?

➡ _____
_____

Reading

The World of Wonderful Jobs

Florist

Hi, I am Tom. A florist is someone who creates beautiful things with
주격 관계대명사

flowers. To become a florist, you need to know many things about
to부정사의 부사적 용법 중 목적(~하기 위해서)

flowers. I attended a high school for florists and gardeners. It was at
attended at(×)

this school that I learned how to grow and care for different types of
It was ~ that 강조 구문(at this school 강조)   ~하는 방법   =look after

flowers. These days, florists can do a lot of different things. I design
=many

movie sets sometimes and I decorate shops with flowers. I am happy

when I create something colorful with fresh flowers and greenery. If
부정대명사는 형용사의 수식을 뒤에서 받음

you like plants and the arts, I highly recommend you become a florist.
recommend (that) you (should) become a florist

Sport Data Analyst

I am Emma. I am a sport data analyst. It sounds like a difficult job,
~처럼 들리다(sound like+명사)

doesn't it? In fact, it is a lot of fun. I work for a baseball team.
부가의문문   =great

My job is to watch recorded games and run a computer program to
보어   to watch와 병렬 (to) run

collect data. Then, I analyze the data to show my team's strengths and
to부정사의 부사적 용법 중 목적(~하기 위해서)

weaknesses. If the team understands their strengths and weaknesses,

they can do better next time. Since I was young, I have been a big fan
다음번에는   ~이었을 때부터   현재완료: 계속

of baseball. Now, in my work, I watch baseball games all the time.
항상

This is a perfect job for me because watching baseball games is my
이유를 이끄는 접속사(~이기 때문에)   동명사 주어 단수 취급

hobby!

wonderful: 놀라운, 경이로운
attend: 참석하다, (~에) 다니다
care for: ~을 보살피다
these days: 요즈음
movie set: 영화 촬영장
decorate: 장식하다, 꾸미다
greenery: 화초
recorded: 녹화된
in fact: 사실
analyze: 분석하다
strength: 강점
weakness: 약점

📎 **확인문제**

● 다음 문장이 본문의 내용과 일치하면 T, 일치하지 않으면 F를 쓰시오.

1 Florists create something beautiful with flowers. ☐

2 Tom's high school taught him how to grow flowers. ☐

3 There's nothing florists can do except growing and caring for different types of

   flowers. ☐

4 Emma is fond of watching basketball. ☐

Director of a Musical Theater

Hi, I am Chris. As a director of a musical theater, I do a lot of things. I
　　　　자격을 나타내는 전치사 (~로서)　　　　　　　　　　=many
audition the actors and I look for good, strong voices. After selecting
　　　　　　　　　　　　　　　　　　전치사 after의 목적어로 쓰인 동명사
the cast, I teach them the songs for each scene.
　　　　　4형식 동사(+사람+사물)
Then, I put the cast and orchestra together for practice. During
　　　　　put A and B together: A와 B를 함께 모으다
the performance, I am in the orchestra area and conduct. It's my
　　　　　　　　　　　　　　　　　　　　　　　　가주어 it ~ 진주어 to V
responsibility to have each song played the same way every time. I
　　　　　사역동사+목적어+과거분사(목적어와 목적격보어의 관계가 수동일 때)　　매번
direct the musicians and the singers to keep the show together.
　　　　　　　　　　　　to부정사의 부사적 용법 중 목적(~하기 위해서)
Conducting and directing is not just about waving my arms around!
　　　　　　　　　　　　　　　　　동명사(전치사의 목적어)

Ocean Scientist

My name is Yeji. I am an ocean scientist. Ocean science is a big field.

It includes studies of the oceans and the creatures living in them.
　　　　　　　　　　　　　　the creatures를 수식하는 현재분사　　=the oceans
Among other things, I have studied many kinds of fish living in the

seas near Korea. It is the growth ring in a fish that interests me. By
　　　　　　　　　　It is ~ that 강조 구문(the growth ring in a fish 강조)
looking at it, I can find out when and where the fish was born. All the
by Ving: V함으로써　　　　　　　　간접의문문(find out의 목적어)
information I get from fish is used to understand sea resources and
　　　　　앞에 관계대명사 that 생략　　be used to V: V하는 데 사용되다
manage the oceans better. My job is important because it makes the
to understand와 병렬
best use of nature possible.

---

audition: 오디션을 보다
select: 선택하다, 선발하다
cast: (영화나 연극의) 출연자들
scene: 장면
orchestra: 오케스트라
performance: 공연, 연주
conduct: 지휘하다
ocean science: 해양 과학
field: 분야
interest: 흥미를 끌다
make the best use of: ~을 최대한 활용하다

 **확인문제**

● 다음 문장이 본문의 내용과 일치하면 T, 일치하지 않으면 F를 쓰시오.

1　Chris directs a musical performance as a job. ☐

2　Chris became a director of a musical theater by audition. ☐

3　Chris do nothing during the performance. ☐

4　Yeji studies not only fish but also oceans. ☐

5　Yeji is interested in the growth ring in a fish. ☐

● 우리말을 참고하여 빈칸에 알맞은 말을 쓰시오.

The World of Wonderful Jobs

Florist

1 Hi, I am Tom. A florist is someone _____ _____ beautiful things _____ flowers.

2 _____ _____ a florist, you _____ _____ _____ many things about flowers.

3 I _____ a high school _____ florists and gardeners.

4 It was _____ _____ _____ that I learned _____ _____ _____ and care _____ different types of flowers.

5 These days, florists can do _____ things.

6 I design _____ _____ sometimes and I _____ shops with flowers.

7 I am happy when I create _____ _____ with fresh flowers and _____.

8 If you like plants and the arts, I _____ _____ you become a florist.

Sport Data Analyst

9 I am Emma. I am a _____ _____ _____.

10 It sounds like a difficult job, _____ _____?

11 In fact, it is _____ _____ _____ _____. I work for a baseball team.

12 My job is _____ _____ _____ _____ _____ and _____ a computer program _____ _____ data.

13 Then, I _____ the data _____ _____ my team's strengths and weaknesses.

14 If the team _____ their strengths and weaknesses, they can _____ _____ next time.

15 _____ I was young, I _____ _____ a big fan of baseball.

플로리스트

1 안녕하세요. 저는 Tom입니다. 플로리스트란 꽃으로 아름다운 것들을 창조하는 사람입니다.

2 플로리스트가 되기 위해서 여러분은 꽃에 관해 많은 것을 알 필요가 있습니다.

3 나는 플로리스트와 정원사를 양성하는 고등학교에 다녔습니다.

4 제가 다양한 종류의 꽃을 기르고 다루는 방법을 배운 곳이 바로 이 학교에서였습니다.

5 오늘날, 플로리스트는 많은 다양한 일을 할 수 있습니다.

6 나는 때때로 영화 세트장을 디자인하고 꽃으로 상점을 꾸밉니다.

7 나는 싱싱한 꽃과 화초로 다채로운 무언가를 창조해 낼 때 행복합니다.

8 만약 당신이 식물과 예술을 좋아한다면, 나는 당신에게 플로리스트가 될 것을 강력히 추천합니다.

스포츠 데이터 분석가

9 나는 Emma입니다. 나는 스포츠 데이터 분석가입니다.

10 어려운 직업처럼 들리죠, 그렇지 않나요?

11 사실, 그것은 매우 재미있습니다. 나는 야구팀을 위해서 일합니다.

12 나의 일은 녹화된 경기를 보고 자료를 수집하기 위해 컴퓨터 프로그램을 실행하는 것입니다.

13 그리고 나서, 나는 내 팀의 강점과 약점을 보여 주기 위해서 그 자료들을 분석합니다.

14 만약 팀이 자신들의 강점과 약점을 이해하면, 그들은 다음번에 더 잘할 수 있습니다.

15 어렸을 때부터, 나는 야구의 열혈 팬이었습니다.

16 Now, in my work, I watch _____ _____ _____ _____ _____.

17 This is a perfect job for me _____ _____ _____ _____ is my hobby!

Director of a Musical Theater

18 Hi, I am Chris. _____ a director of _____ _____ _____, I do a lot of things.

19 I _____ the actors and I _____ _____ good, strong voices.

20 After _____ _____ _____, I teach them the songs _____ _____ _____.

21 Then, I _____ the cast and orchestra _____ for practice.

22 _____ the performance, I am in the orchestra area and _____.

23 It's _____ _____ to have _____ song played the same way every time.

24 I _____ the musicians and the singers _____ _____ the show _____.

25 _____ and _____ is not just about _____ my arms around!

Ocean Scientist

26 My name is Yeji. I am an ocean scientist. Ocean science is _____ _____ _____.

27 It _____ studies of the oceans and the creatures _____ _____ _____.

28 Among other things, I _____ _____ many kinds of fish _____ in the seas near Korea.

29 It is _____ _____ _____ in a fish _____ interests me.

30 _____ _____ at it, I can find out when and where the fish was born.

31 All the information _____ _____ _____ fish _____ _____ _____ _____ sea resources and _____ the oceans better.

32 My job is important _____ it makes _____ _____ of nature possible.

16 지금, 나는 일하는 중에 내내 야구를 봅니다.

17 야구 경기를 보는 것은 나의 취미이기 때문에 이것은 나에게 완벽한 직업입니다!

뮤지컬 극장 감독

18 안녕하세요. 나는 Chris입니다. 뮤지컬 극장 감독으로서 나는 많은 것들을 합니다.

19 나는 배우들을 대상으로 오디션을 실시하고, 훌륭하고 강한 목소리를 찾아냅니다.

20 배역에 맞는 배우를 고른 뒤에, 나는 그들에게 각 장면을 위한 노래를 가르칩니다.

21 그러고 나서, 나는 배우와 오케스트라를 함께 연습시킵니다.

22 공연 동안에, 나는 오케스트라석에 있고 지휘를 합니다.

23 각각의 노래가 매번 동일하게 연주되도록 만드는 것은 나의 책임입니다.

24 나는 공연을 제대로 진행하기 위해 연주자들과 가수들을 감독합니다.

25 지휘하고 감독하는 것은 단지 내 팔을 흔드는 것만이 아닙니다!

해양 과학자

26 나는 예지입니다. 나는 해양 과학자입니다. 해양 과학은 거대한 분야입니다.

27 그것은 바다와 그 안에 살고 있는 생물에 관한 연구를 포함합니다.

28 여러 가지 중에서 나는 한국 주변의 바다에 살고 있는 많은 종류의 물고기를 연구해 왔습니다.

29 나의 흥미를 끄는 것은 바로 물고기 안에 있는 나이테입니다.

30 나이테를 살펴봄으로써, 나는 언제 어디서 그 물고기가 태어났는지 알아낼 수 있습니다.

31 내가 물고기에서 얻은 모든 정보는 바다의 자원을 이해하고 바다를 더 잘 관리하기 위해 사용됩니다.

32 내 직업은 자연을 가장 잘 활용할 수 있게 한다는 점에서 중요합니다.

● 우리말을 참고하여 본문을 영작하시오.

The World of Wonderful Jobs

Florist

1 안녕하세요. 저는 Tom입니다. 플로리스트란 꽃으로 아름다운 것들을 창조하는 사람입니다.

➡ _____

2 플로리스트가 되기 위해서 여러분은 꽃에 관해 많은 것을 알 필요가 있습니다.

➡ _____

3 나는 플로리스트와 정원사를 양성하는 고등학교에 다녔습니다.

➡ _____

4 제가 다양한 종류의 꽃을 기르고 다루는 방법을 배운 곳이 바로 이 학교에서였습니다.

➡ _____

5 오늘날, 플로리스트는 많은 다양한 일을 할 수 있습니다.

➡ _____

6 나는 때때로 영화 세트장을 디자인하고 꽃으로 상점을 꾸밉니다.

➡ _____

7 나는 싱싱한 꽃과 화초로 다채로운 무언가를 창조해 낼 때 행복합니다.

➡ _____

8 만약 당신이 식물과 예술을 좋아한다면, 나는 당신에게 플로리스트가 될 것을 강력히 추천합니다.

➡ _____

Sport Data Analyst

9 나는 Emma입니다. 나는 스포츠 데이터 분석가입니다.

➡ _____

10 어려운 직업처럼 들리죠, 그렇지 않나요?

➡ _____

11 사실, 그것은 매우 재미있습니다. 나는 야구팀을 위해서 일합니다.

➡ _____

12 나의 일은 녹화된 경기를 보고 자료를 수집하기 위해 컴퓨터 프로그램을 실행하는 것입니다.

➡ _____

13 그리고 나서, 나는 내 팀의 강점과 약점을 보여 주기 위해서 그 자료들을 분석합니다.

➡ _____

14 만약 팀이 자신들의 강점과 약점을 이해하면, 그들은 다음번에 더 잘할 수 있습니다.

➡ _____

15 어렸을 때부터, 나는 야구의 열혈 팬이었습니다.

➡ _____

16 지금, 나는 일하는 중에 내내 야구를 봅니다.

➡ _____

17 야구 경기를 보는 것은 나의 취미이기 때문에 이것은 나에게 완벽한 직업입니다!

➡ _____

Director of a Musical Theater

18 안녕하세요. 나는 Chris입니다. 뮤지컬 극장 감독으로서 나는 많은 것들을 합니다.

➡ _____

19 나는 배우들을 대상으로 오디션을 실시하고, 훌륭하고 강한 목소리를 찾아냅니다.

➡ _____

20 배역에 맞는 배우를 고른 뒤에, 나는 그들에게 각 장면을 위한 노래를 가르칩니다.

➡ _____

21 그러고 나서, 나는 배우와 오케스트라를 함께 연습시킵니다.

➡ _____

22 공연 동안에, 나는 오케스트라 석에 있고 지휘를 합니다.

➡ _____

23 각각의 노래가 매번 동일하게 연주되도록 만드는 것은 나의 책임입니다.

➡ _____

24 나는 공연을 제대로 진행하기 위해 연주자들과 가수들을 감독합니다.

➡ _____

25 지휘하고 감독하는 것은 단지 내 팔을 흔드는 것만이 아닙니다!

➡ _____

Ocean Scientist

26 나는 예지입니다. 나는 해양 과학자입니다. 해양 과학은 거대한 분야입니다.

➡ _____

27 그것은 바다와 그 안에 살고 있는 생물에 관한 연구를 포함합니다.

➡ _____

28 여러 가지 중에서 나는 한국 주변의 바다에 살고 있는 많은 종류의 물고기를 연구해 왔습니다.

➡ _____

29 나의 흥미를 끄는 것은 바로 물고기 안에 있는 나이테입니다.

➡ _____

30 나이테를 살펴봄으로써, 나는 언제 어디서 그 물고기가 태어났는지 알아낼 수 있습니다.

➡ _____

31 내가 물고기에서 얻은 모든 정보는 바다의 자원을 이해하고 바다를 더 잘 관리하기 위해 사용됩니다.

➡ _____

32 내 직업은 자연을 가장 잘 활용할 수 있게 한다는 점에서 중요합니다.

➡ _____

[01~03] 다음 글을 읽고 물음에 답하시오.

Hi, I am Tom. A florist is someone who creates beautiful things with flowers. To become a florist, you need to know many things about flowers. I attended a high school for florists and gardeners. It was at this school that I learned how to grow and care for different types of flowers. (A)These days, florists can do a lot of different things. I design movie sets sometimes and I decorate shops with flowers. I am happy when I create something colorful with fresh flowers and greenery. If you like plants and the arts, I highly recommend you become a florist.

01 다음 중 밑줄 친 (A)를 대신하여 쓸 수 있는 것은?

① From time to time ② Nowadays
③ Once in a while ④ Hardly
⑤ Now and then

02 다음 중 위 글의 내용과 일치하는 것은?

① Tom didn't have to know many things about flowers to become a florist.
② Florists care for only flowers.
③ Tom is not satisfied with his job.
④ Tom doesn't recommend his job.
⑤ There is a school for students who want to be florists and gardeners.

03 서답형
According to the passage, who is a florist? Answer in English with a full sentence.

➡ _____

_____

[04~06] 다음 글을 읽고 물음에 답하시오.

I am Emma. I am a sport data analyst. It sounds like a difficult job, doesn't it? In fact, it is a lot of fun. I work for a baseball team. My job is to watch recorded games and run a computer program to collect data. Then, I analyze the data to show my team's strengths and weaknesses. If the team understands their strengths and weaknesses, they can do better next time. Since I was young, I have been a big fan of baseball. Now, in my work, I watch baseball games all the time. This is a perfect job for me (A)_____ watching baseball games is my hobby!

04 다음 중 빈칸 (A)에 들어갈 말로 가장 적절한 것은?

① although ② if ③ because
④ when ⑤ until

05 다음 중 위 글을 읽고 답할 수 있는 것은?

① When did Emma get the job?
② How many games does Emma watch a week?
③ What does Emma do after collecting data?
④ How old is Emma?
⑤ Is Emma good at baseball?

06 서답형
According to the passage, how can the team do better next time? Answer in English with a full sentence.

➡ _____

_____

[07~10] 다음 글을 읽고 물음에 답하시오.

Hi, I am Chris. As a director of a musical theater, I do a lot of things. I audition the actors and I look for good, strong voices. After selecting the cast, I teach them the songs for each scene. Then, I put the cast and orchestra together for practice. During the performance, I am in the orchestra area and conduct. It's my responsibility to have each song (A)_____ the same way every time. I direct the musicians and the singers to keep the show together. Conducting and directing is not just about waving my arms around!

서답형

07 단어 play를 어법에 맞게 빈칸 (A)에 쓰시오.

➡ _____

중요

08 다음 중 뮤지컬 공연 감독이 하는 일이 아닌 것은?

① looking for good, strong voices
② teaching the cast the songs for each scene
③ conducting after the performance
④ directing the musicians and the singers
⑤ choosing actors for a musical performance

서답형

09 What does Chris do after he selects the cast? Answer in English.

➡ _____

_____

서답형

10 다음 빈칸에 들어갈 말을 위 글에서 찾아 쓰시오.

The _____ of a play or film is all the people who act in it.

[11~14] 다음 글을 읽고 물음에 답하시오.

My name is Yeji. I am an ocean scientist. Ocean science is a big field. ①It includes studies of the oceans and the creatures ②living in them. Among other things, I ③have studied many kinds of fish living in the seas near Korea. It is the growth ring in a fish ④that interests me. (A)_____ looking at it, I can find out when and where the fish was born. All the information I get from fish is used to understand sea resources and ⑤manages the oceans better. My job is important because it makes the best use of nature possible.

11 밑줄 친 ①~⑤ 중 어법상 바르지 않은 것은?

①   ②   ③   ④   ⑤

12 다음 중 빈칸 (A)에 들어갈 말과 같은 말이 들어가는 것은? (대·소문자 무시)

① Can you pay attention _____ my speech?
② She is looking forward _____ seeing him.
③ It depends _____ you and your son.
④ Things will get better as time goes _____.
⑤ This medicine will take _____ your pain.

서답형

13 위 글의 내용에 맞게 빈칸에 알맞은 말을 쓰시오.

Ocean scientists study not only _____ _____ but also _____.

서답형

14 What can the growth ring in a fish tell Yeji? Answer in English with a full sentence.

➡ _____

[15~17] 다음 글을 읽고 물음에 답하시오.

Hi, I am Tom. A florist is someone (A)_____ creates beautiful things with flowers. To become a florist, you need to know many things about flowers. I attended a high school for florists and gardeners. It was at this school that I learned how to grow and care for different types of flowers. These days, florists can do a lot of different things. I design movie sets sometimes and I decorate shops with flowers. I am happy when I create something colorful with fresh flowers and greenery. If you like plants and the arts, I highly recommend you become a florist.

15 다음 중 빈칸 (A)에 들어갈 말로 적절한 것을 <u>모두</u> 고르시오.

① which   ② who   ③ that
④ what   ⑤ whose

16 다음 중 위 글의 내용과 일치하지 <u>않는</u> 것은?

① Tom is a florist.
② It is necessary to know many things about flowers to become a florist.
③ Florists always do the same things.
④ Tom creates something with flowers and greenery.
⑤ Tom feels happy when he does his job.

서답형
17 Where did Tom learn how to grow and care for different types of flowers? Answer in English with a full sentence.

➡ _____

_____

[18~21] 다음 글을 읽고 물음에 답하시오.

I am Emma. I am a sport data analyst. It sounds like a difficult job, ⓐ_____?

[A] Then, I analyze the data to show my team's strengths and weaknesses. If the team understands their strengths and weaknesses, they can do better next time. Since I was young, I have been a big fan of baseball.

[B] In fact, it is a lot of fun. I work for a baseball team. My job is to watch recorded games and run a computer program to collect data.

[C] Now, in my work, I watch baseball games all the time. This is a perfect job for me because watching baseball games is my hobby!

서답형
18 빈칸 ⓐ에 알맞은 말을 쓰시오.

➡ _____

19 위 글의 흐름상 [A]~[C]를 바르게 배열한 것은?

① [A]–[C]–[B]   ② [B]–[A]–[C]
③ [B]–[C]–[A]   ④ [C]–[A]–[B]
⑤ [C]–[B]–[A]

20 According to Emma, what does she feel about her job?

① bored   ② tired   ③ annoyed
④ satisfied   ⑤ uninterested

서답형
21 Write the reason why Emma runs a computer program. Use the phrase 'in order to.'

➡ _____

[22~24] 다음 글을 읽고 물음에 답하시오.

Hi, I am Chris. As a director of a musical theater, I do a lot of things. I audition the actors and I look for good, strong voices. After selecting the cast, I teach them the songs for each scene. Then, I put the cast and orchestra together for practice. During the performance, I am in the orchestra area and conduct. It's my responsibility to have each song played the same way every time. I direct the musicians and the singers to keep the show together. Conducting and directing is not just about waving my arms around!

서답형

22 다음 빈칸에 들어갈 말을 위 글에서 찾아 어법에 맞게 쓰시오.

If someone _____ an orchestra or choir, they stand in front of it and direct its performance.

중요

23 다음 중 위 글의 내용과 일치하는 것은?

① Chris acts on the stage of a musical theater.
② Chris has a good and strong voice for the musical.
③ The cast is selected and taught some songs by Chris.
④ Chris writes many songs for the musical and has them played.
⑤ The orchestra doesn't need a conductor.

서답형

24 According to the passage, what is Chris's responsibility? Answer in English with a full sentence.

➡ _____

_____

[25~27] 다음 글을 읽고 물음에 답하시오.

My name is Yeji. I am an ocean scientist. Ocean science is a big field. (①) It includes studies of the oceans and the creatures living in them. (②) Among other things, I have studied many kinds of fish living in the seas near Korea. (③) It is the growth ring in a fish that interests me. (④) All the information I get from fish is used to understand sea resources and manage the oceans better. (⑤) My job is important because it makes the best use of nature possible.

중요

25 ①~⑤ 중 주어진 문장이 들어가기에 가장 적절한 곳은?

By looking at it, I can find out when and where the fish was born.

①   ②   ③   ④   ⑤

26 다음 중 위 글을 읽고 답할 수 있는 것은?

① What did Yeji want to be when she was young?
② How long has Yeji studied ocean science?
③ Why does Yeji study many kinds of fish living in the seas near Korea?
④ Why is Yeji's job important?
⑤ What college did Yeji graduate from?

27 다음 빈칸에 들어갈 말을 위 글에서 찾을 수 없는 것은?

① The price tag ____ tax.
② Damage to the environment affects all wild ____.
③ The country has a lot of energy ____.
④ You pay too much ____ to the news.
⑤ I want to ____ my life better.

[01~04] 다음 글을 읽고 물음에 답하시오.

Hi, I am Tom. A florist is someone who (A) create beautiful things with flowers. To become a florist, you need to know many things about flowers. I attended a high school for florists and gardeners. It was at this school that I learned how to grow and care for different types of flowers. These days, florists can do a lot of different things. I design movie sets sometimes and I decorate shops with flowers. I am happy when I create something colorful with fresh flowers and greenery. If you like plants and the arts, I highly recommend you become a florist.

01 밑줄 친 (A)를 어법에 맞게 고쳐 쓰시오.

➡ _____

02 What kind of high school did Tom attend? Answer in English.

➡ _____

03 What do we need to know in order to become a florist? Answer in English with a full sentence.

➡ _____

04 According to the passage, when does Tom feel happy? Answer in English.

➡ _____

[05~08] 다음 글을 읽고 물음에 답하시오.

I am Emma. I am a sport data analyst. It sounds like a difficult job, doesn't it? In fact, it is a lot of fun. I work for a baseball team. My job is to watch recorded games and run a computer program to collect data. Then, I analyze the data to show my team's strengths and weaknesses. If the team understands their (A)_____, they can do better next time. Since I was young, I have been a big fan of baseball. Now, in my work, I watch baseball games all the time. This is a perfect job for me because watching baseball games is my hobby!

05 빈칸 (A)에 들어갈 말을 위 글에서 찾아 세 단어로 쓰시오.

➡ _____

06 What does Emma do as a sport data analyst? Answer in English.

➡ _____
_____
_____

07 According to Emma, what is her hobby? Answer in English.

➡ _____

08 다음과 같이 풀이되는 말을 위 글에서 찾아 쓰시오.

a person whose job is to analyse a subject and give opinions about it

➡ _____

[09~12] 다음 글을 읽고 물음에 답하시오.

Hi, I am Chris. As a director of a musical theater, I do a lot of things. I audition the actors and I look for good, strong voices. After selecting the cast, I teach them the songs for each scene. Then, I put the cast and orchestra together for practice. During the performance, I am in the orchestra area and conduct. It's my responsibility to have each song played the same way every time. I direct the musicians and the singers to keep the show together. (A) Conducting and directing is not just about waving my arms around!

09 다음은 밑줄 친 (A)와 같은 의미이다. 빈칸에 알맞은 말을 쓰시오.

According to Chris, conducting and directing means much more than just _____ _____ _____ _____.

10 Where is Chris during the performance?

➡ _____

11 What does Chris do to keep the show together? Answer in English with seven words.

➡ _____

12 It is ~ that 강조 구문을 활용하여 다음 대화에 알맞은 답을 쓰시오.

A: Chris, who do you audition?
B: _____

[13~16] 다음 글을 읽고 물음에 답하시오.

My name is Yeji. I am an ocean scientist. Ocean science is a big field. It includes studies of the oceans and the creatures living in them. Among other things, I have studied many kinds of fish living in the seas near Korea. It is the growth ring in a fish that interests me. By looking at it, I can find out when and where the fish was born. All the information I get from fish is used to understand sea resources and manage the oceans better. My job is important because it makes the best use of nature possible.

13 According to the passage, what interests Yeji? Answer in English with a full sentence.

➡ _____

14 Write the reason why Yeji says her job is important. Use the phrase 'It's because.'

➡ _____
_____

15 What has Yeji studied as an ocean scientist? Answer in English with a full sentence.

➡ _____
_____

16 According to the passage, what should we look at if we want to know when and where a fish was born?

➡ _____

Enjoy Writing C

My Dream Job

I like food from around the world and I am good at cooking.
전치사의 목적어

I can also make food look tasty and beautiful. For these reasons, it is a chef
사역동사+목적어+동사원형   look+형용사: ~하게 보이다   it is ~ that ... 강조구문: ~한 것은 바로 …다

that I want to be when I grow up. To achieve my dream, I will read magazines
~할 때   부사적 용법(목적)(= In order to[So as to] achieve)

about cooking. Also, I will go to France to learn various cooking skills. My

role model is my dad. He always thinks of new recipes and then cooks these

new dishes for us. I want to have my name remembered by people who enjoy
to us(×)   사역동사+목적어+과거분사(목적어의 수동 의미): 내 이름이 기억되도록 하다

my food.
주격 관계대명사절로 선행사 people을 수식

구문해설 • be good at: ~을 잘하다 • tasty: 맛있는 • reason: 이유 • chef: 요리사 • achieve: 이루다
• various: 다양한 • recipe: 요리법

Project

HELP WANTED!!
사람 구함

Do you like robots?

If your answer is yes, it is you that we are looking for.
'It is~ that' 강조 구문: you 강조

Please join us to train and fix robots.
to부정사의 부사적 용법(목적 또는 결과를 나타냄)

For more information, visit our website at www.robots.com.

구문해설 • wanted: ~을 구하는 • look for: ~을 찾다

Project Step 3

Are you good at training and fixing robots? If so, we're sure that you'll be a
동명사로 전치사 at의 목적어

good robot specialist. For more information, visit our websites.
셀 수 없는 명사

구문해설 • train: 훈련시키다 • fix: 고치다 • be sure that ~: ~을 확신하다 • specialist: 전문가

01 다음 주어진 두 단어의 관계가 같도록 빈칸에 알맞은 단어를 쓰시오.

> highly : greatly = choose : _____

02 다음 글의 빈칸 (A)와 (B)에 들어갈 단어로 바르게 짝지어진 것은?

> I like food from around the world and I am good at cooking. I can also make food look tasty and beautiful. For these (A)_____, it is a chef that I want to be when I grow up. To (B)_____ my dream, I will read magazines about cooking. Also, I will go to France to learn various cooking skills.

① efforts – report ② efforts – achieve
③ reasons – conduct ④ reasons – fix
⑤ reasons – achieve

[03~04] 다음 영영 풀이에 해당하는 것을 고르시오.

03

> your job or duty to deal with something or someone

① resource ② greenery
③ responsibility ④ historian
⑤ reporter

04

> to contain something as a part of something else, or to make something part of something else

① include ② advise
③ lead ④ collect
⑤ create

05 빈칸에 들어갈 말을 영어 설명을 읽고 주어진 철자로 시작하여 쓰시오. (복수형을 쓸 것)

> Ocean science includes studies of the oceans and the c_____ living in them. Among other things, I have studied many kinds of fish living in the seas near Korea.
> <영어설명> any large or small living thing that can move independently

06 다음 밑줄 친 부분의 뜻이 <u>잘못된</u> 것은?

① It is <u>the growth ring</u> in a fish that interests me. (나이테)
② Giving up smoking <u>reduces</u> the risk of heart disease. (줄이다)
③ I <u>direct</u> the musicians and the singers to keep the show together. (감독하다)
④ <u>Since</u> I was young, I have been a big fan of baseball. (~이기 때문에)
⑤ This is a <u>perfect</u> job for me because watching baseball games is my hobby! (완벽한)

07 다음 대화의 빈칸에 들어갈 말로 적절한 것은?

> A: I want to be a radio program writer. What would help me become one?
> B: It _____ to me that writing your own stories would be helpful.

① leads ② seems ③ is
④ hopes ⑤ happens

[08~10] 다음 대화를 읽고 물음에 답하시오.

Bora: What are you most interested in among the things on this list?

Jessie: I'm most interested in working outside and playing sports.

Bora: Well, (A)내 생각에 너는 현실적인 타입에 속하는 것 같아.

Jessie: What do you mean?

Bora: Most people belong to one of six personality types. Realistic is one of the types.

Jessie: Oh, that's interesting. What kind of jobs do they recommend for realistic types?

Bora: A farmer, a police officer, a soccer player, and so on.

Jessie: Oh, I have always wanted to be a soccer player.

Bora: That's good. I'm quite sure you could become a great soccer player.

08 밑줄 친 (A)의 우리말에 맞게 주어진 단어를 이용하여 영어로 쓰시오. (어형 변화 필수)

(seem / me / belong / the realistic type)

➡ _____

09 위 대화를 읽고 다음 물음에 영어로 답하시오.

Q: What is Jessie most interested in among the things on the list?

➡ _____

_____

10 위 대화의 내용과 일치하지 않는 것은?

① They are talking about personality types.

② Jessie belongs to the realistic type.

③ Bora recommends a soccer player for Jessie.

④ A farmer belongs to the realistic type.

⑤ Jessie wants to be a soccer player.

11 다음 대화의 빈칸에 들어갈 말을 주어진 단어를 알맞은 순서로 배열하여 완성하시오.

B: Do you cook often?

G: Yes, I try to cook every weekend. I want to be a chef someday.

B: What are you doing to make your dream come true?

G: I'm taking a cooking class. I try to think of new and creative dishes.

B: I'm _____.

(chef / good / quite / you / could / sure / be / a)

Grammar

[12~14] 다음 우리말에 맞게 영작한 것을 고르시오.

12

Tom의 아버지는 Tom에게 세차를 시켰다.

① Tom's father had him wash the car.

② Tom's father told him wash the car.

③ Tom's father had the car wash by him.

④ Tom's father let him washing the car.

⑤ Tom's father said him to wash the car.

13

내게 기운을 북돋아 주는 것은 내 아내이다.

① My wife who cheer me up counts.

② It is my wife that cheer me up.

③ My wife encourages me cheer up.

④ It cheers me up that my wife is.

⑤ It is my wife that cheers me up.

14

> Marco는 펜스에 충돌하고 나서 다리가 부러졌다.

① Marco had his leg breaking the fence after hitting.

② Marco had him break his leg after hitting the fence.

③ Marco had got his leg breaking after being hit the fence.

④ Marco had his leg broken after hitting the fence.

⑤ Marco broke his leg after the fence hitting him.

15 다음 중 아래 그림의 내용을 설명하되, 어법상 성격이 <u>다른</u> 한 문장을 고르시오.

① It was a clown that was juggling with red balls.

② It was we that saw a clown juggling.

③ It was on the platform that a clown was performing.

④ It was exciting that my daddy and I were in the amusement park.

⑤ It was my daddy that was holding me up to watch the clown.

16 다음 중 어법상 올바른 문장은?

① David had the repairman fixed the fax machine.

② The police won't let the suspect leaving the country.

③ Her bright smile made Thompson feels so happy.

④ Mom finally allowed me to stay up all night with my friends.

⑤ Amy had her finger break while practicing kick boxing.

17 다음 중 우리말을 영작한 것이 <u>어색한</u> 것을 고르면?

① 어제 오후에 PC방에서 그를 만난 사람은 바로 나였다.

→ It was I that met him at the Internet cafe yesterday afternoon.

② 아빠가 엄마를 처음 만난 것은 바로 아빠가 대학 신입생 때였다.

→ It was when he was a freshman that my daddy first met my mom.

③ Bill이 MS를 만든 해는 1975년이었다.

→ It was 1975 that Bill made MS.

④ 그 트럭을 고장낸 것은 Douglas였다.

→ It was Douglas that broke the truck.

⑤ 오늘 아침에 그녀가 사장에게 받은 것은 바로 해고 통지서였다.

→ It was a notice of dismissal that she received from the boss this morning.

18 다음 중 밑줄 친 부분의 쓰임이 〈보기〉와 같은 것은?

> ┌─ 보기 ─┐
>
> John <u>had</u> the windows replaced an hour ago.

① The food that I <u>had</u> was fantastic.

② The sports complex building <u>has</u> gas-fired central heating.

③ He <u>had</u> his head in his hands.

④ Sarah was <u>having</u> difficulty in staying awake.

⑤ We're <u>having</u> our car painted blue.

19 다음 중 밑줄 친 that의 쓰임이 나머지와 다른 하나는?

① It was on the snow that my dogs left their footprints.

② It is important that the actor should recover from despair.

③ It is this year that you will graduate from Balsan middle school.

④ It is the skill that makes me money.

⑤ It was those pancakes that my daddy sometimes made for me.

20 다음 중 어법상 어색한 문장은?

① The news made Christina cry a lot against her will.

② The designer had the dress to change from green color to orange.

③ Don't let the errors of the past destroy your present.

④ Yewon noticed a boy trying to get on the bus on her way to school.

⑤ Meditation helps you to escape from your grief.

21 다음 주어진 상황을 읽고, Peter가 여동생에게 할 말을 〈조건〉에 맞게 영작하시오.

- Peter's sister just broke her computer.
- Peter doesn't know how to fix the computer.
- He wants to make her relieved today.
- → Peter: I _____ .

─┤ 조건 ├─
fix, have, today, 소유격, 미래시제 등을 활용할 것. 6단어로 빈칸을 채울 것.

Reading

[22~24] 다음 글을 읽고 물음에 답하시오.

Hi, I am Tom. A florist is someone who creates beautiful things with ①flowers. To become a florist, you need to know many things about flowers. I attended a high school for ②florists and gardeners. It was at this school that I learned how to grow and care for different types of flowers. These days, florists can do a lot of ③different things. I design movie sets sometimes and I decorate shops with flowers. I am happy when I create something ④colorful with fresh flowers and greenery. If you like plants and the arts, I ⑤high recommend you become a florist.

22 위 글의 밑줄 친 ①~⑤ 중 글의 흐름상 어색한 것은?

①   ②   ③   ④   ⑤

23 위 글의 내용에 맞게 빈칸에 알맞은 말을 쓰시오.

The high school that Tom attended taught Tom _____
_____ .

24 다음 중 위 글을 읽고 답할 수 없는 것은?

① What does Tom do for a living?

② What do we need to know if we want to become a florist?

③ Where did Tom learn about growing and caring for different types of flowers?

④ Who recommended Tom to become a florist?

⑤ What does Tom do with flowers?

[25~27] 다음 글을 읽고 물음에 답하시오.

I like food from around the world and I am good at cooking. I can also make food look tasty and beautiful.

[A] He always thinks of new recipes and then cooks these new dishes for us. I want to have my name remembered by people who enjoy my food.

[B] Also, I will go to France to learn various cooking skills. My role model is my dad.

[C] For these reasons, it is a chef that I want to be when I grow up. To achieve my dream, I will read magazines about cooking.

25 자연스러운 글이 되도록 [A]~[C]를 바르게 배열한 것은?

① [A]–[C]–[B]　　② [B]–[A]–[C]
③ [B]–[C]–[A]　　④ [C]–[A]–[B]
⑤ [C]–[B]–[A]

26 위 글의 제목으로 가장 적절한 것은?

① France, the Dream Country
② My Dream Job, A Chef
③ My Mentor, My Father
④ Magazines That Will Help You
⑤ A World Famous Restaurant

27 위 글을 읽고 유추할 수 있는 것은?

① The writer wants to look beautiful.
② The writer is reading many books to become a writer.
③ The writer's father is a chef.
④ The writer travels all around the world.
⑤ The writer wants to remember people's name.

[28~30] 다음 글을 읽고 물음에 답하시오.

I am Emma. I am (A)_____. It sounds like a difficult job, doesn't it? In fact, it is a lot of fun. I work for a baseball team. My job is to watch recorded games and run a computer program to collect data. Then, I analyze the data to show my team's strengths and weaknesses. If the team understands their strengths and weaknesses, they can do better next time. Since I was young, I have been a big fan of baseball. Now, in my work, I watch baseball games all the time. This is a perfect job for me because watching baseball games is my hobby!

28 빈칸 (A)에 들어갈 말로 가장 적절한 것은?

① a cartoonist　　② a sport data analyst
③ a florist　　④ a director of musical
⑤ a baseball player

29 다음 중 위 글의 내용과 일치하는 것은?

① Emma thinks her job is very difficult.
② Emma doesn't want to know her team's weaknesses.
③ Emma didn't like baseball when she was young.
④ Emma likes baseball very much.
⑤ Emma always watches baskctball gamcs in her work.

30 According to the passage, what does Emma work for? Answer in English with a full sentence.

➡ _____

01 다음 짝지어진 단어의 관계가 같도록 빈칸에 알맞은 말을 쓰시오.

| weakness : strength = follow : _____ |

02 다음 영영 풀이에 해당하는 단어는?

to give a short performance in order to show that you are suitable for a part in a film, play, show, etc.

① analyze   ② direct
③ audition   ④ display
⑤ exhibit

[03~04] 다음 대화를 읽고 물음에 답하시오.

Girl: I'm glad to meet you, Mr. Han. Could you please tell me what you do?

Mr. Han: Okay. I guide travelers to different places in China and give them information about where they should visit.

Girl: What else do you do?

Mr. Han: I tell them about popular culture and traditional food in China.

Girl: (A)In my opinion, knowing a lot about China is very important. Are you happy with your job?

Mr. Han: Yes. I really love my job.

03 위 글의 밑줄 친 (A)와 같은 의미의 문장을 주어진 단어를 활용하여 쓰시오. (12 words)

| (seem / me) |

➡ _____

04 위 대화의 내용으로 보아 알 수 <u>없는</u> 것은?

① Mr. Han guides travelers to many places in China.
② The girl wants to know what Mr. Han does.
③ Mr. Han gives travelers information about where they should visit.
④ It seems to me that Mr. Han is a tour guide.
⑤ Mr. Han really loves popular culture and traditional food in China.

[05~06] 다음 대화를 읽고 물음에 답하시오.

Mr. Kang: What's wrong, Jisu?

Jisu: I want to be an animator, but my drawing skill is not (a)<u>enough good</u>.

Mr. Kang: Hmm... Being an animator is not just about (b)<u>being</u> a good artist.

Jisu: What should I do (c)<u>to become</u> an animator?

Mr. Kang: Read a lot of books to make good stories and (d)<u>practice</u> drawing every day.

Jisu: Okay, I'll do so.

Mr. Kang: I'm quite sure that you can be a good animator (e)<u>if you try</u> hard.

Jisu: Thank you very much.

05 What does Mr. Kang advise Jisu to do? (대화에서 찾아 2가지를 쓰시오.)

➡ _____

06 위 대화의 밑줄 (a)~(e) 중 어법상 어색한 것은?

① (a)   ② (b)   ③ (c)   ④ (d)   ⑤ (e)

[07~08] 다음 대화를 읽고 물음에 답하시오.

> Bora: What are you most interested in among the things on this list?
>
> Jessie: I'm most interested in working outside and playing sports.
>
> Bora: Well, (A)_____.
>
> Jessie: What do you mean?
>
> Bora: Most people belong to one of six personality types. Realistic is one of the types.
>
> Jessie: Oh, that's interesting. What kind of jobs do they recommend for realistic types?
>
> Bora: A farmer, a police officer, a soccer player, and so on.
>
> Jessie: Oh, I have always wanted to be a soccer player.
>
> Bora: That's good. (B)_____

출제율 95%

07 위 글의 빈칸 (A)에 들어갈 말로 알맞은 것은?

① it seems to me that you belong to the artistic type

② I'm quite sure you'll achieve your dream

③ I'm quite sure that people doing those jobs will be in need

④ it seems to me that you belong to the realistic type

⑤ I think that you belong to the soccer team

출제율 90%

08 위 대화의 빈칸 (B)에 들어갈 말을 주어진 〈조건〉에 맞게 영어로 쓰시오.

┌─── 조건 ───┐
• 확실성 정도를 나타내는 표현을 쓸 것.
• 'quite sure', 'could become'을 사용할 것.
└───────────┘

➡ _____

출제율 90%

09 다음 대화의 밑줄 친 (A)를 do의 구체적인 의미가 나타나도록 바꾸어 쓰시오.

> B: Anne, I'm planning to visit the police station to see my uncle. He is a police officer.
>
> G: Oh, I want to become a police officer someday.
>
> B: (A)You do? Me, too. I have dreamed of becoming a police officer since I was ten.
>
> G: Can I come with you, Matt? I want to meet your uncle and ask him something.
>
> B: Sure. What are you going to ask?
>
> G: I want to ask him what I need to do to become a police officer.
>
> B: I see. I'm sure he would like to meet you.

➡ _____

출제율 95%

10 다음 각 문장에 사용된 어법 사항을 〈보기〉에서 기호를 골라 괄호 안에 쓰시오.

┌─── 보기 ───┐
ⓐ It ~ that 강조 구문 문장
ⓑ It(가주어) ~ that(진주어) 구문 문장
└───────────┘

(1) It is only through practice that you will achieve your goal. (   )

(2) It is wonderful that the whole family gets together on Chuseok. (   )

(3) It is when my kids smile at me that I feel the happiest. (   )

(4) It is Susan's idea that all the club members must gather here. (   )

(5) What was it that motivated Joe to learn engineering? (   )

11 출제율 90%

다음 대화의 밑줄 친 우리말 해석과 같은 표현을 쓸 때 문장의 빈칸에 알맞은 말을 쓰시오.

> B: Did you finish the report about your role model?
> G: Yes, I did. I wrote about my role model, Ms. Shin. I want to be like her.
> B: What does she do?
> G: She teaches people how to stretch. She also helps them reduce stress and calm themselves.
> B: Good. 그녀가 그들의 몸과 마음을 둘 다 건강하게 유지하도록 돕는 것 같아.
> G: Yes, and I think it's great.

➡ _____ _____ that she helps to keep _____ their mind _____ body _____.

12 출제율 95%

아래의 내용을 'It ~ that' 강조 구문으로 다시 설명한 문장 중 내용과 일치하지 않는 것을 고르시오.

> • One day, my uncle Steve accidentally spilled a glass of wine, so my computer broke down. He gave me his credit card and I had the computer repaired at the shop.

① It was my uncle Steve that broke my computer.
② It was by accident that my uncle spilled a glass of wine.
③ It was his credit card that my uncle gave to me.
④ It was my uncle Steve that fixed my computer at the shop.
⑤ It was at the shop that my computer was repaired.

13 출제율 95%

다음 중 어법상 어색한 문장은?

① Laura had her umbrella stolen while she was texting her boyfriend.
② Wasn't it hard to have your son transferred?
③ As her husband was looking away, Gloria had her shoes shone.
④ The VIP customer ordered the clerk to have all her purchases packaged.
⑤ The robber forced her to have the money withdrawn from the ATM.

14 출제율 100%

다음 중 어법상 옳은 것을 고르시오.

① The movie made me moving.
② The principal of my school had us to wait for the mayor to give a speech.
③ Her parents are so strict that they won't let Peggy going out tonight.
④ All the relatives at camping helped my daddy washed the dishes.
⑤ My wife had me stay still during the wedding.

15 출제율 90%

다음 문장의 밑줄 친 ⓐ~ⓓ를 각각 순서대로 'It ~ that' 강조 구문으로 전환하시오.

> The newlyweds bought a table at the mall
>   ⓐ   ⓑ   ⓒ
> 2 weeks ago.
>   ⓓ

➡ (1) ⓐ _____
_____

(2) ⓑ _____
_____

(3) ⓒ _____
_____

(4) ⓓ _____
_____

[16~19] 다음 글을 읽고 물음에 답하시오.

Hi, I am Chris. (A)As a director of a musical theater, I do a lot of things. ① I audition the actors and I look for good, strong voices. ② Then, I put the cast and orchestra together for practice. ③ During the performance, I am in the orchestra area and conduct. ④ It's my responsibility to have each song played the same way every time. ⑤ I direct the musicians and the singers to keep the show together. Conducting and directing is not just about waving my arms around!

16 다음 중 밑줄 친 (A)와 쓰임이 같은 것은?

① As you are here, you need to vote for us.
② This is as light as a feather.
③ He sat watching TV as she got ready.
④ He worked as a doctor for ten years.
⑤ As you were out, I left a message.

17 ①~⑤ 중 다음 주어진 문장이 들어가기에 적절한 곳은?

> After selecting the cast, I teach them the songs for each scene.

①　　　②　　　③　　　④　　　⑤

18 When Chris auditions the actors, what does he look for? Answer in English with a full sentence.

➡ _____

19 Write the reason why Chris directs the musicians and the singers. Answer in English.

➡ _____
_____

[20~23] 다음 글을 읽고 물음에 답하시오.

My name is Yeji. I am an ocean scientist. Ocean science is a big field. It includes studies of the oceans and the creatures living in ⓐ them. Among other things, I have studied many kinds of fish (A)[living / live] in the seas near Korea. It is the growth ring in a fish that interests me. (B)[On / By] looking at it, I can find out when and where the fish was born. All the information I get from fish (C)[is / are] used to understand sea resources and manage the oceans better. My job is important because it makes the best use of nature possible.

20 (A)~(C)에서 어법상 옳은 것끼리 바르게 짝지어진 것은?

① living – On – is　　② live – On – is
③ living – By – is　　④ live – By – are
⑤ living – By – are

21 다음 중 위 글의 내용과 일치하는 것은?

① Yeji doesn't know anything about ocean science.
② What Yeji studies is a big field in Korea.
③ Fish that Yeji has studied live far from Korea.
④ What interests Yeji is the growth ring in a tree.
⑤ The information Yeji gathered about fish helps manage the oceans better.

22 밑줄 친 ⓐ가 가리키는 것을 위 글에서 찾아 쓰시오.

➡ _____

23 위 글의 내용과 일치하도록 빈칸에 알맞은 말을 쓰시오.

> Yeji gets _____ _____ _____ so that she can use it to understand sea resources.

01 다음 그림은 Bora가 관심을 가지고 있는 분야이다. 다음 〈조건〉에 따라 대화를 완성하시오.

technology

┤ 조건 ├

(A) 'interest'를 어형 변화하여 '기술에 관심이 있다'는 표현을 쓸 것.

(B) 확실성 정도를 나타내는 표현을 쓸 것. 'quite'를 사용할 것.

➡ A: _____. Which job would be right for me?

B: _____ an app developer could be a good job for you.

02 다음 대화를 읽고 아래 요약문의 빈칸을 완성하시오.

B: Hello, what are you doing, Sumi?

G: I'm looking for a good recipe on the Internet. I need it for my family dinner today.

B: That is nice. Do you cook often?

G: Yes, I try to cook every weekend. I want to be a chef someday.

B: What are you doing to make your dream come true?

G: I'm taking a cooking class. I try to think of new and creative dishes.

B: I'm quite sure you could be a good chef.

➡ Sumi's _____ is to be a chef. _____ to me _____ class and _____ are important to _____ her dream.

03 다음 대화의 밑줄 친 (A)와 같은 의미가 되도록 주어진 단어를 이용하여 문장의 빈칸을 완성하시오.

M: What's wrong, Jisu?

G: I want to be an animator, but my drawing skill is not good enough.

M: Hmm... Being an animator is not just about being a good artist.

G: What should I do to become an animator?

M: Read a lot of books to make good stories and practice drawing every day.

G: Okay, I'll do so.

M: (A)I'm quite sure that you can be a good animator if you try hard.

G: Thank you very much.

➡ _____

_____ (doubt)

04 다음 그림을 보고, 주어진 어구를 알맞게 배열하여 문맥에 맞게 대화를 완성하시오. (단, 부사구를 강조하는 문장으로 쓰시오.)

Reporter: What is the biggest contribution to your winning this award today?

Winner: It _____

_____.

(award / that / because / received / was / of / my parents / I / this)

05 다음 우리말과 같은 뜻이 되도록 괄호 안에 있는 단어들을 활용하여, 글자 수에 맞게 영작하시오. (동사 형태 변화 가능)

(1) 그녀의 아버지는 Sally에게 Toto를 씻기라고 시켰다. (6 단어)

➡ _____

(2) 그녀의 아버지는 Toto가 Sally에 의해 씻겨지도록 시켰다. (7 단어)

(Sally, Toto, have, wash, father, by, her)

➡ _____

[06~08] 다음 글을 읽고 물음에 답하시오.

I like food from around the world and I am good at cooking. I can also make food look tasty and beautiful. For these reasons, it is a chef that I want to be when I grow up. To achieve my dream, I will read magazines about cooking. Also, I will go to France to learn various cooking skills. My role model is my dad. He always thinks of new recipes and then cooks these new dishes for us. I want to have my name remembered by people who enjoy my food.

06 What does the writer want to be when she grows up? Answer in English with a full sentence.

➡ _____

07 Write the two things that the writer will do in order to achieve her dream. Use the words 'first, second.'

➡ _____
_____
_____

08 What does the writer's father always do?

➡ _____
_____

[09~11] 다음 글을 읽고 물음에 답하시오.

I am Emma. I am a sport data analyst. It sounds like a difficult job, doesn't it? In fact, it is a lot of fun. I work for a baseball team. My job is to watch (A)_____ games and run a computer program to collect data. Then, I analyze the data to show my team's strengths and weaknesses. If the team understands their strengths and weaknesses, they can do better next time. Since I was young, I have been a big fan of baseball. Now, in my work, I watch baseball games all the time. This is a perfect job for me because watching baseball games is my hobby!

09 주어진 단어를 빈칸 (A)에 어법에 맞게 쓰시오.

(record)

➡ _____

10 According to the passage, what is Emma's hobby? Answer in English with a full sentence.

➡ _____

11 What does Emma do all the time in her work? Answer in English with a full sentence.

➡ _____

01 다음 (A)는 관심 있는 분야이고 (B)는 장래 희망이다. 〈보기〉의 문장처럼 대화를 완성하시오.

(A)	(B)
• art	• a designer
• writing	• a poet
• sports	• a soccer player
• nature	• farmer

A: _____. Which job would be right for me?
B: _____ could be a good job for you.

02 다음 그림들을 보고, 괄호 안에 주어진 어휘를 모두 활용하여, 'have+목적어+과거분사'의 표현이 들어간 문장을 만드시오. (원하는 단어를 추가하되, 어법에 유의할 것.)

 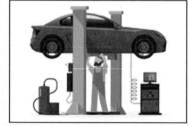

(phone / repair / yesterday)　(Sophia / check / a mechanic / tomorrow)

(1) _____

(2) _____

03 다음 내용을 바탕으로 Jina의 장래 희망을 써 봅시다.

Q: What things do you like?
Jina: I like bags from around the world.
Q: What are you good at?
Jina: I am good at making things. I can also make what I made look beautiful.
Q: What do you want to be when you grow up?
Jina: It is a bag designer that I want to be when I grow up.
Q: What will you do to achieve your dream?
Jina: I will read fashion magazines. Also I will go to France to learn to design bags.

I like _____ the world and I am good at _____. I can also make _____. For these reasons, _____ I want to be when I grow up. To achieve my dream, I will _____. Also, I will _____.

단원별 모의고사

01 다음 단어에 대한 영어 설명이 <u>어색한</u> 것은?

① analyzsis: someone whose job is to analyze and examine something
② bank teller: a person whose job is to pay out and take in money in a bank
③ care for: to protect someone or something and provide the things they need, especially someone who is young, old or ill
④ developer: a person or company that creates new products, especially computer products such as software
⑤ make the best use of: to use something as much as you can

02 다음 중 짝지어진 대화가 <u>어색한</u> 것은?

① A: Did you finish the report about your role model?
   B: Yes, I did. I wrote about my role model, Mr. Kang.
② A: What does she do?
   B: She teaches people how to stretch.
③ A: What are you good at?
   B: I am good at writing stories.
④ A: What are you doing to make your dream come true?
   B: I'm taking a cooking class.
⑤ A: Are you happy with your job?
   B: In my opinion, going to fashion shows would be helpful.

03 다음 짝지어진 단어의 관계가 같도록 빈칸에 알맞은 말을 쓰시오.

fix : repair = operate : _____

04 다음 영영풀이에 해당하는 단어를 고르시오.

to bring a person or thing to a state or place

① handle   ② select
③ lead   ④ create
⑤ fetch

[05~06] 다음 대화를 읽고 물음에 답하시오.

A: I'm interested in animals. (A)_____
B: I think a pet hairdresser can be a good job for you.
A: What is a pet hairdresser?
B: (B)_____ He/She designs different hairstyles for pets.
A: That sounds nice. Why do you think it can be a good job for me?
B: You are interested in animals. And I know you are good at designing and making things.

05 위 대화의 빈칸 (A)에 들어갈 말로 알맞은 것은?

① Are you interested in animals?
② What do you do at a pet hair salon?
③ What is the best thing about a pet hairdresser?
④ Which job is right for me?
⑤ What do you think of a pet hairdresser?

06 위 대화의 A의 물음에 맞게, 주어진 어구를 알맞은 순서로 배열하여 빈칸 (B)를 완성하시오.

(works / that's / a pet / who / at / hair salon / a person)

➡ _____

[07~08] 다음 대화를 읽고 물음에 답하시오.

Bora: What are you most interested in among the things on this list?

Jessie: I'm most interested in working outside and (a)playing sports.

Bora: Well, it (b)seems to me that you belong to the realistic type.

Jessie: What do you mean?

Bora: Most people (c)are belonged to one of six personality types. Realistic is one of the types.

Jessie: Oh, that's (d)interesting. What kind of jobs do they recommend for realistic types?

Bora: A farmer, a police officer, a soccer player, and so on.

Jessie: Oh, I have always (e)wanted to be a soccer player.

Bora: That's good. I'm quite sure you could become a great soccer player.

07 위 대화의 밑줄 친 (a)~(e) 중 어법상 어색한 것은?

① (a) ② (b) ③ (c) ④ (d) ⑤ (e)

08 What jobs do they recommend for the realistic type?

➡ They recommend _____
_____.

[09~10] 다음 대화를 읽고 물음에 답하시오.

M: What's wrong, Jisu?

G: I want to be an animator, but my drawing skill is not good enough.

M: Hmm... Being an animator is not just about being a good artist.

G: _____

M: Read a lot of books to make good stories and practice drawing every day.

G: Okay, I'll do so.

M: (A)나는 네가 열심히 노력하면 훌륭한 만화 영화 제작자가 될 수 있다고 꽤 확신해.

G: Thank you very much.

09 위 대화의 빈칸에 들어갈 말로 알맞은 것은?

① How many books are you going to read?

② What should I do to become an animator?

③ I think that you can be a good novelist.

④ Can I get your advice on what to read?

⑤ What books do I have to read?

10 위 대화의 (A)의 우리말 해석에 맞게 주어진 어구를 알맞은 순서로 배열하시오.

(I'm / you / quite / if / that / can be / a good / you / animator / try hard / sure)

➡ _____
_____

11 다음을 읽고, 각 질문에 대한 답을 'It ~ that' 강조 구문으로 조건에 맞게 영작하시오.

- Lucy started to read the novel last Sunday.
- Austin wrote the novel two months ago.
- Today's Tuesday and Lucy is still reading it.

(1) For how many days has Lucy been reading the novel? (for, 현재완료진행형을 쓸 것, 총 12단어)

➡ _____

(2) What is the name of the author of the novel that Lucy is reading? (who, novel, write를 이용할 것. 형태 변화 가능하며, 총 7단어)

➡ _____

12 다음 그림을 보고, 우리말에 맞게 주어진 어구를 배열하시오.

(1) 엄마는 나에게 쓰지 않는 물건들을 상자에 모으라고 시키셨다.

(me / the unused things / mom / in / had / put / the boxes).

➡ _____

(2) 나는 그 상자들을 자선단체에 기부하게 할 것이다.

(have / charity / will / donated / the boxes / I / to).

➡ _____

13 다음 각각의 그림을 보고, 우리말과 조건에 맞게 영작하시오. (어형 변화 가능)

(1) 엄마는 내가 혼자 힘으로 이를 닦도록 시켰다.
(me, have, brush, myself 활용, 총 8단어).

➡ _____

(2) 그렇게 많은 그릇을 닦고 있는 것은 바로 나의 개 Angel이다.

(dish, wash, so, 'It ~ that' 강조 구문을 활용할 것, 총 11단어)

➡ _____

14 다음 밑줄 친 부분과 어법상 쓰임이 같은 것은?

> The history teacher had all the students go on a field trip to Gyeongju.

① Elizabeth had every reason to get annoyed with that situation.
② Maya had an eye for both modern and ancient paintings.
③ We had him come here earlier.
④ Henry had coffee and cake for dessert.
⑤ Mike had a car accident two years ago.

[15~18] 다음 글을 읽고 물음에 답하시오.

Hi, I am Tom. A florist is someone who creates beautiful things with flowers. ① To become a florist, you need to know many things about flowers. ② It was at this school that I learned how to grow and care for different types of flowers. ③ These days, florists can do a lot of different things. ④ I design movie sets sometimes and I decorate shops with flowers. ⑤ I am happy when I create something colorful with fresh flowers and greenery. If you like (A)_____, I highly recommend you become a florist.

15 ①~⑤ 중 주어진 문장이 들어가기에 가장 적절한 곳은?

> I attended a high school for florists and gardeners.

①   ②   ③   ④   ⑤

16 빈칸 (A)에 들어갈 말로 가장 적절한 것은?

① drawing and writing
② thinking and doing
③ plants and the arts
④ the arts and the artist
⑤ planting and growing

17 다음 중 플로리스트의 일과 관련이 <u>없는</u> 것은?

① making beautiful things with flowers
② knowing many things about flowers
③ growing and caring for different types of flowers
④ decorating flowers with colored paper
⑤ designing movie sets

18 다음 중 위 글을 읽고 답할 수 <u>없는</u> 것은?

① What is a florist?
② What did Tom learn at his high school?
③ When does Tom feel happy?
④ Where does Tom work?
⑤ How does Tom decorate shops?

[19~21] 다음 글을 읽고 물음에 답하시오.

Hi, I am Chris. As a director of a musical theater, I do a lot of things. I audition the actors and I look for good, strong voices. After selecting the cast, I teach them the songs for each scene. Then, I put the cast and orchestra together for practice. During the performance, I am in the orchestra area and conduct. (A)<u>각각의 노래가 매번 동일하게 연주되도록 만드는 것은 나의 책임입니다.</u> I direct the musicians and the singers to keep the show together. Conducting and directing is not just about (B)<u>waving</u> my arms around!

19 According to the passage, when does Chris conduct? Answer in English with a full sentence.

➡ _____

20 다음 주어진 단어를 활용하여 밑줄 친 (A)를 영어로 쓸 때 빈칸에 알맞은 말을 쓰시오. 필요하다면 어형을 바꾸시오.

(responsibility / play / each / have / to / my / song)

➡ It's _____
the same way every time.

21 다음 중 밑줄 친 (B)와 쓰임이 같은 것은?

① Do you hear a baby <u>crying</u> in the room?
② The <u>rising</u> sun is very bright.
③ <u>Making</u> noises here is not helpful.
④ Jason is <u>playing</u> soccer outside.
⑤ We saw a boy <u>dancing</u> on the street.

22 다음 중 글의 흐름상 어색한 것은?

I like food from around the world and I am good at cooking. ①I can also make food look tasty and beautiful. ②For these reasons, it is a chef that I want to be when I grow up. ③To achieve my dream, I will read magazines about cooking. ④ Also, I will go to France to learn various cooking skills. ⑤My dad always thinks of new recipes and then cooks these new dishes for us. I want to have my name remembered by people who enjoy my food.

①   ②   ③   ④   ⑤

INSIGHT
on the textbook

교과서 파헤치기

※ 다음 영어를 우리말로 쓰시오.

01 fantastic	22 save
02 automatically	23 furniture
03 forward	24 guest
04 goal	25 create
05 recognize	26 skill
06 different	27 designed
07 nature	28 floor
08 scene	29 imagine
09 basement	30 humorous
10 countryside	31 motto
11 advise	32 refreshed
12 early adopter	33 photo-taking
13 technology	34 subject
14 free	35 get along with
15 pretty	36 stop -ing
16 forest	37 be full of ~
17 product	38 would like to+동사원형
18 comfortable	39 be interested in
19 among	40 be good at
20 interest	41 here are+복수명사
21 choice	42 look like+명사
	43 wake up

※ 다음 우리말을 영어로 쓰시오.

01	제품		22	만들다
02	그려진, 디자인된		23	언어
03	사진촬영		24	(건물의) 층
04	자동으로		25	손님
05	선택		26	상상하다
06	진짜의		27	지하층[실]
07	편안한		28	장면
08	가구		29	한가한, 다른 계획이 없는
09	조언하다, 충고하다		30	숲
10	매우, 꽤		31	자연
11	~ 중에서		32	기술
12	환상적인, 매우 멋진		33	영웅
13	연습하다		34	(기분이) 상쾌한
14	과목, 주제		35	~을 잘하다
15	앞으로		36	~하고 싶다
16	목표		37	단지 ~가 아닌
17	구하다		38	(잠에서) 깨다, 일어나다
18	관심, 흥미		39	~로 가득 차다
19	인식하다		40	~하는 것을 그만두다
20	시골(지역)		41	~와 잘 지내다
21	재미있는, 유머러스한		42	~처럼 보이다
			43	여기에 ~가 있다

※ 다음 영영풀이에 알맞은 단어를 <보기>에서 골라 쓴 후, 우리말 뜻을 쓰시오.

1 _____ : to go into a place:: _____

2 _____ : in the middle of a group: _____

3 _____ : to make something happen or exist: _____

4 _____ : a large area of land that is covered with trees: _____

5 _____ : to tell someone that they should do something: _____

6 _____ : extremely good, attractive, enjoyable: _____

7 _____ : part of a building that is under the level of the ground: _____

8 _____ : to form or have a mental picture or idea of something: _____

9 _____ : land that is not in towns or cities and may have farms, fields, etc.:

_____

10 _____ : a short sentence or phrase that expresses a belief or purpose: _____

11 _____ : a very brave person, often a man, that a lot of people admire: _____

12 _____ : the possibility of choosing between two or more things: _____

13 _____ : a person who takes photographs, either as a job or hobby: _____

14 _____ : things such as chairs, tables, and beds that you put into a room or building:

_____

15 _____ : an animal that is kept in the home as a companion and treated kindly:

_____

16 _____ : to know someone or something because you have seen or heard him or

her or experienced it before: _____

보기			
advise	motto	among	fantastic
create	hero	furniture	choice
recognize	imagine	enter	countryside
forest	basement	photographer	pet

※ 다음 우리말과 일치하도록 빈칸에 알맞은 말을 쓰시오.

Warm Up

B1: Hello, my name is Kim Chanho. I _____ _____ _____ you about _____ . I'm _____ _____ music. I_____ _____ _____ _____ the drums.

G1: Hi! I am Teri. I _____ _____ in the evening. I feel _____ _____ I exercise.

B2: Hello, my name is Jack. I'_____ _____ in the stars. I _____ _____ _____ _____ _____ stars at night.

G2: I am Lee Bora. I want to be a _____ in the future, so I _____ _____ when I have _____ _____ .

B3: I am Mark. I like dancing. I want to _____ _____ _____ in the dance _____ .

Listen & Speak 1 A

1. **G:** Jiho, _____ was your first day of _____ _____ ?

   B: It was _____ good. The teachers and my new classmates are all good.

   G: That _____ _____ . Who is your _____ _____ ?

   B: My homeroom teacher is Mr. Kim. He _____ math.

   G: _____ _____ _____ _____ more _____ him?

   B: Yes. He is _____ and _____ us some _____ _____ about math. It was _____ .

   G: Cool! I hope you _____ _____ math.

2. **G:** Ted, _____ _____ this movie poster. I want _____ _____ this movie.

   B: It _____ interesting. Can you _____ me about it, Amy?

   G: Yes. It is _____ a hero _____ _____ the Earth.

   B: It _____ _____ an SF movie.

   G: Yes, it is. Actually, SF is my _____ _____ _____ movie. I like the _____ _____ _____ computer _____ . They are _____ and look _____ .

   B: That's _____ . I am free this weekend. _____ _____ to see it together.

   G: _____ good.

해석

B1: 안녕, 내 이름은 김찬호야. 너에게 나에 대해 말해주고 싶어. 나는 음악에 관심이 있어. 나는 드럼을 잘 쳐.
G1: 안녕, 나는 Teri야. 나는 저녁에 달리는 것을 좋아해. 나는 달릴 때 상쾌함을 느껴.
B2: 안녕, 내 이름은 Jack이야. 나는 별들에 관심이 있어. 나는 보통 밤에 별을 보러 나가.
G2: 나는 이보라야. 나는 미래에 디자이너가 되고 싶어서, 시간이 날 때 그림 그리는 연습을 해.
B3: 나는 Mark야. 나는 춤추는 걸 좋아해. 나는 춤 대회에서 1등을 하고 싶어.

1. G: 지호야, 너의 3학년 첫 날은 어땠어?
   B: 꽤 좋았어. 선생님들과 새로운 반 친구들 모두 좋아.
   G: 그거 좋네. 담임 선생님은 누구셔?
   B: 내 담임 선생님은 김 선생님이셔. 그는 수학을 가르치셔.
   G: 나에게 그에 대해 더 말해 줄 수 있니?
   B: 응. 그는 유머가 있으시고 우리에게 수학에 대한 재미있는 몇 가지 이야기를 해 주셨어. 그것은 흥미로웠어.
   G: 멋지네! 네가 수학 공부를 즐기기 바라.

2. G: Ted, 이 영화 포스터 좀 봐. 이 영화 보고 싶어.
   B: 그거 재미있어 보이네. 나에게 그것에 관해 말해 줄 수 있니, Amy?
   G: 응. 그것은 지구를 구하는 영웅에 대한 거야.
   B: 공상 과학 영화 같네.
   G: 응, 맞아. 사실 공상 과학은 내가 가장 좋아하는 영화 장르야. 나는 컴퓨터 기술로 제작된 장면들을 좋아해. 그 장면들은 환상적이고 진짜 같아 보여.
   B: 그거 멋지네. 나 이번 주말에 시간 있어. 같이 그거 보러 가자.
   G: 좋아.

Listen & Speak 1 B

A: _____ you _____ me _____ your plan for this weekend?

B: Yes. I _____ _____ _____ _____ a birthday party.

A: Can you tell me about your _____ _____ _____ _____?

B: Yes. I want _____ _____ _____ fast food.

Listen & Speak 2 A

1. G: I often _____ _____ _____ my family. _____ I like _____ about traveling is _____ new foods.

2. B: My _____ _____ is music. I can _____ _____ _____ and guitar. _____ them, _____ the guitar is _____ I _____ _____.

3. G: This is a picture of Dora. She is my best friend, _____ _____ a pet. _____ _____ her in my free time is _____ I like most.

Real Life Talk

Seho: Nice to meet you. I'_____ _____ _____ _____ your photo club.

Bora: Thank you _____ _____ _____ in the club. Can you tell me _____ _____?

Seho: Yes. My name is Kim Seho. I am _____ the _____ _____, class 8.

Andy: Tell me _____. _____ do you like to do _____ in your _____ _____?

Seho: Well, _____ I like most is _____ _____ pictures.

Bora: That's great. What is your dream _____ _____ _____?

Seho: I want _____ _____ _____ _____.

Andy: Then you made the right _____. You can learn a lot of _____ _____ here. _____ _____ our club.

Seho: Thank you. I'm so _____!

A: 나에게 너의 이번 주말 계획에 대해 말해 줄 수 있니?

B: 응. 나는 생일 파티를 할 거야.

A: 나에게 너의 올해 목표에 대해 말해 줄 수 있니?

B: 응. 나는 패스트푸드를 그만 먹고 싶어.

1. G: 나는 가끔 나의 가족들과 여행을 가. 여행에 관해 내가 가장 좋아하는 것은 새로운 음식들을 먹어보는 거야.

2. B: 내가 가장 좋아하는 과목은 음악이야. 나는 드럼과 기타를 연주할 수 있어. 그것들 중에서, 기타를 연주하는 것이 내가 가장 좋아하는 거야.

3. G: 이것은 Dora 사진이야. 그녀는 단순히 애완동물이 아니라, 나의 가장 친한 친구야. 여가시간에 그녀와 함께 노는 것이 내가 가장 좋아하는 거야.

세호: 만나서 반가워. 나는 너희의 사진 동아리에 가입하고 싶어.

보라: 동아리에 관심을 가져 줘서 고마워. 너에 대해 말해 줄래?

세호: 응. 내 이름은 김세호야. 나는 3학년 8반이야.

Andy: 좀 더 말해 줘. 너는 여가 시간에 무엇을 하는 걸 가장 좋아하니?

세호: 음, 내가 가장 좋아하는 건 사진 찍는 거야.

보라: 멋지다. 너의 장래 희망은 뭐니?

세호: 나는 사진 작가가 되고 싶어.

Andy: 그러면 너는 정말 좋은 선택을 했구나. 너는 여기서 사진 찍는 기술을 많이 배울 수 있어. 우리 동아리에 온 걸 환영해.

세호: 고마워. 나도 기뻐!

Communication Task Step 2

A: What is your _____ ?

B: My nickname is Speedy _____ I can _____ _____ .

C: What do you _____ _____ ?

B: _____ _____ _____ _____ is to play baseball.

D: _____ _____ _____ _____ _____ your dream job?

B: I _____ _____ _____ a baseball player.

A: What is your _____ ?

B: My _____ is "You can go _____ _____ , but _____ _____
_____ ."

A: 너의 별명이 뭐니?

B: 내 별명은 스피디인데 나는 빨리 달릴 수 있기 때문이야.

C: 너는 무엇을 가장 좋아하니?

B: 내가 가장 좋아하는 것은 야구를 하는 거야.

D: 나에게 네가 꿈꾸는 직업에 대해 말해 줄 수 있니?

B: 나는 야구 선수가 되고 싶어.

A: 너의 좌우명은 뭐니?

B: 나의 좌우명은 "앞으로 천천히 나아갈 수 있지만, 절대 물러설 수는 없다"야.

Wrap Up

W: Today, we have a _____ _____ Hojun. Hojun, can you please
_____ _____ to the class?

B: Yes. Hi, my name is Kim Hojun. I am _____ Busan. _____
_____ _____ you.

W: _____ _____ _____ _____ _____ about yourself?

B: Yes. I like sports, _____ soccer. I want _____ _____ a sports
club.

W: Is there _____ _____ you want _____ _____ your new
friends?

B: I want to _____ _____ _____ everyone. Please help me
_____ I'm _____ .

W: Thanks, Hojun. _____ _____ _____ _____ .

W: 오늘, 새로 온 학생 호준이가 있어요. 호준아, 반 친구들에게 너를 소개해 주겠니?

B: 네. 안녕, 내 이름은 김호준이야. 나는 부산에서 왔어. 만나서 반가워.

W: 너에 대해 더 말해 줄 수 있니?

B: 네. 나는 스포츠, 특히 축구를 좋아해. 나는 스포츠 동아리에 가입하고 싶어.

W: 너의 새로운 친구들에게 더 말하고 싶은 게 있니?

B: 모두와 함께 잘 지내고 싶어. 나는 이곳에 새로 왔으니 도와주길 바라.

W: 고마워, 호준아. 우리 반에 온 것을 환영한단다.

※ 다음 우리말에 맞도록 대화를 영어로 쓰시오.

해석

Warm Up

B1: _____

_____

G1: _____

B2: _____

_____

G2: _____

_____

B3: _____

B1: 안녕, 내 이름은 김찬호야. 너에게 나에 대해 말해주고 싶어. 나는 음악에 관심이 있어. 나는 드럼을 잘 쳐.
G1: 안녕. 나는 Teri야. 나는 저녁에 달리는 것을 좋아해. 나는 달릴 때 상쾌함을 느껴.
B2: 안녕, 내 이름은 Jack이야. 나는 별들에 관심이 있어. 나는 보통 밤에 별을 보러 나가.
G2: 나는 이보라야. 나는 미래에 디자이너가 되고 싶어서, 시간이 날 때 그림 그리는 연습을 해.
B3: 나는 Mark야. 나는 춤추는 걸 좋아해. 나는 춤 대회에서 1등을 하고 싶어.

Listen & Speak 1 A

1. G: _____

B: _____

G: _____

B: _____

G: _____

B: _____

_____

G: _____

1. G: 지호야, 너의 3학년 첫 날은 어땠어?
   B: 꽤 좋았어. 선생님들과 새로운 반 친구들 모두 좋아.
   G: 그거 좋네. 담임 선생님은 누구셔?
   B: 내 담임 선생님은 김 선생님이셔. 그는 수학을 가르치셔.
   G: 나에게 그에 대해 더 말해 줄 수 있니?
   B: 응. 그는 유머가 있으시고 우리에게 수학에 대한 재미있는 몇 가지 이야기를 해 주셨어. 그것은 흥미로웠어.
   G: 멋지네! 네가 수학 공부를 즐기기 바라.

2. G: _____

B: _____

G: _____

B: _____

G: _____

_____

B: _____

G: _____

2. G: Ted, 이 영화 포스터 좀 봐. 이 영화 보고 싶어.
   B: 그거 재미있어 보이네. 나에게 그것에 관해 말해 줄 수 있니, Amy?
   G: 응. 그것은 지구를 구하는 영웅에 대한 거야.
   B: 공상 과학 영화 같네.
   G: 응, 맞아. 사실 공상 과학은 내가 가장 좋아하는 영화 장르야. 나는 컴퓨터 기술로 제작된 장면들을 좋아해. 그 장면들은 환상적이고 진짜 같아 보여.
   B: 그거 멋지네. 나 이번 주말에 시간 있어. 같이 그거 보러 가자.
   G: 좋아.

Listen & Speak 1 B

A: _____

B: _____

A: _____

B: _____

A: 나에게 너의 이번 주말 계획에 대해 말해 줄 수 있니?
B: 응. 나는 생일 파티를 할 거야.
A: 나에게 너의 올해 목표에 대해 말해 줄 수 있니?
B: 응. 나는 패스트푸드를 그만 먹고 싶어.

Listen & Speak 2 A

1. G: _____
   _____

2. B: _____
   _____

3. G: _____
   _____

1. G: 나는 가끔 나의 가족들과 여행을 가. 여행에 관해 내가 가장 좋아하는 것은 새로운 음식들을 먹어보는 거야.
2. B: 내가 가장 좋아하는 과목은 음악이야. 나는 드럼과 기타를 연주할 수 있어. 그것들 중에서, 기타를 연주하는 것이 내가 가장 좋아하는 거야.
3. G: 이것은 Dora 사진이야. 그녀는 단순히 애완동물이 아니라, 나의 가장 친한 친구야. 여가시간에 그녀와 함께 노는 것이 내가 가장 좋아하는 거야.

Real Life Talk

Seho: _____

Bora: _____

Seho: _____

Andy: _____

Seho: _____

Bora: _____

Seho: _____

Andy: _____
   _____

Seho: _____

세호: 만나서 반가워. 나는 너희의 사진 동아리에 가입하고 싶어.
보라: 동아리에 관심을 가져 줘서 고마워. 너에 대해 말해 줄래?
세호: 응. 내 이름은 김세호야. 나는 3학년 8반이야.
Andy: 좀 더 말해 줘. 너는 여가 시간에 무엇을 하는 걸 가장 좋아하니?
세호: 음, 내가 가장 좋아하는 건 사진 찍는 거야.
보라: 멋지다. 너의 장래 희망은 뭐니?
세호: 나는 사진 작가가 되고 싶어.
Andy: 그러면 너는 정말 좋은 선택을 했구나. 너는 여기서 사진 찍는 기술을 많이 배울 수 있어. 우리 동아리에 온 걸 환영해.
세호: 고마워. 나도 기뻐!

Communication Task Step 2

A: _____

B: _____

C: _____

B: _____

D: _____

B: _____

A: _____

B: _____

A: 너의 별명이 뭐니?

B: 내 별명은 스피디인데 나는 빨리 달릴 수 있기 때문이야.

C: 너는 무엇을 가장 좋아하니?

B: 내가 가장 좋아하는 것은 야구를 하는 거야.

D: 나에게 네가 꿈꾸는 직업에 대해 말해 줄 수 있니?

B: 나는 야구 선수가 되고 싶어.

A: 너의 좌우명은 뭐니?

B: 나의 좌우명은 "앞으로 천천히 나아갈 수 있지만, 절대 물러설 수는 없다"야.

Wrap Up

W: _____
_____

B: _____

W: _____

B: _____

W: _____

B: _____

W: _____

W: 오늘, 새로 온 학생 호준이가 있어요. 호준아, 반 친구들에게 너를 소개해 주겠니?

B: 네. 안녕, 내 이름은 김호준이야. 나는 부산에서 왔어. 만나서 반가워.

W: 너에 대해 더 말해 줄 수 있니?

B: 네. 나는 스포츠, 특히 축구를 좋아해. 나는 스포츠 동아리에 가입하고 싶어.

W: 너의 새로운 친구들에게 더 말하고 싶은 게 있니?

B: 모두와 함께 잘 지내고 싶어. 나는 이곳에 새로 왔으니 도와주길 바라.

W: 고마워, 호준아. 우리 반에 온 것을 환영한단다.

※ 다음 우리말과 일치하도록 빈칸에 알맞은 것을 골라 쓰시오.

My Dream House

1 _____ you _____ _____ about your dream house?

A. ever   B. have   C. thought

2 Today, _____ _____ , we _____ our dream house.

A. class   B. in   C. created

3 _____ _____ some of the dream houses _____ we _____.

A. are   B. made   C. that   D. here

A House in Nature - Minho

4 _____ is _____ _____ friend.

A. my   B. good   C. nature

5 I do _____ _____ when I _____ in the _____.

A. feel   B. forest   C. good   D. walk

6 I'd _____ _____ a dream house _____ the countryside.

A. in   B. to   C. have   D. like

7 It _____ _____ a big garden _____ many _____ and trees.

A. with   B. have   C. flowers   D. should

8 I _____ always _____ _____ the _____ of birds.

A. excited   B. am   C. sound   D. by

9 It will be _____ to _____ _____ in the morning and listen _____ the songs of the birds.

A. up   B. wonderful   C. to   D. wake

10 Also, I'd _____ to _____ many pets. It will be fun _____ _____ with them!

A. play   B. like   C. to   D. have

A Fun Place - Julie

11 _____ _____ my _____ house!

A. to   B. welcome   C. dream

12 _____ fun is _____ I want most, _____ my dream house is _____ of exciting things.

A. what   B. full   C. so   D. having

13 It _____ a _____ _____ the _____.

A. basement   B. in   C. has   D. theater

14 There, I _____ _____ cookies and _____ my _____ movies.

A. enjoy   B. eat   C. favorite   D. can

15 My dream house _____ a game room _____ the _____ _____.

A. on   B. has   C. floor   D. second

내가 꿈꾸는 집

1 여러분은 꿈의 집에 대해 생각해 본 적이 있나요?

2 오늘, 우리는 수업 시간에 우리가 꿈꾸는 집을 만들었습니다.

3 여기 우리가 만든 몇몇 꿈의 집이 있습니다.

자연 속의 집 – 민호

4 자연은 나의 좋은 친구입니다.

5 나는 숲속에서 걸을 때 기분이 정말 좋습니다.

6 나는 시골에 꿈의 집을 갖고 싶습니다.

7 집에는 많은 꽃과 나무가 있는 큰 정원이 있을 것입니다.

8 나는 항상 새소리에 신이 납니다.

9 아침에 깨어나서 새들의 노래 소리를 듣는 것은 멋질 것입니다.

10 또한 나는 많은 애완동물을 갖고 싶습니다. 그들과 노는 것은 매우 재미있을 것입니다!

재미있는 장소 – Julie

11 나의 꿈의 집에 온 것을 환영합니다!

12 즐겁게 지내는 것은 내가 가장 원하는 것입니다. 그래서 내 꿈의 집은 흥미로운 것들로 가득합니다.

13 집에는 지하에 영화관이 있습니다.

14 그곳에서 나는 쿠키를 먹을 수 있고 내가 좋아하는 영화들을 즐길 수 있습니다.

15 내 꿈의 집에는 2층에 게임방이 있습니다.

16 I can _____ many different _____ _____ _____ there.

   A. kinds   B. play   C. of   D. games

17 My house _____ has a _____ .

   A. swimming   B. also   C. pool

18 I want to do _____ _____ _____ my friends in my house. You can be my _____ !

   A. guest   B. things   C. fun   D. with

A Place for Family - Misun

19 My family is _____ _____ _____ _____ to me.

   A. important   B. the   C. thing   D. most

20 In my dream house, my family _____ _____ and _____ .

   A. safe   B. feels   C. comfortable

21 _____ the gate, you can find a _____ _____ sign with my family's picture _____ it.

   A. on   B. beautifully   C. at   D. designed

22 _____ you _____ the house, you will _____ a _____ living room.

   A. enter   B. see   C. when   D. large

23 My family _____ _____ board games and _____ there.

   A. plays   B. sings   C. sometimes

24 It will _____ a garden _____ a large _____ for family picnics.

   A. with   B. picnic   C. have   D. table

25 There, we _____ _____ barbecues. _____ you _____ my dream house?

   A. like   B. enjoy   C. do   D. will

A House with New Technology - Bryan

26 I am an _____ _____ of new _____ .

   A. adopter   B. early   C. technology

27 I do _____ to use new _____ and technology _____ _____ .

   A. before   B. products   C. others   D. like

28 When I _____ _____ my house, the front door _____ my face and _____ automatically.

   A. recognizes   B. near   C. opens   D. get

29 The furniture _____ the weather _____ and _____ me _____ what to wear.

   A. conditions   B. on   C. advises   D. checks

30 The bathroom mirror _____ me my _____ and the _____ of my _____ .

   A. weight   B. health   C. tells   D. condition

31 A robot _____ the house and _____ me.

   A. for   B. cooks   C. cleans

32 This is _____ _____ _____ _____ about my dream house.

   A. can   B. what   C. imagine   D. I

16 나는 그곳에서 많은 다양한 종류의 게임을 할 수 있습니다.

17 나의 집에는 또한 수영장이 있습니다.

18 나는 나의 집에서 친구들과 함께 즐거운 일들을 하고 싶습니다. 여러분도 나의 손님이 될 수 있습니다!

가족을 위한 장소 – 미선

19 나의 가족은 나에게 가장 중요한 것입니다.

20 내 꿈의 집에서 가족은 안전하고 편안함을 느낍니다.

21 현관에서 여러분은 가족 사진이 있는 아름답게 디자인된 문패를 발견할 수 있습니다.

22 여러분이 집에 들어서면 여러분은 큰 거실을 보게 될 것입니다.

23 나의 가족은 때때로 그곳에서 보드 게임도 하고 노래를 부르기도 합니다.

24 가족 소풍을 위한 커다란 피크닉 테이블이 있는 큰 정원을 갖게 될 것입니다.

25 그곳에서 우리는 바비큐를 즐길 것입니다. 내 꿈의 집이 마음에 드나요?

신기술이 있는 집 – Bryan

26 나는 남들보다 먼저 신기술을 써 보는 것을 좋아하는 사람입니다.

27 나는 새로운 제품이나 기술을 다른 사람보다 먼저 사용하는 것을 정말 좋아합니다.

28 내가 집 근처에 도착할 때, 현관문은 내 얼굴을 인식하고 자동으로 문을 엽니다.

29 가구는 날씨 상태를 확인하여 내게 무엇을 입을지 조언해 줍니다.

30 욕실 거울은 나에게 체중과 건강 상태를 알려 줍니다.

31 로봇은 집을 청소하고 나를 위해 요리합니다.

32 이것이 내가 나의 꿈의 집에 대해 상상할 수 있는 것입니다.

Step2

※ 다음 우리말과 일치하도록 빈칸에 알맞은 말을 쓰시오.

My Dream House

1 _____ you _____ _____ _____ your dream house?

2 Today, _____ _____, we _____ our dream house.

3 Here _____ some of the dream houses _____ we _____.

A House in Nature - Minho

4 _____ is my _____ _____.

5 I _____ _____ _____ when I walk in the _____.

6 I'd _____ _____ _____ a dream house _____ the _____.

7 It _____ _____ a big garden _____ _____ _____ and trees.

8 I _____ _____ _____ _____ _____ the sound of birds.

9 It will be _____ _____ _____ _____ in the morning and _____ _____ the songs of the birds.

10 Also, I'd _____ _____ _____ many pets. It will _____ _____ _____ _____ _____ them!

A Fun Place - Julie

11 _____ _____ my dream house!

12 _____ _____ is _____ I want most, so my dream house _____ _____ _____ _____ _____ .

13 It has a theater _____ _____ _____ .

14 There, I can eat cookies and _____ my _____ _____ .

15 My dream house _____ a game room _____ the _____ _____ .

내가 꿈꾸는 집

1 여러분은 꿈의 집에 대해 생각해 본 적이 있나요?

2 오늘, 우리는 수업 시간에 우리가 꿈꾸는 집을 만들었습니다.

3 여기 우리가 만든 몇몇 꿈의 집이 있습니다.

자연 속의 집 – 민호

4 자연은 나의 좋은 친구입니다.

5 나는 숲속에서 걸을 때 기분이 정말 좋습니다.

6 나는 시골에 꿈의 집을 갖고 싶습니다.

7 집에는 많은 꽃과 나무가 있는 큰 정원이 있을 것입니다.

8 나는 항상 새소리에 신이 납니다.

9 아침에 깨어나서 새들의 노래 소리를 듣는 것은 멋질 것입니다.

10 또한 나는 많은 애완동물을 갖고 싶습니다. 그들과 노는 것은 매우 재미있을 것입니다!

재미있는 장소 – Julie

11 나의 꿈의 집에 온 것을 환영합니다!

12 즐겁게 지내는 것은 내가 가장 원하는 것입니다. 그래서 내 꿈의 집은 흥미로운 것들로 가득합니다.

13 집에는 지하에 영화관이 있습니다.

14 그곳에서 나는 쿠키를 먹을 수 있고 내가 좋아하는 영화들을 즐길 수 있습니다.

15 내 꿈의 집에는 2층에 게임방이 있습니다.

16 I can play many different _____ _____ _____ there.

17 My house _____ has _____ _____.

18 I want to _____ _____ _____ _____ my friends in my house. You can be _____ _____!

A Place for Family - Misun

19 My family is _____ _____ _____ to me.

20 In my dream house, my family _____ _____ and _____.

21 _____ _____ _____, you can find a _____ _____ with my family's picture _____ it.

22 _____ you _____ the house, you will _____ _____ _____ _____.

23 My family sometimes plays _____ _____ and sings there.

24 It will _____ a garden _____ _____ _____ _____ for family picnics.

25 There, we will _____ barbecues. _____ _____ _____ my dream house?

A House with New Technology - Bryan

26 I am _____ _____ _____ of new _____.

27 I _____ _____ to use new products and technology _____.

28 When I _____ _____ my house, the front door _____ my face and _____ _____.

29 The furniture _____ the weather _____ and _____ me _____.

30 The bathroom mirror _____ _____ _____ _____ and the _____ of my health.

31 A robot _____ the house and _____ me.

32 This is _____ _____ _____ _____ about my dream house.

16 나는 그곳에서 많은 다양한 종류의 게임을 할 수 있습니다.

17 나의 집에는 또한 수영장이 있습니다.

18 나는 나의 집에서 친구들과 함께 즐거운 일들을 하고 싶습니다. 여러분도 나의 손님이 될 수 있습니다!

가족을 위한 장소 – 미선

19 나의 가족은 나에게 가장 중요한 것입니다.

20 내 꿈의 집에서 가족은 안전하고 편안함을 느낍니다.

21 현관에서 여러분은 가족 사진이 있는 아름답게 디자인된 문패를 발견할 수 있습니다.

22 여러분이 집에 들어서면 여러분은 큰 거실을 보게 될 것입니다.

23 나의 가족은 때때로 그곳에서 보드 게임도 하고 노래를 부르기도 합니다.

24 가족 소풍을 위한 커다란 피크닉 테이블이 있는 큰 정원을 갖게 될 것입니다.

25 그곳에서 우리는 바비큐를 즐길 것입니다. 내 꿈의 집이 마음에 드나요?

신기술이 있는 집 – Bryan

26 나는 남들보다 먼저 신기술을 써 보는 것을 좋아하는 사람입니다.

27 나는 새로운 제품이나 기술을 다른 사람보다 먼저 사용하는 것을 정말 좋아합니다.

28 내가 집 근처에 도착할 때, 현관문은 내 얼굴을 인식하고 자동으로 문을 엽니다.

29 가구는 날씨 상태를 확인하여 내게 무엇을 입을지 조언해 줍니다.

30 욕실 거울은 나에게 체중과 건강 상태를 알려 줍니다.

31 로봇은 집을 청소하고 나를 위해 요리합니다.

32 이것이 내가 나의 꿈의 집에 대해 상상할 수 있는 것입니다.

※ 다음 문장을 우리말로 쓰시오.

My Dream House

1 Have you ever thought about your dream house?

➡ _____

2 Today, in class, we created our dream house.

➡ _____

3 Here are some of the dream houses that we made.

➡ _____

A House in Nature - Minho

4 Nature is my good friend.

➡ _____

5 I do feel good when I walk in the forest.

➡ _____

6 I'd like to have a dream house in the countryside.

➡ _____

7 It should have a big garden with many flowers and trees.

➡ _____

8 I am always excited by the sound of birds.

➡ _____

9 It will be wonderful to wake up in the morning and listen to the songs of the birds.

➡ _____

10 Also, I'd like to have many pets. It will be fun to play with them!

➡ _____

A Fun Place - Julie

11 Welcome to my dream house!

➡ _____

12 Having fun is what I want most, so my dream house is full of exciting things.

➡ _____

13 It has a theater in the basement.

➡ _____

14 There, I can eat cookies and enjoy my favorite movies.

➡ _____

15 My dream house has a game room on the second floor.

➡ _____

16 I can play many different kinds of games there.

➡ _____

17 My house also has a swimming pool.

➡ _____

18 I want to do fun things with my friends in my house. You can be my guest!

➡ _____

A Place for Family - Misun

19 My family is the most important thing to me.

➡ _____

20 In my dream house, my family feels safe and comfortable.

➡ _____

21 At the gate, you can find a beautifully designed sign with my family's picture on it.

➡ _____

22 When you enter the house, you will see a large living room.

➡ _____

23 My family sometimes plays board games and sings there.

➡ _____

24 It will have a garden with a large picnic table for family picnics.

➡ _____

25 There, we will enjoy barbecues. Do you like my dream house?

➡ _____

A House with New Technology - Bryan

26 I am an early adopter of new technology.

➡ _____

27 I do like to use new products and technology before others.

➡ _____

28 When I get near my house, the front door recognizes my face and opens automatically.

➡ _____

29 The furniture checks the weather conditions and advises me on what to wear.

➡ _____

30 The bathroom mirror tells me my weight and the condition of my health.

➡ _____

31 A robot cleans the house and cooks for me.

➡ _____

32 This is what I can imagine about my dream house.

➡ _____

※ 다음 괄호 안의 단어들을 우리말에 맞도록 바르게 배열하시오.

My Dream House

1 (you / have / thought / ever / your / about / house? / dream)
➡ _____

2 (in / today, / class, / created / we / dream / our / house.)
➡ _____

3 (are / here / of / some / dream / the / that / houses / made. / we)
➡ _____

A House in Nature - Minho

4 (is / nature / good / my / friend.)
➡ _____

5 (do / I / feel / when / good / walk / I / the / in / forest. / in)
➡ _____

6 (like / I'd / have / to / house / a / dream / in / countryside. / the)
➡ _____

7 (should / it / a / have / big / garden / many / with / trees. / and / flowers)
➡ _____

8 (am / I / always / by / excited / the / sound / birds. / of)
➡ _____

9 (will / it / be / to / wonderful / up / wake / the / in / morning / and / to / listen / songs / the / of / birds. / the)
➡ _____

10 (I'd / also, / like / have / to / pets. / many // will / it / be / to / play / fun / them! / with)
➡ _____

A Fun Place - Julie

11 (to / welcome / dream / my / house!)
➡ _____

12 (fun / having / what / is / want / I / most, / my / so / house / dream / full / is / of / things. / exciting)
➡ _____
_____

13 (has / it / theater / a / the / in / basement.)
➡ _____

14 (I / there, / eat / can / cookies / and / my / enjoy / movies. / favorite)
➡ _____

15 (dream / my / house / a / has / game / room / the / on / floor. / second)
➡ _____

내가 꿈꾸는 집

1 여러분은 꿈의 집에 대해 생각해 본 적이 있나요?

2 오늘, 우리는 수업 시간에 우리가 꿈꾸는 집을 만들었습니다.

3 여기 우리가 만든 몇몇 꿈의 집이 있습니다.

자연 속의 집 – 민호

4 자연은 나의 좋은 친구입니다.

5 나는 숲속에서 걸을 때 기분이 정말 좋습니다.

6 나는 시골에 꿈의 집을 갖고 싶습니다.

7 집에는 많은 꽃과 나무가 있는 큰 정원이 있을 것입니다.

8 나는 항상 새소리에 신이 납니다.

9 아침에 깨어나서 새들의 노래 소리를 듣는 것은 멋질 것입니다.

10 또한 나는 많은 애완동물을 갖고 싶습니다. 그들과 노는 것은 매우 재미있을 것입니다!

재미있는 장소 – Julie

11 나의 꿈의 집에 온 것을 환영합니다!

12 즐겁게 지내는 것은 내가 가장 원하는 것입니다. 그래서 내 꿈의 집은 흥미로운 것들로 가득합니다.

13 집에는 지하에 영화관이 있습니다.

14 그곳에서 나는 쿠키를 먹을 수 있고 내가 좋아하는 영화들을 즐길 수 있습니다.

15 내 꿈의 집에는 2층에 게임방이 있습니다.

16 (can / I / play / different / many / of / kinds / games / there.)
➡ _____

17 (house / my / has / also / a / pool. / swimming)
➡ _____

18 (want / I / to / fun / do / things / with / friends / my / in / house. / my // can / you / my / be / guest!)
➡ _____

A Place for Family - Misun

19 (family / my / the / is / important / most / to / me. / thing)
➡ _____

20 (my / in / dream / house, / family / my / safe / feels / comfortable. / and)
➡ _____

21 (the / at / gate, / can / you / a / find / beautifully / sign / designed / my / family's / with / on / it. / picture)
➡ _____

22 (you / when / enter / house, / the / will / you / see / large / a / room. / living)
➡ _____

23 (family / my / plays / sometimes / games / board / and / there. / sings)
➡ _____

24 (will / it / have / garden / a / with / large / a / table / picnic / for / picnics. / family)
➡ _____

25 (we / there, / will / barbecues. / enjoy // you / do / my / like / house? / dream)
➡ _____

A House with New Technology - Bryan

26 (am / I / early / an / of / adopter / technology. / new)
➡ _____

27 (do / I / like / use / to / products / new / and / before / technology / others.)
➡ _____

28 (I / when / get / my / near / house, / front / the / recognizes / door / face / my / and / automatically. / opens)
➡ _____

29 (furniture / the / checks / weather / the / conditions / and / me / advises / what / on / wear. / to)
➡ _____

30 (bathroom / the / tells / mirror / my / me / weight / and / condition / the / my / of / health.)
➡ _____

31 (robot / a / cleans / house / the / and / for / me. / cooks)
➡ _____

32 (is / this / I / what / can / about / imagine / my / house. / dream)
➡ _____

16 나는 그곳에서 많은 다양한 종류의 게임을 할 수 있습니다.

17 나의 집에는 또한 수영장이 있습니다.

18 나는 나의 집에서 친구들과 함께 즐거운 일들을 하고 싶습니다. 여러분도 나의 손님이 될 수 있습니다!

가족을 위한 장소 – 미선

19 나의 가족은 나에게 가장 중요한 것입니다.

20 내 꿈의 집에서 가족은 안전하고 편안함을 느낍니다.

21 현관에서 여러분은 가족 사진이 있는 아름답게 디자인된 문패를 발견할 수 있습니다.

22 여러분이 집에 들어서면 여러분은 큰 거실을 보게 될 것입니다.

23 나의 가족은 때때로 그곳에서 보드 게임도 하고 노래를 부르기도 합니다.

24 가족 소풍을 위한 커다란 피크닉 테이블이 있는 큰 정원을 갖게 될 것입니다.

25 그곳에서 우리는 바비큐를 즐길 것입니다. 내 꿈의 집이 마음에 드나요?

신기술이 있는 집 – Bryan

26 나는 남들보다 먼저 신기술을 써 보는 것을 좋아하는 사람입니다.

27 나는 새로운 제품이나 기술을 다른 사람보다 먼저 사용하는 것을 정말 좋아합니다.

28 내가 집 근처에 도착할 때, 현관문은 내 얼굴을 인식하고 자동으로 문을 엽니다.

29 가구는 날씨 상태를 확인하여 내게 무엇을 입을지 조언해 줍니다.

30 욕실 거울은 나에게 체중과 건강 상태를 알려 줍니다.

31 로봇은 집을 청소하고 나를 위해 요리합니다.

32 이것이 내가 나의 꿈의 집에 대해 상상할 수 있는 것입니다.

※ 다음 우리말을 영어로 쓰시오.

My Dream House

1 여러분은 꿈의 집에 대해 생각해 본 적이 있나요?

➡ _____

2 오늘, 우리는 수업 시간에 우리가 꿈꾸는 집을 만들었습니다.

➡ _____

3 여기 우리가 만든 몇몇 꿈의 집이 있습니다.

➡ _____

A House in Nature - Minho

4 자연은 나의 좋은 친구입니다.

➡ _____

5 나는 숲속에서 걸을 때 기분이 정말 좋습니다.

➡ _____

6 나는 시골에 꿈의 집을 갖고 싶습니다.

➡ _____

7 집에는 많은 꽃과 나무가 있는 큰 정원이 있을 것입니다.

➡ _____

8 나는 항상 새소리에 신이 납니다.

➡ _____

9 아침에 깨어나서 새들의 노래 소리를 듣는 것은 멋질 것입니다.

➡ _____

10 또한 나는 많은 애완동물을 갖고 싶습니다. 그들과 노는 것은 매우 재미있을 것입니다!

➡ _____

A Fun Place - Julie

11 나의 꿈의 집에 온 것을 환영합니다!

➡ _____

12 즐겁게 지내는 것은 내가 가장 원하는 것입니다. 그래서 내 꿈의 집은 흥미로운 것들로 가득합니다.

➡ _____

13 집에는 지하에 영화관이 있습니다.

➡ _____

14 그곳에서 나는 쿠키를 먹을 수 있고 내가 좋아하는 영화들을 즐길 수 있습니다.

➡ _____

15 내 꿈의 집에는 2층에 게임방이 있습니다.

➡ _____

16 나는 그곳에서 많은 다양한 종류의 게임을 할 수 있습니다.

➡ _____

17 나의 집에는 또한 수영장이 있습니다.

➡ _____

18 나는 나의 집에서 친구들과 함께 즐거운 일들을 하고 싶습니다. 여러분도 나의 손님이 될 수 있습니다!

➡ _____

A Place for Family - Misun

19 나의 가족은 나에게 가장 중요한 것입니다.

➡ _____

20 내 꿈의 집에서 가족은 안전하고 편안함을 느낍니다.

➡ _____

21 현관에서 여러분은 가족 사진이 있는 아름답게 디자인된 문패를 발견할 수 있습니다.

➡ _____

22 여러분이 집에 들어서면 여러분은 큰 거실을 보게 될 것입니다.

➡ _____

23 나의 가족은 때때로 그곳에서 보드 게임도 하고 노래를 부르기도 합니다.

➡ _____

24 가족 소풍을 위한 커다란 피크닉 테이블이 있는 큰 정원을 갖게 될 것입니다.

➡ _____

25 그곳에서 우리는 바비큐를 즐길 것입니다. 내 꿈의 집이 마음에 드나요?

➡ _____

A House with New Technology - Bryan

26 나는 남들보다 먼저 신기술을 써 보는 것을 좋아하는 사람입니다.

➡ _____

27 나는 새로운 제품이나 기술을 다른 사람보다 먼저 사용하는 것을 정말 좋아합니다.

➡ _____

28 내가 집 근처에 도착할 때, 현관문은 내 얼굴을 인식하고 자동으로 문을 엽니다.

➡ _____

29 가구는 날씨 상태를 확인하여 내게 무엇을 입을지 조언해 줍니다.

➡ _____

30 욕실 거울은 나에게 체중과 건강 상태를 알려 줍니다.

➡ _____

31 로봇은 집을 청소하고 나를 위해 요리합니다.

➡ _____

32 이것이 내가 나의 꿈의 집에 대해 상상할 수 있는 것입니다.

➡ _____

※ 다음 우리말과 일치하도록 빈칸에 알맞은 말을 쓰시오.

After You Read - Read and Match

1. I like _____ _____ new _____ and _____.

2. _____ _____ m a n y i t e m s _____ _____ _____ _____ in my dream house.

3. _____ _____ my furniture _____ the weather and tells me _____ _____ _____.

4. A robot _____ _____ _____.

1. 나는 새로운 제품과 기술을 이용하는 것이 좋다.
2. 내가 꿈꾸는 집에는 새로운 기술을 이용하는 물건들이 많이 있다.
3. 매일 내 가구들은 날씨를 확인해서 내가 무엇을 입을지 말해 준다.
4. 로봇은 나에게 요리를 해 준다.

Project Step 1

1. A: We _____ _____ _____ know more about you, Minho. What is your _____ _____?

2. B: I _____ pizza _____.

3. C: _____ you _____ _____ _____ your favorite _____?

4. B: Art is _____ I _____ _____. I _____ _____ _____ an art teacher _____ Mr. Kim.

5. D: _____ do you _____ _____ _____ after school?

6. B: I _____ _____ _____ taegwondo and _____ songs.

1. A: 우리는 너에 대해서 더 많이 알고 싶어, 민호야. 네가 가장 좋아하는 음식은 뭐니?
2. B: 나는 피자를 가장 좋아해.
3. C: 나에게 네가 가장 좋아하는 과목에 대해 말해 줄 수 있니?
4. B: 미술이 내가 가장 좋아하는 거야. 나는 김 선생님과 같은 미술 선생님이 되고 싶어.
5. D: 너는 방과 후에 무엇을 하는 것을 좋아하니?
6. B: 나는 태권도를 연습하고, 노래 부르는 것을 좋아해.

Project Step 3

1. We _____ an M and an H _____ _____ Minho _____.

2. Minho likes art and pizza, _____ we made an M _____ a _____ _____, _____ pencils, and _____ _____ _____ pizza.

3. We _____ an H _____ a _____ _____ and taegwondo.

1. 우리는 민호가 좋아하는 것으로 M과 H를 만들었습니다.
2. 민호는 예술과 피자를 좋아합니다. 그래서 우리는 붓, 색연필, 그리고 피자 조각으로 M을 만들었습니다.
3. 우리는 태권도와 음표로 H를 만들었습니다.

※ 다음 우리말을 영어로 쓰시오.

After You Read - Read and Match

1. 나는 새로운 제품과 기술을 이용하는 것이 좋다.

   ➡ _____

2. 내가 꿈꾸는 집에는 새로운 기술을 이용하는 물건들이 많이 있다.

   ➡ _____

3. 매일 내 가구들은 날씨를 확인해서 내가 무엇을 입을지 말해 준다.

   ➡ _____

4. 로봇은 나에게 요리를 해 준다.

   ➡ _____

Project Step 1

1. A: 우리는 너에 대해서 더 많이 알고 싶어, 민호야. 네가 가장 좋아하는 음식은 뭐니?

   ➡ _____

2. B: 나는 피자를 가장 좋아해.

   ➡ _____

3. C: 나에게 네가 가장 좋아하는 과목에 대해 말해 줄 수 있니?

   ➡ _____

4. B: 미술이 내가 가장 좋아하는 거야. 나는 김 선생님과 같은 미술 선생님이 되고 싶어.

   ➡ _____

5. D: 너는 방과 후에 무엇을 하는 것을 좋아하니?

   ➡ _____

6. B: 나는 태권도를 연습하고, 노래 부르는 것을 좋아해.

   ➡ _____

Project Step 3

1. 우리는 민호가 좋아하는 것으로 M과 H를 만들었습니다.

   ➡ _____

2. 민호는 예술과 피자를 좋아합니다. 그래서 우리는 붓, 색연필, 그리고 피자 조각으로 M을 만들었습니다.

   ➡ _____

3. 우리는 태권도와 음표로 H를 만들었습니다.

   ➡ _____

※ 다음 영어를 우리말로 쓰시오.

01 greet

02 bowl

03 place

04 correctly

05 since

06 differ

07 elderly

08 temple

09 experience

10 finally

11 address

12 state

13 goods

14 rate

15 serve

16 present

17 prepare

18 difference

19 hand

20 negative question

21 pack

22 tongue

23 pay

24 exchange

25 uncomfortable

26 wave

27 bump

28 postal code

29 tax

30 entrance fee

31 price tag

32 sales tax

33 death

34 wrap

35 get used to ~

36 between A and B

37 in response to

38 have a bad effect on

39 be regarded as

40 the same as ~

41 remember to V

42 range from A to B

43 place 목적어 together

※ 다음 우리말을 영어로 쓰시오.

01 그릇		22 판매세	
02 긍정의문문		23 우편 번호	
03 죽음		24 세금	
04 율, 비율		25 주	
05 입장료		26 다르다	
06 준비하다		27 (손을) 흔들다	
07 상품, 제품		28 ~에게 인사하다	
08 차이		29 사원	
09 놓다		30 경험하다	
10 주소		31 전통적인	
11 지불하다		32 제공하다, 대접하다	
12 선물		33 문화의, 문화적인	
13 나이 든		34 불편한	
14 가격표		35 서로	
15 부딪치다		36 ~의 대답으로	
16 교환하다, 환전하다		37 ~로 여겨지다	
17 정확하게, 올바르게		38 ~에 익숙해지다	
18 손님		39 반드시 ~하다	
19 마지막으로		40 (범위가) A에서 B에 이르다	
20 포장하다, 싸다		41 A와 B 사이에	
21 혀		42 ~할 것을 기억하다	
		43 ~에 나쁜 영향을 미치다	

※ 다음 영영풀이에 알맞은 단어를 <보기>에서 골라 쓴 후, 우리말 뜻을 쓰시오.

1 _____ : not polite: _____

2 _____ : things for sale, or the things that you own: _____

3 _____ : a tax paid by people when they buy goods or services: _____

4 _____ : to cover or surround something with paper, cloth, or other material:

_____

5 _____ : to raise your hand and move it from side to side as a way of greeting

someone: _____

6 _____ : to hurt part of your body by hitting it against something hard:

_____

7 _____ : to give something to someone and receive something from that person:

_____

8 _____ : not feeling comfortable and pleasant, or not making you feel comfortable

and pleasant: _____

9 _____ : the number of the house, name of the road, and name of the town where

a person lives or works, and where letters can be sent: _____

10 _____ : in a way that is in agreement with the true facts or with what is generally

accepted: _____

11 _____ : an amount of money that you pay in order to be allowed into a cinema,

theater, etc.: _____

12 _____ : an opinion that someone offers you about what you should do or how

you should act in a particular situation: _____

13 _____ : a short series of letters and numbers that is part of an address, and shows

exactly where a place is: _____

14 _____ : a small piece of paper, cloth, or metal with information on it, tied or

stuck onto something larger: _____

15 _____ : money paid to the government that is based on your income or the cost of

goods or services you have bought: _____

16 _____ : following or belonging to the customs or ways of behaving that have

continued in a group of people or society for a long time without

changing: _____

보기			
uncomfortable	traditional	bump	wave
rude	address	sales tax	postal code
exchange	tax	entrance fee	tag
goods	correctly	wrap	advice

※ 다음 우리말과 일치하도록 빈칸에 알맞은 말을 쓰시오.

Warm Up

1. People _____ _____ _____ in _____ .
2. People _____ their hands _____ and say "Namaste" in _____ .
3. Men _____ _____ _____ in the United Arab Emirates.

1. 티베트 사람들은 그들의 혀를 보여준다.
2. 인도 사람들은 손을 모으고 "나마스테"라고 말한다.
3. 아랍에미리트에서 남자들은 코를 부딪친다.

Listen & Speak 1 A

1. G: I want _____ _____ this to my _____ in the USA.
   B: _____ is it?
   G: It's her *hanbok*. Can I _____ your _____ on _____ _____ _____ an _____ _____ ?
   B: Sure. You _____ _____ the _____ _____ first.
   G: _____ this?
   B: Yes. Then, write the name of the city and the _____ and then the _____ _____ . _____ , write the _____ .
   G: Thanks _____ your _____ .

2. G: _____ the people _____ _____ Moroccan clothes. They are really beautiful. I want _____ _____ _____ _____ them.
   M: Wait. _____ _____ an important thing you _____ know _____ _____ pictures.
   G: Oh, really? Can I _____ your _____ _____ it?
   M: Yes. You _____ _____ _____ _____ _____ _____ people _____ _____ .
   G: Why?
   M: They _____ it may have _____ _____ _____ them _____ someone takes their picture.

1. G: 나는 이것을 미국에 계신 이모에게 보내고 싶어.
   B: 그게 뭔데?
   G: 이모의 한복이야. 영어로 주소를 어떻게 쓰는지에 대해 내가 너의 조언을 구할 수 있을까?
   B: 물론이지. 먼저 거리 주소부터 적어야 해.
   G: 이렇게?
   B: 응. 그러고 나서, 도시 이름과 주 그리고 그 다음에 우편 번호를 적어. 마지막으로 국가를 적어.
   G: 도와줘서 고마워.

2. G: 모로코 전통 의상을 입고 있는 사람들을 보세요. 그들은 매우 아름다워요. 그들의 사진을 찍고 싶어요.
   M: 잠깐. 네가 사진을 찍기 전에 알아야 할 중요한 것이 있어.
   G: 오, 정말요? 그것에 대해 조언을 구할 수 있을까요?
   M: 응. 너는 물어보지 않고 모로코 사람들의 사진을 찍으면 안 돼.
   G: 왜요?
   M: 그들은 누군가가 자신의 사진을 찍으면 그것이 그들에게 나쁜 영향을 끼칠 것이라고 믿어.

Listen & Speak 1 B

A: _____ _____ _____ your _____ on _____ the Netherlands?
B: Sure. You _____ _____ on a bike _____ .
A: Can I _____ _____ _____ the USA?
B: Sure. You _____ _____ in the _____ _____ in the taxi.

A: 네덜란드를 방문하는 것에 대해 너의 조언을 구할 수 있을까?
B: 물론이지. 너는 자전거 도로에 서 있으면 안 돼.

A: 미국을 방문하는 것에 대해 너의 조언을 구할 수 있을까?
B: 물론이지. 택시에서는 뒷좌석에 앉아야 해.

Listen & Speak 2 A

1. **B:** Sena, I _____ a _____ for Ms. Han. I _____ _____ at her house here in Korea.

   G: That's great. _____ did you _____ her?

   B: I _____ her a hat. Do you _____ she'll love it?

   G: Yes. _____ _____ you use two hands _____ you it _____ her.

   B: Why?

   G: Because _____ something to _____ people _____ one hand _____ _____ _____ _____ in Korea.

   B: Okay. I'll _____ that.

2. **B:** Did you _____ _____ you _____ for the trip _____ Thailand tomorrow?

   G: Not _____. What _____ I _____?

   B: _____ _____ _____ a pair of long _____ or a long _____.

   G: Why? It's very hot in Thailand, _____ it?

   B: Yes, but _____ _____ many _____ in Thailand. You _____ _____ _____ when you visit a _____.

   G: Okay. Is there _____ _____?

   B: _____ _____ you _____ Korean won _____ Thai baht.

Listen & Speak 2 B

A: Is there _____ I need to _____ when I eat in _____?

B: Yes. _____ _____ you _____ your hands _____ the table _____ _____ _____.

A: Is there _____ I _____ _____ remember _____ I eat in Uzbekistan?

B: Yes. _____ _____ you _____ _____ _____ your hat or shoes _____ _____ a meal.

Real Life Talk

Seho: My _____ friend _____ me _____ his house for dinner this Friday.

Bora: That's good. I hope you _____ _____ dinner at his house.

Seho: I want to _____ a small _____ for him. You lived in China _____ _____ years. Can I get your _____ on _____ _____ _____?

Bora: _____ _____ some tea?

Seho: Tea?

Bora: Yes. _____ Chinese people like to _____ tea _____ a _____. They _____ _____ tea. Also, they _____ _____ tea to _____.

Seho: Oh, thanks. Is there _____ else _____ I know?

Bora: _____ _____ _____ _____ _____ the present in white or black paper. White and black _____ _____ in China.

Seho: Okay. I'll _____ that. Thank you for the _____.

Communication Task Step 2

A: _____ _____ would you _____ _____ _____?

B: I'd like to visit Malaysia. Can I _____ your _____ on there?

C: Sure. _____ _____ you _____ _____ your _____ _____ _____ _____ something to someone.

B: Okay. Thanks.

Wrap Up

1. **B:** I'm _____ to Japan this summer. Can I _____ some _____ on _____ there?

   G: Make sure you _____ when you _____ _____ the bus.

   B: Oh, I didn't know that. Are there any _____ _____ I should _____?

   G: _____ _____ the bowl and _____ it _____ _____. Also, _____ _____ soup, you _____ drink it _____ a spoon.

   B: Okay. Thanks.

2. **M:** I want _____ _____ flowers to my friend _____ Russia. Is there _____ I _____ _____?

   W: _____ _____ you don't give flowers in even numbers.

세호: 그에게 줄 작은 선물을 준비하고 싶어. 너는 몇 년 동안 중국에 살았지. 무엇을 가져가야 할지 조언을 구해도 될까?

보라: 차를 가져가는 게 어때?

세호: 차?

보라: 응. 중국 사람들 대부분은 선물로 차를 받는 것을 좋아해. 그들은 차 마시는 것을 즐기거든. 또 그들은 대개 손님들에게 차를 대접해.

세호: 오, 고마워. 내가 알아야 할 또 다른 것이 있을까?

보라: 선물을 흰색이나 검은색 종이로 포장하지 않도록 해. 흰색과 검은색은 중국에서 죽음을 의미해.

세호: 알겠어. 기억할게. 조언해 줘서 고마워.

A: 너는 어떤 나라를 방문하고 싶니?

B: 나는 말레이시아를 방문하고 싶어. 그곳을 여행하는 것에 대해 너의 조언을 구할 수 있을까?

C: 물론이지. 누군가에게 무엇을 건넬 때 절대 왼손을 사용하지 않도록 해.

B: 알겠어. 고마워.

1. B: 나는 이번 여름에 일본에 갈 거야. 그곳을 방문하는 것에 대해 몇 가지 조언을 구할 수 있을까?

   G: 반드시 버스에서 내릴 때 돈을 내도록 해.

   B: 오, 그걸 몰랐어. 내가 기억해야 할 다른 것들이 또 있니?

   G: 먹는 동안에는 그릇을 들어올리고 그것을 잡고 있어. 또한 국을 먹을 때, 숟가락 없이 그것을 마셔야 해.

   B: 알겠어. 고마워.

2. M: 나는 러시아에서 온 내 친구에게 꽃을 주고 싶어. 내가 기억해야 하는 것이 있니?

   W: 짝수로 꽃을 주지 않도록 해라.

※ 다음 우리말에 맞도록 대화를 영어로 쓰시오.

Warm Up

1. _____
2. _____
3. _____

1. 티베트 사람들은 그들의 혀를 보여준다.
2. 인도 사람들은 손을 모으고 "나마스테"라고 말한다.
3. 아랍에미리트에서 남자들은 코를 부딪친다.

Listen & Speak 1 A

1. G: _____
   B: _____
   G: _____
   B: _____
   G: _____
   B: _____
   G: _____

2. G: _____
   M: _____
   G: _____
   M: _____
   G: _____
   M: _____

1. G: 나는 이것을 미국에 계신 이모에게 보내고 싶어.
   B: 그게 뭔데?
   G: 이모의 한복이야. 영어로 주소를 어떻게 쓰는지에 대해 내가 너의 조언을 구할 수 있을까?
   B: 물론이지. 먼저 거리 주소부터 적어야 해.
   G: 이렇게?
   B: 응. 그러고 나서, 도시 이름과 주 그리고 그 다음에 우편 번호를 적어. 마지막으로 국가를 적어.
   G: 도와줘서 고마워.

2. G: 모로코 전통 의상을 입고 있는 사람들을 보세요. 그들은 매우 아름다워요. 그들의 사진을 찍고 싶어요.
   M: 잠깐. 네가 사진을 찍기 전에 알아야 할 중요한 것이 있어.
   G: 오, 정말요? 그것에 대해 조언을 구할 수 있을까요?
   M: 응. 너는 물어보지 않고 모로코 사람들의 사진을 찍으면 안 돼.
   G: 왜요?
   M: 그들은 누군가가 자신의 사진을 찍으면 그것이 그들에게 나쁜 영향을 끼칠 것이라고 믿어.

Listen & Speak 1 B

A: _____
B: _____
A: _____
B: _____

A: 네덜란드를 방문하는 것에 대해 너의 조언을 구할 수 있을까?
B: 물론이지. 너는 자전거 도로에 서 있으면 안 돼.

A: 미국을 방문하는 것에 대해 너의 조언을 구할 수 있을까?
B: 물론이지. 택시에서는 뒷좌석에 앉아야 해.

Listen & Speak 2 A

1. B: _____
   _____
   G: _____
   B: _____
   G: _____
   B: _____
   G: _____
   _____
   B: _____

2. B: _____
   G: _____
   B: _____
   G: _____
   B: _____
   _____
   G: _____
   B: _____

Listen & Speak 2 B

A: _____
B: _____
A: _____
B: _____

Real Life Talk

Seho: _____
Bora: _____

1. B: 세나야, 나 한 씨 아주머니께 드릴 선물을 샀어. 이곳 한국에서 그녀의 집에 머물고 있거든.
   G: 그거 잘 됐네. 그녀를 위해 무엇을 샀니?
   B: 모자를 샀어. 그녀가 그것을 좋아할 거라고 생각하니?
   G: 응. 그녀에게 그것을 건넬 때 반드시 두 손으로 건네도록 해.
   B: 왜?
   G: 연장자에게 한 손으로 무언가를 주는 것은 한국에서 무례한 것으로 여겨지거든.
   B: 알겠어. 그걸 기억할게.

2. B: 너는 내일 태국 여행에 필요한 모든 것을 챙겼니?
   G: 아니 아직. 무엇을 가져가야 할까?
   B: 긴 바지나 긴 치마를 한 벌 가져가는 것을 기억해.
   G: 왜? 태국은 매우 덥잖아, 그렇지 않니?
   B: 응, 하지만 태국에는 절이 많아. 너는 절을 방문할 때 반바지를 입으면 안 돼.
   G: 알겠어. 다른 것이 또 있니?
   B: 반드시 한국 원화를 태국 바트로 환전하도록 해.

A: 내가 프랑스에서 식사할 때 기억해야 할 것이 있니?
B: 응. 반드시 항상 손을 식탁 위에 올려두도록 해.

A: 내가 우즈베키스탄에서 식사할 때 기억해야 할 것이 있니?
B: 응. 식사할 때 모자나 신발을 절대 벗지 않도록 해.

세호: 나의 중국인 친구가 이번 주 금요일 저녁 식사에 나를 집으로 초대했어.
보라: 좋네. 그 친구 집에서 네가 즐거운 저녁 식사하기를 바라.

Seho: _____

_____

Bora: _____

Seho: _____

Bora: _____

_____

Seho: _____

Bora: _____

_____

Seho: _____

세호: 그에게 줄 작은 선물을 준비하고 싶어. 너는 몇 년 동안 중국에 살았지. 무엇을 가져가야 할지 조언을 구해도 될까?

보라: 차를 가져가는 게 어때?

세호: 차?

보라: 응. 중국 사람들 대부분은 선물로 차를 받는 것을 좋아해. 그들은 차 마시는 것을 즐기거든. 또 그들은 대개 손님들에게 차를 대접해.

세호: 오, 고마워. 내가 알아야 할 또 다른 것이 있을까?

보라: 선물을 흰색이나 검은색 종이로 포장하지 않도록 해. 흰색과 검은색은 중국에서 죽음을 의미해.

세호: 알겠어. 기억할게. 조언해 줘서 고마워.

Communication Task Step 2

A: _____

B: _____

C: _____

B: _____

A: 너는 어떤 나라를 방문하고 싶니?

B: 나는 말레이시아를 방문하고 싶어. 그곳을 여행하는 것에 대해 너의 조언을 구할 수 있을까?

C: 물론이지. 누군가에게 무엇을 건넬 때 절대 왼손을 사용하지 않도록 해.

B: 알겠어. 고마워.

Wrap Up

1. B: _____

G: _____

B: _____

G: _____

B: _____

2. M: _____

W: _____

1. B: 나는 이번 여름에 일본에 갈 거야. 그곳을 방문하는 것에 대해 몇 가지 조언을 구할 수 있을까?

G: 반드시 버스에서 내릴 때 돈을 내도록 해.

B: 오, 그걸 몰랐어. 내가 기억해야 할 다른 것들이 또 있니?

G: 먹는 동안에는 그릇을 들어올리고 그것을 잡고 있어. 또한 국을 먹을 때, 숟가락 없이 그것을 마셔야 해.

B: 알겠어. 고마워.

2. M: 나는 러시아에서 온 내 친구에게 꽃을 주고 싶어. 내가 기억해야 하는 것이 있니?

W: 짝수로 꽃을 주지 않도록 해라.

※ 다음 우리말과 일치하도록 빈칸에 알맞은 것을 골라 쓰시오.

Let's Learn about Cultural Differences

1 Hi! My name is Kim Minhee. I _____ _____ _____ in America _____ three years.

    A. living   B. for   C. have   D. been

2 _____ my family moved here, I have _____ many cultural differences _____ Korea _____ America.

    A. between   B. since   C. and   D. experienced

3 I _____ _____ to _____ some of them _____ you.

    A. like   B. with   C. would   D. share

4 Minhee: Look _____ this shirt. I like _____.

    A. it   B. at

5 Linda: It _____ _____. How _____ is it?

    A. nice   B. much   C. looks

6 Minhee: It's 19 _____ and 99 _____.

    A. cents   B. dollars

7 Linda: That's _____ _____.

    A. expensive   B. not

8 Minhee: Yes, I _____. I want to _____ _____.

    A. buy   B. agree   C. it

9 Clerk: That'll _____ 21 _____ and 20 _____.

    A. dollars   B. be   C. cents

10 Minhee: Really? But the _____ _____ says it's _____ 19 dollars and 99 cents.

    A. only   B. tag   C. price

11 Here in America, in most _____, people _____ a _____ when they buy _____.

    A. goods   B. tax   C. states   D. pay

12 It is _____ a _____ tax. Sales tax _____ _____ by state.

    A. differ   B. called   C. rates   D. sales

13 They _____ from _____ _____ one percent to _____ than ten percent.

    A. more   B. less   C. range   D. than

14 So when you buy _____ in America, you usually need to _____ more than the _____ on the _____.

    A. price   B. goods   C. tag   D. pay

문화적 차이에 대해서 배우자

1 안녕! 내 이름은 김민희야. 나는 미국에 3년 동안 살고 있어.

2 우리 가족이 이곳으로 이민을 온 이후로 나는 한국과 미국의 많은 문화적 차이를 경험하고 있어.

3 나는 그것들 중 몇 가지를 너희들과 공유하고 싶어.

4 민희: 이 셔츠를 봐. 마음에 들어.

5 Linda: 멋져 보인다. 얼마야?

6 민희: 19달러 99센트야.

7 Linda: 비싸지 않네.

8 민희: 응, 나도 그렇게 생각해. 그것을 사고 싶어.

9 점원: 21달러 20센트입니다.

10 민희: 정말이요? 하지만 가격표에는 단지 19달러 99센트라고 쓰여 있는데요.

11 이곳 미국에서는 대부분의 주에서 사람들이 물건을 구입할 때 세금을 내.

12 그것은 판매세라고 불려. 판매세의 비율은 주마다 달라.

13 판매세는 1퍼센트 미만부터 10퍼센트 이상까지 다양해.

14 그래서 미국에서 상품을 살 때, 대개 가격표에 있는 가격보다 더 많은 돈을 지불해야 해.

15 Jessica: Hi, _____ Johnson! Minhee: _____, Mrs. Johnson!
A. hello   B. Mrs.

16 Mrs. Johnson: _____, Jessica! Hi, Minhee! _____ are you?
A. how   B. hi

17 Jessica: Fine, thank you. We are here _____ a burger. _____ your _____.
A. enjoy   B. for   C. meal

18 Mrs. Johnson: _____ you. You, _____!
A. too   B. thank

19 Minhee: Jessica, _____ did you _____ _____ Mrs. Johnson?
A. wave   B. why   C. to

20 In America, people often _____ each _____ by _____.
A. waving   B. other   C. greet

21 _____ to an older person is not _____ _____ rude.
A. regarded   B. waving   C. as

22 When you come to America, you may _____ _____ about it at first, but why _____ you _____ it?
A. uncomfortable   B. don't   C. feel   D. try

23 You can _____ to and smile _____ an _____ man walking on the street. He may wave _____.
A. back   B. at   C. wave   D. elderly

24 Andy: Minhee, _____ this apple _____
A. pie   B. try

25 Minhee: No, _____. I don't _____ _____.
A. to   B. thanks   C. want

26 Andy: Why _____? _____ you _____ apple pie?
A. don't   B. like   C. not

27 _____: _____.
A. yes   B. Minhee

28 Andy: Then, _____ _____. It's _____.
A. some   B. delicious   C. try

15 Jessica: 안녕하세요, Johnson 할머니! 민희: 안녕하세요, Johnson 할머니!

16 Mrs. Johnson: 안녕, Jessica! 안녕, 민희! 잘 지내지?

17 Jessica: 잘 지내요, 감사합니다. 저희는 여기 버거 먹으러 왔어요. 식사 맛있게 하세요.

18 Mrs. Johnson: 고맙구나. 너희들도!

19 민희: Jessica, 왜 너는 Johnson 할머니께 손을 흔들었니?

20 미국에서 사람들은 종종 손을 흔들며 서로에게 인사해.

21 나이가 많은 사람에게 손을 흔드는 것은 무례하다고 여겨지지 않아.

22 네가 미국에 오면 처음에는 그것에 대해 불편하게 느낄 수 있어. 하지만 한번 시도해 보지 않을래?

23 너는 길을 걷고 있는 연세가 많으신 할아버지께 손을 흔들며 미소를 지어도 돼. 그도 너한테 답례로 손을 흔들지도 몰라.

24 Andy: 민희, 이 사과 파이 좀 먹어 봐.

25 민희: 아니야, 고마워. 먹고 싶지 않아.

26 Andy: 왜 안 먹어? 너는 사과 파이를 좋아하지 않니?

27 민희: 응.

28 Andy: 그러면, 좀 먹어 봐. 맛있어.

29 Minhee: No. I _____ _____ I _____ like apple pie.

    A. said   B. just   C. don't

30 _____ : _____ ?

    A. what   B. Andy

31 Americans often ask _____ questions, such _____ " _____ you coming?" and " _____ you go to the hospital?"

    A. aren't   B. as   C. negative   D. didn't

32 It can be _____ to answer _____ questions _____ . Here is some _____ .

    A. correctly   B. difficult   C. advice   D. negative

33 In _____ to negative questions, _____ _____ "Don't you like apple pie?" you should answer "No," _____ you don't like it.

    A. as   B. if   C. response   D. such

34 And you _____ _____ "Yes," if you _____ it.

    A. answer   B. like   C. should

35 These answers are the _____ _____ the answers to _____ _____ , such as "Do you like apple pie?"

    A. positive   B. as   C. questions   D. same

36 Which _____ _____ is most _____ to you?

    A. surprising   B. difference   C. cultural

37 I have _____ _____ about cultural _____ _____ I came to America.

    A. learning   B. since   C. been   D. differences

38 Some _____ me at first, but now I am _____ _____ them.

    A. to   B. used   C. surprised   D. getting

---

29 민희: 아니. 내가 사과 파이를 좋아하지 않는다고 방금 말했잖아.

30 Andy: 뭐라고?

31 미국 사람들은 종종 "너 안 오니?", "너 병원 안 갔니?"와 같은 부정의문문으로 질문해.

32 부정의문문에 바르게 대답하는 것은 어려울 수 있어. 여기 약간의 충고 사항이 있어.

33 "너는 사과 파이를 좋아하지 않니?"와 같은 부정의문문의 대답으로 만약 사과 파이를 좋아하지 않는다면 너는 "No."라고 대답해야 해.

34 그리고 만약 그것을 좋아한다면 "Yes."라고 대답해야 해.

35 이 대답들은 "너는 애플파이를 좋아하니?"와 같은 긍정의문문에 대한 대답들과 같아.

36 어떤 문화적인 차이가 너에게 가장 놀랍니?

37 나는 미국에 온 이후로 문화적인 차이에 대해 계속 배우고 있어.

38 어떤 것들은 처음에 나를 놀라게 했지만, 지금은 그것들에 익숙해지고 있어.

※ 다음 우리말과 일치하도록 빈칸에 알맞은 말을 쓰시오.

Let's Learn about Cultural Differences

1 Hi! My name is Kim Minhee. I _____ _____ _____ in America _____ _____ _____ .

2 _____ my family moved here, I _____ _____ many cultural _____ _____ Korea _____ America.

3 I _____ _____ _____ _____ some of them with you.

4 Minhee: _____ _____ this shirt. I like _____ .

5 Linda: It _____ _____ . _____ _____ is it?

6 Minhee: It's 19 _____ and 99 _____ .

7 Linda: That's _____ _____ .

8 Minhee: Yes, I _____ . I want _____ _____ _____ .

9 Clerk: That'll _____ 21 _____ and 20 _____ .

10 Minhee: Really? But _____ _____ _____ _____ it's _____ 19 dollars and 99 cents.

11 Here in America, in _____ _____ , people _____ _____ _____ when they buy _____ .

12 It _____ _____ a _____ _____ . Sales tax _____ _____ _____ _____ .

13 They _____ from _____ one percent to _____ _____ ten percent.

14 So when you _____ _____ in America, you _____ _____ _____ _____ more than the price on the tag.

1 안녕! 내 이름은 김민희야. 나는 미국에 3년 동안 살고 있어.

2 우리 가족이 이곳으로 이민을 온 이후로 나는 한국과 미국의 많은 문화적 차이를 경험하고 있어.

3 나는 그것들 중 몇 가지를 너희들과 공유하고 싶어.

4 민희: 이 셔츠를 봐. 마음에 들어.

5 Linda: 멋져 보인다. 얼마야?

6 민희: 19달러 99센트야.

7 Linda: 비싸지 않네.

8 민희: 응, 나도 그렇게 생각해. 그것을 사고 싶어.

9 점원: 21달러 20센트입니다.

10 민희: 정말이요? 하지만 가격표에는 단지 19달러 99센트라고 쓰여 있는데요.

11 이곳 미국에서는 대부분의 주에서 사람들이 물건을 구입할 때 세금을 내.

12 그것은 판매세라고 불려. 판매세의 비율은 주마다 달라.

13 판매세는 1퍼센트 미만부터 10퍼센트 이상까지 다양해.

14 그래서 미국에서 상품을 살 때, 대개 가격표에 있는 가격보다 더 많은 돈을 지불해야 해.

15 Jessica: Hi, _____ Johnson! Minhee: Hello, _____ Johnson!

16 Mrs. Johnson: Hi, Jessica! Hi, Minhee! _____ are you?

17 Jessica: Fine, thank you. We are here _____ a burger. _____ _____ _____.

18 Mrs. Johnson: Thank you. You, _____!

19 Minhee: Jessica, _____ _____ you _____ _____ Mrs. Johnson?

20 In America, people _____ _____ _____ _____ by _____.

21 _____ to an older person _____ not _____ _____ _____.

22 When you come to America, you may _____ _____ about it at first, but _____ _____ you _____ _____?

23 You can _____ _____ and _____ _____ an _____ man _____ on the street. He may _____ _____.

24 Andy: Minhee, _____ this _____ _____.

25 Minhee: No, _____. I don't _____ _____.

26 Andy: Why _____? _____ you like apple pie?

27 Minhee: _____.

28 Andy: Then, _____ _____. It's _____.

---

15 Jessica: 안녕하세요, Johnson 할머니! 민희: 안녕하세요, Johnson 할머니!

16 Mrs. Johnson: 안녕, Jessica! 안녕, 민희! 잘 지내지?

17 Jessica: 잘 지내요, 감사합니다. 저희는 여기 버거 먹으러 왔어요. 식사 맛있게 하세요.

18 Mrs. Johnson: 고맙구나. 너희들도!

19 민희: Jessica, 왜 너는 Johnson 할머니께 손을 흔들었니?

20 미국에서 사람들은 종종 손을 흔들며 서로에게 인사해.

21 나이가 많은 사람에게 손을 흔드는 것은 무례하다고 여겨지지 않아.

22 네가 미국에 오면 처음에는 그것에 대해 불편하게 느낄 수 있어. 하지만 한번 시도해 보지 않을래?

23 너는 길을 걷고 있는 연세가 많으신 할아버지께 손을 흔들며 미소를 지어도 돼. 그도 너한테 답례로 손을 흔들지도 몰라.

24 Andy: 민희, 이 사과 파이 좀 먹어 봐.

25 민희: 아니야, 고마워. 먹고 싶지 않아.

26 Andy: 왜 안 먹어? 너는 사과 파이를 좋아하지 않니?

27 민희: 응.

28 Andy: 그러면, 좀 먹어 봐. 맛있어.

29 Minhee: No. I _____ said I _____ _____ apple pie.

30 Andy: _____?

31 Americans _____ _____ _____ _____, such as
"_____ you coming?" and "_____ you _____ to the
hospital?"

32 _____ can be difficult _____ _____ negative questions
_____. Here _____ some advice.

33 In response to _____ _____, _____ _____ "Don't you
like apple pie?" you should _____ "_____," if you don't
like it.

34 And you _____ _____ "_____," _____ you like it.

35 These answers are _____ _____ _____ the answers
_____ _____ _____, such as "Do you like apple pie?"

36 _____ _____ _____ is most _____ to you?

37 I _____ _____ _____ about _____ _____ _____
I came to America.

38 Some _____ me _____ _____, but now I _____
_____ _____ _____ them.

29 민희: 아니. 내가 사과 파이를 좋아하지 않는다고 방금 말했잖아.

30 Andy: 뭐라고?

31 미국 사람들은 종종 "너 안 오니?", "너 병원 안 갔니?"와 같은 부정의문문으로 질문해.

32 부정의문문에 바르게 대답하는 것은 어려울 수 있어. 여기 약간의 충고 사항이 있어.

33 "너는 사과 파이를 좋아하지 않니?"와 같은 부정의문문의 대답으로 만약 사과 파이를 좋아하지 않는다면 너는 "No."라고 대답해야 해.

34 그리고 만약 그것을 좋아한다면 "Yes."라고 대답해야 해.

35 이 대답들은 "너는 애플파이를 좋아하니?"와 같은 긍정의문문에 대한 대답들과 같아.

36 어떤 문화적인 차이가 너에게 가장 놀랍니?

37 나는 미국에 온 이후로 문화적인 차이에 대해 계속 배우고 있어.

38 어떤 것들은 처음에 나를 놀라게 했지만, 지금은 그것들에 익숙해지고 있어.

※ 다음 문장을 우리말로 쓰시오.

1 Hi! My name is Kim Minhee. I have been living in America for three years.

➡ _____

2 Since my family moved here, I have experienced many cultural differences between Korea and America.

➡ _____

3 I would like to share some of them with you.

➡ _____

4 Minhee: Look at this shirt. I like it.

➡ _____

5 Lynda: It looks nice. How much is it?

➡ _____

6 Minhee: It's 19 dollars and 99 cents.

➡ _____

7 Linda: That's not expensive.

➡ _____

8 Minhee: Yes, I agree. I want to buy it.

➡ _____

9 Clerk: That'll be 21 dollars and 20 cents.

➡ _____

10 Minhee: Really? But the price tag says it's only 19 dollars and 99 cents.

➡ _____

11 Here in America, in most states, people pay a tax when they buy goods.

➡ _____

12 It is called a sales tax. Sales tax rates differ by state.

➡ _____

13 They range from less than one percent to more than ten percent.

➡ _____

14 So when you buy goods in America, you usually need to pay more than the price on the tag.

➡ _____

15 ▶ Jessica: Hi, Mrs. Johnson! Minhee: Hello, Mrs. Johnson!

➡ _____

16 ▶ Mrs. Johnson: Hi, Jessica! Hi, Minhee! How are you?

➡ _____

17 ▶ Jessica: Fine, thank you. We are here for a burger. Enjoy your meal.

➡ _____

18 ▶ Mrs. Johnson: Thank you. You, too!

➡ _____

19 ▶ Minhee: Jessica, why did you wave to Mrs. Johnson?

➡ _____

20 ▶ In America, people often greet each other by waving.

➡ _____

21 ▶ Waving to an older person is not regarded as rude.

➡ _____

22 ▶ When you come to America, you may feel uncomfortable about it at first, but why don't you try it?

➡ _____

23 ▶ You can wave to and smile at an elderly man walking on the street. He may wave back.

➡ _____

24 ▶ Andy: Minhee, try this apple pie.

➡ _____

25 ▶ Minhee: No, thanks. I don't want to.

➡ _____

26 ▶ Andy: Why not? Don't you like apple pie?

➡ _____

27 ▶ Minhee: Yes.

➡ _____

28 ▶ Andy: Then, try some. It's delicious.

➡ _____

29 Minhee: No. I just said I don't like apple pie.

➡ _____

30 Andy: What?

➡ _____

31 Americans often ask negative questions, such as "Aren't you coming?" and "Didn't you go to the hospital?"

➡ _____

32 It can be difficult to answer negative questions correctly. Here is some advice.

➡ _____

33 In response to negative questions, such as "Don't you like apple pie?" you should answer "No," if you don't like it.

➡ _____

_____

34 And you should answer "Yes," if you like it.

➡ _____

35 These answers are the same as the answers to positive questions, such as "Do you like apple pie?"

➡ _____

36 Which cultural difference is most surprising to you?

➡ _____

37 I have been learning about cultural differences since I came to America.

➡ _____

38 Some surprised me at first, but now I am getting used to them.

➡ _____

※ 다음 괄호 안의 단어들을 우리말에 맞도록 바르게 배열하시오.

Let's Learn about Cultural Differences

1 (hi! // name / my / is / Minhee. / Kim // living / have / I / been / America / in / three / years. / for)
➡ _____

2 (my / since / family / here, / moved / have / I / many / experienced / cultural / between / differences / Korea / America. / and)
➡ _____

3 (would / I / like / share / to / of / some / them / you. / with)
➡ _____

4 (Minhee: / at / look / shirt. / this // like / it. / I)
➡ _____

5 (Linda: / looks / it / nice. // much / how / it? / is)
➡ _____

6 (Minhee: / 19 / it's / dollars / 99 / and / cents.)
➡ _____

7 (Linda: / not / that's / expensive.)
➡ _____

8 (Minhee: / I / yes, / agree. // want / I / to / it. / buy)
➡ _____

9 (Clerk: / be / that'll / dollars / 21 / and / cents. / 20)
➡ _____

10 (Minhee: / really? // the / but / tag / price / it's / says / 19 / only / dollars / and / cents. / 99)
➡ _____

11 (in / here / America, / most / in / states, / pay / people / tax / a / when / they / goods. / buy)
➡ _____

12 (is / it / called / sales / a / tax. // tax / sales / differ / rates / state. / by)
➡ _____

13 (range / they / less / from / than / percent / one / more / to / ten / than / percent.)
➡ _____

14 (when / so / buy / you / in / goods / America, / usually / you / to / need / pay / than / more / price / the / the / on / tag.)
➡ _____

문화적 차이에 대해서 배우자

1 안녕! 내 이름은 김민희야. 나는 미국에 3년 동안 살고 있어.

2 우리 가족이 이곳으로 이민을 온 이후로 나는 한국과 미국의 많은 문화적 차이를 경험하고 있어.

3 나는 그것들 중 몇 가지를 너희들과 공유하고 싶어.

4 민희: 이 셔츠를 봐. 마음에 들어.

5 Linda: 멋져 보인다. 얼마야?

6 민희: 19달러 99센트야.

7 Linda: 비싸지 않네.

8 민희: 응, 나도 그렇게 생각해. 그것을 사고 싶어.

9 점원: 21달러 20센트입니다.

10 민희: 정말이요? 하지만 가격표에는 단지 19달러 99센트라고 쓰여 있는데요.

11 이곳 미국에서는 대부분의 주에서 사람들이 물건을 구입할 때 세금을 내.

12 그것은 판매세라고 불려. 판매세의 비율은 주마다 달라.

13 판매세는 1퍼센트 미만부터 10퍼센트 이상까지 다양해.

14 그래서 미국에서 상품을 살 때, 대개 가격표에 있는 가격보다 더 많은 돈을 지불해야 해.

15 (Jessica: / Mrs. / hi, / Johnson! // Minhee: / Mrs. / hello, / Johnson!)

➡ _____

16 (Mrs. Johnson: / Jessica! / hi, // Minhee! / hi, // are / you? / how)

➡ _____

17 (Jessica: / thank / fine, / you. // are / we / for / here / burger. / a // your / enjoy / meal.)

➡ _____

18 (Mrs. Johnson: / you. / thank // too! / you,)

➡ _____

19 (Minhee: / why / Jessica, / you / did / to / wave / Johnson? / Mrs.)

➡ _____

20 (America, / in / often / people / each / greet / other / waving. / by)

➡ _____

21 (to / waving / an / person / older / not / is / as / rude. / regarded)

➡ _____

22 (you / when / to / come / America, / may / you / uncomfortable / feel / it / about / first, / at / why / but / you / don't / it? / try)

➡ _____

➡ _____

23 (can / you / to / wave / and / at / smile / elderly / an / walking / man / the / on / street. // may / he / back. / wave)

➡ _____

➡ _____

24 (Andy: / try / Minhee, / apple / this / pie.)

➡ _____

25 (Minhee: / thanks. / no, // don't / I / to. / want)

➡ _____

26 (Andy: / not? / why // you / don't / apple / like / pie?)

➡ _____

27 (Minhee: / yes.)

➡ _____

28 (Andy: / try / then, / some. // delicious. / it's)

➡ _____

15 Jessica: 안녕하세요, Johnson 할머니! 민희: 안녕하세요, Johnson 할머니!

16 Mrs. Johnson: 안녕, Jessica! 안녕, 민희! 잘 지내지?

17 Jessica: 잘 지내요, 감사합니다. 저희는 여기 버거 먹으러 왔어요. 식사 맛있게 하세요.

18 Mrs. Johnson: 고맙구나. 너희들도!

19 민희: Jessica, 왜 너는 Johnson 할머니께 손을 흔들었니?

20 미국에서 사람들은 종종 손을 흔들며 서로에게 인사해.

21 나이가 많은 사람에게 손을 흔드는 것은 무례하다고 여겨지지 않아.

22 네가 미국에 오면 처음에는 그것에 대해 불편하게 느낄 수 있어. 하지만 한번 시도해 보지 않을래?

23 너는 길을 걷고 있는 연세가 많으신 할아버지께 손을 흔들며 미소를 지어도 돼. 그도 너한테 답례로 손을 흔들지도 몰라.

24 Andy: 민희, 이 사과 파이 좀 먹어 봐.

25 민희: 아니야, 고마워. 먹고 싶지 않아.

26 Andy: 왜 안 먹어? 너는 사과 파이를 좋아하지 않니?

27 민희: 응.

28 Andy: 그러면, 좀 먹어 봐. 맛있어.

29 (Minhee: / no. // just / I / said / don't / I / apple / like / pie.)

➡ _____

30 (what? / Andy:)

➡ _____

31 (often / Americans / negative / ask / questions, / as / such / you / coming?" / "aren't / and / "didn't / go / you / the / hospital?" / to)

➡ _____

32 (can / it / difficult / be / answer / to / questions / negative / correctly. // is / here / advice. / some)

➡ _____

_____

33 (response / in / negative / to / questions, / as / such / "don't / like / you / pie?" / apple / should / you / answer / "no," / you / if / like / don't / it.)

➡ _____

_____

34 (you / and / answer / should / "yes," / you / if / it. / like)

➡ _____

35 (answers / these / the / are / same / the / as / to / answers / questions, / positive / as / such / "do / like / you / pie?" / apple)

➡ _____

_____

36 (cultural / which / is / difference / most / to / surprising / you?)

➡ _____

37 (have / I / learning / been / cultural / about / since / differences / I / came / America. / to)

➡ _____

38 (surprised / some / at / me / first, / now / but / am / I / used / getting / them. / to)

➡ _____

29 민희: 아니. 내가 사과 파이를 좋아하지 않는다고 방금 말했잖아.

30 Andy: 뭐라고?

31 미국 사람들은 종종 "너 안 오니?", "너 병원 안 갔니?"와 같은 부정의문문으로 질문해.

32 부정의문문에 바르게 대답하는 것은 어려울 수 있어. 여기 약간의 충고 사항이 있어.

33 "너는 사과 파이를 좋아하지 않니?"와 같은 부정의문문의 대답으로 만약 사과 파이를 좋아하지 않는다면 너는 "No."라고 대답해야 해.

34 그리고 만약 그것을 좋아한다면 "Yes."라고 대답해야 해.

35 이 대답들은 "너는 애플파이를 좋아하니?"와 같은 긍정의문문에 대한 대답들과 같아.

36 어떤 문화적인 차이가 너에게 가장 놀랍니?

37 나는 미국에 온 이후로 문화적인 차이에 대해 계속 배우고 있어.

38 어떤 것들은 처음에 나를 놀라게 했지만, 지금은 그것들에 익숙해지고 있어.

※ 다음 우리말을 영어로 쓰시오.

1 안녕! 내 이름은 김민희야. 나는 미국에 3년 동안 살고 있어.

➡ _____

2 우리 가족이 이곳으로 이민을 온 이후로 나는 한국과 미국의 많은 문화적 차이를 경험하고 있어.

➡ _____

3 나는 그것들 중 몇 가지를 너희들과 공유하고 싶어.

➡ _____

4 민희: 이 셔츠를 봐. 마음에 들어.

➡ _____

5 Linda: 멋져 보인다. 얼마야?

➡ _____

6 민희: 19달러 99센트야.

➡ _____

7 Linda: 비싸지 않네.

➡ _____

8 민희: 응, 나도 그렇게 생각해. 그것을 사고 싶어.

➡ _____

9 점원: 21달러 20센트입니다.

➡ _____

10 민희: 정말이요? 하지만 가격표에는 단지 19달러 99센트라고 쓰여 있는데요.

➡ _____

11 이곳 미국에서는 대부분의 주에서 사람들이 물건을 구입할 때 세금을 내.

➡ _____

12 그것은 판매세라고 불려. 판매세의 비율은 주마다 달라.

➡ _____

13 판매세는 1퍼센트 미만부터 10퍼센트 이상까지 다양해.

➡ _____

14 그래서 미국에서 상품을 살 때, 대개 가격표에 있는 가격보다 더 많은 돈을 지불해야 해.

➡ _____

15 Jessica: 안녕하세요, Johnson 할머니! 민희: 안녕하세요, Johnson 할머니!

➡ _____

16 Mrs. Johnson: 안녕, Jessica! 안녕, 민희! 잘 지내지?

➡ _____

17 Jessica: 잘 지내요, 감사합니다. 저희는 여기 버거 먹으러 왔어요. 식사 맛있게 하세요.

➡ _____

18 Mrs. Johnson: 고맙구나. 너희들도!

➡ _____

19 민희: Jessica, 왜 너는 Johnson 할머니께 손을 흔들었니?

➡ _____

20 미국에서 사람들은 종종 손을 흔들며 서로에게 인사해.

➡ _____

21 나이가 많은 사람에게 손을 흔드는 것은 무례하다고 여겨지지 않아.

➡ _____

22 네가 미국에 오면 처음에는 그것에 대해 불편하게 느낄 수 있어. 하지만 한번 시도해 보지 않을래?

➡ _____

23 너는 길을 걷고 있는 연세가 많으신 할아버지께 손을 흔들며 미소를 지어도 돼. 그도 너한테 답례로 손을 흔들지도 몰라.

➡ _____

24 Andy: 민희, 이 사과 파이 좀 먹어 봐.

➡ _____

25 Minhee: 아니야, 고마워. 먹고 싶지 않아.

➡ _____

26 Andy: 왜 안 먹어? 너는 사과 파이를 좋아하지 않니?

➡ _____

27 Minhee: 응.

➡ _____

28 Andy: 그러면, 좀 먹어 봐. 맛있어.

➡ _____

29 Minhee: 아니. 내가 사과 파이를 좋아하지 않는다고 방금 말했잖아.

➡ _____

30 Andy: 뭐라고?

➡ _____

31 미국 사람들은 종종 "너 안 오니?", "너 병원 안 갔니?"와 같은 부정의문문으로 질문해.

➡ _____

32 부정의문문에 바르게 대답하는 것은 어려울 수 있어. 여기 약간의 충고 사항이 있어.

➡ _____

33 "너는 사과 파이를 좋아하지 않니?"와 같은 부정의문문의 대답으로 만약 사과 파이를 좋아하지 않는다면 너는 "No."라고 대답해야 해.

➡ _____

34 그리고 만약 그것을 좋아한다면 "Yes."라고 대답해야 해.

➡ _____

35 이 대답들은 "너는 애플파이를 좋아하니?"와 같은 긍정의문문에 대한 대답들과 같아.

➡ _____

36 어떤 문화적인 차이가 너에게 가장 놀랍니?

➡ _____

37 나는 미국에 온 이후로 문화적인 차이에 대해 계속 배우고 있어.

➡ _____

38 어떤 것들은 처음에 나를 놀라게 했지만, 지금은 그것들에 익숙해지고 있어.

➡ _____

※ 다음 우리말과 일치하도록 빈칸에 알맞은 말을 쓰시오.

Project Step 1

1. A: Can I get your advice _____ _____ _____ _____?

2. B: _____ _____ you say window shopping _____ _____

   _____ _____.

3. C: _____ _____ _____ _____ _____ Y-shirt. You

   _____ _____ dress shirt _____.

Project Step 3

1. Today, I _____ I _____ _____ _____ many _____

   English expressions.

2. _____ _____, we _____ _____ dress shirt _____

   _____ Y-shirt.

3. Eye shopping is also _____ _____ _____. _____

   _____ _____ _____ _____ it.

Enjoy Writing

1. Holi That I _____ _____.

2. _____ _____ many interesting festivals _____ _____

   _____.

3. _____ them, I'd _____ _____ _____ Holi.

4. People in India _____ _____ _____ this festival _____

   _____ _____.

5. Holi _____ _____ _____ March.

6. I think that _____ _____ _____, I'll experience _____

   _____ _____ _____.

7. First, there are _____ _____ colored powder and water

   _____ _____ _____.

8. It _____ _____ _____!

9. Second, I want _____ _____ _____ _____ _____ on

   the street.

10. I'll also _____ _____ Holi _____.

11. It's _____ _____ be very _____.

12. I _____ _____ _____ the day!

※ 다음 우리말을 영어로 쓰시오.

Project Step 1

1. A: 옳은 영어 표현에 대해 너의 조언을 구할 수 있을까?
   ➡ _____

2. B: 반드시 아이 쇼핑 대신 윈도 쇼핑(구경만 하는 쇼핑)이라고 말하도록 해.
   ➡ _____

3. C: 절대 와이셔츠라고 말하지 않도록 해. 대신 정장용 셔츠라고 말해야 해.
   ➡ _____

Project Step 3

1. 오늘, 나는 내가 많은 잘못된 영어 표현을 사용해 왔다는 것을 알았습니다.
   ➡ _____

2. 예를 들어, 우리는 Y-shirt 대신에 dress shirt라는 말을 써야 합니다.
   ➡ _____

3. 아이 쇼핑도 또한 잘못된 표현입니다. 그것을 사용하지 않도록 명심하세요.
   ➡ _____

Project

1. 놓칠 수 없는 홀리
   ➡ _____

2. 세계에는 많은 흥미로운 축제들이 있다.
   ➡ _____

3. 그 중에서, 나는 홀리에 참여하고 싶다.
   ➡ _____

4. 인도 사람들은 오랫동안 이 축제를 열어오고 있는 중이다.
   ➡ _____

5. 홀리 축제는 3월에 열린다.
   ➡ _____

6. 나는 내가 간다면, 많은 것들을 경험할 것이라고 생각한다.
   ➡ _____

7. 첫째, 서로에게 색색의 가루와 물을 던지는 사람들이 있다.
   ➡ _____

8. 그것은 환상적일 것이다.
   ➡ _____

9. 둘째, 나는 거리에서 다른 사람들과 춤을 추고 싶다.
   ➡ _____

10. 나는 또한 전통적인 홀리 요리를 맛볼 것이다.
    ➡ _____

11. 그것은 정말 신날 것이다.
    ➡ _____

12. 나는 그 날이 정말 기대된다!
    ➡ _____

※ 다음 영어를 우리말로 쓰시오.

01 enough _____

02 analyze _____

03 attend _____

04 figure _____

05 calm _____

06 cast _____

07 personality _____

08 detail _____

09 developer _____

10 highly _____

11 florist _____

12 analyst _____

13 weakness _____

14 include _____

15 among _____

16 resource _____

17 conduct _____

18 reduce _____

19 specialist _____

20 handle _____

21 creature _____

22 recommend _____

23 poet _____

24 veterinarian _____

25 mail carrier _____

26 select _____

27 greenery _____

28 strength _____

29 microphone _____

30 audition _____

31 stethoscope _____

32 performance _____

33 gardener _____

34 realistic _____

35 by -ing _____

36 come true _____

37 care for _____

38 be happy with ~ _____

39 belong to _____

40 make the best use of _____

41 It seems that ~ _____

42 I'm sure that ~ _____

43 dream of ~ _____

※ 다음 우리말을 영어로 쓰시오.

01 성격

02 분석하다

03 출연자들

04 힘, 강점

05 청진기

06 지휘하다, 처신하다

07 수의사

08 약함, 약점

09 세부, 세목

10 선택하다, 고르다

11 정원사

12 전문가

13 개발자

14 마이크

15 매우, 대단히

16 ~ 중에서

17 플로리스트, 화초 연구가

18 오디션을 보다

19 화초, 푸른 잎

20 분석가

21 다루다

22 포함하다

23 진정시키다, 평온하게 하다

24 책임

25 현실적인

26 전통의, 전통적인

27 추천하다

28 공연

29 생물, 생명체

30 자원

31 줄이다, 완화하다

32 언젠가

33 기술자

34 충분히; 충분한

35 ~을 보살피다

36 (단체, 조직에) 소속하다, 속하다

37 ~을 꿈꾸다

38 ~에 만족하다

39 실현되다

40 ~함으로써

41 ~처럼 보이다, ~일 것 같다

42 ~을 확신하다

43 ~을 최대한 활용하다

※ 다음 영영풀이에 알맞은 단어를 <보기>에서 골라 쓴 후, 우리말 뜻을 쓰시오.

1 _____ : the actors in a film, play, or show: _____

2 _____ : facts or information that can be analysed: _____

3 _____ : to take things and put them together: _____

4 _____ : to bring a person or thing to a state or place: _____

5 _____ : to be a member of an organization: _____

6 _____ : your job or duty to deal with something or someone: _____

7 _____ : someone whose job is to analyze and examine something: _____

8 _____ : a person whose job is to pay out and take in money in a bank: _____

9 _____ : green plants or branches, especially when cut and used as decoration: _____

10 _____ : the type of person you are, shown by the way you behave, feel, and think: _____

11 _____ : a useful or valuable possession or quality of a country, organization, or person: _____

12 _____ : to study or examine something in detail, in order to discover more about it: _____

13 _____ : to contain something as a part of something else, or to make something part of something else: _____

14 _____ : to give a short performance in order to show that you are suitable for a part in a film, play, show, etc.: _____

15 _____ : a person or company that creates new products, especially computer products such as software: _____

16 _____ : to protect someone or something and provide the things they need, especially someone who is young, old or ill: _____

보기			
resource	data	belong to	greenery
include	analyst	responsibility	analyze
care for	lead	collect	bank teller
personality	cast	developer	audition

※ 다음 우리말과 일치하도록 빈칸에 알맞은 말을 쓰시오.

Listen & Speak 1 A

1. B: Anne, I'm _____ to visit the _____ _____ to see my
   uncle. He is a _____ _____.

   G: Oh, I want _____ _____ a police officer _____.

   B: You _____? Me, _____. I have _____ _____ _____
   a police officer _____ I was ten.

   G: Can I come _____ you, Matt? I want to meet your uncle and
   _____ him _____.

   B: Sure. What _____ you _____ _____ _____?

   G: I want to ask him _____ I need _____ _____ _____
   _____ a police officer.

   B: I see. I'm _____ he _____ _____ _____ meet you.

2. M: What's _____, Jisu?

   G: I want to be an _____, but my _____ _____ is not good
   _____.

   M: Hmm... _____ _____ _____ is not just about _____
   good _____.

   G: What should I _____ _____ _____ an _____?

   M: Read _____ _____ books _____ _____ good
   stories and _____ _____ every day.

   G: Okay, I'll do so.

   M: I'm _____ _____ _____ you can be a good animator
   _____ you _____ _____.

   G: Thank you very much.

Listen & Speak 1 B

- A: I'm _____ in _____. _____ job would be _____ for
  me?

  B: I'm quite _____ that an app _____ could be a good job for
  you.

- A: I'm _____ _____ _____. _____ _____ would
  _____ _____ _____ me?

  B: I'm _____ _____ that a writer could _____ _____
  _____ _____ _____ you.

1. B: Anne, 나는 우리 삼촌을 보러 경찰서에 갈 예정이야. 그는 경찰관이거든.
   G: 오, 나는 언젠가 경찰관이 되고 싶어.
   B: 그래? 나도야. 나는 10살 때부터 경찰관이 되는 것을 꿈꿔왔어.
   G: 내가 너와 함께 갈 수 있을까, Matt? 나 너희 삼촌을 만나서 몇 가지 물어보고 싶어.
   B: 물론이지. 무엇을 물어볼 거니?
   G: 나는 경찰관이 되기 위해 내가 무엇을 해야 하는지 물어보고 싶어.
   B: 알겠어. 나는 그가 널 만나고 싶어 할 거라고 확신해.

2. M: 무슨 문제 있니, 지수야?
   G: 저는 만화 영화 제작자가 되고 싶은데, 그리기 실력이 좋은 편이 아니에요.
   M: 음... 만화 영화 제작자가 되는 것은 단순히 그림을 잘 그린다고 되는 것만은 아니란다.
   G: 만화 영화 제작자가 되기 위해서 제가 무엇을 해야 하나요?
   M: 좋은 이야기를 만들기 위해 책을 많이 읽고, 그림 그리는 것을 매일 연습하렴.
   G: 알겠어요. 그렇게 할게요.
   M: 나는 네가 열심히 노력하면 훌륭한 만화 영화 제작자가 될 수 있다고 아주 확신해.
   G: 정말 감사해요.

- A: 나는 기술에 관심이 있어. 어떤 직업이 나에게 맞을까?
  B: 나는 앱 개발자가 너에게 좋은 직업이 될 수 있을 거라고 아주 확신해.
- A: 나는 쓰기에 관심이 있어. 어떤 직업이 나에게 맞을까?
  B: 나는 작가가 너에게 좋은 직업이 될 수 있을 거라고 아주 확신해.

Listen & Speak 2 A

1. **G:** I'm _____ _____ _____ you, Mr. Han. Could you please tell me _____ _____ _____?

 M: Okay. I _____ travelers to _____ _____ in China and give them _____ about where they should _____.

 G: What _____ do you do?

 M: I tell them about _____ _____ and _____ food in China.

 G: _____ _____ to me _____ _____ _____ about China is very important. Are you _____ _____ your job?

 M: Yes. I really love _____ _____.

2. **B:** Did you _____ the report about your _____ _____?

 G: Yes, I did. I _____ about my role model, Ms. Shin. I want to _____ _____ her.

 B: What _____ she _____?

 G: She teaches people _____ _____ _____. She _____ _____ them _____ stress and _____ _____.

 B: Good. _____ _____ _____ she helps _____ _____ their mind _____ body healthy.

 G: Yes, and I think it's great.

Listen & Speak 2 B

- **A:** I want to be a radio _____ _____. What would help me _____ one?

 B: It _____ _____ me _____ your own stories would be _____.

- **A:** I want to be a _____ _____. What would _____ _____ _____ one?

 B: It _____ to me _____ _____ _____ _____ at a hospital would _____ _____.

Real Life Talk

Bora: What are you _____ _____ in _____ the things on this list?

Jessie: I'm most _____ _____ _____ outside and playing sports.

---

1. G: 만나 뵙게 되어 반갑습니다, Mr. Han. 당신이 어떤 일을 하시는지 말해 주실 수 있나요?

 M: 그래. 나는 중국에 있는 다양한 장소로 여행객들을 안내하고 그들이 방문해야 할 곳에 대한 정보를 제공해.

 G: 그 외에 또 어떤 일을 하시나요?

 M: 나는 그들에게 중국의 대중문화와 전통 음식에 대해 말해 줘.

 G: 중국에 대해 많이 아는 것이 매우 중요한 것 같네요. 당신의 직업에 만족하시나요?

 M: 응. 나는 내 직업을 정말 사랑해.

2. B: 네 롤 모델에 관한 기사 다 썼니?

 G: 응, 다 썼어. 나는 나의 롤 모델인 신 씨에 관해 썼어. 나는 그녀처럼 되고 싶어.

 B: 그녀는 무슨 일을 하니?

 G: 그녀는 사람들에게 스트레칭하는 방법을 가르쳐. 그녀는 또한 그들이 스트레스를 완화하여 평온해지도록 도와 줘.

 B: 좋구나. 그녀가 사람들의 몸과 마음을 둘 다 건강하게 유지하도록 돕는 것 같아.

 G: 맞아, 그리고 나는 그것이 훌륭하다고 생각해.

- A: 나는 라디오 방송 작가가 되고 싶어. 내가 그것이 되는 데 뭐가 도움이 될까?

 B: 너 자신만의 이야기를 쓰는 것이 도움이 될 것 같아.

- A: 나는 사회복지사가 되고 싶어. 내가 그것이 되는 데 뭐가 도움이 될까?

 B: 병원에서 아이들에게 책을 읽어 주는 것이 도움이 될 것 같아.

보라: 너는 이 목록에 있는 것들 중에서 무엇에 가장 관심이 있니?

Jessie: 나는 밖에서 일하는 것과 스포츠 하는 것에 가장 관심이 있어.

Bora: What are you _____ _____ in _____ the things on this list?

Jessie: I'm most interested in _____ outside and _____ sports.

Bora: Well, _____ _____ _____ _____ _____ you _____ _____ the _____ type.

Jessie: What do you _____ ?

Bora: Most people _____ _____ one of six _____ _____ . _____ is _____ _____ the _____ .

Jessie: Oh, that's _____ . _____ _____ _____ jobs do they _____ for realistic types?

Bora: A farmer, a _____ _____ , a soccer player, _____ _____ _____ .

Jessie: Oh, I have always wanted _____ _____ a soccer player.

Bora: That's good. _____ _____ _____ you could become a great _____ _____ .

Communication Task Step 2

A: I have _____ _____ , _____ _____ , 1 I, and _____ _____ .

B: It _____ _____ me that you _____ _____ Type S.

C: Yes. _____ _____ are _____ for Type S are teacher, nurse, _____ or _____ .

A: Cool. I _____ _____ _____ to be a teacher.

D: That _____ great. I'm _____ _____ _____ _____ _____ be a good teacher.

Wrap Up 1

B: Hello, what _____ you _____ , Sumi?

G: I'm _____ _____ a good _____ on the Internet. I need it for my family dinner today.

B: That is nice. Do you _____ _____ ?

G: Yes, I try _____ _____ every weekend. I want to be a _____ _____ .

B: What are you doing to _____ your dream _____ ?

G: I'm _____ a cooking class. I try _____ _____ _____ new and _____ dishes.

B: _____ _____ _____ you could be a _____ _____ .

보라: 음, 내 생각에 너는 현실적인 타입에 속하는 것 같아.
Jessie: 무슨 의미야?
보라: 대부분의 사람들은 여섯 가지 성격 유형 중 한 가지에 속해. 현실적인 타입도 그중 하나야.
Jessie: 오, 재미있다. 현실적인 타입의 사람들에게 그들이 추천하는 직업은 뭐야?
보라: 농부, 경찰관, 축구 선수 같은 거야.
Jessie: 오, 나는 항상 축구 선수가 되고 싶어 해 왔어.
보라: 멋지다. 나는 네가 훌륭한 축구 선수가 될 수 있을 거라고 아주 확신해.

A: 나는 S가 3개, A가 2개, I가 1개, E가 1개 있어.
B: 너는 S 타입에 속해 있는 것 같아.
C: 응. S 타입에게 추천되는 직업은 선생님, 간호사, 사서, 상담사야.
A: 멋지다. 나는 항상 선생님이 되고 싶었어.
D: 그거 멋지네. 나는 네가 좋은 선생님이 될 수 있다고 아주 확신해.

B: 안녕, 뭐 하고 있니, 수미야?
G: 나는 인터넷으로 좋은 요리법을 찾아보고 있어. 나는 오늘 우리 가족의 저녁 식사를 위해 그것이 필요해.
B: 그거 멋지네. 너는 요리를 자주 하니?
G: 응, 나는 매주 주말에 요리를 하려고 노력해. 나는 언젠가 요리사가 되고 싶어.
B: 네 꿈을 이루기 위해서 무엇을 하고 있니?
G: 나는 요리 수업을 듣고 있어. 새롭고 창의적인 요리를 생각해 내기 위해 노력해.
B: 나는 네가 좋은 요리사가 될 것이라고 아주 확신해.

※ 다음 우리말에 맞도록 대화를 영어로 쓰시오.

Listen & Speak 1 A

1. B: _____
   _____
   G: _____
   B: _____
   _____
   G: _____
   B: _____
   G: _____
   B: _____

2. M: _____
   G: _____
   M: _____
   G: _____
   M: _____
   G: _____
   M: _____
   G: _____

Listen & Speak 1 B

- A: _____
  B: _____
- A: _____
  B: _____

1. B: Anne, 나는 우리 삼촌을 보러 경찰서에 갈 예정이야. 그는 경찰관이거든.
   G: 오, 나는 언젠가 경찰관이 되고 싶어.
   B: 그래? 나도야. 나는 10살 때부터 경찰관이 되는 것을 꿈꿔왔어.
   G: 내가 너와 함께 갈 수 있을까, Matt? 나 너희 삼촌을 만나서 몇 가지 물어보고 싶어.
   B: 물론이지. 무엇을 물어볼 거니?
   G: 나는 경찰관이 되기 위해 내가 무엇을 해야 하는지 물어보고 싶어.
   B: 알겠어. 나는 그가 널 만나고 싶어 할 거라고 확신해.

2. M: 무슨 문제 있니, 지수야?
   G: 저는 만화 영화 제작자가 되고 싶은데, 그리기 실력이 좋은 편이 아니에요.
   M: 음... 만화 영화 제작자가 되는 것은 단순히 그림을 잘 그린다고 되는 것만은 아니란다.
   G: 만화 영화 제작자가 되기 위해서 제가 무엇을 해야 하나요?
   M: 좋은 이야기를 만들기 위해 책을 많이 읽고, 그림 그리는 것을 매일 연습하렴.
   G: 알겠어요. 그렇게 할게요.
   M: 나는 네가 열심히 노력하면 훌륭한 만화 영화 제작자가 될 수 있다고 아주 확신해.
   G: 정말 감사해요.

- A: 나는 기술에 관심이 있어. 어떤 직업이 나에게 맞을까?
  B: 나는 앱 개발자가 너에게 좋은 직업이 될 수 있을 거라고 아주 확신해.
- A: 나는 쓰기에 관심이 있어. 어떤 직업이 나에게 맞을까?
  B: 나는 작가가 너에게 좋은 직업이 될 수 있을 거라고 아주 확신해.

1. G: _____
   M: _____
      _____
   G: _____
   M: _____
   G: _____
      _____
   M: _____

2. B: _____
   G: _____
   B: _____
   G: _____
      _____
   B: _____
   G: _____

Listen & Speak 2 B

• A: _____
  B: _____
• A: _____
  B: _____

Real Life Talk

Bora: _____

Jessie: _____

1. G: 만나 뵙게 되어 반갑습니다, Mr. Han. 당신이 어떤 일을 하시는지 말해 주실 수 있나요?
   M: 그래. 나는 중국에 있는 다양한 장소로 여행객들을 안내하고 그들이 방문해야 할 곳에 대한 정보를 제공해.
   G: 그 외에 또 어떤 일을 하시나요?
   M: 나는 그들에게 중국의 대중문화와 전통 음식에 대해 말해 줘.
   G: 중국에 대해 많이 아는 것이 매우 중요한 것 같네요. 당신의 직업에 만족하시나요?
   M: 응. 나는 내 직업을 정말 사랑해.

2. B: 네 롤 모델에 관한 기사 다 썼니?
   G: 응, 다 썼어. 나는 나의 롤 모델인 신 씨에 관해 썼어. 나는 그녀처럼 되고 싶어.
   B: 그녀는 무슨 일을 하니?
   G: 그녀는 사람들에게 스트레칭하는 방법을 가르쳐. 그녀는 또한 그들이 스트레스를 완화하여 평온해지도록 도와 줘.
   B: 좋구나. 그녀가 사람들의 몸과 마음을 둘 다 건강하게 유지하도록 돕는 것 같아.
   G: 맞아, 그리고 나는 그것이 훌륭하다고 생각해.

• A: 나는 라디오 방송 작가가 되고 싶어. 내가 그것이 되는 데 뭐가 도움이 될까?
  B: 너 자신만의 이야기를 쓰는 것이 도움이 될 것 같아.
• A: 나는 사회복지사가 되고 싶어. 내가 그것이 되는 데 뭐가 도움이 될까?
  B: 병원에서 아이들에게 책을 읽어 주는 것이 도움이 될 것 같아.

보라: 너는 이 목록에 있는 것들 중에서 무엇에 가장 관심이 있니?
Jessie: 나는 밖에서 일하는 것과 스포츠 하는 것에 가장 관심이 있어.

Bora: _____

Jessie: _____

Bora: _____

_____

Jessie: _____

_____

Bora: _____

Jessie: _____

Bora: _____

보라: 음, 내 생각에 너는 현실적인 타입에 속하는 것 같아.

Jessie: 무슨 의미야?

보라: 대부분의 사람들은 여섯 가지 성격 유형 중 한 가지에 속해. 현실적인 타입도 그중 하나야.

Jessie: 오, 재미있다. 현실적인 타입의 사람들에게 그들이 추천하는 직업은 뭐야?

보라: 농부, 경찰관, 축구 선수 같은 거야.

Jessie: 오, 나는 항상 축구 선수가 되고 싶어 해 왔어.

보라: 멋지다. 나는 네가 훌륭한 축구 선수가 될 수 있을 거라고 아주 확신해.

Communication Task Step 2

A: _____

B: _____

C: _____

A: _____

D: _____

A: 나는 S가 3개, A가 2개, I가 1개, E가 1개 있어.

B: 너는 S 타입에 속해 있는 것 같아.

C: 응. S 타입에게 추천되는 직업은 선생님, 간호사, 사서, 상담사야.

A: 멋지다. 나는 항상 선생님이 되고 싶었어.

D: 그거 멋지네. 나는 네가 좋은 선생님이 될 수 있다고 아주 확신해.

Wrap Up 1

B: _____

G: _____

_____

B: _____

G: _____

B: _____

G: _____

B: _____

B: 안녕, 뭐 하고 있니, 수미야?

G: 나는 인터넷으로 좋은 요리법을 찾아보고 있어. 나는 오늘 우리 가족의 저녁 식사를 위해 그것이 필요해.

B: 그거 멋지네. 너는 요리를 자주 하니?

G: 응, 나는 매주 주말에 요리를 하려고 노력해. 나는 언젠가 요리사가 되고 싶어.

B: 네 꿈을 이루기 위해서 무엇을 하고 있니?

G: 나는 요리 수업을 듣고 있어. 새롭고 창의적인 요리를 생각해 내기 위해 노력해.

B: 나는 네가 좋은 요리사가 될 것이라고 아주 확신해.

※ 다음 우리말과 일치하도록 빈칸에 알맞은 것을 골라 쓰시오.

The World of Wonderful Jobs

Florist

1 Hi, I am Tom. A _____ is someone _____ _____ beautiful things _____ flowers.

    A. with   B. who   C. florist   D. creates

2 _____ _____ a florist, you _____ to know many _____ about flowers.

    A. need   B. to   C. things   D. become

3 I _____ a high school _____ florists and _____.

    A. for   B. attended   C. gardeners

4 It was at this school that I learned _____ _____ grow and _____ _____ different types of flowers.

    A. how   B. for   C. to   D. care

5 These _____, florists can do a _____ _____ things.

    A. lot   B. days   C. different   D. of

6 I design _____ _____ sometimes and I _____ shops _____ flowers.

    A. sets   B. decorate   C. movie   D. with

7 I am happy when I create _____ _____ with _____ flowers and _____.

    A. fresh   B. something   C. greenery   D. colorful

8 _____ you like plants and the arts, I _____ _____ you _____ a florist.

    A. recommend   B. highly   C. become   D. if

Sport Data Analyst

9 I am Emma. I am a _____ _____ _____.

    A. data   B. sport   C. analyst

10 It _____ _____ a difficult job, _____ _____?

    A. like   B. doesn't   C. sounds   D. it

11 _____ _____, it is a lot of fun. I _____ _____ a baseball team.

    A. fact   B. for   C. in   D. work

12 My job is to _____ games and _____ a computer program to _____ data.

    A. recorded   B. collect   C. run   D. watch

플로리스트

1 안녕하세요. 저는 Tom입니다. 플로리스트란 꽃으로 아름다운 것들을 창조하는 사람입니다.

2 플로리스트가 되기 위해서 여러분은 꽃에 관해 많은 것을 알 필요가 있습니다.

3 나는 플로리스트와 정원사를 양성하는 고등학교에 다녔습니다.

4 제가 다양한 종류의 꽃을 기르고 다루는 방법을 배운 곳이 바로 이 학교에서였습니다.

5 오늘날, 플로리스트는 많은 다양한 일을 할 수 있습니다.

6 나는 때때로 영화 세트장을 디자인하고 꽃으로 상점을 꾸밉니다.

7 나는 싱싱한 꽃과 화초로 다채로운 무언가를 창조해 낼 때 행복합니다.

8 만약 당신이 식물과 예술을 좋아한다면, 나는 당신에게 플로리스트가 될 것을 강력히 추천합니다.

스포츠 데이터 분석가

9 나는 Emma입니다. 나는 스포츠 데이터 분석가입니다.

10 어려운 직업처럼 들리죠. 그렇지 않나요?

11 사실, 그것은 매우 재미있습니다. 나는 야구팀을 위해서 일합니다.

12 나의 일은 녹화된 경기를 보고 자료를 수집하기 위해 컴퓨터 프로그램을 실행하는 것입니다.

13 Then, I _____ the data to _____ my team's _____ and
_____.

A. weaknesses   B. strengths   C. analyze   D. show

14 _____ the team _____ their strengths and weaknesses, they
can _____ _____ next time.

A. better   B. understands   C. do   D. if

15 _____ I was young, I _____ _____ a _____ fan of
baseball.

A. big   B. since   C. been   D. have

16 Now, in my _____, I _____ baseball games _____ the
_____.

A. time   B. work   C. all   D. watch

17 This is a _____ job for me _____ _____ baseball games
is my _____!

A. watching   B. perfect   C. hobby   D. because

Director of a Musical Theater

18 Hi, I am Chris. _____ a _____ of a musical _____, I do
a _____ of things.

A. theater   B. as   C. director   D. lot

19 I _____ the actors and I _____ _____ good, strong
_____.

A. for   B. audition   C. look

20 After _____ the _____, I teach them the songs for _____
_____.

A. scene   B. selecting   C. each   D. cast

21 Then, I _____ the _____ and orchestra _____ for
_____.

A. together   B. put   C. practice   D. cast

22 _____ the _____, I am in the orchestra _____ and
_____.

A. conduct   B. during   C. performance   D. area

23 It's my _____ to have _____ song _____ the same
_____ every time.

A. played   B. responsibility   C. way   D. each

13 그리고 나서, 나는 내 팀의 강점과 약점을 보여 주기 위해서 그 자료들을 분석합니다.

14 만약 팀이 자신들의 강점과 약점을 이해하면, 그들은 다음번에 더 잘할 수 있습니다.

15 어렸을 때부터, 나는 야구의 열혈 팬이었습니다.

16 지금, 나는 일하는 중에 내내 야구를 봅니다.

17 야구 경기를 보는 것은 나의 취미이기 때문에 이것은 나에게 완벽한 직업입니다!

뮤지컬 극장 감독

18 안녕하세요. 나는 Chris입니다. 뮤지컬 극장 감독으로서 나는 많은 것들을 합니다.

19 나는 배우들을 대상으로 오디션을 실시하고, 훌륭하고 강한 목소리를 찾아냅니다.

20 배역에 맞는 배우를 고른 뒤에, 나는 그들에게 각 장면을 위한 노래를 가르칩니다.

21 그리고 나서, 나는 배우와 오케스트라를 함께 연습시킵니다.

22 공연 동안에, 나는 오케스트라석에 있고 지휘를 합니다.

23 각각의 노래가 매번 동일하게 연주되도록 만드는 것은 나의 책임입니다.

24 I _____ the musicians and the singers _____ _____ the show _____.

    A. keep   B. direct   C. together   D. to

25 _____ and _____ is not just about _____ my arms _____!

    A. waving   B. directing   C. around   D. conducting

Ocean Scientist

26 My name is Yeji. I am an ocean _____. Ocean science is a _____ _____.

    A. big   B. scientist   C. field

27 It _____ _____ of the oceans and the _____ _____ in them.

    A. creatures   B. studies   C. includes   D. living

28 _____ other things, I _____ _____ many kinds of fish _____ in the seas near Korea.

    A. have   B. living   C. among   D. studied

29 It is the _____ _____ in a fish _____ _____ me.

    A. interests   B. growth   C. ring   D. that

30 _____ _____ at it, I can find _____ when and where the fish was _____.

    A. born   B. looking   C. by   D. out

31 All the information I get from fish is _____ _____ understand sea _____ and _____ the oceans better.

    A. to   B. manage   C. used   D. resources

32 My job is important _____ it makes _____ _____ of nature possible.

    A. best   B. because   C. use   D. the

24 나는 공연을 제대로 진행하기 위해 연주자들과 가수들을 감독합니다.

25 지휘하고 감독하는 것은 단지 내 팔을 흔드는 것만이 아닙니다!

해양 과학자

26 나는 예지입니다. 나는 해양 과학자입니다. 해양 과학은 거대한 분야입니다.

27 그것은 바다와 그 안에 살고 있는 생물에 관한 연구를 포함합니다.

28 여러 가지 중에서 나는 한국 주변의 바다에 살고 있는 많은 종류의 물고기를 연구해 왔습니다.

29 나의 흥미를 끄는 것은 바로 물고기 안에 있는 나이테입니다.

30 나이테를 살펴봄으로써, 나는 언제 어디서 그 물고기가 태어났는지 알아낼 수 있습니다.

31 내가 물고기에서 얻은 모든 정보는 바다의 자원을 이해하고 바다를 더 잘 관리하기 위해 사용됩니다.

32 내 직업은 자연을 가장 잘 활용할 수 있게 한다는 점에서 중요합니다.

※ 다음 우리말과 일치하도록 빈칸에 알맞은 말을 쓰시오.

The World of Wonderful Jobs

Florist

1 Hi, I am Tom. A _____ is someone _____ _____ beautiful things _____ flowers.

2 _____ _____ a florist, you _____ _____ _____ _____ _____ about flowers.

3 I _____ a high school _____ florists and _____ .

4 It was _____ _____ _____ that I learned _____ _____ _____ and _____ _____ different types of flowers.

5 _____ _____ , florists can do _____ _____ things.

6 I design _____ _____ sometimes and I _____ shops _____ _____ .

7 I am happy when I create _____ _____ _____ fresh flowers and _____ .

8 If you like _____ and the arts, I _____ _____ you become a florist.

Sport Data Analyst

9 I am Emma. I am a _____ _____ _____ .

10 It _____ _____ a difficult job, _____ _____ ?

11 _____ _____ , it is _____ _____ _____ _____ _____ . I work for a baseball team.

12 My job is _____ _____ _____ _____ and _____ a computer program _____ _____ data.

플로리스트

1 안녕하세요. 저는 Tom입니다. 플로리스트란 꽃으로 아름다운 것들을 창조하는 사람입니다.

2 플로리스트가 되기 위해서 여러분은 꽃에 관해 많은 것을 알 필요가 있습니다.

3 나는 플로리스트와 정원사를 양성하는 고등학교에 다녔습니다.

4 제가 다양한 종류의 꽃을 기르고 다루는 방법을 배운 곳이 바로 이 학교에서였습니다.

5 오늘날, 플로리스트는 많은 다양한 일을 할 수 있습니다.

6 나는 때때로 영화 세트장을 디자인하고 꽃으로 상점을 꾸밉니다.

7 나는 싱싱한 꽃과 화초로 다채로운 무언가를 창조해 낼 때 행복합니다.

8 만약 당신이 식물과 예술을 좋아한다면, 나는 당신에게 플로리스트가 될 것을 강력히 추천합니다.

스포츠 데이터 분석가

9 나는 Emma입니다. 나는 스포츠 데이터 분석가입니다.

10 어려운 직업처럼 들리죠, 그렇지 않나요?

11 사실, 그것은 매우 재미있습니다. 나는 야구팀을 위해서 일합니다.

12 나의 일은 녹화된 경기를 보고 자료를 수집하기 위해 컴퓨터 프로그램을 실행하는 것입니다.

13 Then, I _____ the data _____ _____ my team's strengths and _____.

14 If the team _____ their _____ and weaknesses, they can _____ _____ next time.

15 _____ I was young, I _____ _____ a big fan of baseball.

16 Now, in my work, I watch _____ _____ _____ _____ _____.

17 This is a _____ _____ for me _____ _____ _____ _____ is my _____!

Director of a Musical Theater

18 Hi, I am Chris. _____ a director of _____ _____ _____, I do _____ _____ _____ things.

19 I _____ the actors and I _____ _____ good, strong _____.

20 After _____ _____ _____, I teach them the songs _____ _____ _____.

21 Then, I _____ the _____ and orchestra _____ for practice.

22 _____ the _____, I am in the orchestra area and _____.

23 It's _____ _____ to have _____ song _____ the _____ _____ every time.

---

13 그리고 나서, 나는 내 팀의 강점과 약점을 보여 주기 위해서 그 자료들을 분석합니다.

14 만약 팀이 자신들의 강점과 약점을 이해하면, 그들은 다음번에 더 잘할 수 있습니다.

15 어렸을 때부터, 나는 야구의 열혈 팬이었습니다.

16 지금, 나는 일하는 중에 내내 야구를 봅니다.

17 야구 경기를 보는 것은 나의 취미이기 때문에 이것은 나에게 완벽한 직업입니다!

뮤지컬 극장 감독

18 안녕하세요. 나는 Chris입니다. 뮤지컬 극장 감독으로서 나는 많은 것들을 합니다.

19 나는 배우들을 대상으로 오디션을 실시하고, 훌륭하고 강한 목소리를 찾아냅니다.

20 배역에 맞는 배우를 고른 뒤에, 나는 그들에게 각 장면을 위한 노래를 가르칩니다.

21 그리고 나서, 나는 배우와 오케스트라를 함께 연습시킵니다.

22 공연 동안에, 나는 오케스트라석에 있고 지휘를 합니다.

23 각각의 노래가 매번 동일하게 연주되도록 만드는 것은 나의 책임입니다.

24 I _____ the musicians and the singers _____ _____ the show _____ .

25 _____ and _____ is not just about _____ my arms around!

Ocean Scientist

26 My name is Yeji. I am an _____ _____ . Ocean science is _____ _____ _____ .

27 It _____ studies of the _____ and the _____ _____ _____ .

28 _____ other things, I _____ _____ many kinds of fish _____ in the seas near Korea.

29 It is _____ _____ _____ in a fish _____ _____ me.

30 _____ _____ at it, I can _____ _____ when and where the fish _____ _____ .

31 All the information _____ _____ _____ fish _____ _____ _____ _____ sea resources and _____ the _____ _____ .

32 My job is important _____ it _____ _____ _____ _____ _____ nature possible.

24 나는 공연을 제대로 진행하기 위해 연주자들과 가수들을 감독합니다.

25 지휘하고 감독하는 것은 단지 내 팔을 흔드는 것만이 아닙니다!

해양 과학자

26 나는 예지입니다. 나는 해양 과학자입니다. 해양 과학은 거대한 분야입니다.

27 그것은 바다와 그 안에 살고 있는 생물에 관한 연구를 포함합니다.

28 여러 가지 중에서 나는 한국 주변의 바다에 살고 있는 많은 종류의 물고기를 연구해 왔습니다.

29 나의 흥미를 끄는 것은 바로 물고기 안에 있는 나이테입니다.

30 나이테를 살펴봄으로써, 나는 언제 어디서 그 물고기가 태어났는지 알아낼 수 있습니다.

31 내가 물고기에서 얻은 모든 정보는 바다의 자원을 이해하고 바다를 더 잘 관리하기 위해 사용됩니다.

32 내 직업은 자연을 가장 잘 활용할 수 있게 한다는 점에서 중요합니다.

※ 다음 문장을 우리말로 쓰시오.

The World of Wonderful Jobs

Florist

1 Hi, I am Tom. A florist is someone who creates beautiful things with flowers.

➡ _____

2 To become a florist, you need to know many things about flowers.

➡ _____

3 I attended a high school for florists and gardeners.

➡ _____

4 It was at this school that I learned how to grow and care for different types of flowers.

➡ _____

5 These days, florists can do a lot of different things.

➡ _____

6 I design movie sets sometimes and I decorate shops with flowers.

➡ _____

7 I am happy when I create something colorful with fresh flowers and greenery.

➡ _____

8 If you like plants and the arts, I highly recommend you become a florist.

➡ _____

Sport Data Analyst

9 I am Emma. I am a sport data analyst.

➡ _____

10 It sounds like a difficult job, doesn't it?

➡ _____

11 In fact, it is a lot of fun. I work for a baseball team.

➡ _____

12 My job is to watch recorded games and run a computer program to collect data.

➡ _____

13 Then, I analyze the data to show my team's strengths and weaknesses.

➡ _____

14 If the team understands their strengths and weaknesses, they can do better next time.

➡ _____

15 Since I was young, I have been a big fan of baseball.

➡ _____

16 Now, in my work, I watch baseball games all the time.

➡ _____

17 This is a perfect job for me because watching baseball games is my hobby!

➡ _____

Director of a Musical Theater

18 Hi, I am Chris. As a director of a musical theater, I do a lot of things.

➡ _____

19 I audition the actors and I look for good, strong voices.

➡ _____

20 After selecting the cast, I teach them the songs for each scene.

➡ _____

21 Then, I put the cast and orchestra together for practice.

➡ _____

22 During the performance, I am in the orchestra area and conduct.

➡ _____

23 It's my responsibility to have each song played the same way every time.

➡ _____

24 I direct the musicians and the singers to keep the show together.

➡ _____

25 Conducting and directing is not just about waving my arms around!

➡ _____

Ocean Scientist

26 My name is Yeji. I am an ocean scientist. Ocean science is a big field.

➡ _____

27 It includes studies of the oceans and the creatures living in them.

➡ _____

28 Among other things, I have studied many kinds of fish living in the seas near Korea.

➡ _____

29 It is the growth ring in a fish that interests me.

➡ _____

30 By looking at it, I can find out when and where the fish was born.

➡ _____

31 All the information I get from fish is used to understand sea resources and manage the oceans better.

➡ _____

32 My job is important because it makes the best use of nature possible.

➡ _____

※ 다음 괄호 안의 단어들을 우리말에 맞도록 바르게 배열하시오.

The World of Wonderful Jobs
Florist

1 (hi, / am / I / Tom. // florist / a / someone / is / creates / who / things / beautiful / flowers. / with)
➡ _____
_____

2 (become / to / florist, / a / need / you / know / to / things / many / flowers. / about)
➡ _____

3 (attended / I / a / school / high / florists / for / gardeners. / and)
➡ _____

4 (was / it / this / at / school / that / learned / I / to / how / grow / and / for / care / types / different / flowers. / of)
➡ _____
_____

5 (days, / these / can / florists / do / lot / a / of / things. / different)
➡ _____

6 (design / I / sets / movie / sometimes / and / decorate / I / with / shops / flowers.)
➡ _____

7 (am / I / when / happy / create / I / something / with / colorful / flowers / fresh / greenery. / and)
➡ _____
_____

8 (you / if / like / and / plants / arts, / the / highly / I / you / recommend / become / florist. / a)
➡ _____

Sport Data Analyst

9 (am / I / Emma. // am / I / sport / a / analyst. / data)
➡ _____

10 (sounds / it / a / like / job, / difficult / it? / doesn't)
➡ _____

11 (fact, / in / is / it / lot / a / of // fun. / I / for / work / baseball / team. / a)
➡ _____

12 (job / my / to / is / recorded / watch / games / and / a / run / computer / program / collect / to / data.)
➡ _____

플로리스트

1 안녕하세요. 저는 Tom입니다. 플로리스트란 꽃으로 아름다운 것들을 창조하는 사람입니다.

2 플로리스트가 되기 위해서 여러분은 꽃에 관해 많은 것을 알 필요가 있습니다.

3 나는 플로리스트와 정원사를 양성하는 고등학교에 다녔습니다.

4 제가 다양한 종류의 꽃을 기르고 다루는 방법을 배운 곳이 바로 이 학교에서였습니다.

5 오늘날, 플로리스트는 많은 다양한 일을 할 수 있습니다.

6 나는 때때로 영화 세트장을 디자인하고 꽃으로 상점을 꾸밉니다.

7 나는 싱싱한 꽃과 화초로 다채로운 무언가를 창조해 낼 때 행복합니다.

8 만약 당신이 식물과 예술을 좋아한다면, 나는 당신에게 플로리스트가 될 것을 강력히 추천합니다.

스포츠 데이터 분석가

9 나는 Emma입니다. 나는 스포츠 데이터 분석가입니다.

10 어려운 직업처럼 들리죠, 그렇지 않나요?

11 사실, 그것은 매우 재미있습니다. 나는 야구팀을 위해서 일합니다.

12 나의 일은 녹화된 경기를 보고 자료를 수집하기 위해 컴퓨터 프로그램을 실행하는 것입니다.

13 (then, / analyze / I / data / the / show / to / team's / my / strengths / weaknesses. / and)

➡ _____

14 (the / if / team / understands / strengths / their / weaknesses, / and / can / they / better / do / time. / next)

➡ _____

_____

15 (I / since / young, / was / have / I / been / big / a / fan / baseball. / of)

➡ _____

16 (now, / my / in / work, / watch / I / games / baseball / the / all / time.)

➡ _____

17 (is / this / a / perfect / for / job / me / watching / because / games / baseball / my / is / hobby!)

➡ _____

_____

Director of a Musical Theater

18 (hi, / am / I / Chris. // a / as / director / a / of / theater, / musical / do / I / lot / a / things. / of)

➡ _____

19 (audition / I / actors / the / and / look / I / good, / for / voices. / strong)

➡ _____

20 (selecting / after / cast, / the / teach / I / them / songs / the / each / for / scene.)

➡ _____

21 (then, / put / I / cast / the / and / together / orchestra / practice. / for)

➡ _____

22 (the / during / performace, / am / I / in / orchestra / the / and / area / conduct.)

➡ _____

13 그리고 나서, 나는 내 팀의 강점과 약점을 보여 주기 위해서 그 자료들을 분석합니다.

14 만약 팀이 자신들의 강점과 약점을 이해하면, 그들은 다음번에 더 잘할 수 있습니다.

15 어렸을 때부터, 나는 야구의 열혈 팬이었습니다.

16 지금, 나는 일하는 중에 내내 야구를 봅니다.

17 야구 경기를 보는 것은 나의 취미이기 때문에 이것은 나에게 완벽한 직업입니다!

뮤지컬 극장 감독

18 안녕하세요. 나는 Chris입니다. 뮤지컬 극장 감독으로서 나는 많은 것들을 합니다.

19 나는 배우들을 대상으로 오디션을 실시하고, 훌륭하고 강한 목소리를 찾아냅니다.

20 배역에 맞는 배우를 고른 뒤에, 나는 그들에게 각 장면을 위한 노래를 가르칩니다.

21 그리고 나서, 나는 배우와 오케스트라를 함께 연습시킵니다.

22 공연 동안에, 나는 오케스트라 석에 있고 지휘를 합니다.

23 (my / it's / responsibility / have / to / song / each / played / same / the / every / way / time.)

➡ _____

_____

24 (direct / I / musicians / the / and / singers / the / keep / to / show / the / together.)

➡ _____

25 (directing / and / conducting / is / just / not / waving / about / arms / my / around!)

➡ _____

Ocean Scientist

26 (name / my / Yeji. / is // am / I / ocean / an / scientist. // science / ocean / a / is / field. / big)

➡ _____

27 (includes / it / of / studies / the / oceans / the / and / living / creatures / them. / in)

➡ _____

28 (other / among / things, / have / I / kinds / many / studied / of / living / fish / the / in / seas / Korea. / near)

➡ _____

_____

29 (is / it / growth / the / ring / a / in / fish / interests / that / me.)

➡ _____

30 (looking / by / it, / at / can / I / out / find / where / and / when / fish / the / born. / was)

➡ _____

31 (the / all / information / get / I / fish / from / used / is / to / sea / understand / manage / and / resources / oceans / the / better.)

➡ _____

_____

32 (job / my / is / because / important / makes / it / best / the / use / nature / of / possible.)

➡ _____

23 각각의 노래가 매번 동일하게 연주되도록 만드는 것은 나의 책임입니다.

24 나는 공연을 제대로 진행하기 위해 연주자들과 가수들을 감독합니다.

25 지휘하고 감독하는 것은 단지 내 팔을 흔드는 것만이 아닙니다!

해양 과학자

26 나는 예지입니다. 나는 해양 과학자입니다. 해양 과학은 거대한 분야입니다.

27 그것은 바다와 그 안에 살고 있는 생물에 관한 연구를 포함합니다.

28 여러 가지 중에서 나는 한국 주변의 바다에 살고 있는 많은 종류의 물고기를 연구해 왔습니다.

29 나의 흥미를 끄는 것은 바로 물고기 안에 있는 나이테입니다.

30 나이테를 살펴봄으로써, 나는 언제 어디서 그 물고기가 태어났는지 알아낼 수 있습니다.

31 내가 물고기에서 얻은 모든 정보는 바다의 자원을 이해하고 바다를 더 잘 관리하기 위해 사용됩니다.

32 내 직업은 자연을 가장 잘 활용할 수 있게 한다는 점에서 중요합니다.

※ 다음 우리말을 영어로 쓰시오.

The World of Wonderful Jobs

Florist

1 안녕하세요. 저는 Tom입니다. 플로리스트란 꽃으로 아름다운 것들을 창조하는 사람입니다.

➡ _____

2 플로리스트가 되기 위해서 여러분은 꽃에 관해 많은 것을 알 필요가 있습니다.

➡ _____

3 나는 플로리스트와 정원사를 양성하는 고등학교에 다녔습니다.

➡ _____

4 제가 다양한 종류의 꽃을 기르고 다루는 방법을 배운 곳이 바로 이 학교에서였습니다.

➡ _____

5 오늘날, 플로리스트는 많은 다양한 일을 할 수 있습니다.

➡ _____

6 나는 때때로 영화 세트장을 디자인하고 꽃으로 상점을 꾸밉니다.

➡ _____

7 나는 싱싱한 꽃과 화초로 다채로운 무언가를 창조해 낼 때 행복합니다.

➡ _____

8 만약 당신이 식물과 예술을 좋아한다면, 나는 당신에게 플로리스트가 될 것을 강력히 추천합니다.

➡ _____

Sport Data Analyst

9 나는 Emma입니다. 나는 스포츠 데이터 분석가입니다.

➡ _____

10 어려운 직업처럼 들리죠, 그렇지 않나요?

➡ _____

11 사실, 그것은 매우 재미있습니다. 나는 야구팀을 위해서 일합니다.

➡ _____

12 나의 일은 녹화된 경기를 보고 자료를 수집하기 위해 컴퓨터 프로그램을 실행하는 것입니다.

➡ _____

13 그러고 나서, 나는 내 팀의 강점과 약점을 보여 주기 위해서 그 자료들을 분석합니다.

➡ _____

14 만약 팀이 자신들의 강점과 약점을 이해하면, 그들은 다음번에 더 잘할 수 있습니다.

➡ _____

15 어렸을 때부터, 나는 야구의 열혈 팬이었습니다.

➡ _____

16 지금, 나는 일하는 중에 내내 야구를 봅니다.

➡ _____

17 야구 경기를 보는 것은 나의 취미이기 때문에 이것은 나에게 완벽한 직업입니다!

➡ _____

Director of a Musical Theater

18 안녕하세요. 나는 Chris입니다. 뮤지컬 극장 감독으로서 나는 많은 것들을 합니다.

➡ _____

19 나는 배우들을 대상으로 오디션을 실시하고, 훌륭하고 강한 목소리를 찾아냅니다.

➡ _____

20 배역에 맞는 배우를 고른 뒤에, 나는 그들에게 각 장면을 위한 노래를 가르칩니다.

➡ _____

21 그러고 나서, 나는 배우와 오케스트라를 함께 연습시킵니다.

➡ _____

22 공연 동안에, 나는 오케스트라 석에 있고 지휘를 합니다.

➡ _____

23 각각의 노래가 매번 동일하게 연주되도록 만드는 것은 나의 책임입니다.

➡ _____

24 나는 공연을 제대로 진행하기 위해 연주자들과 가수들을 감독합니다.

➡ _____

25 지휘하고 감독하는 것은 단지 내 팔을 흔드는 것만이 아닙니다!

➡ _____

Ocean Scientist

26 나는 예지입니다. 나는 해양 과학자입니다. 해양 과학은 거대한 분야입니다.

➡ _____

27 그것은 바다와 그 안에 살고 있는 생물에 관한 연구를 포함합니다.

➡ _____

28 여러 가지 중에서 나는 한국 주변의 바다에 살고 있는 많은 종류의 물고기를 연구해 왔습니다.

➡ _____

29 나의 흥미를 끄는 것은 바로 물고기 안에 있는 나이테입니다.

➡ _____

30 나이테를 살펴봄으로써, 나는 언제 어디서 그 물고기가 태어났는지 알아낼 수 있습니다.

➡ _____

31 내가 물고기에서 얻은 모든 정보는 바다의 자원을 이해하고 바다를 더 잘 관리하기 위해 사용됩니다.

➡ _____

32 내 직업은 자연을 가장 잘 활용할 수 있게 한다는 점에서 중요합니다.

➡ _____

※ 다음 우리말과 일치하도록 빈칸에 알맞은 말을 쓰시오.

Enjoy Writing C

1. My _____ _____.

2. I like food from _____ _____ _____ and I _____ _____ _____.

3. I can also _____ _____ _____ _____ _____ and _____.

4. _____ _____ _____, it is a chef _____ I want to be _____ I _____ _____.

5. _____ _____ my dream, I will read magazines _____ _____.

6. Also, I will go to France _____ _____ _____ _____ _____.

7. _____ _____ _____ is my dad.

8. He _____ _____ of new _____ and then cooks these new dishes for us.

9. I want to _____ _____ _____ _____ by people _____ _____ _____ _____.

Project

1. HELP _____!!

2. Do you _____ _____?

3. If your answer is yes, _____ is you that we _____ _____ _____.

4. Please join us _____ _____ and _____ _____.

5. _____ more information, _____ _____ _____ at www. robots.com.

Project Step 3

1. _____ you _____ _____ _____ and _____ robots?

2. If _____, we're sure that you'll be _____ _____ _____ _____.

3. _____ _____ _____ _____, _____ our websites.

1. 내 꿈의 직업
2. 나는 전 세계 음식을 좋아하고 요리를 잘한다.
3. 나는 또한 음식을 맛있고 아름다워 보이게 만들 수 있다.
4. 이러한 이유로 내가 자라서 되고 싶은 것은 요리사이다.
5. 내 꿈을 이루기 위해, 나는 요리에 관한 잡지를 읽을 것이다.
6. 또한 나는 프랑스에 가서 다양한 요리 기술을 익힐 것이다.
7. 내 롤 모델은 나의 아빠이다.
8. 그는 항상 새로운 요리법을 생각해 내시고 우리를 위해 이러한 요리를 만들어 주신다.
9. 나는 내 이름이 내 음식을 좋아하는 사람들에게 기억되도록 하고 싶다.

1. 사람 구합니다!
2. 로봇을 좋아하시나요?
3. 당신의 답이 예스라면, 당신이 바로 우리가 찾는 사람입니다.
4. 우리와 함께 로봇을 훈련시키고, 고쳐 보세요.
5. 더 자세한 사항은 우리 웹사이트 www.robots.com을 방문해 주세요.

1. 당신은 로봇을 훈련시키고 수리하는 것을 잘하나요?
2. 만약 그렇다면, 우리는 당신이 좋은 로봇 전문가가 될 것이라고 확신합니다.
3. 더 많은 정보를 위해서, 우리 웹사이트를 방문하세요.

※ 다음 우리말을 영어로 쓰시오.

Enjoy Writing C

1. 내 꿈의 직업
   ➡ _____

2. 나는 전 세계 음식을 좋아하고 요리를 잘한다.
   ➡ _____

3. 나는 또한 음식을 맛있고 아름다워 보이게 만들 수 있다.
   ➡ _____

4. 이러한 이유로 내가 자라서 되고 싶은 것은 요리사이다.
   ➡ _____

5. 내 꿈을 이루기 위해, 나는 요리에 관한 잡지를 읽을 것이다.
   ➡ _____

6. 또한 나는 프랑스에 가서 다양한 요리 기술을 익힐 것이다.
   ➡ _____

7. 내 롤 모델은 나의 아빠이다.
   ➡ _____

8. 그는 항상 새로운 요리법을 생각해 내시고 우리를 위해 이러한 요리를 만들어 주신다.
   ➡ _____

9. 나는 내 이름이 내 음식을 좋아하는 사람들에게 기억되도록 하고 싶다.
   ➡ _____

Project

1. 사람 구합니다!
   ➡ _____

2. 로봇을 좋아하시나요?
   ➡ _____

3. 당신의 답이 예스라면, 당신이 바로 우리가 찾는 사람입니다.
   ➡ _____

4. 우리와 함께 로봇을 훈련시키고, 고쳐보세요.
   ➡ _____

5. 더 자세한 사항은 우리 웹사이트 www.robots.com을 방문해 주세요.
   ➡ _____

Project Step 3

1. 당신은 로봇을 훈련시키고 수리하는 것을 잘하나요?
   ➡ _____

2. 만약 그렇다면, 우리는 당신이 좋은 로봇 전문가가 될 것이라고 확신합니다.
   ➡ _____

3. 더 많은 정보를 위해서, 우리 웹사이트를 방문하세요.
   ➡ _____

MEMO

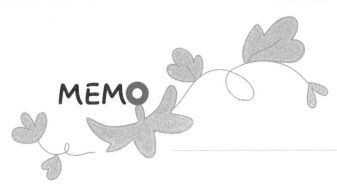

MEMO

영어 기출 문제집

적중100

1학기

정답 및 해설

시사 | 박준언

중 3

적중100

적중"100

중 3

적중"100

All about Me

01 basement   02 ②   03 ④   04 ①
05 feels, comfortable   06 ③
07 counsel   08 ⑤

01 '지면 아래에 있는 건물의 일부'라는 의미로 '지하실'이 적절하다.

02 자연은 좋은 친구라고 했으므로 숲속을 걸을 때 기분이 좋다는 말이 자연스럽다.

03 '전에 보거나 듣고 경험했기 때문에 사람이나 사물을 알다'는 뜻으로 'recognize(인식하다)'가 적절하다.

04 두 가지 이상의 것 중에서 선택할 가능성

05 'feel+형용사'는 '~하게 느끼다'는 의미로, '주어가 3인칭 단수'이므로 동사는 feels를 쓰고 '편안한'은 'comfortable'이다.

06 (A) 남들보다 먼저 신기술을 사용하는 사람을 일컫는 'an early adopter'가 적절하다. (B) 프랑스는 유럽에서 한국 고아들의 가장 큰 입양인이다.

07 유의어 관계이다.

08 (A) '다른 사람들보다 먼저 새로운 제품과 기술을 사용한다.'는 의미로 before가 적절하다. (B) '정문이 얼굴을 인식해서 자동으로 열린다.'로 recognizes가 적절하다.

01 (1) technology   (2) furniture   (3) exciting
    (4) advise

02 (1) stop eating   (2) good at   (3) interested in
    (4) get along with

03 (1) language   (2) nickname   (3) (c)reated

04 (1) fantastic, 환상적인   (2) forward, 앞으로
    (3) imagine, 상상하다

05 (1) (k)ind   (2) (g)oal

01 (1) 나는 컴퓨터 기술(technology)로 만들어진 장면을 좋아해. (2) 그 방은 오래된 가구(furniture)로 가득 차 있다. (3) 내 꿈의 집은 흥미로운(exciting) 것들로 가득 차 있다. (4) 제가 무엇을 해야 할지 조언해(advise) 주시겠어요?

02 (1) '올해 나의 목표는 fast food를 먹는 것을 그만두는 것이다'라는 의미가 적절하다. 'stop+-ing' 형태를 쓴다. (2) '나는 드

럼 연주를 잘한다'라는 의미로 'be good at'이 적절하다. (3) 밤에 별을 보러 나간다고 했으므로 별에 관심이 있다는 의미가 적절하다. 'be interested in'이 '~에 관심이 있다'라는 뜻이다. (4) '동아리에 있는 모든 사람들과 잘 지내기를 바란다'라는 의미로 'get along with'가 적절하다.

03 (1) 언어: language (2) 별명: nickname (3) 만들다: create

04 (1) 매우 좋거나 매력적이고 즐길만한 (2) 당신 앞에 있는 장소나 위치를 향하여 (3) 어떤 것에 대한 마음 속의 그림이나 생각을 형성하거나 가지다

05 (1) kind: 종류; 친절한 / 너는 장래에 어떤 종류의 것들을 원하니? / 친절한 남자가 우리를 도와주었다. (2) goal: 목표; 골, 득점 / 우리의 목표는 쓰레기를 10% 줄이는 것이다. / 리버풀이 3 대 1로 이겼다.

교과서
Conversation

1 ⑤   2 ③

교과서 대화문 익히기

1 T   2 F   3 T   4 F   5 T   6 F   7 T   8 T   9 F

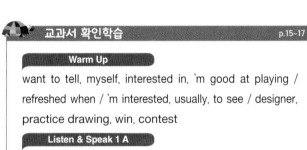

교과서 확인학습   p.15~17

Warm Up
want to tell, myself, interested in, 'm good at playing / refreshed when / 'm interested, usually, to see / designer, practice drawing, win, contest

Listen & Speak 1 A
1. how, grade / pretty / good, homeroom teacher / teaches / Can you tell me, about / humorous, told / fun stories, interesting / enjoy studying
2. to see / looks / about, who saves / looks like / favorite, scenes made, fantastic, real / cool / Sounds

Listen & Speak 1 B
about / have / goal / stop eating

시험대비 기본평가   p.18

01 Can you tell me about   02 ④   03 ⑤
04 refreshed when

01 궁금증을 표현하거나 보다 많은 정보를 알고 싶을 때 사용하는 표현으로 Can you tell me about ...?을 사용한다.

02 B의 대답으로 보아 앞으로의 계획에 관해 물어보는 말이 적절하다.

03 가장 좋아하는 과목이 음악이고, 드럼과 기타를 연주할 수 있다고 말하고 있으므로 빈칸에는 ⑤번이 가장 적절하다.

04 '~하게 느끼다'는 의미로 'feel+형용사' 형태를 사용한다. refreshed는 형용사로 '상쾌한'의 의미고, '~할 때'의 의미를 가진 접속사는 when을 사용한다.

시험대비 실력평가   p.19~20

01 ③, ⑤   02 (a) traveling   (b) Playing[To play]
03 It is about a hero who saves the Earth.
04 ④   05 what I like most   06 ④
07 ③   08 ③   09 (A)mong
10 (B) – (A) – (C)   11 ②
12 What I like most about traveling

01 '내가 가장 좋아하는 것'이라는 의미로 관계대명사 what과 the thing that이 적절하다.

02 (a) 전치사 about 뒤에 동명사 형태가 적절하고, (b) 주어 자리에 동명사나 to부정사 형태가 오는 것이 적절하다.

03 '~에 관한 것이다'는 be about이고, a hero를 수식하는 관계대

명사절을 이용한다. 선행사가 단수 명사 a hero이므로 save는 단수 형태 saves로 쓴다.

04 B가 I like pizza most.라고 답하고 있으므로 좋아하는 음식이 무엇인지 묻는 말이 적절하다.

05 관계대명사 what을 이용하고 '가장 (많이)'의 의미로 most를 쓴다.

06 궁금증을 표현하거나 보다 많은 정보를 알고 싶을 때 사용하는 표현으로 Can you tell me about ...?을 사용한다.

07 '내가 가장 좋아하는 것은'의 의미를 가지며, 주어 자리에 사용되는 관계대명사 what이 적절하다.

08 ③번은 대화에 언급되어 있지 않다.

09 어떤 그룹의 한 가운데에서

10 이번 주말 계획을 묻는 말에 (B) 생일 파티를 할 예정이라는 답을 하고 → (A) 올해 목표를 묻는 말에 → (C) fast food 먹는 것을 그만두겠다는 대답이 오는 것이 적절하다.

11 ②번은 '너에 관해 말해 줄 수 있니?'라는 A의 말에 '내 친구들은 모두 내게 친절해.'라고 말하는 것은 자연스럽지 않다.

12 관계대명사 What으로 문장을 시작하고 뒤에 '주어+동사' 어순이 온다.

서술형 시험대비   p.21

01 Can you tell us more about yourself?
02 I want to get along with everyone.
03 (A) because I can run fast.
   (B) What I like most is to play baseball.
   (C) What is your motto?
04 about a hero who[that] saves the Earth
05 (a) movie   (b) this weekend

01 '~에 관해 더 말해 줄래?'라는 표현은 Can you tell us more about ~?을 이용한다.

02 get along with ~: ~와 잘 지내다

04 '~에 관한 것이다'는 'be about'을 사용하고, 사람을 선행사로 하는 관계대명사 who나 that을 사용한다. 주격 관계대명사의 동사는 단수 동사인 saves를 쓴다.

05 (a) Amy가 보고 싶어 하는 것은 '영화'다. (b) Ted와 영화를 보러 가기로 한 때는 '이번 주말'이다.

교과서
Grammar

1 (1) do   (2) does

2 (1) Janet gave me what she had made.

  (2) What are produced in the factory are cars.

시험대비 기본평가   p.24

01 (1) which → what   (2) does → do

   (3) felt → feel   (4) what → that

02 ②   03 ⑤

04 (1) What he wrote on the paper was interesting.

   (2) She does feel proud of what her mother

     makes.

01 (1) 전치사 by의 목적어와 had의 목적어 두 개의 명사가 필요한 자리에 관계대명사 what을 쓴다. (2) 동사를 강조하는 do는 주어의 인칭과 수 및 시제 등에 맞춘다. They 뒤에는 do를 쓴다. (3) 강조의 do[did]를 쓰면, 동사는 원형이 온다. (4) 선행사 all 뒤에는 관계대명사 that이 온다. 이 문제의 경우, All을 없애고, What만 남겨도 어법상 바르게 된다.

02 ② 강조하는 did가 있으므로 동사 원형 build를 써야 한다.

03 강조하는 do 뒤에는 동사 원형을 써야 한다.

04 (1) 시제에 유의하여 write를 wrote로 쓴다. (2) 인칭과 수 및 시제에 맞춰 does와 makes를 쓴다.

시험대비 실력평가   p.25~27

01 ④	02 that → what	03 ⑤
04 ③	05 ④	06 ①	07 ②
08 ④	09 ①	10 ④, ⑤	11 ②
12 ③	13 ⓓ, ⓕ	14 ④	15 ③
16 what, was 17 ④	18 ③	19 ⑤
20 ④	21 ①	

01 두 문장이 하나가 되었으므로, 앞 문장에서의 보어와 뒤 문장에서의 목적어로 명사 두 개가 필요한데, 이 조건을 충족시키는 것은 관계대명사 what이다.

02 what was worse는 '설상가상으로'라는 뜻이다.

03 'Arthur 왕이 전설의 검을 정말로 찾아냈다.'라는 문장과 '전설의 검을 찾을 수 있었다.'라는 문장은 서로 같지 않다.

04 첫 번째 빈칸 뒤에 동사원형이 있으므로 강조의 does 또는 did 가능, 두 번째 빈칸은 선행사와 관계대명사를 포함하여 명사절

을 이끄는 What이 들어가야 한다.

05 '접속사와 대명사 역할의 관계대명사가 필요한 자리이다. 선행사가 있으므로 that이 들어간다.

06 동사 강조의 do를 현재시제 3인칭 단수형에 맞게 쓴다. do the dishes: 설거지를 하다

07 명령문은 Do로 강조 가능하다. did warned → did warn, did changed → did change, does believed → does believe, do looks → do look

08 관계대명사 what과 의문대명사 what의 문장 구조는 동일할 때가 있다. 이때 구분의 기준은 해석으로서 관계대명사는 '~하는 것'으로, 의문대명사는 '무엇(이/을)'으로 해석한다. ④ 너는 엄마가 무엇을 요리하고 계시는지 모르겠다. (의문대명사)

09 ② a new car와 his wife의 자리를 바꿔야 한다. ③ what → that ④ what → which[that] ⑤ said him → said to him(또는 told him)

10 ④ what → which[that] ⑤ Which → What

11 6년 전 과거의 일이므로 does를 did로 바꿔야 한다.

12 강조의 did를 쓰면 동사는 원형이 와야 한다.

13 ⓐ which → what ⓑ what → which[that] ⓒ The thing → The thing that[which] 또는 What ⓔ that → what ⓖ that → what

14 동사를 강조할 때 do, does, did를 시제와 인칭에 맞게 사용한다.

15 동사 강조의 do(does/did)를 찾는다.

16 과거의 그: what he was, 과거의 그의 재산: what he had 현재의 그: what he is, 현재의 그의 재산: what he has

17 관계대명사 what과 의문대명사 what을 구분하는 문제이다.

18 ① do → does ② made → make ④ what → which[that] ⑤ it 삭제

19 동사 강조의 do(does/did)를 찾는다.

20 Pay attention to what she is saying.

21 ① what → which[that]

서술형 시험대비   p.28~29

01 (1) did build   (2) do think   (3) did write

02 (1) I don't believe what they said to me the other day.

  (2) Show her what you put in your mouth.

  (3) She did feel friendly to Mike.

  (4) I did love Susan, but she left me forever.

  (5) That she asked him to help her was not true.

03 (1) What Sarah bought were comic books.

  (2) Robert couldn't believe what the researchers explained.

  (3) What was discussed was shocking.

04 (1) What she had found in the cave surprised the world.

(2) Do be quiet in this room.

(3) What she bought from the market were all expensive.

05 (1) Charlie did find his missing child.

(2) He does know many K-pop singers.

(3) Jeremy did write those essays last year.

06 (1) Carl himself bought the hamster yesterday.

(2) It was the hamster that Carl bought yesterday.

(3) Carl did buy the hamster yesterday.

(4) It was yesterday that Carl bought the hamster.

07 (1) She finally accepted what he offered.

(2) He did feel satisfied with the result.

(3) It is quite different from what they have been waiting for.

(4) That I saw him yesterday is not true.

(5) What people believed in the past does surprise me.

08 (1) does (2) that 또는 which (3) kill (4) What, are

09 As John did feel a toothache

01 수와 시제 등에 유의하여 do를 활용하되 do 뒤에는 동사원형이 와야 한다.

02 (1) believe의 목적어와 said의 목적어 역할을 하는 what이 적절하다. (2) 그녀에게 '네가 입에 넣은 것'을 보여주라는 문장이므로 접속사 that을 관계대명사 what으로 바꾼다. (3) 강조의 조동사 뒤에는 동사원형이 나온다. (4) 과거시제 동사를 강조할 때는 did + 동사원형이 적절하다. (5) What 뒤에는 불완전한 문장 구조가 나와야 한다. 주어 역할을 하는 명사절을 이끄는 접속사 That이 적절하다.

03 관계대명사 what은 문맥에 따라 단/복수 취급에 유의해야 한다. (1) Sarah가 산 것들은 만화책이었다. (2) Robert는 연구자들이 설명하는 것을 믿을 수 없었다. (3) 논의된 것은 충격적이었다.

04 (1) 관계대명사 what을 활용한다. (2) 명령문의 Be를 강조할 때에도 Do를 사용한다. (3) be동사를 were로 사용하는 것에 주의한다. what은 문맥에 따라 복수 취급도 가능하다.

05 수와 시제 등에 유의하여 do/did/does를 활용하되 강조를 위해 사용한 do 뒤에는 동사 원형이 와야 한다.

06 (1) himself를 문미로 보내도 된다. (2) 'It ~ that 강조 구문'으로 목적어를 강조한다. (3) 'did+동사원형'으로 동사를 강조한다. (4) 부사 yesterday를 'It ~ that 강조 구문'으로 강조한다.

07 (1) '그가 제안하는 것'이므로 what이 적절하다. (2) 강조의 did 뒤에는 동사 원형을 쓴다. (3) '그들이 기다려왔던 것'이므로 what이 적절하다. (4) What 뒤에는 완전한 절이 올 수 없다. 내용상 '내가 어제 그를 보았다는 것'이라는 명사절로서 접속

사 That이 적절하다. (5) does로 강조하면 동사 surprise는 원형을 써야 한다.

08 (1) like가 원형이므로, 부사는 쓸 수 없다. does로 강조한다. (2) 선행사가 있으므로 관계대명사 that 또는 which를 쓴다. (3) 강조의 did 뒤에는 원형동사 kill이 적절하다. (4) 중요한 '것'이므로 주어는 What이 적절하며, what절 내의 동사가 are인 것으로 보아, 본동사도 are가 적절하다.

09 동사를 강조하는 'do'를 시제에 맞게 활용한다.

Reading

확인문제   p.30

1 T 2 T 3 F 4 F 5 T

확인문제   p.31

1 F 2 F 3 T 4 T 5 F

교과서 확인학습 A   p.32~33

01 Have, ever thought   02 created

03 are, that

04 Nature   05 do feel good

06 like to have, in

07 should have, with

08 am, excited by

09 wonderful to wake up, listen to

10 like to have, to play   11 to

12 Having fun, what, is full of

13 in the basement

14 enjoy, movies   15 has, on, floor

16 kinds of games

17 a swimming pool

18 do fun things, my guest

19 the most important thing

20 feels safe, comfortable

21 At, beautifully designed sign, on

22 enter, see a large living room

23 board games

24 a large picnic table

25 enjoy, Do you like

26 an early adopter

27 do like, before

28 get near, recognizes, opens

29 checks, conditions, advises, on

30 tells me, condition

31 cleans, cooks for

32 what I can imagine

1 Have you ever thought about your dream house?

2 Today, in class, we created our dream house.

3 Here are some of the dream houses that we made.

4 Nature is my good friend.

5 I do feel good when I walk in the forest.

6 I'd like to have a dream house in the countryside.

7 It should have a big garden with many flowers and trees.

8 I am always excited by the sound of birds.

9 It will be wonderful to wake up in the morning and listen to the songs of the birds.

10 Also, I'd like to have many pets. It will be fun to play with them!

11 Welcome to my dream house!

12 Having fun is what I want most, so my dream house is full of exciting things.

13 It has a theater in the basement.

14 There, I can eat cookies and enjoy my favorite movies.

15 My dream house has a game room on the second floor.

16 I can play many different kinds of games there.

17 My house also has a swimming pool.

18 I want to do fun things with my friends in my house. You can be my guest!

19 My family is the most important thing to me.

20 In my dream house, my family feels safe and comfortable.

21 At the gate, you can find a beautifully designed sign with my family's picture on it.

22 When you enter the house, you will see a large living room.

23 My family sometimes plays board games and sings there.

24 It will have a garden with a large picnic table for family picnics.

25 There, we will enjoy barbecues. Do you like my dream house?

26 I am an early adopter of new technology.

27 I do like to use new products and technology before others.

28 When I get near my house, the front door recognizes my face and opens automatically.

29 The furniture checks the weather conditions and advises me on what to wear.

30 The bathroom mirror tells me my weight and the condition of my health.

31 A robot cleans the house and cooks for me.

32 This is what I can imagine about my dream house.

01 ⑤   02 ④

03 He wants to have his dream house in the countryside.   04 ⑤

05 ③   06 guest   07 ②   08 ④

09 Her family is the most important thing to her.

10 ③   11 ⑤

12 A robot cleans the house and cooks for him in his dream house.

13 ⑤   14 ③

15 They created their dream house in class.

16 ②   17 ⑤

18 A theater, a game room, and a swimming pool.

19 ②   20 ③   21 ④

22 New Technology   23 ⑤   24 ②

25 ③

01 이어지는 말로 보아 기분이 좋다는 말이 들어가는 것이 적절하다.

02 민호는 자신이 만든 꿈의 집에 대해 말하고 있다.

03 '민호는 시골에 자신의 꿈의 집을 갖기를 원한다고 하였다.

04 주어진 문장의 there가 가리키는 것은 2층에 있는 게임방이라고 보는 것이 적절하다.

05 Julie는 지하실(basement)에 극장을 둔다고 하였다. ground floor: 1층

06 '당신이 초대하여서 당신을 방문한 사람'은 '손님'이다.

07 미선이는 자신의 꿈의 집에 관해 말하고 있으며, 자신에게 가장 중요한 가족을 위한 공간임을 말하고 있다.

08 미선의 가족은 거실에서 보드 게임을 하거나 노래를 부른다고 하였다.

09 미선이는 그녀에게 가족이 가장 중요하다고 하였다.

10 빈칸 ⓐ에 들어갈 말은 관계대명사 what이다. ①, ②, ④에는 관계대명사 that, ⑤에는 명사절 접속사 That이 쓰이며 ③번에

는 what이 쓰인다.

11 adapter: (별개의 전기 기구를 연결하는 데 쓰는) 어댑터, adopter: (신기술) 사용자, get near: 가까워지다, get away: 떠나다, 멀어지다, 날씨 상태를 보고 '무엇을 입을지' 조언한다는 표현이 적절하다.

12 꿈의 집에서 로봇은 Bryan을 위해 청소를 하고 요리를 해준다고 하였다.

13 also는 '또한, 게다가'라는 의미이다. ① 그러나 ② 그럼에도 불구하고 ③ 그러므로 ④ 예를 들어 ⑤ 게다가

14 우리가 만든 꿈의 집 몇 개가 있다'고 말하며 민호의 집을 소개하고 있으므로 이어질 내용으로는 다른 학생이 만든 꿈의 집을 소개하는 내용이 이어진다고 보는 것이 적절하다.

15 수업 시간에 꿈의 집을 만들었다고 하였다.

16 글의 내용으로 미루어 보아 민호는 자연친화적임을 알 수 있다.

17 빈칸 (A)에는 전치사 of가 쓰인다. ① be interested in: ~에 흥미가 있다 ② pay attention to: ~에 주의를 기울이다 ③ depend on: ~에 의존하다 ④ belong to: ~에 속하다 ⑤ get rid of: ~을 없애다

18 Julie가 만든 꿈의 집에는 극장, 게임방, 그리고 수영장이 있다고 하였다.

19 (B)는 '~하는 용도'라는 의미로 쓰인 동명사이다. 모두 현재분사로 명사를 수식하거나 설명하지만 ②번은 동명사이다.

20 각각 ① safe ② large ④ comfortable ⑤ important의 반의어이다.

21 정원에서 바비큐를 즐길 것이라고 하였다. ① 미선은 가족들과 함께 살 것이며, ② 가족들이 집을 안전하고 편안하게 느낄 것이라고 하였다. ③ 꿈의 집에는 거실이 있고, ⑤ 가족들과의 소풍을 위한 피크닉 테이블이 있다.

22 글의 내용으로 보아 'New Technology(새로운 기술)'를 쓰는 것이 적절하다.

23 is의 보어와 imagine의 목적어 역할을 할 수 있는 what을 쓰는 것이 가장 적절하다.

24 새로운 상품이나 기술을 다른 사람들보다 먼저 사용하는 것을 좋아하는 사람이 early adopter이다. 따라서 before라고 쓰는 것이 적절하다.

25 Bryan이 집에 가까워지면 현관이 그의 얼굴을 인식하여 자동으로 문이 열린다고 하였다. story: (건물 등의) 층

서술형 시험대비 p.40~41

01 He feels good when he walks in the forest.
02 They made their dream house in class today.
03 We can find many flowers and trees in the garden of Minho's house.
04 many pets

05 Having fun is what she wants most.
06 We can find a theater in the basement.
07 strange → exciting
08 We can find the game room on the second floor.
09 my family does feel safe and comfortable
10 We can see a beautifully designed sign with her family's picture on it.
11 Misun's dream house
12 like to use new products and technology before others
13 It checks the weather conditions and advises Bryan on what to wear.
14 What
15 It's because she does want to remember what happened in her middle school days.

01 민호는 숲 속을 걸을 때 기분이 좋다고 하였다.

02 학생들은 오늘 수업 시간에 자신들의 꿈의 집을 만들었다고 하였다.

03 많은 꽃과 나무를 가진 큰 정원이 있는 집이라고 하였다.

04 앞 문장의 'many pets'를 지칭하는 말이다.

05 Julie가 가장 원하는 것은 즐거운 시간을 보내는 것이라고 하였다.

06 극장은 지하실에 있다고 하였다.

07 집에는 이상한 것들이 아니라 신나는 것들로 가득 차 있다고 하였다.

08 게임방은 2층에 있다고 하였다.

09 밑줄 친 문장의 동사는 feels이므로 does를 이용하여 강조하는 문장을 만들 수 있다.

10 미선이의 가족 사진이 있는 아름답게 꾸며진 문패를 볼 수 있다.

11 미선이의 꿈의 집을 가리키는 말이다.

12 Early adopter는 신기술 사용자를 의미하며 다른 사람보다 먼저 신제품이나 신기술을 이용하는 것을 좋아하는 사람이다.

13 Bryan의 꿈의 집에서는 가구가 날씨를 확인하고 그에게 무엇을 입을지 조언해 준다고 하였다.

14 put의 목적어와 are의 주어 역할을 할 수 있는 'what'이 적절하다.

15 자신의 중학교 시절에 무슨 일이 일어났는지를 정말로 기억하고 싶어서라고 하였다.

영역별 핵심문제 p.43~47

01 forward   02 ④   03 ③   04 ①
05 technology / technology 06 ⑤   07 ④
08 ⑤   09 ③   10 ①, ④   11 ③

7

12 What I like most is to play baseball.

13 ⑤

14 (1) Peter that[who] solved the problems

　(2) did solve the problems in the last class

　(3) in the last class that Peter solved the

　　problems

15 ①　　　　16 ④, ⑤　　　17 what

18 does/did　19 what　　　20 ②　　　　21 ⑤

22 ③, ④　　　23 ①, ④

24 The dream house

25 The sound of birds always makes Minho excited.

26 ④　　　　27 ③　　　　28 ③　　　　29 ③

30 It's because it shows what good friends they are.

31 ⑤

32 things Jina wants to put into her memory box

01 반의어 관계다. 넓은 : 좁은 = 뒤로 : 앞으로

02 (a): 우리가 만든 몇 개의 꿈의 집이 여기에 있다는 말로 보아 꿈의 집을 만들었다가 적절하다. (b): 나의 꿈의 집에서 친구들과 재미있는 것을 하고 싶다고 했으므로 너는 내 손님이 될 수 있다는 말이 적절하다.

03 집에서 동반자로 길러지고 친절하게 대접받는 동물

04 믿음이나 목적을 표현하는 짧은 문장이나 문구

05 가구가 날씨를 확인하고 무엇을 입을지 말해 준다고 했기 때문에 새로운 '기술'이 적절하고, 로마인들은 콘크리트를 만드는 데 매우 진보적인 '기술'을 갖고 있었다.

07 (a)는 저녁에 달리는 것을 좋아한다고 했기 때문에 'refreshed'가 적절하고, (b)는 밤에 별을 보러 나간다고 했기 때문에 '~에 관심이 있다'라는 interested가 적절하다.

08 3학년 첫날이 어땠는지 묻는 말에 → (C) 매우 좋았다고 답하고, 담임 선생님이 누군지 묻는 G의 질문에 → (B) 담임 선생님에 대한 설명이 오고, 선생님에 대해 더 말해 달라는 G의 물음에 → (A) 긍정의 답을 하고 선생님에 대한 추가적인 설명을 하는 것이 적절하다.

09 제시문의 여가 시간에 무엇을 하는지 묻는 말은 사진을 찍는 것을 가장 좋아한다는 대답 앞에 오는 것이 적절하다.

10 Seho의 대답이 사진작가가 되고 싶다고 했으므로 (A)에는 미래의 직업이나 꿈을 묻는 말이 적절하다.

11 Seho가 이미 많은 사진촬영 기술을 알고 있는지는 대화에 언급되어 있지 않다.

13 ① Jenny가 3인칭 단수이므로 does look이 적절하다. ② They look handsome on the stage. be동사와 상태를 나타내는 look이 같이 쓰였다. are를 생략하거나 do look으로 강조해야 한다. ③ does believe가 적절하다. ④ 과거동사 met을 강조할 때는 did meet이 적절하다.

14 원래의 문장을 영작하면, Peter solved the problems in the

last class.이다. (1) 주어인 Peter 강조 (2) 동사 solve를 강조하기 위해 did 사용 (3) 부사구인 in the last class를 강조하기 위해 'It ~ that 강조 구문' 사용

15 첫 번째 문장에서는 '백악관 앞에서 찍힌 것들(사진들)'을 가리키는 말이므로 what이 적절하다. 두 번째 문장에서는 동사 원형 start로 보아 did가 적절하다.

16 ④ does like가 적절하다. ⑤ 강조의 did 뒤에는 동사 원형을 써야 한다.

17 the thing(s) that[which] = what

18 '노인과 바다'는 3인칭 단수이고, 동사원형 make가 쓰였으므로, 강조의 조동사 does 또는 did가 적절하다.

19 showed와 believed의 목적어가 들어갈 자리이므로 what이 적절하다.

20 do some laundry '빨래를 하다'라는 뜻의 본동사이다. 다른 문장들의 do[does, did]는 강조를 위해 사용되었다. villain role: 악역

21 ① (A) 본동사 (B) 강조 ② (A) 강조 (B) 본동사 ③ (A) 본동사 (B) 강조 ④ (A) 강조 (B) 의문문을 만드는 조동사 ⑤ (A) 본동사 (B) 본동사

22 ③ said의 목적어와 was의 주어 두 가지 역할을 하는 자리이므로 That을 What으로 고쳐야 한다. ④ 선행사가 있으므로 what이 아닌 관계대명사 which나 that이 적절하다.

23 사물을 선행사로 받아주는 목적격 관계대명사 which나 that이 적절하다.

24 앞 문장에서 제시한 꿈의 집을 가리키는 말이다.

25 민호는 새 소리에 항상 신난다고 하였다.

26 (B)는 가주어 It이다. ①, ② 비인칭 주어 ③, ⑤ 인칭대명사

27 민호의 꿈의 집은 도시 한 가운데가 아닌 시골에 있다고 하였다.

28 spend+시간+Ving: V하느라 시간을 보내다

29 (A)는 '마지막으로'라는 의미이다.

30 세민이로부터 온 편지를 넣으려는 이유는 그들이 얼마나 좋은 친구인지를 보여 주어서이다.

31 지나가 언제 축구를 시작했는지는 위 글을 읽고 알 수 없다.

32 위 글은 지나가 자신의 기억 상자에 넣기를 원하는 것들에 관한 것이다.

단원별 예상문제　　　　　　　　p.48~51

01 advise　　　02 ②

03 really curious about your dream job

04 (1) He is from Busan.　(2) He likes soccer.

　(3) He wants to get along with everyone.

05 Is there anything else you want to tell your new friends?

06 (1) What Jiho likes most about traveling is trying new foods.

　(2) What Bora likes most is playing the guitar.

(3) What Jenny likes most is playing with her pet[Dora] in her free time.

07 ④ 08 ③ 09 ②

10 what I like most is to take pictures 11 ⑤

12 things which 13 ①, ②, ④ 14 ③, ⑤

15 (1) That is not what Harry has always wanted.

(2) My parents already know what happened three weeks ago.

(3) Tell her what have been bothering you.

16 ⓐ the soccer ball ⓑ the school newspaper ⓒ the letter

17 What I hope from you 18 ④ 19 ④

20 ③ 21 ③ 22 recognize

23 It tells him his weight and the condition of his health.

01 유의어 관계다. 대답하다 = 조언하다

02 도시에 있지 않고 농장, 밭 등을 가질 수도 있는 땅

03 궁금증을 표현하거나 보다 많은 정보를 알고 싶을 때 'be curious about+명사'를 사용할 수 있다.

04 (1) Hojun의 출신지는 부산이고, (2) 축구를 좋아한다. (3) 모두와 잘 지내기를 원한다.

06 '~가 가장 좋아하는 것은'의 의미로 관계대명사 what을 이용하여 'What+주어+likes most is ~'를 쓴다.

07 명사 the scenes를 수식하는 분사 형태로 '컴퓨터 기술로 만들어진 장면'이므로 수동의 의미를 갖는 과거분사 made가 적절하다.

08 영화는 지구를 구하는 영웅에 관한 것이다.

09 Seho의 대답으로 보아 빈칸 (A)에는 '너에 대해 말해 줄래?'라는 표현이 적절하다. ⑤번은 대답이 No로 나와야 하므로 적절하지 않다.

10 '내가 가장 좋아하는 것은'의 의미로 관계대명사 what을 이용하여 'What+주어(I)+동사(like) most is ~'를 쓴다.

11 Seho의 사진작가가 되고 싶다는 말에 대해 '그렇다면 올바른 선택을 했어.'라는 말이 오는 것이 적절하다.

12 본동사가 were이므로 선행사를 복수로 쓴다.

13 ① 선행사 the only one이 있으므로 선행사를 포함하는 관계대명사 what은 불가능하다. who도 좋지만 the only가 선행사 앞에 올 때는 관계대명사 that을 더 자주 쓴다. ② 강조의 did 뒤에 과거형 동사가 있다. 원형동사로 바꿔 줘야 적절하다. ④ 'It ~ that 강조 구문'의 be동사는 is/was 둘 뿐이다.

14 what이 관계대명사인지 의문대명사인지 구분하는 것은 해석으로 판단한다. 때로는 구분이 모호한 경우도 많다. 일반적으로 의문대명사 what은 '무엇'으로, 관계대명사 what은 '~하는 것'으

로 해석한다. ① 의문대명사 ② 의문대명사 ③ 관계대명사 ④ 의문대명사 ⑤ 관계대명사 (과거에 예의바른 것으로 여겨졌던 것이 오늘날 항상 그렇게 여겨지는 것은 아니다.)

15 관계대명사 what은 선행사를 포함하며, 문맥에 따라 단/복수 취급한다. (1) 그것은 Harry가 항상 원해 왔던 것이 아니다. (2) 나의 부모님은 3주 전에 생긴 일들을 이미 알고 있다. (3) 그녀에게 너를 괴롭혀 오고 있는 것들을 말하라.

16 축구를 하며 시간을 많이 보내기 때문에 축구공을, 중학교 시절에 무슨 일이 일어났는지 기억하고 싶으므로 신문을, 진짜 친구임을 보여주는 것이므로 편지를 넣는다고 보는 것이 적절하다.

17 '~하는 것'이므로 what을 써서 문장을 만든다.

18 Jina는 3가지 물건을 추억 상자에 넣으며 자신이 이것을 영원히 간직하기를 원한다.

19 enter는 '~로 들어가다'라는 의미의 타동사로, 전치사 없이 목적어를 취한다. 따라서 into 없이 enter만 쓰는 것이 적절하다.

20 큰 피크닉 테이블은 정원에 있다고 하였다.

21 현관문이 Bryan의 얼굴을 알아보고 자동으로 문을 열어준다고 하였다. identify: (신원 등을) 확인하다, 알아보다

22 사람이나 사물을 알아보는 것은 'recognize'이다.

23 욕실 거울은 그의 체중과 건강 상태에 대해 말해 준다고 하였다.

서술형 실전문제
p.52~53

01 (A) how was your first day of third grade?
(B) Can you tell me more about him?

02 I like the scenes made with computer technology.

03 (1) He likes to take pictures most.
(2) He can learn a lot of photo-taking skills.

04 (1) I must make the most of what I have.
(2) What you do is much more important than what you say.

05 (1) People in Hong Kong do love freedom.
(2) Was it yesterday that he broke the door?
(3) The wall was painted by Mr. Lee himself.

06 (1) the furniture
(2) a robot
(3) the bathroom mirror

07 It does open automatically

08 what to do → what to wear /
my classroom → the house

09 a beautifully designed sign

10 They will enjoy barbecues in the garden.

02 '주어(I)+동사(like)+목적어(the scenes)' 어순으로 문장을 시작하고, the scenes 뒤에 과거분사 made with computer

9

technology를 써서 명사 the scenes를 수식한다.

03 (1) Seho는 여가 시간에 무엇을 하는 것을 가장 좋아하는가?

(2) Seho는 사진 동아리에서 무엇을 배울 수 있는가?

04 (1) make the most of: ~을 최대한 이용하다 (2) 관계대명사 what을 이용해야 글자 수에 맞는 영작이 가능하다.

05 (1) 동사의 강조는 do를 사용한다. (2) 부사를 강조할 때는 'It ~ that 강조 구문'을 쓴다. 의문문이므로, 의문문의 형식으로 be동사 was와 it의 위치를 바꿔 준다. (3) 명사의 강조를 위해 재귀대명사를 사용한다. Mr.는 남성이므로 himself가 적절하다.

06 날씨를 확인하는 것은 가구, 요리를 하는 것은 로봇, 건강 상태를 말해 주는 것은 화장실 거울이다.

07 정말로 문이 자동으로 열리는지 묻고 있으므로 동사를 강조하여 '정말로 자동으로 문이 열린다'라고 쓸 수 있다.

08 가구가 날씨를 확인하고 무엇을 입을지 알려준다고 하였고, 로봇은 집을 청소한다고 하였다.

09 아름답게 만들어진 문패를 가리키는 말이다.

10 정원에서 바비큐를 즐길 것이라고 하였다.

창의사고력 서술형 문제   p.54

|모범답안|

01 Can you tell me about / to have a birthday party / Can you tell me about / stop eating fast food

02 (1) |모범답안| I know what Ms. Smith was looking for in the kitchen.

(2) |모범답안| What Brian bought at the market was the bag.

(3) |모범답안| This book is what Kathy found at the library.

03 my dancing shoes, the first prize from a dancing performance, some pictures with friends / my dancing shoes, they are related to my future dream / the first prize from a dancing performance, I can remember my happiest moment / put in some pictures with friends, I don't want to forget my friends from middle school

단원별 모의고사   p.55~58

01 ④　　02 draw　　03 ①　　04 ④

05 ③　　06 ②, ⑤　　07 ③

08 He wants to join a sports club. / He wants to get along with everyone.

09 Can you tell me about your best friend?

10 What do you like most / What I like most / What I

like most, listen to

11 ④　　12 ⑤

13 (1) what Sarah wrote in her mail

(2) what Gloria wants to visit someday

14 ③　　15 ③, ⑤

16 (1) This is what she purchased from a Japanese carpenter last year.

(2) It was the English teacher who moved the heavy box.

(3) What John fixed in the office was a photocopy machine.

17 pet　　18 ⑤

19 He feels good when he walks in the forest.

20 ①, ③　　21 It means an elephant.　　22 ⑤

23 It's because having fun is what she wants most.

24 She can eat cookies and enjoy her favorite movies.

01 ④번은 create에 대한 설명이다.

02 유의어 관계이다. 들어가다 : 그리다

03 나무로 덮여 있는 넓은 지역의 땅

04 A가 '가장 좋아하는 과목에 관해 말해 줄래?'라는 말에 B가 '미술 교사가 되고 싶어.'라고 말하는 것은 어색하다.

05 B가 '내가 가장 좋아하는 것은 야구를 하는 거야.'라고 대답하고 있으므로 C는 무엇을 가장 좋아하는지 묻는 것이 자연스럽다.

06 B의 대답으로 보아 가장 좋아하는 과목을 묻는 말이 적절하다.

07 빈칸 다음의 말이 '여기 새로 왔기 때문에 나를 도와줘.'라고 했으므로 모두와 잘 지내고 싶다는 ③번이 가장 적절하다.

10 가장 좋아하는 것을 묻는 표현은 'What do you like most?'를 사용하고, 가장 좋아하는 것을 말하는 표현은 'What I like most is ~'를 사용한다.

11 (A)와 (B)에 공통으로 들어갈 수 있는 말은 '내가 가장 좋아하는 것'이다.

12 motto는 자신의 믿음이나 인생의 가치관, 신념을 표현하는 짧은 문장이나 문구를 말하는 것으로 ⑤번은 속담(proverb)으로 '집 만한 곳은 없다'는 모토가 되기에 어색하다.

13 (1)과 (2) 각각의 선행사와 관계대명사를 써보면, the words that, the place which가 되는데, 문맥상 what으로 바꾸는 데 무리가 없다.

14 '①, ②, ③은 모두 'It ~ that 강조 구문'의 형식을 취하고 있는데, ③에서 보어인 very hungry는 'It ~ that 강조 구문'의 강조 대상이 될 수 없다. ④, ⑤는 동사를 강조하는 형태로 문법적으로 어색한 부분이 없다.

15 ①, ②, ④는 모두 조동사로서 각각 부정문, 의문문, 명령의 조동사로 사용됐다. ③, ⑤는 동사를 강조하는 do/did로 사용되었고, 주어진 문장의 밑줄 친 does와 같은 기능을 한다.

17 우리 곁에 있으면서 즐거움을 주기 위해 집에 데리고 있는 동물
    은 '애완동물'이다.

18 [B]의 첫 문장에서 It이 가리키는 것은 [C]에 나오는 시골의 꿈
    의 집이다. [B]에서 새 소리에 신난다고 하였고 [A]에서 새 소
    리를 들으며 잠에서 깨는 것이 아주 멋질 것이라고 하였다. 따라
    서 [C]-[B]-[A]가 가장 자연스럽다.

19 숲 속을 걸을 때 기분이 좋다고 하였다.

20 사람들은 Tanabat을 Chang이라고 부른다. Carl의 이름은 부
    모님이 지어준 것이 아니라 어떤 목록에서 선택된 것이라고 하
    였다.

21 Chang은 코끼리를 의미한다고 하였다.

22 수영장이 2층에 있다는 말은 나와 있지 않다.

23 Julie의 꿈의 집에 신나는 것들이 가득 차 있는 이유는 그녀가 가
    장 원하는 것이 즐거움이기 때문이다.

24 Julie는 극장 안에서 쿠키를 먹고 자신이 가장 좋아하는 영화를
    볼 수 있다고 하였다.

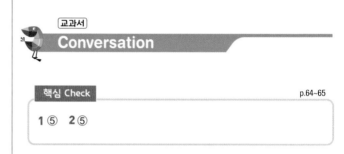

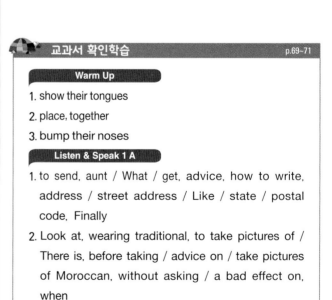

<Lesson 2 / logo>

Experience Different Cultures!

시험대비 실력평가
p.62

01 (d)ifferences 02 ③ 03 ⑤ 04 ①
05 regarded as 06 ④
07 Chinese 08 ⑤

01 '민희의 가족이 미국으로 이사 온 이후로, 그들은 한국과 미국의 문화적 차이를 많이 경험했다.

02 대화의 내용상 A가 영어로 주소를 쓰는 방법에 대해 조언(advice)을 해줄 수 있니?라고 묻는 말이 적절하다.

03 '영화관, 극장 등에 들어갈 수 있도록 지불하는 돈'의 의미로 '입장료'가 적절하다.

04 '편안하고 쾌적하지 않거나, 편안하고 쾌적하지 못하도록 하는'의 의미로 '불편한'이 적절하다.

05 '…로 여겨지다'는 'be regarded as …'이다.

06 (A) 미국인들은 "너 오고 있지 않니?"와 같은 부정의문문으로 종종 묻는다. (B) 과학자들은 그 이론에 대해 상당히 부정적인 태도를 취하고 있다.

07 한국-한국인, 한국어의 관계와 같이 중국(China)-중국인 또는 중국어를 나타내는 Chinese가 적절하다.

08 (A) 미국에서는 제품을 구매할 때 판매세라는 세금을 지불한다는 내용이므로 '세금'을 뜻하는 tax가 적절하다. (B) They는 Sales tax rates를 가리키므로 '판매세의 비율'이 '~의 범위에 이르다'라는 range가 적절하다.

서술형 시험대비
p.63

01 (1) stayed (2) Make (3) tag (4) cultural
02 (A) In response to (B) the same as (C) positive
03 (1) rude (2) prepare (3) shorts, temple
04 (1) wave, 흔들다 (2) correctly, 정확하게
   (3) exchange, 교환하다
05 (1) (g)ood (2) (h)and

01 (1) 집에 머물렀다는 과거형 stayed가 적절하다. (2) '반드시 ~해라'라는 의미로 'Make sure+주어+동사'를 사용한다. (3) 가격표에 있는 가격보다 많이 지불한다는 의미로 tag가 적절하다. (4) 명사를 수식하는 형용사 형태로 cultural이 적절하다.

02 (A) ~의 대답으로: in response to (B) ~와 같은: the same as (C) 긍정의: positive

03 (1) 무례한: rude (2) 준비하다: prepare (3) 반바지: shorts, 사원: temple

04 (1) 누군가에게 인사하기 위한 방법으로 손을 들고 좌우로 움직이다 (2) 참된 사실 또는 일반적으로 받아들여지는 것과 일치하는 방식으로 (3) 누군가에게 무언가를 주고 그 사람에게서 무언가를 받다

05 (1) good: (형) 좋은, (명) (-s) 상품 / 그들은 또한 우리들을 잘 돌보아 줍니다. / 그날 그 가게는 있는 상품을 모조리 진열했다. (2) hand: (명) 손, (동) 건네주다 / 그녀에게 그것을 건네줄 때 두 손을 사용해야 해.

교과서 Conversation

핵심 Check
p.64~65

1 ⑤ 2 ⑤

교과서 대화문 익히기

Check(√) True or False
p.66~67

1 F 2 T 3 F 4 T 5 T 6 F 7 F 8 T

교과서 확인학습
p.69~71

Warm Up
1. show their tongues
2. place, together
3. bump their noses

Listen & Speak 1 A
1. to send, aunt / What / get, advice, how to write, address / street address / Like / state / postal code, Finally
2. Look at, wearing traditional, to take pictures of / There is, before taking / advice on / take pictures of Moroccan, without asking / a bad effect on, when

Listen & Speak 1 B
Can I get, advice, visiting / shouldn't, path / get your

advice on visiting / should sit, back seat

Listen & Speak 2 A
1. present, have stayed / What, buy / bought / Make sure, hand, to / giving, is regarded as rude
2. pack / yet, take / Remember to bring / isn't / there are, temples, shorts, temple / else / Make sure, exchange, to

Listen & Speak 2 B
remember, France / Make sure, keep, on, at all times / anything, when / Make sure, take off, when having

Real Life Talk
Chinese, invited / having / prepare, several, advice, what to bring / How about / Most, receive, as, present, drinking, serve, guests / that / Make sure, wrap, mean death / advice

Communication Task Step 2
Which / get, advice, traveling / Make sure, hand

Wrap Up
1. going, get, visiting / pay, get off / remember / Pick, while eating, when having, without
2. to give, from, remember / Make sure

시험대비 기본평가　　　　　　　p.72

01 Can I get your advice on what to wear?
02 ⑤　　　　03 ③　　　　04 place, together

01 'Can I get your advice on ~?'이 '제가 당신의 조언을 구할 수 있을까요?'라는 의미이다. '무엇을 입을지'는 '의문사+to V'를 이용한다.
02 상대방에게 충고하는 표현으로 'had better+동사원형 ~', 'Don't forget to+동사원형 ~', 'remember to+동사원형 ~'을 사용할 수 있다.
03 B가 '자전거 도로에 서 있으면 안 돼.'라고 말하는 것으로 보아 빈칸에는 주의해야 할 일에 대해 물어보는 말이 자연스럽다.
04 '~을 모으다'는 'place 목적어 together'를 쓴다.

시험대비 실력평가　　　　　　　p.73~74

01 ③　　　02 ②　　　03 ③　　　04 ⑤
05 Make sure 06 ④
07 Remember to bring a pair of long pants or a long skirt.
08 ②　　　09 ④　　　10 ⑤

---

01 B가 'You should write the street address first.'라고 말하고 있으므로 영어로 주소를 쓰는 방법을 물어보는 말이 적절하다.
02 여학생이 한복을 입을지 말지를 결정해야 하는 내용은 대화에 언급되어 있지 않다.
03 어떤 나라를 방문하고 싶은지 묻는 말에 (B) 말레이시아를 방문하고 싶다고 말하고, 여행할 때 조언을 구하고 있다. → (C) 여행할 때 주의해야 할 일에 대해 말해주자 → (A) 고맙다고 답한다.
04 B의 대답이 '거리에서 껌을 씹으면 안 돼.'라고 주의를 주고 있으므로, 싱가포르에서 주의해야 할 조언을 구하는 질문이 적절하다.
05 남자의 질문이 '러시아에서 온 친구에게 꽃을 줄 때 기억해야 할 것이 있니?'라고 묻고 있으므로, 상대방에게 경고하는 표현으로 'Make sure+주어+동사 ~'의 형태를 사용한다.
06 ④번은 '그녀가 그것을 좋아할까?'라는 A의 물음에 '반드시 그것을 줄 때는 두 손을 사용해라.'라고 말하는 것은 자연스럽지 않다.
07 '~할 것을 기억하다'는 'remember to V'를 사용한다. 바지는 항상 복수형을 사용해야 하는 pants를 사용해야 한다.
08 'Make sure+주어+동사 ~'는 상대방에게 주의나 경고를 할 때 사용하는 표현이다.
09 제시문은 '내가 알아야 할 또 다른 것이 있을까?'라는 뜻으로 또 다른 조언을 구한다는 것을 알 수 있다. 두 번째 조언을 구하는 부분으로 ④가 적절하다.
10 어떤 색깔로 선물을 포장해야 하는지는 언급되어 있지 않다.

서술형 시험대비　　　　　　　p.75

01 Can I get your advice on what to bring?
02 Make sure you don't wrap the present in white or black paper.
03 (A) What should I take?
　 (B) You shouldn't wear shorts when you visit a temple.
　 (C) Make sure you exchange Korean won to Thai baht.
04 123 Van Ness Street, San Francisco, California 94101, USA

01 조언을 구할 때는 'Can I get your advice on ~?'으로 표현할 수 있다.
02 make sure 다음에 접속사 that을 생략할 수 있고 당부하고자 하는 내용을 주어와 동사를 갖춘 문장으로 쓴다.
04 영어로 주소를 쓸 때는 '거리 주소, 도시, 주, 우편번호, 나라'의 순서로 쓴다.

핵심 Check p.76~77

1 (1) since (2) for

2 (1) repaired (2) broken

시험대비 기본평가 p.78

01 (1) understanding → understood

(2) gone → been (3) studied → studying

(4) writing → written

02 ④   **03** ②

04 (1) The picture taken by Peter was interesting.

(2) Billy's mom has been cooking for five hours.

---

01 (1) 불어로 자기 자신을 이해받게(남들이 이해하도록) 만드는 것이므로, 과거분사를 써야 한다. make oneself understood: 소통하다, 이해시키다 (2) 1, 2인칭의 주어 뒤에 have gone은 어법상 부적절하다. (3) 작년 이후로 수학을 공부하는 중이라는 현재완료진행시제이므로, have been+V-ing 형태가 적절하다. (4) 스페인어로 쓰여진 편지이므로, written이 적절하다.

02 현재완료진행시제는 '동작'이 아닌 '상태'를 나타내는 know 등의 동사는 쓸 수 없다.

03 피곤함을 느끼는 것은 능동이 아니라 수동의 과거분사를 써야 한다.

04 (1) take를 과거분사로 써야 함에 유의한다. (2) 수와 시제에 맞춰 has been cooking을 쓴다.

시험대비 실력평가 p.79~81

01 ③   **02** making → made

03 (1) many people watching

(2) built by my father is

04 ③   **05** has been playing, for   **06** ②

07 wearing a yellow T-shirt is sitting under the maple

08 ⑤   **09** ①, ④, ⑤   **10** ⑤

11 (1) writing → witten (2) making → made

(3) cried → crying   **12** ⑤   **13** ①, ④

14 ⑤   **15** ⑤

16 (1) has been listening (2) have been painting

(3) has been teaching (4) has been taking

(5) have been traveling

17 (A) written (B) known (C) named (D) related

18 ②   **19** sitting, nothing

---

01 '과거+현재진행'은 현재완료진행시제로 표현한다. has been writing이 적절하다.

02 필리핀에서 제조된 가방이므로 과거분사가 적절하다.

03 분사가 명사의 뒤에서 꾸며주는 것을 적절히 활용한다. (1)은 watching fireworks가 people을 꾸며주고(능동), (2)는 built by my father가 warehouse를 뒤에서 꾸민다.(수동)

04 (1) 쓰레기를 줍는 소녀(능동) (2) 휴가에 쓰인 돈(수동) (3) 지루한 강의(능동) 등에 적절하게 분사를 활용한다.

05 과거에 시작된 일이 현재에도 진행되고 있을 때, 현재완료진행시제로 표현한다. 동사는 has been playing이 적절하고, 전치사는 기간(~ 동안)을 나타내는 for가 알맞다.

06 ②는 tried의 목적어로 쓰인 동명사이고, 나머지는 모두 명사를 앞 또는 뒤에서 꾸며주는 현재분사이다.

07 분사가 명사 뒤에서 꾸며주는 것을 활용한다. 능동이므로 wearing을 사용하고, 본동사는 'be동사+sitting'을 쓴다.

08 ⓐ 타는 불, ⓑ 지나가는 학생들 모두 '진행'의 의미를 갖고 있으며, 명사를 앞, 뒤에서 꾸며주고 있다.

09 ① 이야기책을 읽는 소녀이므로 reads → reading ④ '거짓말을 해오고 있다'는 뜻으로 현재완료진행형을 써야 한다. lied → lying, ⑤ 내 가족이 만난 사람들이므로, 분사가 아니라 관계사절의 동사가 적절하다. meeting → met

10 ① 직업을 잃는 것은 현재완료진행형으로 쓸 수 없다. has been losing→ has lost ② 관계대명사 뒤에는 동사를 써야 한다. who 뒤에 was를 추가하거나, sitting을 sat으로 바꾼다. ③ rides→ riding ④ 남겨진 과자가 없는 것이므로 leaving → left가 적절하다.

11 (1) 쓰인 책(수동) (2) 만들어진 쿠키(수동) (3) 우는 아기(능동)

12 <보기>는 현재완료시제의 용법 중 '경험'이며, ⑤는 'Emily가 가족과 하와이로 떠나서 현재 여기 없다'는 내용의 '결과' 용법으로 사용되었다.

13 ① 신나는 날 excited→ exciting ④ 감동적인 장면들 touched → touching

14 현재완료시제의 '계속' 용법, 또는 현재완료진행시제가 적절하다.

15 현재완료진행시제는 과거에 시작한 일이 현재까지 진행되고 있음을 의미하며, ⑤를 제외하고 모두 가능하다. ⑤는 명백한 과거시제 표현이므로 부적절하다.

16 (1) 라디오 프로그램 청취 (2) 낙후된 마을 벽에 그림 그리기 (3) 수학 강의 (4) 약 복용 (5) 유럽 여행 등의 내용에 적절하게 동사를 선택하고, 주어의 수에 has/have 등을 활용하여 현재완료진행시제를 쓴다.

17 (A) 쓰여진 소설 (B) ~로서 알려진 악기를 연주하는 (C) ~라고 이름 불리는 (D) 관련된 영화

18 <보기>는 현재완료의 용법 중 '계속'이며, 과거에 시작된 일이 현재에도 지속되고 있음을 나타낸다. ②는 '청소를 끝냈다'는 내용으로, '완료' 용법으로 사용되었다.

19 어법에 맞게 배열하면, 'Have you been sitting here calmly and doing nothing to help them?'이 된다.

서술형 시험대비   p.82~83

01 (1) David has been chewing gum after dinner for an hour.
  (2) Margaret has been blogging since she first started the Internet.
  (3) Our team members have been working out in the gym for over six hours.

02 (1) has been practicing playing the drums for 6 weeks
  (2) has been writing letters for 3 hours

03 (1) flying   (2) washing   (3) standing   (4) sitting
  (5) closed   (6) sent   (7) written

04 (1) old lady standing across the street
  (2) boys performing on that stage
  (3) the flowers planted in an old boat

05 ⓐ calling → called
  해석: Hoop King이라고 불리는 뛰어난 선수는 정말 농구 경기를 잘했다.
  ⓑ taken → taking
  해석: 우리는 오스트리아의 한 오래된 광장에서 사진을 찍는 많은 관광객들을 볼 수 있었다.
  ⓒ producing → produced
  해석: 스위스에서 생산된 시계들이 세계 최고의 명성을 누린다.
  ⓓ writing → written
  해석: 북 콘서트에 참가한 모든 사람들은 그의 어린 딸에 의해 쓰여진 책 제목을 알게 되었다.
  ⓔ flown → flying
  해석: 하늘 위로 날아가는 철새 무리들이 격려의 소리를 내고 있었다.

06 Frank has been doing his son's homework for three hours.

07 (A) has been suffering   (B) pulled

08 (1) with the crying baby
  (2) an illegally parked truck
  (3) the birds flying over the buildings

01 현재완료진행시제에 맞게 각 단어를 적절히 활용한다.

03 (1)~(4)는 현재분사, (5)~(7)은 과거분사를 쓴다.

04 명사의 뒤에서 꾸미는 분사 활용 (1) 서 있는 할머니(능동) (2) 공연하는 소년들(능동) (3) 심어진 꽃들(수동)

05 ⓐ Hoop King이라고 불리는 선수(수동) ⓑ 사진을 찍는 관광객들(능동) ⓒ 생산된 시계(수동) ⓓ 쓰인 제목(수동) ⓔ 날아가는 철새들(능동) 등에 맞게 분사를 적절히 고치고, 분사의 의미에 맞게 우리말로 해석한다.

06 3시간 전에 집에 도착한 아들이, 집에 도착하자마자 아버지에게 숙제를 보여줬고, 즉시 아들 대신 숙제를 시작한 아버지 Frank가 3시간 동안 숙제를 하고 있는 중이므로, 현재완료진행시제를 활용하여 영작한다.

07 (A) 빈칸이 3개이고, 내용상 현재완료진행형이므로, has been suffering이 적절하다. (B) 이가 뽑히는(수동) 것이므로 과거분사 pulled가 적절하다.

08 (1) 울고 있는 아기 (2) 불법으로 주차된 트럭(부정관사 an에 유의한다.) (3) 건물들 위로 날아가고 있는 새들

교과서 Reading

확인문제   p.84

1 F   2 F   3 F

확인문제   p.85

1 T   2 F   3 F   4 F

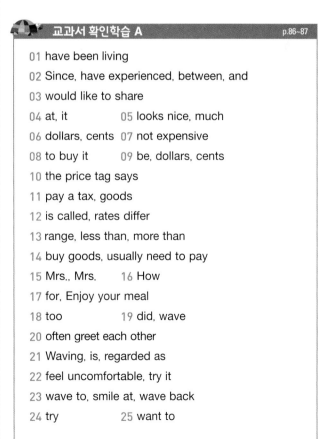

교과서 확인학습 A   p.86~87

01 have been living
02 Since, have experienced, between, and
03 would like to share
04 at, it   05 looks nice, much
06 dollars, cents   07 not expensive
08 to buy it   09 be, dollars, cents
10 the price tag says
11 pay a tax, goods
12 is called, rates differ
13 range, less than, more than
14 buy goods, usually need to pay
15 Mrs., Mrs.   16 How
17 for, Enjoy your meal
18 too   19 did, wave
20 often greet each other
21 Waving, is, regarded as
22 feel uncomfortable, try it
23 wave to, smile at, wave back
24 try   25 want to

26 Don't   27 Yes

28 try some, delicious

29 don't like   30 What

31 negative questions, Aren't, Didn't, go

32 to answer, is

33 negative questions, answer, No

34 answer, Yes

35 the same as, to positive questions

36 Which cultural difference

37 have been learning, since

38 surprised, am getting used to

---

1 Hi! My name is Kim Minhee. I have been living in America for three years.

2 Since my family moved here, I have experienced many cultural differences between Korea and America.

3 I would like to share some of them with you.

4 Minhee: Look at this shirt. I like it.

5 Linda: It looks nice. How much is it?

6 Minhee: It's 19 dollars and 99 cents.

7 Linda: That's not expensive.

8 Minhee: Yes, I agree. I want to buy it.

9 Clerk: That'll be 21 dollars and 20 cents.

10 Minhee: Really? But the price tag says it's only 19 dollars and 99 cents.

11 Here in America, in most states, people pay a tax when they buy goods.

12 It is called a sales tax. Sales tax rates differ by state.

13 They range from less than one percent to more than ten percent.

14 So when you buy goods in America, you usually need to pay more than the price on the tag.

15 Jessica: Hi, Mrs. Johnson! Minhee: Hello, Mrs. Johnson!

16 Mrs. Johnson: Hi, Jessica! Hi, Minhee! How are you?

17 Jessica: Fine, thank you. We are here for a burger. Enjoy your meal.

18 Mrs. Johnson: Thank you. You, too!

19 Minhee: Jessica, why did you wave to Mrs. Johnson?

20 In America, people often greet each other by waving.

21 Waving to an older person is not regarded as rude.

22 When you come to America, you may feel uncomfortable about it at first, but why don't you try it?

23 You can wave to and smile at an elderly man walking on the street. He may wave back.

24 Andy: Minhee, try this apple pie.

25 Minhee: No, thanks. I don't want to.

26 Andy: Why not? Don't you like apple pie?

27 Minhee: Yes.

28 Andy: Then, try some. It's delicious.

29 Minhee: No. I just said I don't like apple pie.

30 Andy: What?

31 Americans often ask negative questions, such as "Aren't you coming?" and "Didn't you go to the hospital?"

32 It can be difficult to answer negative questions correctly. Here is some advice.

33 In response to negative questions, such as "Don't you like apple pie?" you should answer "No," if you don't like it.

34 And you should answer "Yes," if you like it.

35 These answers are the same as the answers to positive questions, such as "Do you like apple pie?"

36 Which cultural difference is most surprising to you?

37 I have been learning about cultural differences since I came to America.

38 Some surprised me at first, but now I am getting used to them.

---

01 ④   02 ③   03 ②   04 states

05 ④   06 ④   07 ③

08 People in America greet each other by waving.

09 ③   10 ③   11 No, I don't like them.

12 ④   13 ④

14 We need to pay a sales tax.

15 She moved to America three years ago.

16 ③   17 waving to an older person

18 ⑤   19 ④   20 Yes, I am (hungry).

21 ⑤   22 cultural

23 The writer has been learning about cultural differences.   24 ②

01 가족들이 미국으로 이사 온 이래로 많은 문화적 차이를 경험해왔다는 의미가 적절하다. 따라서 '~한 이래로'라는 의미의 since가 적절하다.

02 민희는 자신이 경험한 문화적 차이를 말하고 싶다고 하였다.

03 미국에서는 물건을 살 때 가격표 금액에 더하여 판매세를 지불해야 한다. 따라서 19달러 99센트에 판매세가 붙어서이다.

04 미국과 같은 큰 나라는 '주'라고 불리는 작은 지역으로 나뉘어져 있다. sate는 '주(州)'라는 의미로 쓰이고 있다.

05 물건을 살 때 지불하는 세금이 판매세이며, 미국 대부분의 주에서 판매세가 붙고 판매세의 비율은 주마다 다르다.

06 미국에 오면 처음에는 나이든 사람에게 손을 흔들며 인사하는 것이 불편하게 느껴질 수도 있다고 하였으므로, 이것이 '무례한' 것으로 여겨지지 않는다고 말하는 것이 가장 적절하다.

07 Jessica는 민희와 함께 버거를 먹기 위해 이곳에 왔다고 하였다.

08 미국 사람들은 손을 흔들면서 서로 인사한다고 하였다.

09 부정의문문에 올바르게 대답하기가 어려울 수 있다고 말하며 조언을 주는 말이 들어간 후 부정의문문에 답변하는 방법을 말해주는 것이 가장 자연스럽다.

10 밑줄 친 (A)는 '먹어보다'라는 의미로 쓰였다. ① ~을 시험 삼아 써보다 ② ~하려고 노력하다 ③ 먹어보다, 마셔보다 ④ ~인지 아닌지 시험해 보다 ⑤ try one's best: 최선을 다하다

11 좋아하지 않을 경우 'No.'라고 답하면 된다고 하였다.

12 (A) 미국과 한국의 문화적 차이에 대해 말하고 있다. similarity: 유사성 (B) 판매세는 물건을 살 때 지불하는 것이다. (C) 가격표에 판매세를 더하여 물건 값을 지불하므로 more가 적절하다.

13 판매세 비율의 범위는 1퍼센트 이하부터 10퍼센트 이상이라고 하였다.

14 미국에서 물건을 살 때 우리는 판매세를 지불해야 한다.

15 미국에 3년 동안 살고 있다고 하였으므로 3년 전에 미국으로 이사를 간 것이다.

16 미국에서 나이든 사람들에게 손을 흔들며 인사하는 것은 무례하다고 여겨지지 않으며 사람들은 서로 손을 흔들며 인사한다고 하였다. 따라서 ③번이 가장 적절하다.

17 나이든 사람에게 손을 흔드는 것을 의미한다.

18 Johnson 할머니가 친구와 함께 대회를 나누는 모습은 찾아볼 수 없다.

19 [C] 부정의문문에 바르게 대답하기 어렵다고 말하며 조언을 줌 [B] 대답하는 방법을 제시하며, 싫으면 'No'라고 답하고 [A] 좋으면 'Yes'라고 답해야 한다고 말함.

20 부정의문문에 대한 대답은 긍정의문문에 대한 대답과 똑같다고 하였다. 배가 고프면 '그렇다'라고 대답하면 된다.

21 부정의문문에 대한 대답은 긍정의문문에 대한 대답과 같다고 하였다.

22 특정한 사회와 그것의 생각, 관습, 그리고 예술과 관련된 것은 'cultural(문화와 관련된, 문화의)'이다.

23 글쓴이는 문화적 차이에 관해 배워오고 있다고 하였다.

24 문화적 차이를 배워 오고 있다고 하였으므로 ②번이 적절하다.
① 놀란 ② 익숙한 ③ 무서운 ④ 충격적인 ⑤ 즐거운

서술형 시험대비 p.94~95

01 She has been living in America for three years.

02 She wants to share some cultural differences between Korea and America.

03 It's 19 dollars and 99 cents.

04 People in America pay a sales tax when they buy goods.

05 are equal in most states → differ by state

06 It doesn't include a sales tax.

07 wave

08 Jessica waved to Mrs. Johnson.

09 Minhee, greet each other by waving

10 How to Answer Negative Questions Correctly

11 No, I don't like it.

12 Yes, I did

13 Answering negative questions, the same, positive questions

01 민희는 3년 동안 미국에서 살고 있다고 하였다.

02 민희는 한국과 미국 사이의 문화적 차이를 공유하고 싶다고 하였다.

03 가격표에 따르면 셔츠 가격은 19달러 99센트이다.

04 미국 사람들은 물건을 살 때 판매세를 낸다고 하였다.

05 주마다 판매세 비율이 다르다고 하였다.

06 가격표에는 판매세가 포함되어 있지 않다.

07 나이가 많은 사람에게 손을 흔들며 인사하라고 제안하고 있으므로 wave가 적절하다.

08 Johnson 할머니에게 손을 흔든 것은 Jessica이다.

09 해석: 민희는 미국에서 사람들이 손을 흔들며 서로 인사하는 방식에 익숙하지 않다.

10 위 글은 부정의문문에 올바르게 대답하는 방법을 제시하고 있다.

11 긍정의문문과 부정의문문의 대답은 같다고 하였다. 민희는 사과 파이를 좋아하지 않는다고 하였으므로 부정의문문에 'No, I don't like it.'이라고 답하는 것이 적절하다.

12 긍정의문문에 대한 대답과 부정의문문에 대한 대답은 같다고 하였다. 책을 지루하게 여겼다고 하였으므로 부정 의문문에 대한 대답은 'Yes, I did.'라고 하는 것이 적절하다.

13 해석: 부정의문문에 답하는 것은 그렇게 어렵지 않다. 당신이 미

국에 있다면, 단지 이것만 기억해라. 부정의문문에 대한 대답은 긍정의문문에 대한 대답과 같다.

영역별 핵심문제 p.97~101

01 positive 02 ⑤ 03 ③ 04 ①
05 waving, Waving 06 ④ 07 ②
08 Make sure you don't ask, age
09 ② 10 ③ 11 ⑤
12 Make sure you drink it without a spoon.
13 ③
14 (A) has been trying to solve (B) since
15 ① 16 ①, ⑤
17 staying in Kenya to study wild animals is Ms. Baker
18 (1) moving (2) found 19 ② 20 ③
21 ④ 22 (B)-(A)-(C) 23 ③
24 It is a tax that people pay when they buy goods in America.
25 ④ 26 Interesting, Festival 27 ③
28 People throw colored powder and water on each other.
29 ④

01 반의어 관계이다. 차이 : 닮음 = 부정적인 : 긍정적인

02 (a)는 현재완료(have experienced)를 사용하고 있기 때문에 'since(~한 이후로)'가 적절하고, (b)는 '나는 그것들 중 몇 가지를 너희들과 공유하고 싶어.'라는 말이 적절하다.

03 집의 번호, 도로의 이름, 사람이 살거나 일하는 마을의 이름, 그리고 편지가 발송될 수 있는 곳

04 당신의 수입이나 구입한 상품이나 서비스의 비용에 근거해서 정부에 지불되는 돈

05 영어 설명은 '누군가에게 인사하기 위한 방법으로 손을 들고 좌우로 움직이다'라는 의미로 동사 'wave'에 대한 설명이다. 전치사 by 뒤와, 주어 자리에는 동명사 형태가 와야 하므로 동명사 waving이 적절하다.

06 get used to ...: …에 익숙해지다

07 미국을 방문하는 것에 대해 조언을 구하는 표현이다.

08 서양 문화권에서는 사람의 나이를 물어보는 것이 예의바르지 않다. 이 상황에서 소녀가 경고할 말은 '절대 다른 사람의 나이를 묻지 않도록 해'가 적절하다.

09 무엇을 가져가야 할지에 대한 조언을 구하는 말이므로 Bora의 '차는 어때?'라고 묻는 말 앞에 오는 것이 적절하다.

10 흰색과 검은색은 중국에서 죽음을 의미한다고 했으므로 선물을 흰색이나 검은색 종이로 포장하지 말라는 조언이 적절하다.

11 세호가 보라에게 차를 대접받는다는 내용은 대화에 언급되어 있지 않다.

12 '~해야 한다'라는 의미로 Make sure를 이용할 수 있다.

13 ① Toto라고 '이름이 불리는' 것이므로 named가 적절하다. ② Bong-Junho에 의해 '연출된 영화들'이 되어야 하므로 directed를 써야 한다. ④ which 뒤에 be동사를 써주거나 which를 생략해서 뒤에서 명사를 꾸미는 형태로 쓰는 것이 적절하다. ⑤ 축제에 '초대 받은 유명인사들'이므로 invited가 적절하다.

14 대학에 입학한 이후로 지금까지 문제를 풀기 위해 노력해 오고 있다는 말로 보아 try to solve 표현을 활용하여, 현재완료진행 시제로 쓰도록 한다.

15 첫 번째 문장에서는 '런던에서 찍힌 사진(수동)'을 가리키는 말이므로 taken이 적절하다. 두 번째 문장에서도 '떨어진 잎들'(수동)을 가리키므로 fallen이 적절하다.

16 ① 방이 춥게 느껴지는 '상태'이므로, 진행형은 부적절하다. has felt 또는 feels가 적절하다. ⑤ have been being ~ing 형태는 어색한 구문이다. I have fallen in love with ~ 로 쓰면 적절하다.

17 분사가 명사의 앞, 뒤에서 꾸미는 것을 적절히 활용하여 영작한다.

18 (1) 책에서 발견한 감동적인(감동을 주는) 문장(능동)이므로, moving이 적절하다. (2) Giza에서 발견된 pyramids(수동)이므로, 과거분사 found가 적절하다.

19 ② be busy ~ing는 '~하느라 바쁘다'라는 뜻의 동명사의 관용적 표현이다. 다른 문장들에서는 밑줄 친 부분들 모두가 현재분사로 사용되었다. 단, ①, ③, ④는 명사 뒤에서 수식하는 역할인데 반해, ⑤는 서술적 용법으로 쓰였다.

20 with+A+형용사/분사 형태는 A의 능동/수동 여부에 따라 현재분사 또는 과거분사를 쓴다. ③ with one's legs crossed '다리를 꼰 상태로'인데, crossing은 부적절하다. ① with one's arms folded: 팔짱을 낀 채로 ② with one's eyes closed: 눈을 감은 채로 ④ with the window open: 창문이 열린 채로 ⑤ with one's shirts wet: 셔츠가 젖은 채로

21 현재완료진행시제는 과거에 시작한 일이 현재까지 진행되고 있음을 의미하며, '동작의 진행'을 나타내기 때문에 상태 표현에 사용할 수 없다. ④ own은 '소유하고 있다'는 뜻으로 진행형으로 쓰지 않는다.

22 (B)의 It이 가리키는 것은 a tax이며, (A)의 They가 가리키는 것은 (B) 문장의 sales tax rates이다. 주 별로 판매세가 다르다고 끝맺으며 1퍼센트 이하에서부터 10퍼센트 이상에까지 걸쳐 있다고 설명하고, 그래서 가격표에 있는 가격보다 더 많은 금액을 지불해야 한다고 말하는 것이 적절하다.

23 (A)는 '~한 이래로'라는 의미로 쓰인 접속사이다. 모두 같은 의미로 쓰였지만 ③번은 '~ 때문에'라는 의미로 쓰이고 있다.

24 판매세는 미국에서 사람들이 물건을 살 때 지불하는 세금이라고 하였다.

25 가격표에 있던 가격을 본 민희는 비싸지 않다고 생각했다.

26 전 세계의 흥미로운 축제 중 인도의 Holi에 대해 소개하고 있다.

27 기간을 이끄는 말이 이어지고 있으므로 for를 쓰는 것이 적절하다. since는 특정 시점을 이끈다.

28 사람들은 홀리 축제에서 서로에게 형형색색의 가루와 물을 던진다고 하였다.

29 글쓴이는 사람들과 함께 길거리에서 춤추고 싶다고 하였다. look forward to: ~을 고대하다

단원별 예상문제
p.102~105

01 Japanese 02 ②

03 sure you don't use your left hand

04 She wants to send it[the hanbok] to her aunt in the USA.

05 how to write an address in English

06 Make sure (that) you show your tongue

07 Look at the people wearing traditional Moroccan clothes.

08 ④ 09 ② 10 ④

11 get your advice, to take 12 ③

13 ⓐ since → for ⓑ taught → teaching
ⓒ speak → spoken ⓓ risen → rising 14 ③

15 ⑤ 16 tax

17 from less than, to more than 18 ⑤

19 ④ 20 ③ 21 cultural differences

22 She has been learning about cultural differences since she came to America.

01 국가 – 국민(언어) 관계이다.

02 어떤 상황에서 무엇을 해야 하는지, 어떻게 행동해야 하는지에 대해 누군가가 여러분에게 제안하는 의견

03 had better not은 '~하지 않는 게 낫다'라는 의미로 '~하지 않도록 확실히 해라'라는 의미로 'Make sure you don't'를 사용하는 것이 적절하다.

04 미국에 계신 이모에게 한복을 보내기를 원한다.

05 영어로 주소를 쓰는 방법에 관한 충고를 얻고자 한다.

06 Tibet에서 인사하는 방법에 대해 조언을 구하고 있다. 'Make sure+주어+동사'를 이용하여 '반드시 혀를 보여주도록 해라'라고 조언한다.

07 동사원형으로 시작하는 명령문 형태로 Look at을 먼저 쓰고, 현재분사 wearing(입고 있는)이 명사 people을 뒤에서 수식한다.

08 모로코 사람들에게 물어보지 않고 사진을 찍으면 안 된다고 했기 때문에 빈칸에는 그 이유로 부정적인 의미가 오는 것이 적절하다.

09 G의 마지막 말에 연장자에게 한 손으로 무언가를 주는 것은 한국에서 무례한 것으로 여겨진다고 말하고 있으므로 ②가 적절하다.

10 태국에는 절이 많기 때문에 절을 방문할 때 짧은 옷을 입으면 안된다는 것이 적절하다. should wear를 shouldn't wear로 바꾸어 준다.

11 조언을 구하는 표현으로 바꾸어 말할 수 있다. 'Can I get your advice on ~' 구문과 '의문사+to부정사'를 이용한다.

12 모든 문장들에 현재완료진행시제가 사용되었다. ③번 문장은 시제 자체에는 문제가 없으나, during the last winter party가 '명백한 과거 시점'을 지칭하므로, '과거에 시작된 일이 지금도 진행되고 있다'는 의미의 현재완료진행시제로 표현할 수 없다. during을 since로 바꾸면, '지난 겨울 파티 이후로 Donald의 친지들이 포커 게임을 해오고 있는 중이다'가 된다.

13 ⓐ '2달 동안'이므로 for (단, '2달 전부터 가능하기 때문에 그 경우 months뒤에 ago를 추가하면 된다.) ⓑ '수영을 가르치는 강사'(능동) ⓒ '대부분의 라틴 아메리카 국가들에서 말해지는 스페인어'라는 뜻의 수동이므로 과거분사를 써야 한다. ⓓ 가격이 꾸준히 상승해 오고 있다.(현재완료진행형)

14 ③번은 전치사의 목적어로 쓰인 동명사이다. 그 외에는 모두 명사의 뒤에서 꾸미는 분사로 사용되었다.

15 가격표에 있는 가격에 판매세를 더해서 물건 가격을 지불해야 하므로 ⑤번이 가장 적절하다.

16 정부가 공공 서비스를 위해 쓸 수 있도록 당신이 정부에 지불하는 돈은 '세금'이다.

17 판매세율은 주마다 다른데, 1퍼센트 이하에서부터 10퍼센트 이상에 이른다고 하였다.

18 판매세율은 주마다 다르다고 하였다..

19 민희가 부정의문문에 긍정으로 답하였으므로 Andy는 민희가 사과파이를 좋아한다고 이해하였다. 따라서 한 번 더 사과파이를 권한 것이다.

20 (B)는 진주어로 쓰인 to부정사이다. ①, ④ 부사적 용법 중 목적 ② 부사적 용법 중 감정의 원인 ③ 진주어 ⑤ 형용사적 용법으로 something을 수식

21 문화적 차이를 가리키는 말이다.

22 글쓴이는 미국에 온 이래로 문화적인 차이에 대해 배워오고 있다고 하였다.

서술형 실전문제
p.106~107

01 A: Can I get your advice on visiting
B: not eat food or drink water in the subway

02 she shouldn't wear shorts when she visits a temple

03 (1) most Chinese people like to receive tea as a present
(2) Is there anything else that I need to know?

19

04 I have been teaching Korean in an Indian middle school for thirteen years.

05 ⓐ crying ⓑ leaving ⓒ sleeping ⓓ covered ⓔ written

이유: ⓒ만 동명사이고, 나머지는 모두 분사이다.

06 positive questions

07 ⓐ Yes, I do. ⓑ No, I don't.

08 Yes, I did

09 (A) interesting (B) throwing

10 They have been celebrating Holi for many years.

01 (A) 조언을 구하는 표현으로 'Can I get your advice on ~?'을 이용하고, 전치사 on 뒤에는 동명사 visiting이 적절하다. (B) 주어진 그림은 음식과 음료 금지를 나타내므로 should not을 이용한다.

02 긴 바지와 치마를 챙겨야 하는 이유는 태국에서 절을 방문할 때 짧은 옷을 입으면 안 되기 때문이다.

03 (1) 대부분의 중국인들은 차를 선물로 받는 것을 좋아하기 때문이다. (2) '~가 있다'라는 there is를 이용한 의문문을 사용하고, 형용사 else는 anything을 뒤에서 수식한다. 목적격 관계대명사 that[which]을 사용하고 need는 to부정사를 사용하므로 need to know를 쓴다.

05 ⓐ '울고 있는 아이'(능동) ⓑ '5시에 출발하는 기차'(능동) ⓒ '침낭'은 '잠을 자고 있는 가방'이 아니라, '잠을 자기 위한 용도의 가방'이므로 동명사 ⓓ '담쟁이로 덮인 건물 벽'(수동) ⓔ '에머슨에 의해 쓰여진 시'(수동)

06 예를 들어 이어지는 의문문의 형태로 보아 '긍정의문문'이라는 말이 들어가는 것이 가장 적절하다.

07 부정의문문에 대한 대답과 긍정의문문에 대한 대답이 같다고 하였으므로 위와 같이 쓰는 것이 적절하다.

08 부정의문문으로 묻는다 하더라도 의문문에 대한 대답이 사실이면 'Yes, I did.'로 답하는 것이 적절하다.

09 (A) 흥미를 유발하는 축제이므로 interesting, (B) '가루와 물을 던지는 사람들'이라는 의미이므로 현재분사 throwing을 쓴다.

10 인도 사람들은 수년 동안 Holi 축제를 기념해 오고 있다고 하였다.

창의사고력 서술형 문제 p.108

|모범답안|

01 A: Can I get your advice on visiting Russia?
   B: Make sure, don't give flowers in even numbers

02 (1) |모범답안| John has been singing since he ate lunch.

   (2) |모범답안| Susan's brother has been cleaning the table with a towel for ten minutes.

03 Pizza Festival, Italy, in June, try different kinds of pizza from all around the world, selecting the best chef

단원별 모의고사 p.109~112

01 ④   02 impolite   03 ②   04 ③

05 ④   06 ⑤   07 ⑤

08 white and black mean death in China

09 Make sure

10 There is an important thing you need to know before taking pictures.

11 ②

12 (1) have been reading the novel written by Sarah for three

    (2) has been working at a bank founded by Bill for

13 ③

14 My English teacher has been carrying the heavy boxes since this morning.

15 ③   16 ②   17 ④   18 ⑤

19 ⑤   20 ④

21 She greeted Mrs. Johnson by waving.

01 ④번은 '당신의 수입이나 구입한 상품이나 서비스의 비용에 근거해서 정부에 지불되는 돈'의 의미로 tax에 관한 설명이다.

02 유의어 관계이다. 나이 든 : 무례한

03 take off: 벗다 at first: 처음에

04 A가 부정의문문으로 '배고프지 않니?'라고 물었을 때 B가 'Yes'라고 긍정의 대답을 하고 있으므로 'I am'으로 하는 것이 적절하다.

05 B의 대답으로 보아 올바른 영어 표현에 대한 조언을 구하고 있다는 것을 알 수 있다.

06 G의 대답으로 보아 또 다른 조언을 구하고 있다는 것을 알 수 있다.

07 make sure는 뒤에 '주어+동사'가 와야 한다. Make sure (that) you don't wrap이 되어야 적절하다.

08 Q: 왜 Seho는 선물을 흰색이나 검은색 종이로 포장해서는 안 되는가?

09 A가 '프랑스에서 식사할 때 기억해야 할 것이 있니?'라고 묻고 있으므로 B의 빈칸에는 주의해야 할 일을 경고하는 표현이 적절하다.

10 '~가 있다'는 'There is+단수 명사(an important thing)'로 문장을 시작하고, thing을 수식하는 관계대명사절을 뒤에 사용한다. 마지막으로 'before+동명사'를 사용한다.

11 빈칸 다음에 '너는 물어보지 않고 모로코 사람들의 사진을 찍으면 안 돼.'라고 말하고 있으므로, (B)에는 모로코 사람을 사진 찍는 것에 대한 조언을 구하는 말이 적절하다.

12 조건을 충족시키면서 10단어를 넘지 않도록 하고, 명사를 뒤에서 꾸미는 분사의 능동/수동에 유의한다. (1) 지난 일요일에 읽기 시작해서 오늘이 화요일이므로 기간은 3일 동안이 된다. (2) 글자 수에 유의하여 마지막에 for가 오도록 영작한다.

13 주어진 문장과 ①, ②, ④, ⑤는 모두 수동의 의미로 명사를 뒤에서 꾸미는 과거분사가 적절하다. ③번만 현재분사이다.

15 명사의 뒤에서 꾸며주는 분사의 능동/수동을 적절하게 구분해야 한다. ① called ② wearing ④ taken ⑤ written이 적절하고, ③의 hanging은 자동사로서 '매달려 있다, 늘어져 있다'는 뜻으로 어법상 옳게 쓰였다.

16 민희는 자신이 경험한 문화적 차이를 공유하고 싶다고 하였다. 따라서 ②번이 가장 적절하다.

17 민희는 가족과 함께 미국으로 이사를 가서 한국과 미국의 문화적 차이를 경험하고 있다고 하였다. 미국에서는 가격표에 제시된 금액에 더해서 판매세를 내야 하는 것을 문화적 차이로 소개하고 있으므로 한국에서는 가격표의 금액만큼을 지불한다는 것을 유추할 수 있다.

18 한국이 아닌 미국에서 물건을 살 때 판매세를 내는 것이다.

19 ① by+Ving: V함으로써 ② at first: 처음에 ③ wave to: ~에게 손을 흔들다 ④ smile at: ~을 향해 웃다 ⑤ on the street: 거리에서

20 글의 내용상 나이 든 사람에게 손을 흔들며 인사하는 것은 무례하게 여겨지지 않으므로 한번 시도해 보라고 말하는 것이 자연스럽다. 미소 지으며 손을 흔들며 인사하면 그 사람도 손을 흔들며 인사할 것이라고 말하는 것이 적절하다.

21 Jessica는 Johnson 할머니에게 손을 흔들며 인사를 하였다.

Future Dreams, Future Jobs

시험대비 실력평가   p.116

01 ④   02 florist   03 ②   04 ③
05 analyze, strength, weakness   06 ⑤
07 repair   08 ④

01 '학교에 다니다'와 '결혼식에 참석하다'는 의미를 가지는 'attend'가 적절하다.

02 꽃으로 아름다운 것들을 창조하는 사람이라는 의미로 florist(플로리스트)가 적절하다.

03 '조직의 일원이 되다'는 의미로 '~에 속하다'는 belong to가 적절하다.

04 '국가, 조직 또는 개인의 유용하거나 가치 있는 소유물 또는 자질'의 의미로 'resource(자원)'가 적절하다.

05 analyze: 분석하다, strength: 강점, weakness: 약점

06 (A) 아이들의 그림이 교실 벽을 장식한다. (B) 아름다운 꽃으로 집을 장식하는 것은 아주 재미있다.

07 유의어 관계다. 고치다 : 다루다

08 (A) 뮤지컬 극장의 감독으로서, '나는 배우들을 대상으로 오디션을 실시하고'가 적절하다. (B) 오디션을 본 다음 '배역에 맞는 배우를 고른 뒤에'라는 말이 적절하므로 'cast'가 와야 한다.

서술형 시험대비   p.117

01 (1) reduce, calm   (2) among   (3) belong to
     (4) field
02 (A) something colorful   (B) highly recommend
03 (1) analyst   (2) recorded   (3) During, performance
04 (1) collect, 모으다   (2) personality, 성격
     (3) greenery, 화초, 푸른 잎
05 conduct

01 (1) 그녀는 그들이 스트레스를 완화하고 평온해지도록(calm) 도와줘. (2) 너는 이 목록에 있는 것들 중에서(among) 무엇에 가장 관심이 있니? (3) 대부분의 사람들은 여섯 가지 성격 유형 중 한 가지에 속해(belong to). 현실적인 타입도 그 중 하나야. (4) 나는 해양 과학자입니다. 해양 과학은 거대한 분야(field)입니다.

02 (A) something은 형용사가 뒤에서 수식을 한다. 다채로운: colorful (B) '매우, 대단히'의 의미로 부사 highly를 사용한다.

03 (1) analyst: 분석가 (2) record: 녹화하다. 명사 games를 꾸며주며 수동의 의미('녹화된')로 과거분사 recorded가 적절하다. (3) '~ 동안에'의 의미로 'the+명사'가 뒤에 있기 때문에 전치사 during이 적절하다. performance: 공연

04 (1) 물건을 가져가서 함께 모으다 (2) 당신이 어떤 사람인지, 행동하고 느끼고 생각하는 방식으로 보여 지는 것 (3) 특히 잘려서 장식으로 사용되는 녹색 식물이나 가지

05 • 오케스트라를 지휘하려면, 여러분은 머릿속에서 음악을 들을 수 있어야 합니다. • 경찰관들은 1년에 네 번 인천에서 학교 폭력 예방 캠페인을 실시합니다.

Conversation

핵심 Check   p.118~119

1 ①, ②, ④   2 ⑤

교과서 대화문 익히기

Check(√) True or False   p.120~121

1 T   2 T   3 T   4 F   5 F   6 T   7 T   8 F

교과서 확인학습   p.123~125

Listen & Speak 1 A

1. planning, police station, officer / to become, someday / do, dreamed, becoming, since / with, ask, something / going / what, to do / sure, would like to
2. wrong / animator, drawing, enough / Being, a, artist / animator / a lot of, practice drawing / quite sure that, if

Listen & Speak 1 B

interested, technology, Which, right / sure, developer in writing. Which job, be right for / quite sure, be a good job for

Listen & Speak 2 A

1. glad, what you do / guide, information, visit / else / popular culture, traditional / It seems, knowing, happy with

2. role model / be like / does, do / how to stretch / reduce, calm themselves / It seems that, to keep both, and

Listen & Speak 2 B

program writer, become / writing, helpful
social worker, help me become / seems, reading books to kids, be helpful

Real Life Talk

most interested, among / working / it seems to me that, belong to, realistic / mean / belong to, personality types. Realistic, types / interesting, What kind of, recommend / and so on / to be / I'm quite sure

Communication Task Step 2

3 Ss, 2 As, 1 E / seems to, belong to / Jobs that, recommended / have always wanted / sounds, quite sure that you could

Wrap Up 1

doing / recipe, cook / to cook, chef / make / taking, to think of, creative / I'm quite sure

---

시험대비 기본평가   p.126

01 It seems, that   02 ③   03 ⑤
04 ②

01 'It seems to me that 주어+동사 ~.'는 '~인 것 같다'라는 의미로 자신의 의견이나 생각을 나타내는 표현이다.

02 어떤 직업이 맞는지 묻는 말에 '나는 ~라고 확신해.'라는 의미로 확실성을 표현하는 말이 적절하다.

03 라디오 방송 작가가 되고 싶어 하는 A에게 도움이 되는 말로 ⑤가 적절하다.

04 'I'm sure (that) ~.'은 '나는 ~을 확신해.'라는 의미로 확실성 정도를 표현하는 말이다.

시험대비 실력평가   p.127~128

01 ③   02 ①   03 ④   04 ③
05 In my opinion   06 ⑤
07 Being an animator is not just about being a good artist.
08 ②   09 ⑤   10 ③

01 전치사 of 뒤에 동사가 올 때는 동명사를 사용해야 한다. become을 becoming으로 고쳐야 한다.

02 ① Matt가 이번 주말에 삼촌을 만날 것인지는 대화에서 언급되어 있지 않다.

03 동물에 관심이 있어서 어떤 직업이 나에게 맞는지 묻는 말에 → (C) 애완동물 미용사가 적합한 직업이라 말하고 → (B) 애완동물 미용사가 무엇인지 묻고 → (A) 직업을 설명한다. → 마지막으로 (D) 멋지다고 답하는 것이 적절하다.

04 A가 패션 디자이너가 되고 싶다는 말에 B가 패션쇼에 가는 것이 도움이 될 것 같다고 했으므로 빈칸에는 '내가 그것이 되는 데 뭐가 도움이 될까?'라는 말이 적절하다.

05 의견을 말하는 표현으로 'It seems to me ~' 대신 'In my opinion, ~'을 사용할 수 있다.

06 ⑤번은 '나는 기술에 관심이 있어. 어떤 직업이 나에게 맞을까?'라는 물음에 '네가 훌륭한 축구 선수가 될 수 있을 것이라고 꽤 확신한다.'라는 대답은 어색하다.

07 주어 자리에 동사 be를 동명사 Being으로 바꾸고, 동사 is를 추가한다. 전치사 about 뒤에도 동명사 being을 추가하여 문장을 완성한다.

08 'It seems to me that ~.'은 '~처럼 보인다, ~인 것 같다'라는 의미로 자신의 의견이나 생각을 나타내는 표현이다.

09 현실적인 타입이고, 항상 축구선수가 되기를 원하는 Jessie의 말에 '멋지다'라고 말한 다음 훌륭한 축구선수가 될 수 있을 거라고 확신하지 못한다고 말하는 것은 어색하다.

10 ③ 보라가 Jessie에게 어떤 직업을 제안했는지는 대화에 언급되어 있지 않다.

서술형 시험대비   p.129

01 I have dreamed of becoming a police officer since I was ten.
02 I'm (quite) sure (that) he would like to meet you.
03 (A) Could you please tell me what you do?
   (B) What else do you do?
   (C) It seems to me knowing a lot about China is very important.
04 (A) What does she do?   (B) It seems to me that

01 '10살 때부터'는 'since I was ten'을 쓰고, 주절에는 현재완료 'have dreamed'를 쓴다. '~이 되는 것을 꿈꾸다'는 'dream of'와 동명사 being을 사용한다.

02 확실성의 정도를 나타내는 말은 'I'm (quite) sure (that) 주어+동사'를 이용한다.

핵심 Check   p.130~131

1 (1) which   (2) that

2 (1) Peter had his legs broken several times.

(2) I will have my hair cut this Saturday.

시험대비 기본평가   p.132

01 (1) watched → watch

(2) injure → injured   (3) which → that

(4) encourage → encourages

02 ④   **03** ④

04 It is those books that[which] Barbara has always wanted to buy.

01 (1) 소녀가 다른 학생을 관찰하는 것이므로, 수동의 과거분사 watched는 부적절하다. 동사원형 watch를 써야 한다. (2) 다리를 부상당한 것이므로 수동의 과거분사 injured로 고쳐야 한다. (3) 'It ~ that' 강조구문으로 부사구 last Friday를 강조한다. (4) 삼촌이 격려하는 것이므로 현재시제, 3인칭 단수 주어에 맞는 동사형을 써야 한다.

02 the taxi를 강조하면, that 뒤에는 불완전한 문장이 와야 하는데, 구조가 완전하다. 내용상 Frank가 Nancy에게 청혼을 한 장소를 강조하는 문장이 되어야 하기 때문에 It was in the taxi that Frank proposed to Nancy.가 적절하다.

03 목적보어 자리에 동사원형이 왔으므로, 사역동사 had가 적절하다.

04 목적어를 강조하는 것이므로, 'It ~ that' 강조구문을 사용한다. 강조되는 대상이 복수라 하더라도 be동사는 is/was만 가능하며, 주절의 문장이 현재완료 시제이므로, 강조구문의 시제도 is로 하는 것에 유의한다.

시험대비 실력평가   p.133~135

01 ②   **02** ③   **03** ①

04 ③   **05** it was Poppy that tore the letter

06 ⓑ gain → to gain,   ⓒ to take → take,

ⓓ performing → (to) perform, ⓕ stops → to stop

07 ③   **08** ②   **09** ①   **10** ⑤

11 ④

12 Laura had Tom help her husband to repair the washing machine.

13 It is James who is responsible for taking care of

plants.   **14** ⑤   **15** ②   **16** ③

17 ③, ⑤   **18** break → broken

01 'It is[was] ~ that' 강조구문의 강조 대상은 문장 내의 명사(주어, 목적어)와 부사(구/절) 뿐이다.

02 ③의 that은 진주어로 쓰였다. 나머지는 모두 'It ~ that' 강조 구문의 that이다.

03 'have/has/had+목적어+목적보어' 형태에서 목적어의 능동/수동에 따라 목적보어 자리에 동사원형 또는 과거분사를 쓴다. 집이 '칠해지는' 것이므로, 과거분사 painted가 적절하다.

04 자동차가 '수리되는' 것이므로 fixed가 적절하다.

05 과거시제 동사 tore 형태에 유의하여, 'It is[was] ~ that' 강조 구문을 글자 수에 맞게 쓴다.

06 ⓑ order+목적어+to부정사 ⓒ let+목적어+원형부정사 ⓓ help+목적어+(to)부정사 ⓕ get+목적어+to부정사 등의 형태로 쓰는 것이 적절하다. the addict: 중독자

07 ③은 가주어 It과 진주어 명사절을 이끄는 접속사 that이 쓰였다. 나머지는 모두 'It ~ that' 강조 구문이다.

08 ②는 가주어 It과 진주어 명사절을 이끄는 접속사 that이 쓰였다. 나머지는 모두 'It ~ that' 강조 구문이다.

09 ①번 문장은 '그는 아들의 사고에 의해서도 마음이 바뀌지 않았다'는 내용이며, 전치사 by와 문맥을 통해 수동임을 알 수 있다. change를 changed로 고치는 것이 적절하다.

10 (A), (C)는 사역동사 have, make 뒤의 목적보어 자리이므로 원형부정사를, (B), (D)는 order, expect이므로 목적보어로 to 부정사를 쓰는 것이 적절하다.

11 ④의 allow는 목적보어 자리에 to부정사를 사용한다. ① to wash → wash, ② eat → to eat, ③ to use → use, ⑤ help → to help

12 사역동사 'have+목적어+동사원형'과 'help+목적어+(to) V' 형태를 적절하게 활용하여 영작한다.

13 내용상 아버지가 기르는 화초에 대한 책임을 맡고 있는 사람에 대한 강조 문장이므로 'It ~ who' 강조 구문을 사용한다. 전치사 for 뒤의 동명사 taking의 형태에 주의한다.

14 ⑤번 문장의 that은 접속사로 쓰였다. 나머지는 모두 'It ~ that' 강조 구문의 that이다.

15 'It ~ that' 강조구문에서는 강조되는 명사의 성격에 따라 that을 who 또는 which로 대체할 수 있다. ②는 진주어 명사절을 이끄는 접속사 that이며 다른 단어로 대체 불가하다.

16 옳은 문장은 ⓒ, ⓔ, ⓖ 3개이다. ⓐ fix → fixed, ⓑ clean → to clean, ⓓ 'It ~ that' 강조구문에서는 형용사를 강조할 수 없다. ⓕ pick → to pick ⓗ do → done

17 사역동사 'have+목적어+원형/과거분사' 형태를 적절하게 활용한 문장을 선택한다. ①은 우리말과 일치하지 않으며, ②도 내용뿐 아니라 어법상 be taken 뒤에 by가 와야 한다. ④는 to take

의 to를 삭제하는 것이 적절하다.

18 '시합 중 그 축구 선수의 다리가 부러졌다'라는 의미가 정확하게 표현되려면, 수동의 과거분사가 목적보어 자리에 와야 한다. break를 broken으로 고치는 것이 적절하다.

서술형 시험대비
p.136~137

01 (A) It is John that[who] is going to buy the masks at a party this Friday.
  (B) It is the masks that[which] John is going to buy at a party this Friday.
  (C) It is at a party that John is going to buy the masks this Friday.
  (D) It is this Friday that John is going to buy the masks at a party.

02 had me help him to make

03 (1) the Hongdae street → on(in) the Hongdae street
  (2) He rescued the injured carefully.
  (3) Bush was chairman of the council.
  (4) the playground → on[in] the playground
  (5) who → that[which]

04 (1) clean (2) come[coming] (3) cry[crying]
  (4) go (5) to look

05 on March 14, 1879 that Einstein was

06 (1) check → checked (2) sing → to sing
  (3) meet → to meet (4) playing → play
  (5) was → was 삭제 (6) looks → look

07 (1) The teacher had Susan clean her desk.
  (2) The tie made his father look much younger.
  (3) Allow her to enjoy the film.

08 (1) 답변 불가
  (2) It was Alicia that[who] had John's phone repaired.
  (3) It was two weeks ago that Alicia had John's phone repaired.
  (4) 답변 불가
  (5) It was at the repair shop that John's phone was repaired two weeks ago.

01 강조하는 대상에 따라 알맞게 강조하는 대상이 사람일 때는 who, 사물일 때는 which를 써도 좋다. 'It ~ that 강조 구문'으로 표현한다.

02 '시키다'의 의미를 갖는 사역동사 have를 시제에 맞게 had로 사용하는 것에 유의하여, 단어들을 배열한다.

03 (1) '부사구'로 장소를 강조하는 것이므로 전치사를 써야 한다.
  (2) 태도를 나타내는 '양태 부사'는 'It ~ that' 강조 구문의 강조

대상이 될 수 없다. (3) '주격보어'도 'It ~ that' 강조 구문의 강조 대상이 될 수 없다. (4) '부사구'로서 장소를 강조하는 것이므로 전치사를 써야 한다. (5) 강조 대상이 사람이 아니므로 who는 쓸 수 없다. which 또는 that이 적절하다.

04 (1)~(4)는 사역/지각동사 (5)는 일반 5형식 동사이다. (5)의 목적보어 자리에는 to look의 형태가 적절하다.

05 '1879년 3월 14일이 Einstein이 태어난 날'이라는 문장을 '부사구'를 강조하는 'It ~ that 강조 구문'으로 표현해야 한다. 전치사 on과 함께 쓰는 것에 유의하여 영작한다.

06 (1) '짐 검사를 당하는 것'이니까 수동의 표현이 필요하다. 'have+목적어+과거분사' 형태가 적절하다. (2) get+목적어+to V (3) allow+목적어+to V (4) let+목적어+원형동사 (5) break one's legs 다리가 부러지다 (6) make+목적어+원형동사

07 (1) 사역동사 had + 목적어 + 동사원형. (2) 사역동사 made + 목적어 + 동사원형. (3) 일반 5형식 동사 allow 뒤에 나오는 목적보어 자리에는 to 부정사를 쓰는 것이 적절하다.

08 (1) 사역동사 'have +목적어+ p.p.' 형태에서는 행위자를 파악할 수 없다. 일반적으로 제3자가 행위자이므로, 보기의 문장만으로는 누가 전화기를 수리했는지 답변할 수 없다. (4) 주어진 문장만으로는 수리 시점(2주 전)만을 알 수 있고, 수리 기간은 파악할 수 없으므로 답변 불가임. (2), (3), (5)번은 'It ~ that' 강조 구문에 맞춰 적절히 영작한다.

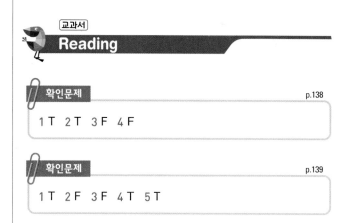

교과서 Reading

확인문제
p.138

1 T 2 T 3 F 4 F

확인문제
p.139

1 T 2 F 3 F 4 T 5 T

교과서 확인학습 A
p.140~141

01 who creates, with
02 To become, need to know
03 attended, for
04 at this school, how to grow, for
05 a lot of different
06 movie sets, decorate
07 something colorful, greenery

08 highly recommend
09 sport data analyst
10 doesn't it   11 a lot of fun
12 to watch recorded games, run, to collect
13 analyze, to show
14 understands, do better
15 Since, have been
16 baseball games all the time
17 because watching baseball games
18 As, a musical theater
19 audition, look for
20 selecting the cast, for each scene
21 put, together
22 During, conduct
23 my responsibility, each
24 direct, to keep, together
25 Conducting, directing, waving
26 a big field   27 includes, living in them
28 have studied, living
29 the growth ring, that
30 By looking
31 I get from, is used to understand, manage
32 because, the best use

교과서 확인학습 B   p.142~143

1 Hi, I am Tom. A florist is someone who creates beautiful things with flowers.

2 To become a florist, you need to know many things about flowers.

3 I attended a high school for florists and gardeners.

4 It was at this school that I learned how to grow and care for different types of flowers.

5 These days, florists can do a lot of different things.

6 I design movie sets sometimes and I decorate shops with flowers.

7 I am happy when I create something colorful with fresh flowers and greenery.

8 If you like plants and the arts, I highly recommend you become a florist.

9 I am Emma. I am a sport data analyst.

10 It sounds like a difficult job, doesn't it?

11 In fact, it is a lot of fun. I work for a baseball team.

12 My job is to watch recorded games and run a computer program to collect data.

13 Then, I analyze the data to show my team's strengths and weaknesses.

14 If the team understands their strengths and weaknesses, they can do better next time.

15 Since I was young, I have been a big fan of baseball.

16 Now, in my work, I watch baseball games all the time.

17 This is a perfect job for me because watching baseball games is my hobby!

18 Hi, I am Chris. As a director of a musical theater, I do a lot of things.

19 I audition the actors and I look for good, strong voices.

20 After selecting the cast, I teach them the songs for each scene.

21 Then, I put the cast and orchestra together for practic

22 During the performance, I am in the orchestra area and conduct.

23 It's my responsibility to have each song played the same way every time.

24 I direct the musicians and the singers to keep the show together.

25 Conducting and directing is not just about waving my arms around!

26 My name is Yeji. I am an ocean scientist. Ocean science is a big field.

27 It includes studies of the oceans and the creatures living in them.

28 Among other things, I have studied many kinds of fish living in the seas near Korea.

29 It is the growth ring in a fish that interests me.

30 By looking at it, I can find out when and where the fish was born.

31 All the information I get from fish is used to understand sea resources and manage the oceans better."

32 My job is important because it makes the best use of nature possible.

시험대비 실력평가   p.144~147

01 ②   02 ⑤

03 A florist is someone who creates beautiful things with flowers.

04 ③   05 ③

06 They can do better next time if the team understands their strengths and weaknesses.

07 played   08 ③

09 (After selecting the cast,) He teaches them the songs for each scene.

10 cast   11 ⑤   12 ④

13 the oceans, the creatures living in them

14 It can tell Yeji when and where the fish was born.

15 ②, ③   16 ③

17 He learned how to grow and care for different types of flowers at a school for florists and gardeners.

18 doesn't it   19 ②   20 ④

21 She does it in order to collect data.

22 conducts   23 ③

24 His responsibility is to have each song played the same way every time.

25 ④   26 ④   27 ④

01 (A)는 '오늘날'이라는 의미이다. 따라서 ②번이 적절하다. ①, ③, ⑤ 가끔 ④ 거의 ~하지 않는

02 Tom은 플로리스트와 정원사들을 양성하는 학교에 다녔다고 하였으므로 ⑤번이 글의 내용과 일치한다.

03 플로리스트는 꽃으로 아름다운 것들을 창조하는 사람이라고 하였다.

04 야구 경기를 보는 것이 자신의 취미이기 때문에 완벽한 직업이라고 말하는 것이 적절하다.

05 자료를 수집한 후 분석한다고 하였다.

06 팀이 자신들의 강점과 약점을 알면 다음번에 더 잘할 수 있다고 하였다.

07 각각의 노래가 연주되도록 하는 것이므로 과거분사 형태를 쓰는 것이 적절하다.

08 ③ 공연 중에 지휘한다고 하였다.

09 배역에 맞는 배우를 고른 뒤에, Chris는 그들에게 각 장면을 위한 노래를 가르친다고 하였다.

10 어떤 영화나 연극에 출연하는 사람들은 '출연자들(배역진)'이다.

11 to understand와 병렬 관계이므로 manage라고 쓰는 것이 적절하다.

12 빈칸 (A)에는 By가 들어간다. ① pay attention to: ~에 주의를 기울이다 ② look forward to: ~을 기대하다 ③ depend on: ~에 의존하다 ④ go by: 지나가다, 흐르다 ⑤ take away: ~을 없애주다

13 해양 과학자들은 바다뿐만 아니라 바다에 사는 생명체를 연구한다고 하였다.

14 물고기의 나이테로 물고기가 언제 어디에서 태어났는지를 알 수 있다고 하였다.

15 사람을 선행사로 받는 주격 관계대명사 who가 쓰이며, who를 대신하여 that을 써도 무방하다.

16 항상 같은 일을 하는 것이 아니라 여러 가지 일을 한다고 하였다.

17 Tom은 플로리스트와 정원사들을 위한 학교에서 갖가지 종류의 꽃을 키우고 관리하는 방법을 배웠다고 하였다. 'It was at a high school for florists and gardeners that he learned how to grow and care for different types of flowers.'라고 답해도 좋다.

18 일반동사의 부가의문문이고, 주어가 it이므로 doesn't it이라고 쓰는 것이 적절하다.

19 어려운 직업처럼 들리지만 [B] 사실 매우 재미있다고 말하며 녹화된 경기를 보고 자료를 수집한다고 말함 [A] 수집한 자료를 분석하여 팀에게 보여주는 일을 한다고 설명. 어릴 때부터 야구의 열혈 팬이었고 [C] 지금 일하는 내내 야구를 보므로 자신에게 완벽한 직업이라고 함.

20 어렸을 때부터 야구의 열혈 팬이었던 Emma는 자신의 직업에 만족하고 있다는 것을 글을 통해 알 수 있다.

21 Emma는 자료를 수집하기 위하여 컴퓨터 프로그램을 실행한다고 하였다.

22 오케스트라나 합창단 앞에 서서 공연을 지시하는 것은 '지휘하다'이다.

23 Chris는 배역에 맞는 배우를 고르고 그들에게 각 장면을 위한 노래를 가르친다고 하였다. 따라서 ③번이 일치한다.

24 각각의 노래가 매번 동일하게 연주되도록 만드는 것이 Chris의 책임이라고 하였다.

25 주어진 문장의 it이 가리키는 것은 the growth ring in a fish 이다.

26 예지의 작업은 자연을 가장 잘 활용할 수 있게 한다는 점에서 중요하다고 하였다.

27 ① includes ② creatures ③ resources ④ attention ⑤ manage

서술형 시험대비   p.148~149

01 creates

02 He attended a high school for florists and gardeners.

03 We need to know many things about flowers to become a florist.

04 He feels happy when he creates something colorful with fresh flowers and greenery.

05 strengths and weaknesses

06 She watches recorded games and runs a computer program to collect data. Then, she analyzes the data to show her team's strengths and weaknesses.

07 Her hobby is watching baseball games.

08 analyst

09 waving his arms around

10 He is in the orchestra area during the performance.

11 He directs the musicians and the singers.

12 It is the actors that I audition.

13 It is the growth ring in a fish that interests Yeji.

14 It's because her job makes the best use of nature possible.

15 As an ocean scientist, she has studied many kinds of fish living in the seas near Korea.

16 We should look at the growth ring in a fish.

---

01 주격 관계대명사의 선행사가 someone이므로 단수 동사를 쓰는 것이 적절하다.

02 Tom은 플로리스트와 정원사들을 위한 학교를 다녔다고 하였다.

03 플로리스트가 되기 위해서 여러분은 꽃에 관해 많은 것을 알 필요가 있다고 하였다.

04 그는 싱싱한 꽃과 화초로 다채로운 무언가를 창조해 낼 때 행복하다고 하였다.

05 팀이 자신들의 강점과 약점을 이해하면 다음번에 더 잘할 수 있다는 의미이다.

06 스포츠 데이터 분석가로서 Emma는 녹화된 경기를 보고 자료를 수집하기 위해 컴퓨터 프로그램을 실행한 후 팀의 강점과 약점을 보여주기 위해서 자료를 분석하는 일을 한다고 하였다.

07 Emma는 자신의 취미가 야구 경기를 보는 것이라고 하였다.

08 어떠한 주제를 분석하여 그것에 관한 의견을 주는 사람은 '분석가'이다.

09 Chris에 따르면 지휘하고 감독하는 것은 단지 그의 팔을 흔드는 것 이상을 의미한다.

10 Chris는 공연 동안에 오케스트라 석에 있다고 하였다.

11 공연을 제대로 진행하기 위해 그는 연주자들과 가수들을 감독한다고 하였다.

12 Chris는 배우들을 대상으로 오디션을 실시한다고 하였다. 따라서 강조하는 대상을 the actors로 하여 답할 수 있다.

13 'The growth ring in a fish interests Yeji.'라고 답해도 좋다.

14 그녀의 직업은 자연을 가장 잘 활용할 수 있게 한다는 점에서 중요하다고 하였다.

15 예지는 해양 과학자로서 한국 주변의 바다에 살고 있는 많은 종류의 물고기를 연구해 왔다고 하였다.

16 물고기가 언제 어디서 태어났는지 알고 싶으면 물고기 안에 있

는 나이테를 보면 된다고 하였다.

01 select   02 ⑤   03 ③   04 ①

05 (c)reatures 06 ④   07 ②

08 it seems to me that you belong to the realistic type.

09 She is most interested in working outside and playing sports.

10 ③

11 quite sure you could be a good chef   12 ①

13 ⑤   14 ④   15 ④   16 ④

17 ③   18 ⑤   19 ②   20 ②

21 will have your computer fixed today   22 ⑤

23 how to grow and care for different types of flowers   24 ④   25 ⑤   26 ②

27 ③   28 ②   29 ④

30 She works for a baseball team.

---

01 유의어 관계다. 매우, 대단히 = 고르다, 선택하다

02 (A)의 앞 문장에 전 세계의 요리를 좋아하고 요리를 잘할 수 있으며 음식을 맛있고 아름답게 만들 수 있다는 말을 하고 있고 그에 대한 결과로 요리사가 되고 싶다고 했기 때문에 의미상 '이러한 이유로'가 적절하다. (B)는 '내 꿈을 이루기 위해'가 의미상 적절하다.

03 어떤 것 또는 어떤 사람을 처리해야 할 일이나 의무

04 무언가를 다른 것의 일부로 포함하거나 다른 것의 일부로 만들다

05 영어 설명은 '독립적으로 움직일 수 있는 크거나 작은 생물'이란 의미로 creature가 적절하다.

06 since가 현재완료와 함께 사용이 될 때는 '~일 때부터'의 의미가 된다.

07 자산의 의견을 나타내는 표현으로 '~처럼 보이다'는 의미로 'It seems to me that ~'을 사용한다.

08 '~인 것 같다'는 의미로 'it seems to me that 주어+동사 ~'를 쓴다.

09 목록에 있는 것 중에서 Jessie가 가장 관심이 있는 것은 무엇인가?

10 Jessie에게 축구 선수를 추천한 것은 보라가 아니라 the things on the list에서 추천한 것이다.

11 확실성 정도를 표현하는 말로 'I'm quite sure+주어+동사' 어순이 적절하고 '나는 네가 좋은 요리사가 될 것이라고 꽤 확신해'라는 의미가 된다.

12 have+목적어+동사원형: ~하게 시키다

13 'It ~ that' 강조 구문으로 표현한다. ②는 cheer 동사의 수의 일치가 부적절하고, ③은 to cheer가 어법상 적절하다.

14 'have+목적어+과거분사' 문장이다. ⑤번의 break one's leg 도 '다리가 부러지다'라는 뜻이지만, '펜스가 그를 쳤다'는 내용 이 부적절하다.

15 ④는 가주어 It과 진주어 명사절을 이끄는 접속사 that이 쓰인 문장이다. 나머지는 모두 'It ~ that' 강조 구문이 쓰였다.

16 ① fixed → fix ② leaving → leave ③ feels → feel ④ allow의 목적보어 자리에 to부정사는 적절하다. ⑤ break → broken

17 'It ~ that' 강조 구문에서 일어난 해를 가리키는 표현은 연도 앞 에 in을 쓰는 것이 적절하다.

18 <보기>의 have는 'have+목적어+p.p.' 형태로 '목적어가 ~되도 록 시키다'라는 의미이다. 같은 의미로 쓰인 문장은 ⑤번이다. 다 른 문장들의 have는 ① 먹다 ② (특징)으로 ~이 있다 ③ (잡고) 있다 ④ 겪다 등의 의미로 쓰였다.

19 ②는 가주어 It과 진주어 명사절을 이끄는 접속사 that으로 쓰 였다. 나머지는 모두 'It ~ that' 강조 구문의 that이다.

20 'have+목적어+과거분사' 형태이다. to change를 changed로 고치는 것이 적절하다. grief: 슬픔

21 주어진 조건대로 영작할 때, '오늘 네 컴퓨터를 고쳐줄게'라고 해 야 한다. Peter는 컴퓨터를 고칠 줄 모르기 때문에, 누군가 제 3자가 고치도록 해야 하므로, 그에 맞는 표현인 'have+목적어 +p.p.'를 활용한다.

22 '매우' 추천한다는 의미이므로 highly라고 쓰는 것이 적절하다.

23 Tom이 다닌 학교는 다양한 종류의 꽃을 기르고 다루는 방법을 그에게 가르쳐 주었다.

24 누가 Tom이 플로리스트가 되도록 권했는지는 위 글을 읽고 알 수 없다.

25 [C]에서 말하는 these reasons는 주어진 문장에서 언급한 '자 신이 잘하는 것들'을 가리키는 말이다. [C]에서 꿈을 위해 요리 잡지를 보고 [B]에서 또한 프랑스로 가서 다양한 요리 기술을 배우겠다고 말하며 자신의 롤 모델이 아버지라고 언급한다. [A] 아버지에 대한 이야기가 기술되고 있다.

26 자신의 꿈의 직업인 요리사에 관한 글이다.

27 요리사가 되고 싶은 글쓴이의 롤 모델이 아버지라고 하였고, 아 버지는 항상 새로운 조리법에 대해 생각하고 이것을 요리해준다 고 하였으므로 ③번을 유추할 수 있다.

28 스포츠 경기를 보고 컴퓨터 프로그램을 돌려 분석하는 직업으로 ②번이 가장 적절하다.

29 Emma는 어렸을 때부터 야구의 열혈 팬이었고 야구 경기를 보 는 것이 자신의 취미라고 하였으므로 ④번이 글의 내용과 일치 한다.

30 Emma는 야구팀을 위해서 일한다고 하였다.

01 lead   02 ③

03 It seems to me knowing a lot about China is very important. 04 ⑤

05 Read a lot of books and practice drawing every day.   06 ①   07 ④

08 I'm quite sure (that) you could become a (great) soccer player.

09 Do you want to become a police officer?

10 (1) ⓐ   (2) ⓑ   (3) ⓐ   (4) ⓑ   (5) ⓐ

11 It seems, both, and, healthy   12 ④

13 ③   14 ⑤

15 (1) ⓐ It was the newlyweds that bought a table at the mall 2 weeks ago.
   (2) ⓑ It was a table that the newlyweds bought at the mall 2 weeks ago.
   (3) ⓒ It was at the mall that the newlyweds bought a table 2 weeks ago.
   (4) ⓓ It was 2 weeks ago that the newlyweds bought a table at the mall.

16 ④   17 ②

18 He looks for good, strong voices.

19 He directs the musicians and the singers to keep the show together.   20 ③   21 ⑤

22 the oceans   23 information from fish

01 반의어 관계다. 약함 - 강함 : 따르다 - 이끌다

02 영화, 연극, 쇼 등의 한 부분에 적합하다는 것을 보여주기 위해 짧은 공연을 하다.

03 'In my opinion, 주어+동사 ~'는 의견을 말할 때 사용하는 표 현으로 'It seems to me (that)+주어+동사 ~'로 바꾸어 쓸 수 있다.

05 지수에게 많은 책을 읽고, 매일 그리기 연습을 하라고 조언하고 있다.

06 enough는 형용사를 뒤에서 수식하므로 good enough로 바꾸 어야 한다.

07 Jessie의 '무슨 의미야?'라는 질문에 대한 보라의 대답으로 보아 '너는 현실적인 타입에 속하는 것 같아.'라는 말이 적절하다.

08 확실성 정도를 나타내는 표현은 'I'm quite sure (that) 주어+ 동사'를 이용한다.

09 'You do?'의 do는 대동사로 앞 문장의 become a police officer를 대신하는 말이다. 구어체에서 일반동사 의문문의 Do 가 생략되어 'You want to ~?' 형태로 사용하기도 한다.

10 (2), (4) 문장들은 접속사 that이 이끄는 진주어 명사절과 형용 사 보어(2), 명사보어(4)로 이뤄진 문장이다. (1) 부사구를 강조 (3) 부사절을 강조 (5) 의문사를 강조하는 'It ~ that' 강조 구문 이다.

11 '~인 것 같다'는 'It seems that ~'을 이용하고, 'A와 B 둘 다'는 'both A and B' 구문을 사용한다. '건강하게'는 우리말로 부사로 해석되지만 'keep+목적어+목적보어' 구문으로 목적보어 자리에는 형용사 healthy를 사용해야 한다.

12 ④ 글의 내용상 나의 컴퓨터가 shop에서 수리되었으므로, '컴퓨터를 수리한 것은 삼촌이다'라는 내용의 문장은 부적절하다.

13 'have+목적어+p.p.' 형태의 문장들이다. 각각 ① '우산을 도둑맞다' ② '아들을 전학보내다' ④ '구매품들을 포장시키다' ⑤ '돈을 인출하다'를 뜻하며, ③번 '신발을 닦다'라는 의미로 쓰려면, shone을 shined로 쓰는 것이 적절하다.

14 ⑤ 'have+목적어+동사원형'이 쓰였다. ① moving → moved ② to wait → wait ③ going → go ④ washed → (to) wash 로 고치는 것이 적절하다.

16 (A)는 자격을 나타내어 '~로서'라고 해석되는 전치사이다. ① ~ 때문에, ~이므로 ② ~만큼 ③ ~하는 동안에 ④ ~로서 ⑤ ~ 때문에

17 the cast는 Chris가 오디션을 실시하여 고른 배우들을 의미한다. 이들에게 노래를 가르친 후 배우와 오케스트라를 함께 연습시킨다는 흐름이 자연스럽다.

18 Chris는 훌륭하고 강한 목소리를 찾아낸다고 하였다.

19 Chris는 공연을 제대로 진행하기 위해 연주자들과 가수들을 감독한다고 하였다.

20 (A) '한국 주변의 바다에 살고 있는'이 fish를 수식하므로 현재분사 형태, (B) by Ving: V함으로써, on Ving: V하자마자 (C) 핵심 주어가 all the information이므로 단수 동사를 쓰는 것이 적절하다.

21 예지가 물고기에 대해 얻은 정보는 바다의 지원을 이해하고 바다를 더 잘 관리하기 위해 사용된다고 하였다.

22 바다를 가리키는 말이다.

23 예지는 물고기로부터 정보를 얻어서 바다 자원을 이해한다고 하였다.

서술형 실전문제 p.160~161

01 A: I'm interested in technology
   B: I'm quite sure that

02 dream, It seems, taking a cooking, trying to think of new and creative dishes, achieve

03 I have no doubt that you can be a good animator if you try hard.

04 was because of my parents that I received this award

05 (1) Her father had Sally wash Toto.
   (2) Her father had Toto washed by Sally.

06 She wants to be a chef (when she grows up).

07 First, she will read magazines about cooking. Second, she will go to France to learn various cooking skills.

08 He always thinks of new recipes and then cooks these new dishes for his family.

09 recorded

10 Her hobby is watching baseball games.

11 She watches baseball games all the time in her work.

01 (A) '~에 관심이 있다'는 'be interested in'을 사용한다. (B) 확실성 정도는 'I'm quite sure that ~'을 사용한다.

02 수미의 꿈은 요리사가 되는 것이다. 요리 수업을 듣고 새롭고 창조적인 요리를 생각해 내기 위해 노력하는 것이 그녀의 꿈을 이루는 데 중요한 것 같다.

03 확실성 정도를 표현하는 말은 'I'm quite sure (that)+주어+동사'나 'I have no doubt that+주어+동사'를 사용할 수 있다.

04 기자의 질문이 '수상에 가장 크게 기여한 것'을 묻는 것이므로, 부모님 때문이라는 내용으로 'because of my parents'를 'it ~ that' 구문으로 강조하는 문장을 쓰는 것이 적절하다.

05 사역동사 'have+목적어+원형[과거분사]' 형태를 적절하게 활용하도록 한다.

06 글쓴이는 자라서 요리사가 되기를 원한다.

07 글쓴이는 꿈을 이루기 위해 요리 잡지를 읽고, 다양한 요리 기술을 배우기 위하여 프랑스로 갈 것이라고 하였다.

08 아버지는 항상 새로운 조리법에 대해 생각하고 그것을 요리해 준다고 하였다.

09 녹화된 경기라는 의미이므로 과거분사를 쓰는 것이 적절하다.

10 그녀의 취미는 야구 경기를 보는 것이라고 하였다.

11 그녀는 일하는 중에 내내 야구를 본다고 하였다.

창의사고력 서술형 문제 p.162

|모범답안|

01 A: I'm interested in art.
   B: I'm quite sure that a designer

02 (1) |모범답안| I had my phone repaired yesterday.
   (2) |모범답안| Sophia will have her car checked by a mechanic at the repair shop tomorrow.

03 bags from around, making things, what I made look beautiful, it is a bag designer that, read fashion magazines, go to France to learn to design bags

01 ①　　02 ⑤　　03 run　　04 ③
05 ④
06 That's a person who works at a pet hair salon.
07 ③
08 a farmer, a police officer, a soccer player, and so on
09 ②
10 I'm quite sure that you can be a good animator if you try hard.
11 (1) It is for three days that Lucy has been reading the novel.
　　(2) It is Austin who wrote the novel.
12 (1) Mom had me put the unused things in the boxes.
　　(2) I will have the boxes donated to charity.
13 (1) Mom had me brush my teeth for myself.
　　(2) It is my dog Angel that is washing so many dishes.
14 ③　　15 ②　　16 ③　　17 ④
18 ④
19 He conducts during the performance.
20 my responsibility to have each song played
21 ③　　22 ⑤

01 ①번은 'analyst(분석가)'에 관한 설명이다.
02 '직업에 만족하나요?'라는 A의 말에 B가 '내 생각으로는, 패션쇼에 가는 것이 도움이 될 거야.'라고 말하는 것은 자연스럽지 못하다.
03 유의어 관계다. 고치다 : 실행하다
04 사람이나 사물을 어떤 상태나 장소로 데려오다[가져오다]
05 '애완동물 미용사가 너에게 좋은 직업이 될 거라고 생각한다.'는 B의 대답으로 보아 (A)에는 자신에게 맞는 직업의 종류를 물어보는 것이 자연스럽다.
06 '애완동물 미용사는 무엇이니?'라는 A의 질문에 대한 답으로 '그것은 애완동물 미용실에서 일하는 사람이다'라는 답이 적절하다. 주격 관계대명사 who를 이용하여 선행사 a person을 수식한다.
07 belong to는 자동사이므로 수동태를 사용할 수 없다.
08 Q: 현실적인 타입의 사람들에게 그들이 추천하는 직업은 무엇인가?
09 빈칸 다음에 좋은 이야기를 만들기 위해 책을 많이 읽고, 그림 그리는 것을 매일 연습하라고 조언하고 있으므로 빈칸에는 만화영화 제작자가 되기 위해 조언을 구하는 말이 적절하다.
10 '~을 꽤 확신해'는 'I'm quite sure that+주어+동사' 구문을 이용하고, '노력한다면'은 'if+주어+동사'를 이용한다.
11 내용을 정확히 이해하고, 조건에 맞게 질문에 답하도록 한다.
　(1) 일요일에 시작해서 화요일이므로 '3일 동안'이다. (2) who를 쓰는 것이 조건이므로 that을 쓰지 않는 것에 유의한다.

12 시제와 능동/수동에 유의하여, 'have+목적어+원형/과거분사' 형태로 주어진 단어를 배열한다.
13 (1) 혼자 힘으로: for myself (2) '그릇을 닦고 있는'이라는 우리말로 보아 현재진행시제로 영작하는 것이 적절하다.
14 주어진 문장과 ③번은 사역동사 have로서 '시키다'라는 의미로 쓰였다. 각 문장에 쓰인 have의 의미는 ①, ② '갖고 있다' ④ '먹다' ⑤ '경험하다' 등이다.
15 ②번 이후의 문장에서 말하는 at this school은 주어진 문장의 a high school for florists and gardeners이다.
16 글의 내용상 '식물과 예술'을 좋아한다면 플로리스트가 될 것을 강력히 추천한다는 말이 가장 적절하다.
17 색종이로 꽃을 장식하는 것은 위 글에 나와 있지 않다.
18 Tom이 어디에서 일하는지는 위 글을 읽고 알 수 없다.
19 Chris는 공연 중에 지휘를 한다고 하였다.
20 노래가 연주되도록 하는 것이므로 사역동사 have의 목적격 보어로 과거분사 played를 쓰는 것이 적절하다.
21 (B)는 전치사 about의 목적어로 쓰인 동명사이다. 모두 명사를 수식하는 현재분사이지만 ③번은 '~하는 것'으로 해석되는 동명사이다.
22 자신의 꿈에 관하여 이야기하고 있으므로 아버지가 항상 새로운 요리법에 관해 생각한다는 것은 글의 흐름상 어색하다.

교과서 파헤치기

Lesson 1

단어 TEST Step 3   p.04

1 enter, 들어가다   2 among, ~ 중에서
3 create, 만들다, 창출하다   4 forest, 숲
5 advise, 충고하다   6 fantastic, 환상적인
7 basement, 지하실[층]   8 imagine, 상상하다
9 countryside, 시골   10 motto, 좌우명, 모토
11 hero, 영웅   12 choice, 선택
13 photographer, 사진사   14 furniture, 가구
15 pet, 애완동물   16 recognize, 인식하다, 알아차리다

단어 TEST Step 1   p.02

01 환상적인, 매우 멋진		02 자동으로
03 앞으로	04 목표	05 인식하다
06 다른, 다양한	07 자연	08 장면
09 지하층[실]	10 시골(지역)	11 조언하다, 충고하다
12 (남들보다 먼저 신기술을 사서 써 보는 사람) 얼리 어답터		
13 기술	14 한가한, 다른 계획이 없는	
15 매우, 꽤	16 숲	17 제품
18 편안한	19 ~ 중에서	20 관심, 흥미
21 선택	22 구하다	23 가구
24 손님	25 만들다	26 기술
27 그려진, 디자인된	28 (건물의) 층	29 상상하다
30 재미있는, 유머러스한		31 좌우명, 모토
32 (기분이) 상쾌한	33 사진촬영	34 과목, 주제
35 ~와 잘 지내다	36 ~하는 것을 그만두다	
37 ~로 가득 차다	38 ~하고 싶다	39 ~에 관심이 있다
40 ~을 잘하다	41 여기에 ~가 있다	42 ~처럼 보이다
43 (잠에서) 깨다, 일어나다		

단어 TEST Step 2   p.03

01 product	02 designed	03 photo-taking
04 automatically	05 choice	06 real
07 comfortable	08 furniture	09 advise
10 pretty	11 among	12 fantastic
13 practice	14 subject	15 forward
16 goal	17 save	18 interest
19 recognize	20 countryside	21 humorous
22 create	23 language	24 floor
25 guest	26 imagine	27 basement
28 scene	29 free	30 forest
31 nature	32 technology	33 hero
34 refreshed	35 be good at	
36 would like to+동사원형		37 not just ~
38 wake up	39 be full of[be filled with]	
40 stop -ing	41 get along with	42 look like+명사
43 here are+복수명사		

대화문 TEST Step 1   p.05~07

Warm Up

want to tell, myself, interested in, 'm good at playing / like running, refreshed when / 'm interested, usually go out to see / designer, practice drawing, free time / win first prize, contest

Listen & Speak 1 A

1 how, third grade / pretty / sounds good, homeroom teacher / teaches / Can you tell me, about / humorous, told, fun stories, interesting / enjoy studying

2 look at, to see / looks, tell / about, who saves / looks like / favorite kind of, scenes made with, technology, fantastic, real / cool, Let's go / Sounds

Listen & Speak 1 B

Can, tell, about / am going to have / goal for the year / to stop eating

Listen & Speak 2 A

1 go traveling with, What, most, trying

2 favorite subject, play the drums, Among, playing, what, like most

3 not just / Playing with, what

Real Life Talk

'd like to join / for your interest, about yourself / in, third grade / more, What, most, free time / what, to take / for the future / to be a photographer / choice, photo-taking, skills, Welcome to / glad

Communication Task Step 2

nickname / because, run fast / like most / What I like most / Can you tell me about / want to be / motto / motto, forward slowly, never go back

Wrap Up

new student, introduce yourself / from, Nice to meet / Can you tell us more / especially, to join / anything else, to tell / get along with, because, new here / Welcome to our class

Warm Up

B1: Hello, my name is Kim Chanho. I want to tell you about myself. I'm interested in music. I'm good at playing the drums.

G1: Hi! I am Teri. I like running in the evening. I feel refreshed when I exercise.

B2: Hello, my name is Jack. I'm interested in the stars. I usually go out to see stars at night.

G2: I am Lee Bora. I want to be a designer in the future, so I practice drawing when I have free time.

B3: I am Mark. I like dancing. I want to win first prize in the dance contest.

Listen & Speak 1 A

1 G: Jiho, how was your first day of third grade?

　B: It was pretty good. The teachers and my new classmates are all good.

　G: That sounds good. Who is your homeroom teacher?

　B: My homeroom teacher is Mr. Kim. He teaches math.

　G: Can you tell me more about him?

　B: Yes. He is humorous and told us some fun stories about math. It was interesting.

　G: Cool! I hope you enjoy studying math.

2 G: Ted, look at this movie poster. I want to see this movie.

　B: It looks interesting. Can you tell me about it, Amy?

　G: Yes. It is about a hero who saves the Earth.

　B: It looks like an SF movie.

　G: Yes, it is. Actually, SF is my favorite kind of movie. I like the scenes made with computer technology. They are fantastic and look real.

　B: That's cool. I am free this weekend. Let's go to see it together.

　G: Sounds good

Listen & Speak 1 B

A: Can you tell me about your plan for this weekend?

B: Yes. I am going to have a birthday party.

A: Can you tell me about your goal for the year?

B: Yes. I want to stop eating fast food.

Listen & Speak 2 A

1 G: I often go traveling with my family. What I like most about traveling is trying new foods.

2 B: My favorite subject is music. I can play the drums and guitar. Among them, playing the guitar is what I like most.

3 G: This is a picture of Dora. She is my best friend, not just a pet. Playing with her in my free time is what I like most.

Real Life Talk

Seho: Nice to meet you. I'd like to join your photo club.

Bora: Thank you for your interest in the club. Can you tell me about yourself?

Seho: Yes. My name is Kim Seho. I am in the third grade, class 8.

Andy: Tell me more. What do you like to do most in your free time?

Seho: Well, what I like most is to take pictures.

Bora: That's great. What is your dream for the future?

Seho: I want to be a photographer.

Andy: Then you made the right choice. You can learn a lot of photo-taking skills here. Welcome to our club.

Seho: Thank you. I'm so glad!

Communication Task Step 2

A: What is your nickname?

B: My nickname is Speedy because I can run fast.

C: What do you like most?

B: What I like most is to play baseball.

D: Can you tell me about your dream job?

B: I want to be a baseball player.

A: What is your motto?

B: My motto is "You can go forward slowly, but never go back."

Wrap Up

W: Today, we have a new student Hojun. Hojun, can you please introduce yourself to the class?

B: Yes. Hi, my name is Kim Hojun. I am from Busan. Nice to meet you.

W: Can you tell us more about yourself?

B: Yes. I like sports, especially soccer. I want to join a sports club.

W: Is there anything else you want to tell your new friends?

B: I want to get along with everyone. Please help me because I'm new here.

W: Thanks, Hojun. Welcome to our class.

01 Have, ever thought
02 in class, created
03 Here are, that, made
04 Nature, my good
05 feel good, walk, forest
06 like to have, in
07 should have, with, flowers
08 am, excited by, sound
09 wonderful, wake up
10 like, have, to play
11 Welcome to, dream
12 Having, what, so, full
13 has, theater in, basement
14 can eat, enjoy, favorite
15 has, on, second floor
16 play, kinds of games
17 also, swimming pool
18 fun things with, guest
19 the most important thing
20 feels safe, comfortable
21 At, beautifully designed, on
22 When, enter, see, large
23 sometimes plays, signs
24 have, with, picnic table
25 will enjoy, Do, like
26 early adopter, technology
27 like, products, before others
28 get near, recognizes, opens
29 checks, conditions, advises, on
30 tells, weight, condition, health
31 cleans, cooks for
32 what I can imagine

01 Have, ever thought about
02 in class, created
03 are, that, made
04 Nature, good friend
05 do feel good, forest
06 like to have, in, countryside
07 should have, with many flowers
08 am always excited by
09 wonderful to wake up, listen to
10 like to have, be fun to play with
11 Welcome to

12 Having fun, what, is full of exciting things
13 in the basement
14 enjoy, favorite movies
15 has, on, second floor
16 kinds of games
17 also, a swimming pool
18 do fun things with, my guest
19 the most important thing
20 feels safe, comfortable
21 At the gate, beautifully designed sign, on
22 When, enter, see a large living room
23 board games
24 have, with a large picnic table
25 enjoy, Do you like
26 an early adopter, technology
27 do like, before others
28 get near, recognizes, opens automatically
29 checks, conditions, advises, on what to wear
30 tells me my weight, condition
31 cleans, cooks for
32 what I can imagine

1 여러분은 꿈의 집에 대해 생각해 본 적이 있나요?
2 오늘, 우리는 수업 시간에 우리가 꿈꾸는 집을 만들었습니다.
3 여기 우리가 만든 몇몇 꿈의 집이 있습니다.
4 자연은 나의 좋은 친구입니다.
5 나는 숲속에서 걸을 때 기분이 정말 좋습니다.
6 나는 시골에 꿈의 집을 갖고 싶습니다.
7 집에는 많은 꽃과 나무가 있는 큰 정원이 있을 것입니다.
8 나는 항상 새소리에 신이 납니다.
9 아침에 깨어나서 새들의 노래 소리를 듣는 것은 멋질 것입니다.
10 또한 나는 많은 애완동물을 갖고 싶습니다. 그들과 노는 것은 매우 재미있을 것입니다!
11 나의 꿈의 집에 온 것을 환영합니다!
12 즐겁게 지내는 것은 내가 가장 원하는 것입니다. 그래서 내 꿈의 집은 흥미로운 것들로 가득합니다.
13 집에는 지하에 영화관이 있습니다.
14 그곳에서 나는 쿠키를 먹을 수 있고 내가 좋아하는 영화들을 즐길 수 있습니다.
15 내 꿈의 집에는 2층에 게임방이 있습니다.
16 나는 그곳에서 많은 다양한 종류의 게임을 할 수 있습니다.
17 나의 집에는 또한 수영장이 있습니다.
18 나는 나의 집에서 친구들과 함께 즐거운 일들을 하고 싶습니다. 여러분도 나의 손님이 될 수 있습니다!
19 나의 가족은 나에게 가장 중요한 것입니다.
20 내 꿈의 집에서 가족은 안전하고 편안함을 느낍니다.

21 여러분은 가족 사진이 있는 아름답게 디자인된 문패를 발견할 수 있습니다.

22 여러분이 집에 들어서면 여러분은 큰 거실을 보게 될 것입니다.

23 나의 가족은 때때로 그곳에서 보드 게임도 하고 노래를 부르기도 합니다.

24 가족 소풍을 위한 커다란 피크닉 테이블이 있는 큰 정원을 갖게 될 것입니다.

25 그곳에서 우리는 바비큐를 즐길 것입니다. 내 꿈의 집이 마음에 드나요?

26 나는 남들보다 먼저 신기술을 써 보는 것을 좋아하는 사람입니다.

27 나는 새로운 제품이나 기술을 다른 사람보다 먼저 사용하는 것을 정말 좋아합니다.

28 내가 집 근처에 도착할 때, 현관문은 내 얼굴을 인식하고 자동으로 문을 엽니다.

29 가구는 날씨 상태를 확인하여 내게 무엇을 입을지 조언해 줍니다.

30 욕실 거울은 나에게 체중과 건강 상태를 알려 줍니다.

31 로봇은 집을 청소하고 나를 위해 요리합니다.

32 이것이 내가 나의 꿈의 집에 대해 상상할 수 있는 것입니다.

본문 TEST Step 4 - Step 5 p.17~20

1 Have you ever thought about your dream house?

2 Today, in class, we created our dream house.

3 Here are some of the dream houses that we made.

4 Nature is my good friend.

5 I do feel good when I walk in the forest.

6 I'd like to have a dream house in the countryside.

7 It should have a big garden with many flowers and trees.

8 I am always excited by the sound of birds.

9 It will be wonderful to wake up in the morning and listen to the songs of the birds.

10 Also, I'd like to have many pets. It will be fun to play with them!

11 Welcome to my dream house!

12 Having fun is what I want most, so my dream house is full of exciting things.

13 It has a theater in the basement.

14 There, I can eat cookies and enjoy my favorite movies.

15 My dream house has a game room on the second floor.

16 I can play many different kinds of games there.

17 My house also has a swimming pool.

18 I want to do fun things with my friends in my

house. You can be my guest!

19 My family is the most important thing to me.

20 In my dream house, my family feels safe and comfortable.

21 At the gate, you can find a beautifully designed sign with my family's picture on it.

22 When you enter the house, you will see a large living room.

23 My family sometimes plays board games and sings there.

24 It will have a garden with a large picnic table for family picnics.

25 There, we will enjoy barbecues. Do you like my dream house?

26 I am an early adopter of new technology.

27 I do like to use new products and technology before others.

28 When I get near my house, the front door recognizes my face and opens automatically.

29 The furniture checks the weather conditions and advises me on what to wear.

30 The bathroom mirror tells me my weight and the condition of my health.

31 A robot cleans the house and cooks for me.

32 This is what I can imagine about my dream house.

구석구석지문 TEST Step 1 p.21

After You Read - Read and Match

1. to use, products, technology

2. There are, that use new technology

3. Every day, checks, what to wear

4. cooks for me

Project Step 1

1. would like to, favorite food

2. like, most

3. Can, tell me about, subject

4. what, like most, want to become, like

5. What, like to do

6. like to practice, sing

Project Step 3

1. made, with what, likes

2. so, with, paint brush, colored, a piece of

3. made, with, musical note

After You Read - Read and Match

1. I like to use new products and technology.
2. There are many items that use new technology in my dream house.
3. Every day my furniture checks the weather and tells me what to wear.
4. A robot cooks for me.

Project Step 1

1. A: We would like to know more about you, Minho. What is your favorite food?
2. B: I like pizza most.
3. C: Can you tell me about your favorite subject?
4. B: Art is what I like most. I want to become an art teacher like Mr. Kim.
5. D: What do you like to do after school?
6. B: I like to practice taegwondo and sing songs.

Project Step 3

1. We made an M and an H with what Minho likes.
2. Minho likes art and pizza, so we made an M with a paint brush, colored pencils, and a piece of pizza.
3. We made an H with a musical note and taegwondo.

Lesson **2**

01 ~에게 인사하다	02 그릇	03 놓다
04 정확하게, 올바르게		05 ~한 이후로
06 다르다	07 나이 든	08 사원
09 경험하다	10 마지막으로	11 주소
12 주	13 상품, 제품	14 율, 비율
15 제공하다, 대접하다		16 선물
17 준비하다	18 차이	19 건네주다
20 부정의문문	21 (짐을) 싸다, 꾸리다	
22 혀	23 지불하다	
24 교환하다, 환전하다		25 불편한
26 (손을) 흔들다	27 부딪치다	28 우편 번호
29 세금	30 입장료	31 가격표
32 판매세	33 죽음	34 포장하다, 싸다
35 ~에 익숙해지다	36 A와 B 사이에	37 ~의 대답으로
38 ~에 나쁜 영향을 미치다		39 ~로 여겨지다
40 ~와 똑같은	41 ~할 것을 기억하다	
42 (범위가) A에서 B에 이르다		43 ~을 모으다

01 bowl	02 positive question	
03 death	04 rate	05 entrance fee
06 prepare	07 goods	08 difference
09 place	10 address	11 pay
12 present	13 elderly	14 price tag
15 bump	16 exchange	17 correctly
18 guest	19 finally	20 wrap
21 tongue	22 sales tax	23 postal code
24 tax	25 state	26 differ
27 wave	28 greet	29 temple
30 experience	31 traditional	32 serve
33 cultural	34 uncomfortable	35 each other
36 in response to	37 be regarded as	
38 get used to ~	39 make sure (that)+주어 ~	
40 range from A to B		
41 between A and B		42 remember to V
43 have a bad effect on		

1 rude, 무례한   2 goods, 상품, 제품   3 sales tax, 판매세
4 wrap, 포장하다   5 wave, 흔들다   6 bump, 부딪히다
7 exchange, 교환하다   8 uncomfortable, 불편한
9 address, 주소   10 correctly, 올바르게, 맞게
11 entrance fee, 입장료   12 advice, 충고, 조언
13 postal code, 우편번호   14 tag, 꼬리표
15 tax, 세금   16 traditional, 전통적인

Warm Up

1 show their tongues, Tibet
2 place, together, India
3 bump their noses

Listen & Speak 1 A

1 to send, aunt / What / get, advice, how to write, address in English / should write, street address / Like / state, postal code, Finally, country / for, help
2 Look at, wearing traditional, to take pictures of / There is, need to, before taking / get, advice on / shouldn't take pictures of Moroccan, without asking / believe, a bad effect on, when

Listen & Speak 1 B

Can I get, advice, visiting / shouldn't stand, path / get your advice on visiting / should sit, back seat

Listen & Speak 2 A

1 bought, present, have stayed / What, buy / bought, think / Make sure, when, hand, to / giving, older, with, is regarded as rude / remember
2 pack everything, need, to / yet, should, take / Remember to bring, pants, skirt / isn't / there are, temples, shouldn't wear shorts, temple / anything else / Make sure, exchange, to

Listen & Speak 2 B

anything, remember, France / Make sure, Keep, on, at all times / anything, need to, when / Make sure, don't take off / when having

Real Life Talk

Chinese, invited, to / enjoy having / prepare, gift, for several, advice, what to bring / How about / Most, receive, as, present, enjoy drinking, usually serve, guests / Make sure you don't wrap / mean death / remember, advice

Communication Task Step 2

Which country, like to visit / get, advice, traveling / Make sure, don't use, left hand to hand

Wrap Up

1 going, get, advice, visiting / pay, get off / other things, remember / Pick up, hold, while eating, when having, should, without
2 to give, from, anything, should remember / Make sure

Warm Up

1 People show their tongues in Tibet.
2 People place their hands together and say "Namaste" in India.
3 Men bump their noses in the United Arab Emirates.

Listen & Speak 1 A

1 G: I want to send this to my aunt in the USA.
 B: What is it?
 G: It's her hanbok. Can I get your advice on how to write an address in English?
 B: Sure. You should write the street address first.
 G: Like this?
 B: Yes. Then, write the name of the city and the state and then the postal code. Finally, write the country.
 G: Thanks for your help.
2 G: Look at the people wearing traditional Moroccan clothes. They are really beautiful. I want to take pictures of them.
 M: Wait. There is an important thing you need to know before taking pictures.
 G: Oh, really? Can I get your advice on it?
 M: Yes. You shouldn't take pictures of Moroccan people without asking.
 G: Why?
 M: They believe it may have a bad effect on them when someone takes their pictures.

Listen & Speak 1 B

A: Can I get your advice on visiting the Netherlands?
B: Sure. You shouldn't stand on a bike path.

A: Can I get your advice on visiting the USA?
B: Sure. You should sit in the back seat in the taxi.

Listen & Speak 2 A

1 B: Sena, I bought a present for Ms. Han. I have stayed at her house here in Korea.
 G: That's great. What did you buy her?
 B: I bought her a hat. Do you think she'll love it?
 G: Yes. Make sure you use two hands when you

hand it to her.

B: Why?

G: Because giving something to older people with one hand is regarded as rude in Korea.

B: Okay. I'll remember that.

2 B: Did you pack everything you need for the trip to Thailand tomorrow?

G: Not yet. What should I take?

B: Remember to bring a pair of long pants or a long skirt.

G: Why? It's very hot in Thailand, isn't it?

B: Yes, but there are many temples in Thailand. You shouldn't wear shorts when you visit a temple.

G: Okay. Is there anything else?

B: Make sure you exchange Korean won to Thai baht.

A: Is there anything I need to remember when I eat in France?

B: Yes. Make sure you keep your hands on the table at all times.

A: Is there anything I need to remember when I eat in Uzbekistan?

B: Yes. Make sure you don't take off your hat or shoes when having a meal.

Seho: My Chinese friend invited me to his house for dinner this Friday.

Bora: That's good. I hope you enjoy having dinner at his house.

Seho: I want to prepare a small gift for him. You lived in China for several years. Can I get your advice on what to bring?

Bora: How about some tea?

Seho: Tea?

Bora: Yes. Most Chinese people like to receive tea as a present. They enjoy drinking tea. Also, they usually serve tea to guests.

Seho: Oh, thanks. Is there anything else that I need to know?

Bora: Make sure you don't wrap the present in white or black paper. White and black mean death in China.

Seho: Okay. I'll remember that. Thank you for the advice.

A: Which country would you like to visit?

B: I'd like to visit Malaysia. Can I get your advice on

traveling there?

C: Sure. Make sure you don't use your left hand to hand something to someone.

B: Okay. Thanks.

1 B: I'm going to Japan this summer. Can I get some advice on visiting there?

G: Make sure you pay when you get off the bus.

B: Oh, I didn't know that. Are there any other things I should remember?

G: Pick up the bowl and hold it while eating. Also, when having soup, you should drink it without a spoon.

B: Okay. Thanks.

2 M: I want to give flowers to my friend from Russia. Is there anything I should remember?

W: Make sure you don't give flowers in even numbers.

---

01 have been living, for

02 Since, experienced, between, and

03 would like, share, with

04 at, it　　　　05 looks nice, much

06 dollars, cents　07 not expensive

08 agree, buy it　09 be, dollars, cents

10 price tag, only 11 states, pay, tax, goods

12 called, sales, rates differ

13 range, less than, more

14 goods, pay, price, tag　　　15 Mrs., Hello

16 Hi, How　　　17 for, Enjoy, meal

18 Thank, too　　19 why, wave to

20 greet, other, waving

21 Waving, regarded as

22 feel uncomfortable, don't, try

23 wave, at, elderly, back　　　24 try, pie

25 thanks, want to　　　　26 not, Don't, like

27 Minhee, Yes　28 try some, delicious

29 just said, don't　　　　30 Andy, What

31 negative as, Aren't, Didn't

32 difficult, negative, correctly, advice

33 response, such as, if

34 should answer, like

35 same as, positive questions

36 cultural difference, surprising

37 been learning, differences since

38 surprised, getting used to

01 have been living, for three years
02 Since, have experienced, differences between, and
03 would like to share
04 Look at, it 05 looks nice, How much
06 dollars, cents 07 not expensive
08 agree, to buy it
09 be, dollars, cents
10 the price tag says, only
11 most states, pay a tax, goods
12 is called, sales tax, rates differ by state
13 range, less than, more than
14 buy goods, usually need to pay
15 Mrs., Mrs. 16 How
17 for, Enjoy your meal
18 too 19 why did, wave to
20 often greet each other, waving
21 Waving, is, regarded as rude
22 feel uncomfortable, why don't, try it
23 wave to, smile at, elderly, walking, wave back
24 try, apple pie 25 thanks, want to
26 not, Don't 27 Yes
28 try some, delicious
29 just, don't like 30 What
31 often ask negative questions, Aren't, Didn't, go
32 It, to answer, correctly, is
33 negative questions, such as, answer, No
34 should nswer, Yes, if
35 the same as, to positive questions
36 Which cultural difference, surprising
37 have been learning, cultural differences since
38 surprised, at first, am getting used to

1 안녕! 내 이름은 김민희야. 나는 미국에 3년 동안 살고 있어.
2 우리 가족이 이곳으로 이민을 온 이후로 나는 한국과 미국의 많은 문화적 차이를 경험하고 있어.
3 나는 그것들 중 몇 가지를 너희들과 공유하고 싶어.
4 민희: 이 셔츠를 봐. 마음에 들어.
5 Linda: 멋져 보인다. 얼마야?
6 민희: 19달러 99센트야.
7 Linda: 비싸지 않네.
8 민희: 응, 나도 그렇게 생각해. 그것을 사고 싶어.
9 점원: 21달러 20센트입니다.
10 민희: 정말이요? 하지만 가격표에는 단지 19달러 99센트라고 쓰여 있는데요.

11 이곳 미국에서는 대부분의 주에서 사람들이 물건을 구입할 때 세금을 내.
12 그것은 판매세라고 불려. 판매세의 비율은 주마다 달라.
13 판매세는 1퍼센트 미만부터 10퍼센트 이상까지 다양해.
14 그래서 미국에서 상품을 살 때, 대개 가격표에 있는 가격보다 더 많은 돈을 지불해야 해.
15 Jessica: 안녕하세요, Johnson 할머니! 민희: 안녕하세요, Johnson 할머니!
16 Mrs. Johnson: 안녕, Jessica! 안녕, 민희! 잘 지내지?
17 Jessica: 잘 지내요, 감사합니다. 저희는 여기 버거 먹으러 왔어요. 식사 맛있게 하세요.
18 Mrs. Johnson: 고맙구나. 너희들도!
19 민희: Jessica, 왜 너는 Johnson 할머니께 손을 흔들었니?
20 미국에서 사람들은 종종 손을 흔들며 서로에게 인사해.
21 나이가 많은 사람에게 손을 흔드는 것은 무례하다고 여겨지지 않아.
22 네가 미국에 오면 처음에는 그것에 대해 불편하게 느낄 수 있어. 하지만 한번 시도해 보지 않을래?
23 너는 길을 걷고 있는 연세가 많으신 할아버지께 손을 흔들며 미소를 지어도 돼. 그도 너한테 답례로 손을 흔들지도 몰라.
24 Andy: 민희, 이 사과 파이 좀 먹어 봐.
25 Minhee: 아니야, 고마워. 먹고 싶지 않아.
26 Andy: 왜 안 먹어? 너는 사과 파이를 좋아하지 않니?
27 Minhee: 응.
28 Andy: 그러면, 좀 먹어 봐. 맛있어.
29 Minhee: 아니. 내가 사과 파이를 좋아하지 않는다고 방금 말했잖아.
30 Andy: 뭐라고?
31 미국 사람들은 종종 "너 안 오니?", "너 병원 안 갔니?"와 같은 부정의문문으로 질문해.
32 부정의문문에 바르게 대답하는 것은 어려울 수 있어. 여기 약간의 충고 사항이 있어.
33 "너는 사과 파이를 좋아하지 않니?"와 같은 부정의문문의 대답으로 만약 사과 파이를 좋아하지 않는다면 너는 "No."라고 대답해야 해.
34 그리고 만약 그것을 좋아한다면 "Yes."라고 대답해야 해.
35 이 대답들은 "너는 애플파이를 좋아하니?"와 같은 긍정의문문에 대한 대답들과 같아.
36 어떤 문화적인 차이가 너에게 가장 놀랍니?
37 나는 미국에 온 이후로 문화적인 차이에 대해 계속 배우고 있어.
38 어떤 것들은 처음에 나를 놀라게 했지만, 지금은 그것들에 익숙해지고 있어.

1 Hi! My name is Kim Minhee. I have been living in America for three years.

2 Since my family moved here, I have experienced many cultural differences between Korea and America.

3 I would like to share some of them with you.

4 Minhee: Look at this shirt. I like it.

5 Linda: It looks nice. How much is it?

6 Minhee: It's 19 dollars and 99 cents.

7 Linda: That's not expensive.

8 Minhee: Yes, I agree. I want to buy it.

9 Clerk: That'll be 21 dollars and 20 cents.

10 Minhee: Really? But the price tag says it's only 19 dollars and 99 cents.

11 Here in America, in most states, people pay a tax when they buy goods.

12 It is called a sales tax. Sales tax rates differ by state.

13 They range from less than one percent to more than ten percent.

14 So when you buy goods in America, you usually need to pay more than the price on the tag.

15 Jessica: Hi, Mrs. Johnson! Minhee: Hello, Mrs. Johnson!

16 Mrs. Johnson: Hi, Jessica! Hi, Minhee! How are you?

17 Jessica: Fine, thank you. We are here for a burger. Enjoy your meal.

18 Mrs. Johnson: Thank you. You, too!

19 Minhee: Jessica, why did you wave to Mrs Johnson?

20 In America, people often greet each other by waving.

21 Waving to an older person is not regarded as rude.

22 When you come to America, you may feel uncomfortable about it at first, but why don't you try it?

23 You can wave to and smile at an elderly man walking on the street. He may wave back.

24 Andy: Minhee, try this apple pie.

25 Minhee: No, thanks. I don't want to.

26 Andy: Why not? Don't you like apple pie?

27 Minhee: Yes.

28 Andy: Then, try some. It's delicious.

29 Minhee: No. I just said I don't like apple pie.

30 Andy: What?

31 Americans often ask negative questions, such as "Aren't you coming?" and "Didn't you go to the hospital?"

32 It can be difficult to answer negative questions correctly. Here is some advice.

33 In response to negative questions, such as "Don't you like apple pie?" you should answer "No," if you don't like it.

34 And you should answer "Yes," if you like it.

35 These answers are the same as the answers to positive questions, such as "Do you like apple pie?"

36 Which cultural difference is most surprising to you?

37 I have been learning about cultural differences since I came to America.

38 Some surprised me at first, but now I am getting used to them.

Project Step 1

1. on correct English expressions

2. Make sure, instead of eye shopping

3. Make sure you don't say, should say, instead

Project Step 3

1. realized, have been using, incorrect

2. For example, should say, instead of

3. an incorrect expression, Make sure you don't use

Enjoy Writing

1. Can't Miss

2. There are, around the world

3. Among, like to attend

4. have been celebrating, for many years

5. is held in

6. if I go, a lot of things

7. people throwing, on each other

8. will be fantastic

9. to dance with other people

10. taste traditional, dishes

11. going to, exciting

12. can't wait for

Project Step 1

1. A: Can I get your advice on correct English expressions?
2. B: Make sure you say window shopping instead of eye shopping.
3. C: Make sure you don't say Y-shirt. You should say dress shirt instead.

Project Step 3

1. Today, I realized I have been using many incorrect English expressions.
2. For example, we should say dress shirt instead of Y-shirt.
3. Eye shopping is also an incorrect expression. Make sure you don't use it.

Enjoy Writing

1. Holi That I Can't Miss
2. There are many interesting festivals around the world.
3. Among them, I'd like to attend Holi.
4. People in India have been celebrating this festival for many years.
5. Holi is held in March.
6. I think that if I go, I'll experience a lot of things.
7. First, there are people throwing colored powder and water on each other.
8. It will be fantastic!
9. Second, I want to dance with other people on the street.
10. I'll also taste traditional Holi dishes.
11. It's going to be very exciting.
12. I can't wait for the day!

Lesson **3**

01 충분히; 충분한	02 분석하다	03 출석하다, 참석하다
04 인물, 형상, 사람 모양의 장난감		
05 진정시키다, 평온하게 하다		06 출연자들
07 성격	08 세부, 세목	09 개발자
10 매우, 대단히	11 플로리스트, 화초 연구가	
12 분석가	13 약함, 약점	14 포함하다
15 ~ 중에서	16 자원	17 지휘하다, 처신하다
18 줄이다, 완화하다	19 전문가	20 다루다
21 생물, 생명체	22 추천하다	23 시인
24 수의사	25 우편집배원	26 선택하다, 고르다
27 화초, 푸른 잎	28 힘, 강점	29 마이크
30 오디션을 보다	31 청진기	32 공연
33 정원사	34 현실적인	35 ~함으로써
36 실현되다	37 ~을 보살피다	38 ~에 만족하다
39 (단체, 조직에) 소속하다, 속하다		
40 ~을 최대한 활용하다		
41 ~처럼 보이다, ~일 것 같다		42 ~을 확신하다
43 ~을 꿈꾸다		

01 personality	02 analyze	03 cast
04 strength	05 stethoscope	06 conduct
07 veterinarian	08 weakness	09 detail
10 select	11 gardener	12 specialist
13 developer	14 microphone	15 highly
16 among	17 florist	18 audition
19 greenery	20 analyst	21 handle
22 include	23 calm	24 responsibility
25 realistic	26 traditional	27 recommend
28 performance	29 creature	30 resource
31 reduce	32 someday	33 engineer
34 enough	35 care for	36 belong to
37 dream of ~	38 be happy with ~	
39 come true	40 by -ing	41 It seems that ~
42 I'm sure that ~	43 make the best use of	

1 cast, 출연자들　2 data, 자료　3 collect, 모으다
4 lead, 이끌다　5 belong to, 소속하다, 속하다
6 responsibility, 책임　7 analyst, 분석가

8 bank teller, 은행 창구 직원   9 greenery, 푸른 잎, 화초

10 personality, 성격   11 resource, 자원

12 analyze, 분석하다   13 include, 포함하다

14 audition, 오디션을 보다   15 developer, 개발자

16 care for, 보살피다

Listen & Speak 1 A

1 planning, police station, police officer / to become, someday / do, too, dreamed of becoming, since / with, ask, something / are, going to ask / what, to do to become / sure, would like to

2 wrong / animator, drawing skill, enough / Being an animator, a, artist / do to become, animator / a lot of, to make, practice drawing / quite sure that, if, try hard

Listen & Speak 1 B

• interested, technology, Which, right / sure, developer

• interested in writing. Which job, be right for / quite sure, be a good job for

Listen & Speak 2 A

1 glad to meet, what you do / guide, different places, information, visit / else / popular culture, traditional / It seems, knowing a lot, happy with, my job

2 finish, role model / wrote, be like / does, do / how to stretch, also helps, reduce, calm themselves / It seems that, to keep both, and

Listen & Speak 2 B

• program writer, become / seems to, writing, helpful

• social worker, help me become / seems, reading books to kids, be helpful

Real Life Talk

most interested, among / interested in working / most interested, among / working, playing / it seems to me that, belong to, realistic / mean / belong to, personality types, Realistic, one of, types / interesting, What kind of, recommend / police officer, and so on / to be / I'm quite sure, soccer player

Communication Task Step 2

3 Ss, 2 As, 1 E / seems to, belong to / Jobs that, recommended, librarian, counselor / have always wanted / sounds, quite sure that you could

Wrap Up 1

are, doing / looking for, recipe / cook often / to cook, chef someday / make, come true / taking, to think of, creative / I'm quite sure, good chef

Listen & Speak 1 A

1 B: Anne, I'm planning to visit the police station to see my uncle. He is a police officer.

G: Oh, I want to become a police officer someday.

B: You do? Me, too. I have dreamed of becoming a police officer since I was ten.

G: Can I come with you, Matt? I want to meet your uncle and ask him something.

B: Sure. What are you going to ask?

G: I want to ask him what I need to do to become a police officer.

B: I see. I'm sure he would like to meet you.

2 M: What's wrong, Jisu?

G: I want to be an animator, but my drawing skill is not good enough.

M: Hmm... Being an animator is not just about a good artist.

G: What should I do to become an animator?

M: Read a lot of books to make good stories and practice drawing every day.

G: Okay, I'll do so.

M: I'm quite sure that you can be a good animator if you try hard.

G: Thank you very much.

Listen & Speak 1 B

• A: I'm interested in technology. Which job would be right for me?

B: I'm quite sure that an app developer could be a good job for you.

• A: I'm interested in writing. Which job would be right for me?

B: I'm quite sure that a writer could be a good job for you.

Listen & Speak 2 A

1 G: I'm glad to meet you, Mr. Han. Could you please tell me what you do?

M: Okay. I guide travelers to different places in China and give them information about where they should visit.

G: What else do you do?

M: I tell them about popular culture and traditional food in China.

G: It seems to me knowing a lot about China is very important. Are you happy with your job?

M: Yes. I really love my job.

2 B: Did you finish the report about your role model?

G: Yes, I did. I wrote about my role model, Ms.

Shin. I want to be like her.

B: What does she do?

G: She teaches people how to stretch. She also helps them reduce stress and calm themselves.

B: Good. It seems that she helps to keep both their mind and body healthy.

G: Yes, and I think it's great.

Listen & Speak 2 B

• A: I want to be a radio program writer. What would help me become one?

B: It seems to me writing your own stories would be helpful.

• A: I want to be a social worker. What would help me become one?

B: It seems to me reading books to kids at a hospital would be helpful.

Real Life Talk

Bora: What are you most interested in among the things on this list?

Jessie: I'm most interested in working outside and playing sports.

Bora: Well, it seems to me that you belong to the realistic type.

Jessie: What do you mean?

Bora: Most people belong to one of six personality types. Realistic is one of the types.

Jessie: Oh, that's interesting. What kind of jobs do they recommend for realistic types?

Bora: A farmer, a police officer, a soccer player, and so on.

Jessie: Oh, I have always wanted to be a soccer player.

Bora: That's good. I'm quite sure you could become a great soccer player.

Communication Task Step 2

A: I have 3 Ss, 2 As, 1 I, and 1 E.

B: It seems to me that you belong to Type S.

C: Yes. Jobs that are recommended for Type S are teacher, nurse, librarian or counselor.

A: Cool. I have always wanted to be a teacher.

D: That sounds great. I'm quite sure that you could be a good teacher.

Wrap Up 1

B: Hello, what are you doing, Sumi?

G: I'm looking for a good recipe on the Internet. I need it for my family dinner today.

B: That is nice. Do you cook often?

G: Yes, I try to cook every weekend. I want to be a chef someday.

B: What are you doing to make your dream come true?

G: I'm taking a cooking class. I try to think of new and creative dishes.

B: I'm quite sure you could be a good chef.

본문 TEST Step 1   p.58~60

01 florist, who creates, with

02 To become, need, things

03 attended, for, gardeners

04 how to, care for

05 days, lot of different

06 movie sets, decorate, with

07 something colorful, fresh, greenery

08 If, highly recommend, become

09 sport data analyst

10 sounds like, doesn't it

11 In fact, work for

12 watch recorded, run, collect

13 analyze, show, strengths, weaknesses

14 If, understands, do better

15 Since, have been, big

16 work, watch, all, time

17 perfect, because watching, hobby

18 As, director, theater, lot

19 audition, look for, voices

20 selecting, cast, each scene

21 put, cast, together, practice

22 During, performance, area, conduct

23 responsibility, each, played, way

24 direct, to keep, together

25 Conducting, directing, waving, around

26 scientist, big field

27 includes studies, creatures living

28 Among, have studied, living

29 growth ring, that interests

30 By looking, out, born

31 used to, resources, manage

32 because, the best use

본문 TEST Step 2   p.61~63

01 florist, who creates, with

02 To become, need to know many things

03 attended, for, gardeners

04 at this school, how to grow, care for

05 These days, a lot of different

06 movie sets, decorate, with flowers

07 something colorful with, greenery

08 plants, highly recommend

09 sport data analyst

10 sounds like, doesn't it

11 In fact, a lot of fun

12 to watch recorded games, run, to collect

13 analyze, to show, weaknesses

14 understands, strengths, do better

15 Since, have been

16 baseball games all the time

17 perfect job, because watching baseball games, hobby

18 As, a musical theater, a lot of

19 audition, look for, voices

20 selecting the cast, for each scene

21 put, cast, together

22 During, performance, conduct

23 my responsibility, each, played, same way

24 direct, to keep, together

25 Conducting, directing, waving

26 ocean scientist, a big field

27 includes, oceans, creatures living in them

28 Among, have studied, living

29 the growth ring, that interests

30 By looking, find out, was born

31 I get from, is used to understand, manage, oceans better

32 because, makes the best use of

본문 TEST Step 3   p.64~65

1 안녕하세요. 저는 Tom입니다. 플로리스트란 꽃으로 아름다운 것들을 창조하는 사람입니다.

2 플로리스트가 되기 위해서 여러분은 꽃에 관해 많은 것을 알 필요가 있습니다.

3 나는 플로리스트와 정원사를 양성하는 고등학교에 다녔습니다.

4 제가 다양한 종류의 꽃을 기르고 다루는 방법을 배운 곳이 바로 이 학교에서였습니다.

5 오늘날, 플로리스트는 많은 다양한 일을 할 수 있습니다.

6 나는 때때로 영화 세트장을 디자인하고 꽃으로 상점을 꾸밉니다.

7 나는 싱싱한 꽃과 화초로 다채로운 무언가를 창조해 낼 때 행복합니다.

8 만약 당신이 식물과 예술을 좋아한다면, 나는 당신에게 플로리스트가 될 것을 강력히 추천합니다.

9 나는 Emma입니다. 나는 스포츠 데이터 분석가입니다.

---

10 어려운 직업처럼 들리죠, 그렇지 않나요?

11 사실, 그것은 매우 재미있습니다. 나는 야구팀을 위해서 일합니다.

12 나의 일은 녹화된 경기를 보고 자료를 수집하기 위해 컴퓨터 프로그램을 실행하는 것입니다.

13 그리고 나서, 나는 내 팀의 강점과 약점을 보여 주기 위해서 그 자료들을 분석합니다.

14 만약 팀이 자신들의 강점과 약점을 이해하면, 그들은 다음번에 더 잘할 수 있습니다.

15 어렸을 때부터, 나는 야구의 열혈 팬이었습니다.

16 지금, 나는 일하는 중에 내내 야구를 봅니다.

17 야구 경기를 보는 것은 나의 취미이기 때문에 이것은 나에게 완벽한 직업입니다!

18 안녕하세요. 나는 Chris입니다. 뮤지컬 극장 감독으로서 나는 많은 것들을 합니다.

19 나는 배우들을 대상으로 오디션을 실시하고, 훌륭하고 강한 목소리를 찾아냅니다.

20 배역에 맞는 배우를 고른 뒤에, 나는 그들에게 각 장면을 위한 노래를 가르칩니다.

21 그리고 나서, 나는 배우와 오케스트라를 함께 연습시킵니다.

22 공연 동안에, 나는 오케스트라 석에 있고 지휘를 합니다.

23 각각의 노래가 매번 동일하게 연주되도록 만드는 것은 나의 책임입니다.

24 나는 공연을 제대로 진행하기 위해 연주자들과 가수들을 감독합니다.

25 지휘하고 감독하는 것은 단지 내 팔을 흔드는 것만이 아닙니다!

26 나는 예지입니다. 나는 해양 과학자입니다. 해양 과학은 거대한 분야입니다.

27 그것은 바다와 그 안에 살고 있는 생물에 관한 연구를 포함합니다.

28 여러 가지 중에서 나는 한국 주변의 바다에 살고 있는 많은 종류의 물고기를 연구해 왔습니다.

29 나의 흥미를 끄는 것은 바로 물고기 안에 있는 나이테입니다.

30 나이테를 살펴봄으로써, 나는 언제 어디서 그 물고기가 태어났는지 알아낼 수 있습니다.

31 내가 물고기에서 얻은 모든 정보는 바다의 자원을 이해하고 바다를 더 잘 관리하기 위해 사용됩니다.

32 내 직업은 자연을 가장 잘 활용할 수 있게 한다는 점에서 중요합니다.

본문 TEST Step 4 - Step 5   p.66~70

1 Hi, I am Tom. A florist is someone who creates beautiful things with flowers.

2 To become a florist, you need to know many things about flowers.

3 I attended a high school for florists and gardeners.

4 It was at this school that I learned how to grow

and care for different types of flowers.

5 These days, florists can do a lot of different things.

6 I design movie sets sometimes and I decorate shops with flowers.

7 I am happy when I create something colorful with fresh flowers and greenery.

8 If you like plants and the arts, I highly recommend you become a florist.

9 I am Emma. I am a sport data analyst.

10 It sounds like a difficult job, doesn't it?

11 In fact, it is a lot of fun. I work for a baseball team.

12 My job is to watch recorded games and run a computer program to collect data.

13 Then, I analyze the data to show my team's strengths and weaknesses.

14 If the team understands their strengths and weaknesses, they can do better next time.

15 Since I was young, I have been a big fan of baseball.

16 Now, in my work, I watch baseball games all the time.

17 This is a perfect job for me because watching baseball games is my hobby!

18 Hi, I am Chris. As a director of a musical theater, I do a lot of things.

19 I audition the actors and I look for good, strong voices.

20 After selecting the cast, I teach them the songs for each scene.

21 Then, I put the cast and orchestra together for practice.

22 During the performance, I am in the orchestra area and conduct.

23 It's my responsibility to have each song played the same way every time.

24 I direct the musicians and the singers to keep the show together.

25 Conducting and directing is not just about waving my arms around!

26 My name is Yeji. I am an ocean scientist. Ocean science is a big field.

27 It includes studies of the oceans and the creatures living in them.

28 Among other things, I have studied many kinds of fish living in the seas near Korea.

29 It is the growth ring in a fish that interests me.

30 By looking at it, I can find out when and where the fish was born.

31 All the information I get from fish is used to understand sea resources and manage the oceans better.

32 My job is important because it makes the best use of nature possible.

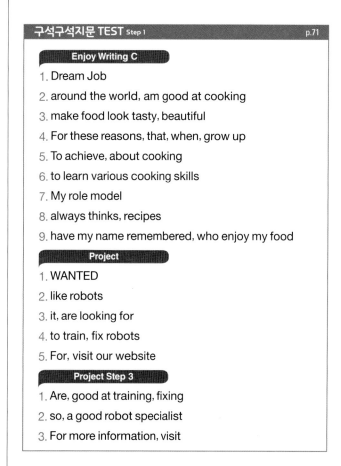

구석구석지문 TEST Step 1   p.71

Enjoy Writing C

1. Dream Job
2. around the world, am good at cooking
3. make food look tasty, beautiful
4. For these reasons, that, when, grow up
5. To achieve, about cooking
6. to learn various cooking skills
7. My role model
8. always thinks, recipes
9. have my name remembered, who enjoy my food

Project

1. WANTED
2. like robots
3. it, are looking for
4. to train, fix robots
5. For, visit our website

Project Step 3

1. Are, good at training, fixing
2. so, a good robot specialist
3. For more information, visit

구석구석지문 TEST Step 2   p.72

Enjoy Writing C

1. My Dream Job
2. I like food from around the world and I am good at cooking.
3. I can also make food look tasty and beautiful.
4. For these reasons, it is a chef that I want to be when I grow up.
5. To achieve my dream, I will read magazines about cooking.
6. Also, I will go to France to learn various cooking skills.
7. My role model is my dad.
8. He always thinks of new recipes and then cooks these new dishes for us.
9. I want to have my name remembered by people who enjoy my food.

1. HELP WANTED!!

2. Do you like robots?

3. If your answer is yes, it is you that we are looking for.

4. Please join us to train and fix robots.

5. For more information, visit our website at www. robots.com.

1. Are you good at training and fixing robots?

2. If so, we're sure that you'll be a good robot specialist.

3. For more information, visit our websites.

MEMO